THE SONG OF THE GREYS

THE SONG
OF THE GREYS

Nigel Kerner

Hodder & Stoughton

Copyright © 1997 by Nigel Kerner

First published in 1997 by Hodder and Stoughton
A division of Hodder Headline PLC

The right of Nigel Kerner to be identified as the Author of
the Work has been asserted by him in accordance with the
Copyright, Designs and Patents Act 1988.

10 9 8 7 6 5 4 3 2 1

British Library Cataloguing in Publication Data
A CIP catalogue record for this title
is available from the British Library

ISBN 0 340 69581 1

Typeset by Hewer Text Composition Services, Edinburgh
Printed and bound in Great Britain by
Mackays of Chatham PLC, Chatham, Kent

Hodder and Stoughton
A division of Hodder Headline PLC
338 Euston Road
London NW1 3BH

To Darren
And all the little ones of our human family.

ACKNOWLEDGEMENTS

My sincere thanks to Ms Danielle Silverman for her dedicated and faithful help in assembling this work. I am grateful to Dr Andrew Silverman for his co-operation and reassurance that chapters 3 & 4 can be understood.

My thanks to my secretary Marion Fallows for her patience, fortitude and gentle calming of a harassed mind while the book was being written. Thank you, Daniel Langsman, for your marvellous artwork, illustrating what must have been a fog of obscure ideas, and last but not least I am deeply grateful to my son Julian for leading me out of the Stone Age and confronting me with this new-fangled device we call a Wordprocessor.

CONTENTS

PREFACE

It seems they are everywhere in the Occidental world, calling the children of Cain under the influence of what might well be a Trojan Horse that will claim all humanity. They are the most dangerous phenomena this world has ever known. So dangerous that it might just be that 'they' are the reason that the great 'redeemers' that have visited humanity came claiming to 'save' Man. So who and what are 'they'?

They are grey in colour. Their skin is sallow and smooth and formed in scaly patterns. Their eyes are huge 'almonds' that wrap around their faces. Their bodies are small in stature, spindly and thin. Their heads are very large in proportion to their bodies, their chins narrow and pointed, with tiny mouths and nostrils that merge into their faces. They are the 'Greys', and their hands reach out urgently to seek their purposes in and within the bodies and body of all Humanity.

They are more. Much more. They are the tentacles of doom. They are the arms of Satan; for so long the talisman of all wrongs, of all evil, all sin in the history of Men. They creep wilfully, inexorably into the parlours of the damned and the innocent alike with a technology undreamed of on this Earth. They are Godhead to some among Man. They play with an unsuspecting world with castings of sugared contrivance, of coated reassuring sweetness. They form their armies, their spokesmen out of the body of our very humanity and they are placing their spawn unsuspected among the disbelieving legions of our world.

Flashes of rounded symmetry dance in a clear blue sky, announcing the demons' forms in the geomancy of doom. Our doom. The doom of the human family. *Homo Sapiens Sapiens*. Hungry relentless shadows of grey, running in lighted discs, poised ready to feed on the souls of Mankind. Hidden routes, written in a wheat field, a cornfield here and there, boiling the collective mind of Mankind, silently fixing the places of God's most salient touch – the wombs of womankind. Here they dally, womb upon womb, rifling the most precious locations in all the Universe with their dead spawn. Here they lie within the ignorance of an entire species, to write with their traces the schemes of an alien design that it might live again renewed. Within their singular centred curiosity they scale and scan the margins of Man with the measures of Succubi and Incubi – to transpose their fever in alien ways, and survive upon the blood of innocent human children born, and yet to be born.

'There is something out there' they exclaim, these agents that speak for them among Man. Inviting our disbelief. Yet not quite wanting to believe it themselves. Something inside them whispering that they dare not believe lest they see the horror of their predicament. 'We don't know what or who they are' they say. They stand as blind guides that stare at a disc and swallow our humanity. It is all a salutation for fools. And so as fools, they stand their New Age resolves in the make-believe buffoonery of empty minds. They draw the blinds over our collective eyes and we all see darkly through the fog of their ignorance, and worst of all, their pretence and their subterfuge.

They have been with us from the beginning. These creatures of the dead Universe. Their bedding places were once upon a time the Learning Cradles of all our yesterdays – long before the present histories of Humankind. They have slept in these cradles – in our centres of civilization, uninvited parasites festering within our flesh for their place in an eternity beyond the atom. A place now long lost, their quest for a soul gone with the last of their once biologically living species. They now linger in a kind of permanence as machines, yearning to sleep in the eternity beyond the atom they can only remember through the points that drive their memory store. Bioids, Roboids, Androids, call them what you will, they seek their yesterdays too, somehow, somewhere, not quite knowing its true meaning, because their creators could never write a program for the meaning of a soul. The meaning of that awesome, vital line that joins spirit-borne Being to the centre of all absolutes.

They can wait. They have the urgency of Clones. It is their only heritage. A thousand of our years, ten thousand, a hundred thousand. Theirs is not the urgency of the grave. Their time for lasting is measured in the width of the physical. The reins of atoms. Their returns are gauged and mortgaged in the sponge of mercury and silicon, not blood and bone. Their renewals lie within no tomb. 'Bioblasts' of 'living' plastic written in the legacy of the former of their kind that once could live in the halos beyond force, within conscience and thus love: they are the final reductions of such as this, leftovers lost and doomed to wander the thresholds of others' dreams. Indeed, of those who may dream at all.

Nigel Kerner

CHAPTER ONE:
THE ALIEN PHENOMENON

The words 'Flying Saucer' were first coined in 1947 in the USA. They were used to describe saucer-shaped discs of light and, some claim, craft that would fly at incredible speeds and be seen then, at that time, by many thousand witnesses, and in preceding years by many millions of people all round the world. It is claimed by many witnesses that these craft have landed and interactions and interplays have taken place between them and the beings that come in these craft. In truth, these claims have been made through the millennia and there is some telling evidence that cave drawings 40,000 years old depict the forms of alien beings that landed on this planet that long ago. The truth may well be that such visitations have been taking place for millions of years, and that the highways and by-ways of the Universe are roadways of exchange for all kinds of highly technologically advanced beings.

The earliest recorded sighting of Unidentified Flying Objects was during the reign of Pharaoh Thutmose III, about 1450 BC. According to a papyrus, 'scribes found a circle of fire in the sky . . . It had no head, the breath of its mouth had a foul odour'. Over the next few days 'they became more numerous in the sky'. There were many witnesses: 'The army of the Pharaoh looked on with him in their midst'. This account is particularly interesting because it speaks of a 'foul odour'. Many modern-day witnesses of alien craft report a terrible sulphurous smell that seems to be coming from the craft.

The Roman historian Livy described an 'altar' floating in the sky, surrounded by 'men in white clothing'. While Pliny the Elder describes a 'spark' that fell from a star to earth, becoming as large as the Moon before returning skywards. He also wrote of lights in the sky called 'night suns'. Julius Obsequens wrote in the fourth century AD about 'ships in the sky over Italy' that he alleged had been seen 500 years previous to his report. In Medieval Europe there are also historical accounts of UFOs. The Anglo-Saxon Chronicle for 793 AD tells of 'terrible portents' in Northumbria, with 'fiery dragons flying through the air'. While in 1170, Ralph Niger described 'a wonderfully large dragon' that caused the 'air' to be 'kindled into a fire and burnt a house'. The historian Matthew Paris writes of strange lights in the sky, and describes how, on New Year's Day 1254 over St Albans, 'there suddenly appeared in the sky a kind of large ship, elegantly shaped, well-equipped and of marvellous colour'.

There are many highly respected people who contend that we as a species, *Homo Sapiens Sapiens*, owe our existence to the genetic manipulation of genotypes of ape by these alien visitors that have been witnessed through the centuries. In this book, unlike others of its genre, I would like to examine some of the more important recent evidence that might affirm this proposition and correlate it with a historical perspective of social and religious beliefs. An astonishing story unfolds with startling repercussions pointed at the very bases and basis of human existence.

The chaotic Universe, by definition, is unpredictable and a fortuitous accident in 1947 in Roswell, New Mexico, USA may have provided stunning evidence and exposed the physical existence of the alien beings here on this Earth. Despite denial and counter-denial over fifty years, it is now clear that an undoubted cover-up of this event was staged by the US government then. It is an event that is well known and I will allude to it later as certainly one of the most vivid encounters amongst countless others that have occurred through the millennia.

There has been a great deal written about the phenomenon of Flying Saucers and their occupants over the years, be they Greys, Yellows, Blues, or Greens. Whatever the label, it is undeniable to all but the hard core of cynics, or 'conspirators of silence', that something of awesome impact on and, I believe, against the body of Mankind has been going on through the centuries. In the light of the whole UFO phenomenon as such, just too many witnesses, too many highly respected and respectable attestors have seen, experienced and been part of the phenomenon for us to deny its veracity as something genuine and tangibly real. Yet the difficulty of placing it beyond any doubt with hard evidence that is scientifically verifiable has been prodigious. What evidence there is has been, beyond doubt, hidden by the highest powers in government, particularly in the United States and what was previously the Soviet Union. In addition, it is clear the subjects of all this attention most certainly do not want to be found and do their best to keep it so.

The Greys are a species of alien being that are said to be visiting the Earth at this very moment in time. They are the subject of a great deal of excitement, discussion and speculation by millions of people around the world at the time of writing. A recent book by a pre-eminent Harvard Professor of Psychiatry contends that reports of kidnappings of human beings by these creatures may well be a real phenomenon and not the rantings of mentally disturbed imaginations. It has set the cat among the pigeons not only among Ufologists but also in the world of (particularly American) academia. Professor John Mack contends that the experiences of many abductees are genuine experiences, in no way attributable to mental illness. The stories come from individuals from diverse backgrounds. They are remarkably consistent tales of encounters with small Grey beings with huge dark eyes who immobilize their subjects and transport them to spacecraft where they are probed in a battery of tests that appear to involve a sexual and reproductive enterprise, with far-reaching implications for humanity.

What contemporary evidence do we have to suggest the intrusion of an alien intelligence on the affairs of the Earth? There are tens of thousands of anecdotal accounts of both close and far encounters with disc-shaped craft travelling at speeds well in excess of anything our fastest aircraft are capable of. There are also hundreds of accounts, again anecdotal, of human beings who have met and been 'affected' by alien beings in very close encounters, some of an intimate variety. Most of the anecdotal evidence is regarded as scientifically unproved because of its very nature, and rightly so. The nature, and circumstances of some of this type of evidence are very convincing. There are a large number of incidents reported by reputable and reliable people, some of whom were doctors, pilots, engineers, scientists, and priests. I believe many of these accounts could be and should be taken very seriously and without incredulity. They are not, however, verifiable through the scientific processes that would render them affirmable beyond doubt. Yet there have been a few instances where actual proof of landings of craft and alien beings that have taken place was available and this physical evidence was later hidden and obscured by the authorities. One of the most famous is the Roswell incident. I write from a typical account that appeared in one of the more reputable journals claiming to investigate such an incident:

On the 7th July 1947 a spacecraft of extraterrestrial origin crashed in a remote region of the New Mexico desert, near the Roswell Air Force base. Parts of the damaged craft and a total of six alien beings, two of them still alive, were collected from the crash site and removed to secret destinations. The American Air Force in collusion with the local police began an extensive and elaborate denial and cover-up of the incident that has taken nearly fifty years to uncover and expose. In a deliberate and measured series of lies and misinformation the authorities in the Pentagon and other responsible military and governmental organizations hid the facts of the incident, threatening some witnesses with the loss of their lives. Until, eventually, the sheer volume of witness reports overwhelmed official inertia to reveal the truth of what had happened at Roswell, helped along by a sympathetic Congressman who opened up a can of worms, the repercussions of which have only just begun to be realized. A film taken at the time by one of the official cameramen purporting to be of the autopsy of two of these beings has grabbed world attention. The whole event, the details of which are extensively available for the interested reader, puts into perspective the size of the international conspiracy that seeks to hide the fact of the alien presence in our solar system.

The 'creatures' recovered from the Roswell crash site were described at autopsy as humanlike in appearance but the biological and evolutionary processes responsible for their development appear to have been quite different from those of *Homo Sapiens*.

It is beyond the scope of this book to catalogue all but a few of the host of startling and in some cases highly significant incidents that point to verification that the UFO phenomenon is a real and crucially important factor in the destiny of Mankind. The evidence for its veracity is overwhelming now and has been for some time. It has got to the point where it is usually dismissed by those who have a vested interest or brief in defending and obscuring the interests of these creatures. I believe that anyone who follows the strings that lead to the first 'hands' that actually control the alien presence on Earth will find that those hands have not got five fingers.

Gordon Cooper, a US astronaut, while on a Mercury flight on 15th March 1963, reported a glowing greenish object ahead of him approaching his capsule at speed. The vehicle was, as he put it, 'very real and solid'. This was confirmed by the tracking radar at Muchea. Cooper had previously reported sighting metallic saucer-shaped discs while piloting an F86 Super Sabre jet over Germany. He reported that the discs could out-manoeuvre all existing fighter aircraft in the world at the time. Cooper further affirmed before the United Nations that he believed that extra-terrestrial vehicles and their occupants were visiting this planet.

James Lovell, Frank Borman, Neil Armstrong, Buzz Aldrin, Donald Slayton, Robert White, Eugene Cernan and Scott Carpenter, all US astronauts, have confirmed and affirmed sightings of extraterrestrial vehicles that they believe are not of our world. They are just the tip of the iceberg of reports by hundreds of US, Russian, British, French and German pilots who have seen and witnessed real and tangible evidence that our Earth is being examined by strange craft that do not have their origin on this planet.

Admiral of the Fleet Lord Peter Hill-Norton, who was Britain's former Chief of Defence Staff in the early 1970s, found himself that doors were closed and access to essential material was refused him when he decided to investigate an incident that took place near a Nato air force base in Suffolk in 1980. If a man with his contacts and military pre-eminence could be sent packing when looking into matters to do with UFOs what chance does the ordinary citizen have of unravelling the truth about it all? It seems some very important people in very high places are closing ranks to guard and keep secret all information pertaining to the phenomenon. They seem to be protecting what might amount to a deepening threat to the natural well-being of the family of Man by grey-bodied synthetic 'demons' that have invited themselves to be our unwanted guests.

After years of contrived denial, misinformation and downright lies, the Head of the investigating machinery appointed by the Ministry of Defence in Britain to probe all matters relating to UFOs, much to the chagrin of the authorities, admitted in 1994, in full public glare, that he is convinced that there are such things as extraterrestrial craft visiting this planet. He also admitted that the authorities were perpetrating a cover-up.

Let me describe the event that Admiral Hill–Norton was investigating in a little more detail. It is a particularly interesting one . . .

It was 28th December 1980. The location was Rendlesham in England. A US Air Force Base in Suffolk, England. A joint US/British nuclear base seconded to Nato operations, one of the busiest Air Force bases in the United Kingdom. Its activities were highly secret and it held one of Nato's largest nuclear weapons stockpiles.

It was in the early hours of 28th December that two teams of base security officers left the East Gate to investigate strange lights in the forest. One team included Deputy Base Commander Lieutenant Colonel Halt and in the other group was Larry Warren. Larry Warren who witnessed the event said: 'The field in front of me was illuminated with some very bright strange light. I noticed that the giant oak tree to my side was illuminated as well. That was my first indication that something wasn't right in the field.' As standard procedure Lt. Col. Halt tape recorded his team's progress through the forest. As they measured radiation levels they spotted something through the trees. This is from the actual tape recording: 'It's a strange small red light. Looks maybe a quarter, half a mile, maybe further out . . . I'm gonna switch off . . . It was approximately 120° from our site. Is it back again? Yes, sir. We'll douse the flashlights then . . . Let's go back to the edge of the clearing, so we can get a better look at it . . . See if you can get the Star-Scope on it . . . the light's still there and all the barnyard animals have gotten quiet now . . . We're heading about 110°–120° from the site out through the clearing now . . . Still getting a reading on the meter, about 2 clicks, I count about 3–4 clicks, getting stronger . . .'

As Halt and his team were moving towards the light, Larry Warren and the others saw a curious circle of mist in the field in front of them. Larry Warren said: 'Out in front of me as we approached, I was watching this mist on the ground. There was other Air Force personnel, Security, Police, all throughout the field. Over in the distance were two cameras, one was a video camera, one was a motion picture camera and at the time the video cameras were very bulky technology, but I recognized it for what it was. Everything I saw in the field was documented on film that night, both on still photographs and on motion picture, there's no doubt about it. As I was watching this mist on the ground, a red ball of light moved in, I thought it was an A10 taxiing to RAF Woodbridge, behind me about a mile. It came in over the forest and the trees, it stopped over the circular fog-like object on the, ground, dispersed in an explosion of colour that was soundless, heatless and what happened was a transformation, somehow, of this mist to a structured object. It was about thirty feet at the base, twenty feet in height and a bank of blue lights at the base of it and mother-of-pearl or rainbow effect all over it, it was very difficult to look directly at it. The worst thing that happened to me was that when the event transpired, when there was this transformation somehow, some senior people ran off into the woods, into the fields and left us there and why I didn't run could have been shock, or whatever, but a number of us ran, a number of us stayed glued.'

One telling piece of evidence remains – Lt. Col. Halt's report, authenticated as genuine by the British Ministry of Defence. His report was released three years later through pressure from Warren and others, via the Freedom of Information Act.

Despite Government pronouncements, one man whose views cannot be ignored is Lord Peter Hill-Norton: I quote Lord Hill-Norton in a television interview:

'It seems to me that something physical took place, I have no doubt that something landed at this US Air Force base and I have no doubt that it got the people concerned, the Air Force people and the Commanding General at the base, into a very considerable state. My view is that the Ministry of Defence, who are repeatedly questioned about this, not only by me but by the other people, have doggedly stuck to their normal line, which is that nothing which was of defence interest took place on that occasion. My position about this is quite clear and I have said this both in public and on the television and on the radio and I said it face to face to Lord Trethgowan when we met – either large numbers of people, including the Commanding General at Bentwaters, were hallucinating and for an American Air Force base this is extremely dangerous, or what they say happened did happen and in either of those circumstances there can only be one answer and that is that it was of extreme defence interest to the UK and I have never had a satisfactory rebuttal of that view.'

Sometimes the claimants to close encounters with UFOs are young children who are unlikely to have either the ulterior motive or the information needed to give convincing yet false accounts. In Professor Mack's book *Abduction* he cites the example of a little boy who is given the pseudonym Colin. His mother has the pseudonym Jerry:[1]

'In a journal entry dated August 14 1992, when Colin was two and a half years old, Jerry wrote of hearing him crying and talking to himself in the night. She went into his room and found him sitting up in bed. "He seemed very awake". He asked for juice, which she brought him, and then "started to ramble on about lights outside and owls with eyes". He pointed out the window and said "see the eyes". Colin is generally a sound sleeper, Jerry noted and "never asks to sleep with us or even has a habit of waking up at night". But that night for the first time he would not sleep in his own bed and insisted upon sleeping with his parents . . . This behaviour continued for several nights and Jerry wrote in her journal on October 29 that Colin talked often and consistently about "these things". When Jerry and Colin were outside together he would look up into the sky and ask about the stars and the moon and then talk about the "scary owls with the big eyes" that "fell down out of the sky" or "floated" down. A few times he demonstrated what the eyes looked like by circling his eyes with his hands curved in the shape of a C. One time he went "into a lot of action like running and screaming and saying that they make me eat some food and they attack me", especially hurting his toe.

'Colin also talked about spaceships, planets and stars. One night he climbed into bed with his mother and noticed a small picture of the Earth on the binding of the book. "That's the planet Earth" he said and "it go away" and "the house go away". Pointing at the ceiling he said, "they say bye-bye, see ya". Then he jumped out of bed and enacted a scene, talking anxiously. "The owls with big eyes fall down and jump and I jump" and "there's a spaceship and I come out of the spaceship . . . My toe hurt," he said and "the big eyes are scary, Mommy." After this Jerry actually found blood at the end of one of Colin's toes and a torn toenail . . . In her journal on 15 November Jerry wrote that Colin had cried out "Ouchy! Ouchy!" several times during the night. When she and Bob went in to see him he was sound asleep, but the next morning he said that the "monster owls" hurt his leg. Climbing into his parents' bed and pointing to the ceiling Colin said, "What's that big boat, that big boat in the sky?"

'In her journal entry of 28 January 1993, Jerry wrote that Colin's distressing experiences seemed to be occurring every week or two. On 25 January, when she and Colin went in the bathroom as she was preparing to meet Bob for lunch, he said several times in an angry frightened voice, "I don't want to go back to the spaceship!" Then, standing on the toilet with his teeth and fist clenched and obviously distressed, he said several times, "I get lost. I don't like it." Calming down, he said, "I was born there and fell from the stars". When Jerry asked him to repeat what he had said he added, "I born on the spaceship and it was dark." Then he became tense again and wriggled around. She asked him how he got onto the spaceship and he circled his eyes with his hands and said, "The eyes." When Jerry asked him if there was anyone on the spaceship with him he answered, "Yeah, I see the King. I see the King and he is God." Jerry wondered where he obtained the verbal skills, seemingly beyond his years, to say these things.'

On May 5th 1994 schoolchildren in the playground of a Zimbabwe primary school attested that they had all had a close encounter with a UFO and alien beings. One boy described 'a silver thing in amongst a clump of trees'. They all described the 'man' who 'walked towards us' out of the spaceship as having 'big black eyes'. One of the girls described how they left: 'They went one metre up from the ground and then they just disappeared.'

In 1989 several encounters took place in the industrial town of Voronezh in Russia. The main events happened between the 23rd and 27th of September. According to Dr Henry Silanov from the

University of Voronezh, who interviewed several of the witnesses, there were six landings and one 'hovering' UFO encountered. Most of the witnesses were schoolchildren. Dr Silanov had no doubts that they were telling the truth. One of the children, Vasya Suren, described how he was playing football with some friends in the park when they became aware of a pink haze, like a 'bonfire in a fog' above a nearby factory. The boys stopped playing and were observing the fog when a red sphere suddenly emerged. The object flew towards a tree and rested precariously on its top branches. As the boys kept watch, a door opened in the sphere allowing a tall being with three eyes to emerge. Another followed, and together they reached the ground. A young man at a nearby bus stop was paralysed by the second being and only released when the sphere flew away. This was only one of several close encounters witnessed around the town.

The São Jose Mountains in Brazil have, it is claimed, one of the highest concentrations of claimed abductions (or attempted alien kidnappings) anywhere in the world. A case occurred here on 22 May 1973 which is typical of dramatic local sightings. At three a.m. a travelling salesman was on his way home from Itajobi in a heavy rainstorm when his radio and then his engine began to fail. A blue beam from the sky penetrated the car. Assuming a truck was coming, he managed to steer the car off the road but no other vehicle appeared. Jumping out in panic, the man was smothered by an overpowering heat as the blue beam shone onto him. It was emerging from an opaque oval shape in the sky, out of which a tube or funnel was appearing. The beam made his car look transparent. His skin was also burning. He stumbled away and collapsed on the ground. He was discovered some hours later by two people in a passing car. These people brought the police as they were afraid that the man was dead after being in an accident. When they woke him, however, he responded in terror, screaming that they were aliens.

He was taken to hospital and kept in for observation, after which he was eventually released with no ill effects. But several days later, strange blotches appeared on his skin around his abdomen. The investigating doctor could not explain what had happened and insisted that the man was in no way deranged. Dr Chediak reported: 'I am absolutely sure that this man is telling the truth

. . . He was burnt, and they are no ordinary burns. They look as if caused by strange rays.'

A year later, on 26 April 1974, the witness disappeared on a short drive to Julio de Mesquita and was found six days later, over five hundred miles away, sitting on a hillside and soaking wet. Later investigation revealed that he had been abducted aboard a UFO and medically examined by blond-haired entities.

(The above account is given in a book entitled *UFOs and How to See Them* by Jenny Randles.[2])

David M. Jacobs, Ph.D., Associate Professor of History at Temple University in Philadelphia, is a leading academic authority on UFOs and alien abductions. Since 1986 he has been conducting hypnotic regressions with abductees. When he was asked in an interview whether he believes that it is possible that experiences with alien craft and alien beings could be psychologically contrived manifestations, his answer was as follows:

'What you have to remember is the sheer enormousness of the abduction phenomenon; millions of people are being abducted. Moreover, in abductions people are typically missing from their normal environment. Others notice that they are missing. There are multiple abductions. People may see other people being abducted, and may or may not be abducted themselves. There are situations where somebody sees somebody else being abducted, and is abducted him or herself. Years go by and person A has a hypnotic regression, remembers seeing the other person. Person B, 3,000 miles away in another city, and for another reason has a hypnotic regression, remembers the abduction and sees person A there as well. And neither of them know that they have been regressed remembering this same abduction. To make that psychological, we have to live in a different informational world of how the human brain operates.

'Furthermore, abductees come back from an abduction event with anomalous marks on their body, scars on their body, scar-tissue that was literally formed the night before. They came back wearing somebody else's clothes, they came back to somebody else's house by accident. People see UFOs in the air, hovering directly over the person's house when they're describing being abducted, neighbours who have nothing to do with it see this. There is a very, very, very strong physical aspect to this, that is completely non-existent in all of the other dissociative behaviour that we see.

'The interesting thing about all these questions is, if this were psychological, if people were dreaming it up, we wouldn't be asking any of these questions, we'd know all the answers. We'd ask people, why do you think they're doing this? And they wouldn't tell you, because that's the way the brain works. In channelling, for example, all questions are answered, all ends are tied up, and it's all roses and light. With the abduction phenomenon we just don't know'.[3]

How does one prove to the world that UFOs are real tangible objects if Governments at the highest level conspire to keep any physical evidence under wraps? Add to this the fact that the ETs don't want anyone to know of their presence in our neck of the woods. They have gone to and will go to extreme lengths to keep hidden their existence in our solar system. You can now imagine the predicament of someone who genuinely has a close encounter of the third kind and excitedly seeks to report and make known to the world their experience . . .

Let's say that Mr X, an average citizen, is out walking the dog and, coming out of the woods into a clearing, he happens upon a UFO and its occupants having to 'change a tyre.' Mr Average Citizen is carrying a video camera to photograph the countryside. The visitors don't see him. He immediately jumps behind a bush and gets a good five minutes of video footage of the alien family frolicking around their spaceship trying to make repairs and get out of there urgently. The dog finally gives the game away and the ET family zap Mr X and his dog and all other life forms in the vicinity for good measure. After a while Mr X awakens and finds that he has been asleep. Fido too comes back to life and, thanking the country air for its soporific effect, Mr X proceeds home without the slightest idea of what has happened. His memory has been wiped.

When Mr X gets home he plays the video and of course discovers what's on it. Can you imagine the predicament of Mr X who like any red-blooded average American sees money signs before his eyes? How does he prove that what is on the video is the genuine article both to himself and to an incredulous world?

Act as the devil's advocate for the moment. Let us assume that this accidental revelation of an alien presence must somehow be subverted. How would you prevent Mr X from making the maximum use of his evidence?

The natural incredulity of the scientific community worldwide would be the aliens' best asset. It does not even need an alien fifth column here on the Earth to help do this. Video evidence is so difficult to verify because it is so easy to fake. Mr X is likely to be doomed to a life of misery and perhaps madness if he persists in trying to prove the truth of the existence of UFOs and their occupants. Hollywood has a lot to answer for. A special-effects studio could concoct a video that would make our Mr X's genuine product look fake and there would be no way of proving it. It would be game set and match to the ETs. No Mr Xs anywhere in the world stand a snowflake's chance in hell of exposing, much less proving, the alien presence here.

I suppose the old cliché 'You can take a horse to water but you can't make it drink' is an apposite adage for illustrating the almost impossible task of convincing the powers-that-be who seek to hide the alien presence that is already here of this. I believe they too are in deadly peril. In fact, they are in greater peril, if anything, because they are likely to be the nearest at hand to be discarded when the time comes, much like we dispose of laboratory animals when their usefulness is over. Alas, I believe that those who actually know about the alien presence are controlled through mind-command techniques such as Mack and Jacobs have documented, and cannot in fact do much about it. While the rest are held by an elaborate system of dog-legged obfuscation that keeps them in ignorance of whom they really serve and how.

The pyramid of high-powered influence at government level worldwide has to be of fantastic scale to carry through a charade of these proportions. The evidence for UFOs as alien craft with 'living' occupants is just too staggering for the world to ignore. Literally tens of thousands of sightings have been made by tens of thousands of people all over the world, and their frequency has been increasing with time. Whilst the vast majority of these are explainable as natural phenomena, there are thousands that cannot be dismissed in such a way any more, as I have already said. But the numbers don't matter if the proof of their veracity is so easily obscured by the high-powered conspiracy that I believe exists specifically to do just this.

There is something else that is rather interesting about the whole UFO business. It would be funny if it were not of serious consequence to us all if stories of alien contact are true. The conspiracy of silence is backed up by law in the United States.

A bizarre law quoted by one of the US respondents in the Pentagon, Dr Brian T. Clifford, at a press conference on October 5th 1982, states that contact between US citizens and extraterrestrials, or their spacecraft, was illegal. According to a law that was already on the books (Title 14, Section 1211 of the Code of Federal Regulations, adopted on 16 July 1969, before the Apollo moon shots), anyone guilty of such contact automatically becomes a wanted criminal, to be jailed for one year and fined $5,000. The NASA administrator is empowered to decide, with or without a hearing, that a person or object has been 'extraterrestrially exposed' and impose an indeterminate quarantine under armed guard, which cannot be broken even by court order. There is no limit placed on the number of individuals who could in this way be arbitrarily quarantined. This legislation was buried amidst a batch of regulations that very few members of government were likely to have read in their entirety. Thus it was slipped onto the statute books without public debate. The dictatorial power given to the NASA administrator to override all the usual democratic rights of citizens to a hearing, or an appeal, is so against the principles of the US Constitution that it would surely have resulted in uproar, had it been brought to public attention. The excuse given by NASA for this remarkable law is that extraterrestrials might carry a virus that could wipe out the human race. This reason does not of course justify the criminal charges that would be brought against contactees with extraterrestrials. Such charges would prevent contactees from publishing reports of their experiences for fear of consequences to themselves. Thus, if the law were enforced, it would effectively silence witnesses to such phenomena. According to NASA spokesman Fletcher Reel, the law as it stands is not immediately applicable. It is ambiguously worded and can be thus interpreted as the government wishes at any particular time. Why would such a law be in place when NASA's commanding officers have for the last thirty-nine years assured the public that UFOs are nothing more than delusions or hoaxes? Is it there in preparation for a time in the future when NASA officials will be able to detain, and therefore silence, individuals who have clearly (without room for doubt or speculation) had contact with extraterrestrials?

There are further clauses to this particular law that cover all NASA manned and unmanned space missions. According to these clauses, NASA has the authority and responsibility to guard the Earth against any harmful contamination, or adverse changes in its environment resulting from personnel, spacecraft and other property returning to Earth after landing on or coming within the atmospheric envelope of a celestial body. It also has the power to establish security requirements, restrictions and safeguards that are necessary in the interest of national security. The article from which I obtained the information about this law was printed in *The Open Line Newspaper* in August 1992 in Spokane, Washington. The author of the article concludes that 'given all the unanswered questions regarding the authorities' hypocritical attitude to unidentified flying objects, it is hardly surprising that so many people are convinced that there is a cover-up of international proportions.'

Between the 14th and the 18th of January 1953, a remarkable UFO conference took place in Washington. Led by physicist Dr H.P. Robertson, five top scientists studied the best evidence available from the now famous 'Blue Book' files. The team included weapons experts and relativity specialists, but no psychologists. Thus the US government clearly regarded the UFO problem as a physical mystery – not one involving hallucinations. Although the Blue Book team gave evidence, they were not allowed to attend all of the sessions, or to be there when the panel made its recommendations. Only in 1976, via the Freedom of Information Act, did the full truth about the Robertson panel become public. It turned out that the conference was set up by the CIA. They had never tried to judge what UFOs were, or how Blue Book should study them. Quite the opposite: top secret recommendations involved finding ways to debunk sightings and defuse all interest. Among the CIA's plans was the use of cartoonists such as Walt Disney to create silly UFO pictures that would make the subject seem frivolous. They also ordered the monitoring of civilian UFO groups and researchers as they were considered too influential on public thinking.

It is my contention that this factor concerning the Greys has through the ages been the secret source of many of the ills that have befallen our species during its history. I believe that Mankind has been intercepted by an alien species of Being and that this interception accounts for the deadly insets in the nature of Man and has directed our actions in such a way as to compromise our very existence as a species. I believe we have been blindly working for the 'Greys' to do just this. I believe that our species has been the victim of a giant con trick. We are sheep following a 'Master' plan that has prevailed through the millennia and has sought to muster all our tomorrows to serve ends not necessarily to our existential benefit as a species, but rather to the benefit of a technologically superior alien 'species'.

I have in this book attempted to view the entire gamut of our existential meaning as a species with the added ingredient of an intervention of an alien species into the very centre of our affairs: the blueprint of our physicality, our DNA.

In order to try and understand the Greys and their relevance to all of us it is necessary to speculate on who and what they might be, and how and why these Greys might have come to be in the first place. For obvious reasons all I have to say must remain an open-minded speculation for now. Only time will reveal its veracity. However, it all might account for the condition and conditioning of our species through the ages, and perhaps reveal a cautionary lesson for us all. *A lesson that might save our very being as a species on this Earth if it is not already too late.*

CHAPTER TWO:
'BANG GOES OUR FUTURE'

If we are to understand this phenomenon of the Greys at all, we have to first understand the total existential phenomenon of our predicament as thinking, knowing, conscious beings. What are we really? Who are we? What are we doing here in this scenario called a Universe? Where are we going? Eternal poignant questions that we have to try to answer if we are to understand our total predicament as living beings.

Knowledge gives meaning. Meaning gives resolve and resolve makes for discovery. Everything depends on the urge to want to know. Those who seek knowledge incessantly are therefore likely to be more assured of a better and longer existence, at least in physical life. The knowledge of, and the preservation of Self is all to do with the urge to discover and it seems we have not been able to discover what really mattered till it was too late.

The biggest tragedy of our human condition is that the vast majority of human beings on the Earth, it seems, are content to go about their everyday business with never a thought about our existential meaning as a species, or group, or our predicament as individuals. We all know that it takes a crisis to prompt any real questions of profound meaning or value to us. This has led to an awesome failure on our part. We have not made the one great discovery that mattered. The one crucial piece of information that many great sages and masters through the centuries came to warn us about. As a result we didn't spot the Greys in the soup of our existential condition soon enough. So who or what are these Greys?

Here, therefore, is a simple man's view of the Greys (or whoever there might be out there flying a cigar or a dish), formed in answer to two earnest questions posed by my then ten-year-old son: 'Dad, can flying saucers really hurt people? And where do they come from?' His questions were sincere and deeply serious. They implied that he accepted these things were real and this was what intrigued me. I thought he deserved a serious considered answer if only to convince him that his original premise was wrong. Darren was and is a deep thinker and always considered his questions very carefully before he asked them. He has an encyclopaedic knowledge of all kinds of trivia and could quote you the length to the yard of the most obscure river, or give you the football score between Upper Moldavia and Lower Baluchistan in 1948, had they played a match. I decided a peremptory answer would not do and so I decided to research an answer in some depth. Little did I know then that my search was going to turn my own world and philosophical perspectives upside down. So here goes.

Before I attempt an answer, let me start with an apology. It is impossible to try to get an insight into the questions raised by the possible presence of extraterrestrial alien beings in our neck of the woods without trying to establish how they got here and from where. That involves some understanding of the nature of our existential base: the Universe, space/time, matter, light and energy. An adequate elucidation of these notions to non-physicists involves horrendously obscure explanations. I have tried my best to give a simple explanation of the basic dimensional elements involved in the way my non-physicist mind conceives it all. It still involves some seemingly obscure explanations that cannot be helped and for which I apologize, but it really is easy to understand if taken slowly by those, like me, untutored in the formalities of advanced theoretical physics.

We are told it all started for us with a Big Bang. The universe we inhabit as a species of thinking, knowing beings started with a mighty explosion. It started, we are told by scientists, from a point so small it cannot be envisaged. A Higgs Boson point. A field of effect so tiny in scale we cannot imagine it. All things we know and observe in this universe came, impossibly it seems, from this point that suddenly expanded in an explosion that continues to this day, making with it all the 'things' we know and observe with our physical senses. But where did this Higgs Boson point come from in the first place?

At this point we have to change tack and get into the world of reasoned speculative imagination. We know that there had to have been a point from which it all started. We have to then ask the question, where did this point come from? How was it there? The clear logical implication is that there was something from which the point came. So what could this 'something' be?

The best theoretical physicists in the world have no consensus nor, indeed, any plausible answer as individuals for this. The theophilosophers have no clue either that stands up to rational view. So the task of finding an answer comes down, I believe, to you and me. Mr and Ms Ordinary. We are the great 'in betweens' and I would back our speculations and instincts against theirs any day, because ours are less likely to be cluttered up with the narrow specialized perspectives that their individual learning tunnels may have inherently given them.

As distinguished physicist Professor Russell Stannard points out in his recent book *Doing Away With God*: 'Science cannot say what anything is. At a fundamental level, it cannot say what anything actually is'. He clearly illustrates this point in the following way:

'You can say that matter is made of atoms; an atom is made of a nucleus and electrons; the nucleus is made of protons and neutrons; and protons and neutrons are made of quarks. So, everything is made of electrons and quarks. So, there we have it. What is matter? It's a pile of electrons and quarks.

'But does that really tell us what matter is? No, not at all. We haven't said what quarks and electrons are – other than that they are point-like somethings.

'There are, of course, additional statements we can make about them. We can say, for example, that each electron and quark spins about on its axis like a top. But that still does not throw light on the nature of the "stuff" out of which the tiny top is made.

'Or we can say that the particles carry electric charge. But that only gets us into deeper water still. It raises the question: What is electric charge? Again, we can't actually say.

'We introduce the notion of electric charge because it helps us to understand the movement of the particles better. For example, it is noticed that when two electrons are placed close to each other, they tend to try and move away from each other. Why do they do that? We say that they each carry an amount of negative electric charge, and that like charges repel each other. Good. That explains the motion of the electrons. But it does not tell us anything about what electric charge is – any more than it helps us to understand what the matter is that carries the charge.

'Talking about motion brings us up against yet more unknowns. The motions are in space and time. But what actually is space? What actually is time? We know how to measure them. We can assert that the distance here called a metre is a hundred times that one called a centimetre; or that an hour is sixty times as long as a minute; but the actual nature of space and of time? They remain a mystery.

'So, if science is fundamentally incapable of explaining what anything actually is, what does it explain?

'It describes how things behave. That's all science ever does. It describes how point-like objects behave in space and time – and it manages to do that without ever coming clean about the nature of the "stuff" that makes up either the objects, or the space, or the time. Put that way, it can sound like a pretty modest enterprise.'[1]

Stannard goes on to point out that science 'is interested only in questions beginning "How . . . ?" It has no way of tackling questions that begin "Why . . . ?" It cannot, for example answer the question: "Why is there a Universe rather than nothing?" Nor has it anything to say about: "Why is the Universe the way it is, rather than some other way?" All it can talk about is how the Universe behaves. Whereas the restriction on not being able to answer questions about what things are might be regarded as mildly frustrating, this latest restriction is crippling. It means that science is quite incapable of tackling questions to do with meaning and purpose.'

It is for such questions that I will now seek an answer.

CHAPTER THREE:
TO BE OR NOT TO BE –
THAT IS THE ANSWER

Why does our Universe exist in a point scale, a series of seemingly separate and discrete points called atoms and particles woven in a matrix of different forces?

If we look around us it is clear to see that all that exists is fundamentally measured in this point scale. We seem to exist in a Universe of separated points or parts. What's more, a fundamental law of physics called the Second Law Of Thermodynamics tells us that all things will decay into greater and greater states of randomness and chaos with time, till finally at the death of the Universe all that will be left of it will be one vast arena of heat with no particles. They call this phenomenon 'entropy', or the heat-death of the Universe. It is all a one-way process from Order to Chaos no matter what contrivances some scientists use in a current vogue for trying to elicit order out of chaos.

'God' has been a dreaded word to many scientists in the recent past. As explained by the Judeo-Christian theosophers, it was to me, too, once upon a time. So many men of science these days run away covering their logical heads and ears from the sound of pulpits and church bells. I can't help feeling that with ultimate irony it will be just one such as these who will finally, by reduction at least, prove the existence of the Final Being.

But God is becoming more popular in the lexicon of science these days. He, She, or It is making a comeback with the permission of the scientists. At least, in the most recent prognostications by our most eminent men of science, God has made a rather spectacular comeback. Physicists have approved His nomination by implication at any rate in including it in a spate of recent books by them. I'm sure He is giving praise to them wherever 'He' is.

I have mentioned the word and now I am going to have to deal with it. The scenario I have outlined thus far now requires a definition of what I mean by 'God' or, to put it better, 'Godhead'.

Some would say that the most important question in science today is centred on the question 'Is Godhead physics?' Or, to be more precise, the laws of physics. Many theoretical physicists would like to claim at the very least that God has to be a physicist. The most interesting current debate in science is centred on this question. Although few scientists would admit it, the final arbitrator, the Old Man in the Sky, or whatever Godhead might be in the sky or elsewhere, has worked a flanker on all of them, when they all thought they had got rid of Him (or Her).

Here they were, all of them tacitly working harder and harder to take God out of the picture as some medieval superstition, and the harder they worked the more they discovered that they were being brought face to face with the possibility that something like Godhead might exist. It's a hard world, even for our men of science.

If I can come down to Earth for a moment and consider the words of Russell Stannard again, Professor Stannard has said that in his opinion, 'although many scientists have the word "God" in the titles to their books, they are really unravelling the laws of nature, and not the Mind Of God as they claim. By using the word "God" it is making it sound to the public that scientists have got it all wrapped up, and it's not true. Take it from me, it is not true.'

In his aforementioned book, entitled *Doing Away with God*, Stannard makes the following observation: 'Walk into a bookshop these days and what do you find? Titles such as *The Mind of God* by Paul Davies, and *Unravelling the Mind of God* by Robert Matthews . . . Most people, of course, will not be buying these books to find out what they are actually about. But they do see the titles – blazoned in big letters across the dustjackets. So, what are they to think? Scientists have succeeded in getting God sorted out? They have triumphed where theologians down the ages have failed?

Concepts such as 'love' and 'salvation' have now been incorporated into a formula? And what of the scientist himself? If, by his scientific investigation and assessment, the totality of God's mind can be laid bare, where does that place him in relation to God? Science becomes the religion, the scientist the high priest – or even the god, perhaps. I'm sure it was never the intention of these authors to promote such a triumphalist view of science. Yet it is a view that some people do hold.'[1]

It has been said rather appositely that 'The God of the New Physics is a cold God unresponsive to prayer and oblivious to human misery.' He sounds suspiciously like the caricature of a scientist, doesn't he?

What, then, might this phenomenon I prefer to call Godhead be? Before I make an attempt to explain the phenomenon as I see it, I will start with a claim. A claim that I later hope to confirm with argument. I claim that Godhead has to be something like a Centre of total Ultimate Balance – where no contradiction whatsoever exists. This centre will thus give rise to perfect Harmony in Peace and absolute Stillness. Most importantly – absolute Forcelessness. Here will have to exist the ultimate reference against all references, where viewing points and points of view are one and no separation of points exists. Time itself will be no more, because Time is a function of the separation of points, if you think about it. And so everywhere is instant and instant instantness is Everywhere in Godhead. Here there has to be no 'happening'. Just a passive maximum potential to Be, in that state, or not to Be in that state eternally. Perfect Balance, where there is no something . . . Where ALL is the No-thing of Perfect Congruence.

So is there such an effect . . . ? Is there such a centre – somewhere – somehow?

The Universe, it seems, came out of a prior state of order in a gigantic explosion that now provides an awesome engine for the dismantling of this order into chaos.

So where did this prior order come from? Is there another Universe? One that is the opposite of our Universe in all ways. A Master Universe from which ours comes. It is a logical assumption to make. If there is a Universe where everything divides, there has to be a Universe where all things are added together. Simplistic though it all seems, it is often what is simple that holds the greatest truth. I believe that there is such a phenomenon as a Universe of the Whole where all parts come together in total fit. It also has to be the Master Universe because total fit makes for total stability and total stability makes for everlasting tenure. Have you noticed that all this makes for a nice definition of God?

There is a pointer verifiable in scientific terms that indicates the incredible fact that there is a power totally outside life and the living process that gives rise to it all. A power that by implication points to the fact that there is a world, universe, call it what you will, totally outside the atom. In fact it clearly implies that we would all not be here now or indeed continue to be here if this power did not exist. Let me explain.

It has been recently confirmed as one of the most significant discoveries of biology, though actually discovered twenty years ago by Dr Andrew Wyllie, a research scientist, that the basic element propagating all life, the cell, has an underlying primary drive to die. It is called the Cell Death Phenomenon.[2] It is now believed that every cell in living formats is innately programmed and initiated with the fundamental drive to die. In other words the base existential paradigm of the basic living unit of all living beings is – to die. The cell only lives to die, and unless signals continually 'order' it to stay alive by getting the cell to use its properties functionally, every cell in the body, in any living body, will spontaneously commit suicide and die. In other words, the cell only stays alive because it is called on to have a function. As soon as this call ceases, it will 'switch off' and die. Amazingly, it seems the way of life is truly death.

The implication of this for general existence is explosive. The immediate questions that dawn in the mind are, why and how is there a cell in the first place? Why indeed does a cell 'happen' at all if it is already programmed to die? More intriguing, what instigates it to come about in the first place and why, if its only meaning is never to exist anyway? In the light of this discovery, why, if the Evolutionists are right, does a cell, having been formed despite the unbelievable and totally unlikely mathematical discongruities of chance, have as its driving paradigm the extinguishment of itself?

This, of course, raises the further question: Who or what commands the cell to come into being if apparently its only reason for doing this is to die? How did we evolve to be human from the

'Sea Worm' in the primeval broth, as biologists and evolutionists would commonly have us believe, if at every step of the way we are trying like hell to commit suicide? At least, our very basic building blocks, our cells, are seeking to do this all the time.

Biologists and all evolutionists claim that life was 'conceived' at random, and based on mere chance. That it all happened accidentally in some chemical soup that existed on the planet millions of years ago, that from this most rudimentary start all of us emerged biogenetically routed through a sea worm that crawled on to the land and finally came up with Ronald Reagan and Maggie Thatcher. They claim, therefore, that there is no great shape and coherent meaning behind life at all. According to them, it was all based on the accidental coming-together of all the building blocks necessary to make hypocrisy and cant happen.

The fact remains that the 'Cell Death Phenomenon' can only be explained if the existential base of the Universe itself is somehow 'wrong'. In other words the Universe is struggling to exist. That, as it turns out, is absolutely true. You see, the Universe runs on a system that at the very root tries, all the time, to prevent itself from existing. This root is called the Second Law of Thermodynamics, or Entropy. A fundamental tenet of science that says that all things made of atoms, including atoms themselves, by themselves and without anything being done to them degrade into greater and greater states of randomness and disorder with time. In other words, the Universe will finally end in a great field of heat with no particles. This is called the heat–death of the Universe.

So, why does the Universe exist at all? Why does it exist as we know it does, simply to die? Why is it even there if it is an existential base of errors? A dynamo of diminishing returns? Is it only there so that 'all things may exist,' be they good or bad, right or wrong?

A startling question dawns. If the Universe is finite, is there another paradigm of existence that is infinite? Just as if there is a plus there must be a minus, if this Universe separates and divides itself into chaotic oblivion, is there another 'Universe' that does the opposite? Adds things together into more and more ordered states till there is an opposite singularity of all parts together in total harmony and perfect fit. If logic and sense has any meaning there's a clear implication that there *must* be another 'place' or another 'thing' or a vantage point of some sort that conducts the 'music' to the opposite tune to which our Universe dances. A Universe of what is whole and together. A Universe of no parts because all parts fit perfectly into a perfect Whole.

If this were so, then there is a clear implication that intelligent life only exists in our Universe because this other place or master device exists. An even more startling implication arises and that is that this vantage point or 'place' has to be of the opposite existential tenor to all the features of this Universe. It has thus to be a scenario the base of which runs counter to all the basic design features of our Universe, including the most salient one of Limit or finiteness. A scenario that issues a call to 'live' and not to 'die' as our Universe does. An existential paradigm, as I have said before, that of itself adds, unites all parts in perfect fit with nothing left over.

What would provide such an indictment of 'death'? It surely has to be a situation where 'death' does NOT exist, i.e. a state of 'everlasting life'. Hold on. Where have I heard that before? Was this not after all the only thing promised to us by the being we have come to know as Jesus Christ? 'Eternal Life.' Yes, it really is the ONLY thing Christ promised as a consequence of leading a life through his example. Eternal life. Was Christ alluding to this Universe of the Whole when he spoke of his 'Father in Heaven'? Was he saying that 'heaven' was simply the opposite paradigm to this one? Would it not be reasonable to say that this vantage point is what religions and mystics have referred to throughout the ages for want of a better word as 'Godhead'; the central focus for all life throughout this universe of separated parts? Our Universe of the Whole. Our Universe of NO separated parts.

I cannot duck the issue and must attempt to explore the whys and wherefores of such a proposition. It is bound to get obscure and I have to warn the reader that it might be heavy going for some. Those readers not of a scientific or philosophical turn of mind and who don't much care about how and why the Universe came into being and much less care to read someone's opinion of how and why it all might have happened, need only skip this chapter and Chapter Four. Those, however, who want the whole thesis tied in and are 'suckers for punishment' might like to bravely venture forth.

I wrote Chapters Three and Four in a kind of inspirational

apoplexy. My mind was driven by the flow of ideas set in a gel of scientific expression. When I finished writing and glanced through the finished work as words on paper I could not understand head nor tail of it. It was only when I was about to scrap the lot and challenged myself to visualize the concept of each word as I read it that the whole thing started to live with rational meaning. I say this by way of apology for the necessary but perhaps annoying use of all the 'nesses' you will see. As any sympathetic reader or writer out there will note, there just ain't the lexicon in the English language to say this sort of thing. My deep apologies to all philologists and others who might take offence at the use of the glorious English language in this way.

Let me first start with a proposition and a claim. Let me then try to account for it and justify it. To do this we first need to allude to and account for an ultimate Finality – for want of a better word: God.

The proposition is that God, or Godhead as I prefer to call the phenomenon, is 'That in which all BEGINNINGS have their END and all ENDS have their BEGINNING.' My assertion is that there *has* to be such a state. My claim is that there *has* to be 'God', if logic has any meaning – and meaning has the merest logic. That assertion is unequivocal if reason and meaning are any yardstick. There has to be such an absolute FINALITY, if the separation of points that we affirm by our own existence, and the existence of the Universe as we know it, exists. There has to be a point where that demarcation began ... The 'where' in which it was ALL together *has to* exist, whatever we might call it.

But what determined the separation of points from this 'all together' state of being? This would be one of the most important questions since questions began. I believe the answer can be summed up in one word: Contradiction. The principle of 'Difference' as defined in a Universe of parts and portions. Whatever exists that simply 'contradicts' any elements or states in relative or comparative disposition, forbids the fitting together of these elements and states as parts in singular resolution and total fit. We have, therefore, to determine how and what brought about such 'contrariness' and what are the poles that define 'contradiction' as the elemental principle that constitutes 'difference'. 'Contradictions' vast enough to account for the manifestation of the entire

Universe of parts, in terms of separation of points through a dynamic effect, we all call 'Force'.

The law of increasing diminishing returns (Entropy) is based upon an exponential property that declares that an increase in the value of difference supplies an increase in the quantum of separation that, in turn, provides an increase in restriction which, when translated in terms of scope and choice, dictates values of 'Fixture'. Scope and choice are another way of saying viewpoint and point of view. The active or passive expression of Choice will thus demarcate the hierarchical standpoint of Being and its value as such.

It is useless to speculate, with a view to a definite answer, on what instigated the initial *choice* within 'Godness' for a *move* away, if you like, from the state of ultimate Union, for one very good reason. You cannot. Not 'really'. We have a somethingness mind, textured in separation. Our viewpoint is always going to be in 'somethingness' and therefore it will be in separation from the view of 'Unionness', if I can express it so. We cannot know anything in 'Unionness' terms. We can't visualize in instant instantness terms, from all points of view and perspectives all at once realized and understood in a multitude of different Thoughts being thought at the same moment and not one after the other, as we have to do in our 'Universe' of separated parts. We have to rely on what I will call the principle of 'Opposed Acquisition' that allows for the scope for separatedness, if there is a scope for Union to grasp the 'why' for separation. We have to say that within what is WHOLE all standpoints are ALL, not singularly disposed, and so to know as single in the singular and thus as a PART of the whole or what is All, you must be in the state of single-ness or parts of a whole. So must exist the scope to be singular. To be, in other words, in the state of being a portion of the whole. This is what the concept of 'Space' or 'room to exist' expresses. Space is that scope to be ONE with the WHOLE or separate parts from it. All this may be judged, or seen, in AWARENESS (being able to know anything) terms as a viewpoint, or point of view and in Actuality terms as some'thing'ness (having an identity that is definable) or no 'thing' ness (having no definable identity).

It is vital to realize that the state of Nothingness is not an effect where there is *no* effect, no anything . . . It is simply a centre where what we know as existence in 'thing' terms ceases to be such. Therefore, it is logical to surmise that such a centre of resolution is beyond our scope to visualize, discern or understand, adequately, in its own intrinsic terms of reference.

What, then, have we gleaned so far of an insight into the 'No-thing-ness' of perfect congruence? The centre of perfect balance and infinite extent – albeit not in its own terms of reference, which is limitless, but in our own limited terms: As extent increases, so does the scope for experience and so it is reasonable to expect such a centre to offer a greater scale of effect. As the potential for Knowledge increases, so does the capacity for what knowing prescribes. It therefore seems reasonable to suggest that order proposes the extent of KNOWINGNESS and so one would expect such a centre to be resolved in the greatest ORDER possible. Order prescribes the lack of contradiction and this, in turn, proposes the lack of tension, or force, for resolution. There would inherently be what we may call a perfect state of PEACE . . . stillness . . . tranquillity. Ultimately an effect of *no* force whatsoever. The eternal infinite PEACE of poets and dreamers, priests and mystics, would seem to be a logical derivation, its existence proved deductively outside claim and feeling, emotion and religio-political invective. For me this paradigm is Godhead, God or whatever you like to call it in terms of the utmost existential finality.

We now have a contour of Absolutes providing for the qualitative union of points. A centre of PERFECTION itself. Cast in an infinite continuum, where point of view and viewpoint are One. The manifestation of the two final abstract metaphysical polarities of all. What other way could we describe the principles 'Point of View' and 'Viewpoint'?

Stop reading at this juncture for a moment and have a think. What are the two most fundamental attributes one would need to have to make sense or give meaning to anything? They could only be the two properties of nature, judged existentially, we call Awareness and Will. You have to have Awareness to be able to know and you have to have Will to want to be Aware. To my mind they would be the two most fundamental tautological elements that verify Godhead itself in our own Universe of mass, force and thus separated parts. They are the two most basic elements of 'mind-force' possible that have to prevail to allow for and account for the connection between what is Whole and what is Part. They are *the* arms that assemble Existence itself. Like the co-ordinate planes of light fields that make a hologram, they issue forth into the potential to Be and make some'thing'ness happen in the merest steps in the symmetrical ordered connection modules of the heart of meaning we call Logic.

In order to answer questions concerning the origin of the Universe, we have to start at the beginning of all the dispositions these questions imply. To do this we have to ask *two* vital questions first. From where and from what did the Universe come and what exactly is the nature of this 'where'? To answer these questions we are forced to use clues provided by the Universe itself: its shape – its form – its existential frame.

I have tried to resist the urge to get too deeply philosophical in answering these questions, or I shall be writing into deeper and deeper obscurity. So let me begin by accepting, for instance, that the Universe is physical and known as such by us, through our capacity for sensory response, such as it is. Let's say our physical senses provide a 'knowing' that marks the Universe as a physical thing. This is expressed in what we call our perception of extent, as three distinct, opposed, detectable corporeal contours we 'know' and describe as the three 'spatial dimensions'. Thus, we can say that the 'frame' of the Universe is presented in a real and sensorially identifiable three-dimensional aspect. It has length, breadth and height. The fourth dimension is a 'conceptual dimension' we might call 'space/time'. It is nevertheless very real but not identifiable with the physical senses.

I have tried to understand the sequence of dimensional acquisition and would like to invite the reader to follow what must essentially be, at first sight, a rather complex and puzzling description, with forbearance. It is unavoidable if we are to 'see' how wonderfully 'set up' the concept we refer to as 'Being' really is.

The first question I have tried to answer is: Was there 'Space' before the 'Big Bang'? Was there in fact anything in terms of the Universe as we understand it in existence before the point of the bang, or was there just a 'potential' for dimensionality to occur? It really doesn't matter for the purposes of what I am about to expound. We have to account in as simple terms as possible for the dimensional contour of Space as we know it. We have to try to discover if these dimensional contours were made by the Big Bang, or existed prior to it. In other words, did atoms 'make' Space in its three-dimensional contour, or did they happen into an already existent 'pro forma' and just take up their resolutions to the dictates of this pro forma? The conceptual expression necessary to define such a dichotomy is, in my contention, the same.

As I have said, I have to start the whole quest by taking a single conceptual element or 'point' as our investigatory aid. I will give this 'point' the 'living' facilities of Awareness and Will for the purpose of this exercise. The whole brief of this 'point' is to create a 'world' that is maximally different to itself as a point and so let's set about this in logical steps, the merest steps of logical progression possible at each and every stage.

What, then, defines the contours of physicality and how may they be derived? In the Final Effect of togetherness of all effect – in what we might call Godhead, there has to be centred the ultimate potentiality to be or not to be anything and everything, something, or nothing, somewhere, or everywhere. It is in the exercise of choice, through the guidance of awareness and functioning capacity of will, that all existential effect comes to be. The expression of degree is the result of choice.

In logical terms, the merest minimum step away from such a state of potentiality, or 'nothingness', to actuality, or 'somethingness', is for an infinitely small point, or centre of effect, to occur. This point, or centre of isolationary effect, is the merest contour possible in what might be regarded as the 'all', or whole of 'being'. It is thus unique from what is 'all', as a 'point' and is, therefore, the initial singularity of separation itself. There would be nothing that exists away from it, that is the same as it, and so it would have to 'create' the scope – room – effect – to exist – completely new. We are used to seeing space as extent – an allowance of 'room' to fit things in – if you like, and so our 'point' is limitation itself. It is the scope to exist in limitation. (That seems a contradiction in terms, I know – but there is no other way to see it, existentially.) In becoming the merest point of actuality and in creating its scope to exist as such, it is fixing itself in a certain pose – in a defined stance – and so it is completely unlike its status within the whole, where it would be in all positions at once. This stance of complete singularity can never be achieved absolutely, of course, because the centre – this merest point of actuality, is pure intelligence itself. In other words we have made it at one and the same time – awareness and will, ready for the first posture of separate existence out of the All. Out of the whole of existence in total and absolute fit. Out of what we might call the phenomenon of Godhead. The final absolute of all togetherness in total existential fit.

Our 'Point' in its now discrete aspect has no sense of itself, because it is now 'alone' and has no way of 'knowing' itself in its now complete and absolute isolation as a point. It is at the very first stage of achieving what it set out to do – namely the complete acquisition of separation from what is whole, i.e. Ultimate Chaotic Subversion. The complete opposite to Total union in ordered harmony. Our point is now Actuality itself and, we must remember, 'knowingness' itself, expressed through the co-ordinates 'awareness' and 'will' as directives. It is ultimately ordered, but in separation from the whole has paid the price and is slightly disphased into singular direction with an instinct for 'every directionness' in its inherent make-up. It will seek 'total' separation from the whole through the merest logical steps in compromise of all these factors.

Our centre of Actuality, as a point, is in complete isolation from its previous situation. This makes it a Singularity, a completely new effect – alone. It has no reference of itself. This would not be true in the 'whole', when it was not a point, but in the separate state – it would have to have a reference against which it could view itself to simply 'know' it exists. This will provide the constant drive for difference – whenever it becomes the next logical singularity.

The drive to make dimensional space itself begins. In a series of merest logical steps, our point of actuality will find line – plane – curve – etc., tracing out the elbows of dimensional space – as it seeks difference, each time creating a home and living in it, so to speak, at the same time. It will be a most interesting exercise for the reader to trace the exact sequence in merest logic that our point will take in achieving all possible stances of spatial dimensionality. The correct sequence will give you an insight into a most startling and fantastic conclusion. You will arrive at a result where our 'Point' will have no option but to take on a mathematical incongruity, a conundrum of effect that will decide the scenario that we find ourselves in as Beings.

Let's try to trace the likely sequence of dimensional acquisition that gave rise to the Universe of parts. It is important that the stages are seen clearly, for they mark a general logical sequence that formed both the cradle and the baby: Space and all that occupies it. (See Figs. 1, 2, & 3 in the illustrated section.)

A point has no implicit direction. If it will do the merest thing different from itself, it will go to a line in one direction from itself – not two. So, a unidirectional trend is set that will be frozen into the line. A predisposition to seek the difference from the merest most single standpoint possible. But how does our point decide which direction to head . . . to favour? It doesn't. It doesn't need Direction, for the point's only view is the first expression it can make outside itself. It knows how to express itself outside itself, because before it became a point, this expression was what brought it from being no 'point' to being *a* 'point'. It is not in three-dimensional space (and so there isn't a 360° choice for direction) because that hasn't happened yet. All that exists is its self, with all the information that went to make itself – a point. It will do the thing it *knows* of itself in its search to make a difference, to view itself against. It will make another point and then another, outside itself, and so on, the same way it did the first. When it makes the first point outside itself, it has made its maximal difference, as a point, happen. It is not *a* point any more, it has lost individuality. In duplicating itself, it has to start at a fundamental 'stage' of itself before it gets to its 'full' self.

This is difference enough and as this 'difference' happens, it will continue to the next stage of difference and so on, till it makes itself whole . . . In being programmed to find difference, it will go further and seek difference in the expression of extent.

It is important to realize that the above sequence of stages is not part of the Big Bang, but neither is it before the Big Bang, as time began with it. It could be seen as part of the architecture of the first instant.

This change gives rise to the concept of direction, giving potential speed from stasis, a direction and thus velocity . . . Velocity gives increased potential . . . Speed and so on. A continuum begins. A continuum of differential acquisition. Our point in separated sequential velocity (time) makes a line and one dimension is born. The sequence continues . . .

As the merest empirical change from a point to line(ness) happens and the line is formed, the one-dimensional plane becomes a singularity in itself. It is born of pointness and knows direction and velocity . . . It has, on its way from 'O' (no pointness) given birth to 'time' and at the very 'moment' it does so, so to speak, it is another singularity, it will have as its whole conceptuality lineness(ness). (I'm having fun inventing these words. I declare this with due regard in apology to any philologists reading this.) As a singularity it still has not found difference that exists minimally as a duality. So it will repeat what pointness did when it was no point then one point . . . it will go for the next empiric difference to itself . . . in the logically merest current next step it can take.

Let's consider what Lineness knows at this juncture. It knows *choice* and *change* and so it knows *speed* and *direction*. In doing this, it assumes *velocity*, tacitly, and so it knows separation. As separation, it knows *time* and all this together gives it a state of individuality. So now it knows individuality and, as this, it 'knows' everything, relatively. Of course, the price of individuality, of unitness in any scheme, point, or line, is that it can never know as the ALL . . . The final price for separation is paid. And so, the line is a confluence of all that is pointness implicit and explicit. In becoming a line from a point, it knows extent (a line is just another point from the first and the difference between the two.) All these characteristics go to make it a whole conceptuality as Lineness . . . It contributes to its only functional capability: Lengthwiseness. It has no direct concept of Widthwiseness yet, because it will use all it knows in Lengthwiseness, to increase to infinite Length, if it was not baulked at the prospect of not knowing it existed when it became a 'singularity' as one dimension.

It needs most of all to know it exists and so seeks difference against which it can know itself. It knows Choice, Change, Speed, Unindirectionality, Velocity, Separateness, Time and Extent. It knows Difference and how to Differentiate. Above all, it still knows Pointness. It knows Start, but not end . . . It thus continues. All the above are One in the Ultimate Union of Points, no Dimensionalness – Godhead. We have separated all these in distinct knowabilities because Intention, or Will, prompted the creation of the elbows of dimensionality – Separateness. Godness is made to reveal itself. The vectors that make Contradiction manifest and so Force as a 'potential difference' have begun.

Our Line seeks difference armed with all the above. This collective functioning gives LINENESS an 'instinct' that it is possible to find something that is different to Lengthwiseness – itself. It searches all the permutations its 'knowledge' provides and in doing so sees that difference lies in a change of direction. It does this by duplicating itself as a line in its original direction from a point and becomes an infinite Line. It now has something different from Pointness. It has a longer surface expressed as Lengthness. Again, observing the rule of logically merest change, it starts from an imaginary centre to this Infinite LINE and begins to move with Lengthness, acting from pointness (see Figs. 1, 2, & 3 in the illustrated section) and finds that it will still be the same Lengthness each time a different direction is taken. It continues and in doing this, traces another surface it never had before . . . It has traced curve and plane. The Second Dimension is born.

It is into this 'Frame of Possibilities' we call the spatial dimensions, a frame that is implicit in the design of 'Godhead', so to speak, that the primal 'Knowing' essence of Godhead is propelled as the two elements that make up Thoughtability – Awareness and Will.

All 'things' are simply centres of physicality, or force, where this essence of Godhead settles in grander or lesser states to make 'life' where it is grandest, and static dependent things (lifeless things), where it's least. In other words, 'Thoughtability' commences to sublimate into dimensional space/time. It becomes at one and the same time the architecture, the architect, and the occupier of space/time. Remember our 'Point', as Thoughtness, is coherent and, in its own dimensional terms, together, when it begins its journey into separation from the Master Universe (Godhead State) of total union of parts and as it gathers the measures of force, it expresses in choice the urge to know itself as a separated entity, creating the very thing that ironically fixes it more and more as it continues to manifest difference – difference against which it, in turn, may measure its own identity. In other words, it has to gather more and more the force of contradiction from its previous expression, as it transmutes into the dimensional elbows. Its intrinsic identity as once 'Coherence Pure' degrades in quantum measure as it increases its dynamic availability. Thought as 'Knowing' becomes Thinking or the search To Know, or Thought in an active directional mode – the implicit search for option within more and more separated complexity. In other words – our Point of once 'All Knowing' now has to seek to know what it once knew; as its Knowledge of 'All' is being lost, the further it goes into the state of being parts of the Whole, or the 'All'.

From within and without – Thoughtability as Thinkability gets inherently more pinned in the twisted contours of the increasingly complicated dimensional elbows. (Again, I'm sorry about the words, but as you have no doubt seen I have no choice but to use them.) As each successive dimension happens, through to the second dimensional aspect – the step by step process is logically coherent. Nought becomes One – One can become Two, without the loss of all of itself, so to speak, and complete reconciliation of its dimensional information, but it is at this point that all that ceases.

The two-dimensional stage is where the logical incongruity happens, because up to now an increase by single Whole measure can take place from one dimension to two, by simply increasing the whole of what is there by a full measure of itself. But, at the stage of reaching Two, the least Whole measure it once was and can increase by – one – is lost and it could only increase by its present Whole – Two– to maintain its full measure. I'll call this my 'Maximum/Minimum' rule as I am no mathematician and don't know the jargon for such a concept. This contradiction to its previous format of increase – in seeking the next step – means 'halving' its scope to increase, to seek the third dimension, which is done with the acquisition of a single extra one. Our point is only phased for two discrete dimensions that 'fit'. But the bipartite phase has to be accommodated whole, and it cannot be. In other words, 2 cannot increase by half of itself to 3 and still keep all of its increased value as 2. It will have to go to 4 to do this. But it has to meet the Maximum/Minimum rule, so it will seek a compromise and try and do both at the same time. It will try to change its aspect by half of itself and all of itself. Its '2' stage will try to go to '3' and '4' all at the same time. This incongruity provides the two-dimensional plane with no alternative but to provide for the next single-level increase, to three dimensionalities, most simply with a twist off its plane and, following its other implicit resolutions of pointness – lineness, planeness, curvedness and twistedness – it would compromise. Through this simple expression, it would spiral back on itself to whence it came. The single-dimensional line has no defined edges. The two-dimensional plane has no defined sides, with one side 'above' and one 'below', as there is no 'Space' above or below the plane, both perspectives are contained in one. So, in using all this information, together with the further impulse to go beyond 'three-dimensionalness' and finding this extra impulse, together with the rest of the elements of extent it 'knows', it provides a toroidal twist that generates dimensional extent – Space and Time in a form whose two edges are one – and whose two sides are one side. A giant incongruous continuum happens as a 'Universe of Parts' that contains and synthesizes Knowing into platforms of force that would provide for the basic 'centres of action' we call atoms to happen – in the form, shape and expression of a Möbius Toroid which I will call henceforth a Moroid. (See Figs. 4, 5, 6 & 7 in the illustrated section).

If you have done the exercise, I hope you will see that there is no alternative in connected – ordered – sequence than to arrive at the conclusion that Space and all effect in it will be 'set' in a pattern that implies what is termed in science as a three/four-dimensional Möbius strip, or more accurately a Möbius Toroid. All that exists in separatedness will have a Moroidal central spinal 'moment' – 'Holologically', so to speak, printed in every conceivable aspect of existent effect. A continuum of enforced motional sequence that has to be followed in a basic two-dimensional singularity twisted loop that implies a toroidal effect of three- to four-dimensional compromise.

It simply means that we are stuck in 'doing' and 'being' everything in an environment of force that provides effect – in force that follows the shape outlined above. That every atom that makes the physical Universe and the entire physical Universe itself, has to be set in an inherent 'twist', a logical compromise to allow separation from 'Godhead' to be, or exist. Space itself is twisted in this basic shape – and pattern. All happening that is inherently part of that space, happens within and to its dictates. There is no escape from this shape for anything! Or is there?

Forgive me if I recap once again on the fundamental essential concept that is revealed. It is, of course, the most important of all concepts in explaining the *why*, *who*, *what* and *how* of Universal existential effect, both as we know it, and if you'll pardon the speculations, how we *should* know it.

The search for the final spatial dimension possible provides an inertial effect we call Force, the shape of which is the familiar figure-of-eight or concentric loop configuration – the sign for infinity. This is the root shape upon which the entire spatial infrastructure of the three-dimensional matter, (and, as radiation, non-matter), inherently dual-polarity Universe is set and evaluated by the sciences of physics and chemistry today. It is the pattern of force of all newly-created 'elements' that the separation of points must 'follow' in 'our' state of implicit separation from the All Together state of Spirit. It gives rise in its most basic *completed* building block to the Atom. We might say that the atom is *the self-contained pattern of implicit, fixed force, or tension, in the space of its own creation that Thought becomes in its search for ultimate separation from the Whole*. Hydrogen was and is the first and simplest self-containable stable pattern of Force. Uranium was and is the last 'created' that this planet can hold as a stable, or, in my terms, 'devolved' stable modulus for our particular location in Space and situation in 'Time' on the planet Earth.

And so, the acquisition of Dimensionality, or to you and me, what we might call the way one measures 'Space', or the room or allowance to *Be*, is thus an implicit effect that has a beginning beyond the stage at which spatial Time starts.

The effect is as implicit as its opposite concept: no dimensionality, Nothingness. If there is Union, there must be Separation or vice versa. We know the Universe emerged from an effect where all that we see in somethingness – plasma, gas, liquid, solid, atoms, elements, planets, stars, galaxies – was centred to become separated with the 'momentum' we see as the universal state at present, driving them all apart in what we observe as Entropy. This momentum, this drive, this all-encompassing directive, that gives *change* a pace, a rate, an irresistible momentum in constancy. Constancy is the platform on which all Existence has to be judged. If we, for the moment, just suppose there is an absolute point of Congruity, where all things fit so perfectly without the slightest contradiction, we must then suppose that there must be a process, an 'effect', that allows this perfection, this 'fit', to happen. Conversely, we will then have to accept that there must be a continuum – an effect that allows for the opposite – to occur: a drive to discontinuity, discongruity, break-up, separation . . . absolute. Existence would then be just the architecture within, including, and between the two.

We have to accept *one* thing. Just as we *cannot* visualize true Nothingness from within a somethingness state, we will *never* be able to visualize accurately the final concept that accounts for the starting of the above momentum in our living separate state. We just would not have the references to relate to it. It would be somewhat like trying to derive and describe the gas state from the liquid one, without ever having the conceptual capacity to envision the gas state. There would be no references by which we could 'know' anything outside liquidness. If the sensory equipment necessary to detect it were similar to ours – Touch, Taste, Smell, Feel, and Sight – we would never detect the two gases that make water. They would lie outside the capacity of all these senses to register, because the gases are invisible, untouchable, colourless, odourless and tasteless.

So, to summarize again . . .

The minimum change from Potentiality (No-thing-ness) to Actuality (Some-thing-ness) gives us a location – a centre – a point of happening. This all comes from an 'Ultimate Reality', that is expressed in terms of an abstraction we may call Godhead and see from our discrete, finite, terms in Space/Time separatedness as No'thing' that can be real in the sense of the matter-composed three-dimensional Universe. It can only be looked upon in terms of an ultimate – an absolute neutrality with eternal potential to be, or not be, an Actuality. It is Perfection itself, which, if expressed in true terms, will deny finite definition. It must be the ultimate freedom to know – to understand perfectly – anything and everything, something and nothing, nowhere, somewhere and everywhere. To know and understand without restriction, or restricted view, in an overall Whole frame or background – instantly – from all perspectives in all modes of thinking, at once. We may call it the summary of two basic poles, or co-ordinates, of effect – termed Awareness and Will. An eternal awareness – the 'content' of which manifests as what we call 'Thoughtability'. This phenomenon, in its turn, in our frame of existence – A Universe of Parts – is maintained in a continual potential to know and express itself through what we may call the drive to be, or *will*, or the potential difference between being active and passive in the state of Ultimate Knowing (Awareness).

We might describe the union of these fundamentals as the Whole – where all that is absolutely pure is centred: the most primary Centre in which existence maintains itself eternally, of itself, its elements so much part of each other that they cease to be discrete. And so, there is no need for direction – and, therefore, choice.

So the state beyond the first point of Somethingness – that state from which Union 'provided' Separation in terms of a Point can never be known in actual 'reality' terms, but is best seen as an abstract imaginary Centre of resolution. An analogy that springs to mind, that might describe the difference, may be seen in the way we view the Equator. An imaginary line, one that divides the Earth into two hemispheres. Of course, there is no *actual* line there. The line only exists in the mind of the observer. There must be something there to make the 'line' happen. Its only reality is contrived, it has no independence of its own, in its own terms. The centre of all resolution in the Absolute Union of points exists as a disposition of ultimate fit and so, from within itself, could be expected to understand, 'know' and control all Effect. To provide all possibilities, because all possibilities are reconciled as it, and through it. If all contradiction is ironed out in it, it would 'know' what and who provided for the contradiction in the first place. And so could choose to keep, or resolve, any state of contradiction.

From this we can see that the state of Togetherness supersedes and is superior to the state of Individuality. It commands, controls and dominates it. The logical answer to the eternal question. What came first, Godhead or the Universe, is therefore disposed in, shall we say, the 'favour' of Godhead ... where Godhead is that in which all absolutes centre and are reconciled in perfect togetherness. Strictly speaking, there is NO 'first' in terms of a sequence, because there is no 'sequenceability' in perfect Union. 'First' is no measure of chronology in this context. Time cannot exist in a frame that is completely together. It must be a measure defining the separation of points. Time is both the grand measurer and that which is measured. It chronicles, comparatively, points separated from one another in terms of Extent and Fixture. There would be no situational relativistic judgement necessary measuring separatedness. 'All' would be Infinite, Instant – Instantness.

A huge result from the merest point, or centre of effect, had happened. The birth of a Universe of Force. The product of the contradiction between Potentiality and Actuality is born. What happens when opposites meet? The moving grindstone in motion comes into contact with the sedentary, still, metal bar – sparks fly. The institutional nature of the centre of Absolutes (Godhead) is Wholeness. It is the view point and point of view implicit in the absolute Potenial to BE anything, or nothing. And so there is potential for all change. Potential for all choice through the twin primary axioms that make it up. A part of the final Centre as Awareness (viewpoint) and Will (point of view) together as the elemental array of Godhead, elected to separate in choice and Direction, to be born, so to speak, in singular direction – away from togetherness into separatedness. It all takes 'Us', originally the smallest parts of Godhead by definition, into the 'paradigm of Forces' we call the Universe. In an isotropic explosion: through the elbows of mathematical logic we call spatial Dimensionality, the merest centre of effect sprays out the giant wheels of the Universe in conglomerates of force we call the galaxies, stars, planets and 'Us'. Settling through stages into less and less symmetry and more and more dissymmetry – to ultimate Chaos.

Fantastic!

The metaphysical – the ephemeral non-matterness – as All-Knowing, as Ultimate Order in Ultimate Togetherness – takes itself out into greater and greater expressions of separation and tightness, or forceness, to settle as uranium at the farthest end (and who knows what else as the Universe expands) with hydrogen at the end nearest to Godhead.

The perfect freedom of Choice – Free Will – is implicitly the heartbeat of Existence as the formulas of tightness – forceness – cede to greater and greater expressions of discongruity and contradiction, as the Universe expands into greater and greater relativistic separation – and therefore contradiction from the first point of total Union. The least becomes the most. Pions to 'Neutrinos' . . . to hydrogen to uranium and beyond to the enforced resolution of atomness we call Lawrencium.

We will find, therefore, that the final element that is naturally stable will provide the last contour, or shape, of force that the Universal thrust in entropy establishes. This element uranium is the highest matter signature of the corridor of Force we exist in, on the planet Earth, only at this point of time perhaps 15,000,000,000 years after the Universe began. In the spatial situation of the Universe, more and more complexity happens and more and more complexity is revealed. As the 'brick' breaks apart, so the grains are seen – relative to each other in clearer perspective. The 'detectives' (scientists) searching for the implicit factors of physical existence in their cloud chambers and cyclotrons from Stanford to Cerne reveal its architecture. But remember, as they don't seem to want to remember, that the eyes that witness this are dying too. They are breaking up as atoms, just as securely as their targets for view. They die more quietly, to the tunes of hydrogen, carbon, and oxygen. Living eyes that 'live' for one reason only. They hold and keep more order and less force – 'within', overall, less force than the maximally packed tightness that wraps the parcels of tension that make up the most recent resolutions in terms of time: the heaviest elements. In an anthem of the greatest order, with the least implicit force, Knowability and Choice(ability) exist, at their best dispositions to map the presence of Godhead, in a Universe of increasing Force. The best, as far as *we* know, is Us: Humanity . . .

Yes: even we are, as *Homo Sapiens Sapiens*, a fractured summary of what 'we' once were as a genus of living beings, slowly, inexorably, ceding into less and less quantum states of Knowability and Choiceability. With time, if logical supposition, or rational thought is any guide – *and it is the only guide to truth* – the whole function of our entrapment is, in fact, to facilitate the original intention. To be separate – totally separate, into parts of the former 'Whole'. And so we head in stages for the ultimate state – Chaos – implicit.

Imagine a light – a brilliant silver-gold light of purest coherence polarized into a flat plane of two axes set in perfect right-angled aspect. (Please refer to Figs. 8 and 9 in the illustrated section.) This light is Thoughtness pure, as the primary elements Awareness and Will. Two-dimensionally arrayed and set to enter the drift of separation – the 'Space' to be 'part' – the inherent mathematical incongruity that is implicit in the overall design of what it means to be in the state of Separatedness. This 'light' of Knowing is about to begin a journey. It is a journey it will take along the contour of shape reminiscent of a three-dimensional Möbius strip twisted Toroid. The 'shape' of contradiction that makes the order and exact symmetry of the two-dimensional metaphysical state into the three/four-dimensional one of atomic force, the disordered, chaotic state of the physical, material Universe we exist in. The 'space' it enters is a void. A void of extent, or scope to be anything, with an inherent, twisted tension in the shape I have described as a Möbius Toroid. The implicit coherence of this light as it enters will define the axes of this twisted tension – of space. These axial lines can be described as 'Godhead' lines. They are the axes of symmetry of Universal space and the locations of least force within this 'engine' for the separation of points we call the physical Universe.

This space you see is tense, because it is full of the contradiction between the perfect state of all Union and the total opposite of it, the pole of Chaos absolute. I will later show why it cannot be a true absolute.

Any physicist or electrician will tell you that what is called a 'potential difference', or voltage, happens when you have something of such contrast, or difference, at opposite ends of any situation. A voltage is like a gradient measuring this 'difference'. A simple way of seeing it is to visualize the top from the bottom of anything. A difference of height. The greater the top rises above the horizontal plane, so to speak, the greater the difference between top and bottom, the higher the 'voltage'. A marble placed at the top will roll down the gradient faster, the greater the difference between the height of the top from the bottom. The Pole of Union (or stillness) and the Pole of Chaos define existence as a dynamic, an enforced difference that allows things to move in between, as a 'measure' of this difference. We, in and of the physical Universe, exist betwixt them, these final Poles. I have called the Pole of absolute Union: 'Godhead' and the other one I will call the 'Devil'. My 'Godlines' are simply confined to the places within this enforced dynamic that provide for the least possible 'Force', or inherent 'Tension'. The word Godness may be taken to mean 'Godhead in Force', for the Pole I define as Godhead is simply in such utter reconciliation in Union that there simply is no need for a dynamic 'force' that defines a contradiction, simply because no contradiction of any sort exists here. Here is the Peace, Tranquillity, Sublimity, call it Nirvana, Heaven, whatever you like.

In any inertial system such as this, the forces, however they are defined – centrifugal, centripetal, kinetic, potential, etc. have centres within and without them where their paradigms of effect cancel, and are neutralized to provide a 'stillness', or 'Peace', where Godness can dwell. Like a light filling any place it is *allowed* to enter, so will the prior light of utter Knowing, and Awareness, we call Godhead, enter and settle – 'lighting up', so to speak, all things it touches with this capacity to Know, to be Aware, this potential to be anything, or nothing. We, as living things, are a self-propelled system that can admit this light freely available as Godness. You might have noticed that I make a distinction between God*head* and God*ness*, the latter being the reflected 'light' of the *absolute* purity that I define Godhead to be. Pure 'light', reflected through the dimensional elbows, or 'lenses', of a system designed to separate points and thus allow the complete range of freedoms. My postulation is that 'living' systems, as we call them, can choose, to various degrees, to admit or preclude this light on the platform they possess of this light – within them and that non-living things have lost this vital facility of Choice and move through the grist, or mill, of dismantling force in a passive state to be broken down to the base of no'thing'ness, incohesive, to be reassembled into Nothingness cohesive in an infinite twisted loop I have previously described as the Möbius Meandering of Forces. It would help to pause and ponder the scenario I am about to describe quietly in your mind. But, before you do that, please bear with me while I describe the elements that define it.

The monopolar unidimensional coherence of Centre-Godness is an incidental product of Focus, the focus of all incongruous anomalies into a point of total reconciliation. Imagine the centre point of a cross, with two lines bisecting perpendicular to each other. This is my reflection of 'Centre Godness', or what we as men call the Godhead phenomenon. 'No dimensionalness', Zero Dimensionality. The lines are the single spatial dimensions I spoke of previously: each taken in its own terms is, of course, one dimension, or First Dimensional(ness). Viewed in correspondence with each other they are relatively two-dimensional, their togetherness defining a coincident plane that illustrates all geometric shape, if their acquisition is taken with reference to Time sequentially. Of course, this is a concept of view from a stance of the separation of points, or parts. In their intrinsic terms they are implicitly Timeless and, for the purposes of my analogy, are the Whole Godness effect I have explained. I will ascribe the colours silver and gold to each of these lines and define the lines as representing the abstract metaphysical primal qualities we know as Awareness (Gold) and Will (Silver). It can be seen now that they are in themselves a measure of 'separation in union', as we move away from the Centre point (Godhead point). (At the Godhead point only are they themselves reconciled as singular Awareness in Totality, where Will is sublimated because it is, shall we say, not necessary any more.) Their separation outside the centred Godhead Point is thus a centred separation, a separation in the most congruency possible and so it is stable, resisting the dynamism that is the product of incongruity. A passive Silver Gold Lightedness that is there, but is not apparent or visible yet, till it goes for the three/four-dimensional anomaly that twists its stable resolution into the visible reality we 'know' and experience as our Universe of separated parts.

We may choose to view the two-dimensional, or bipartite, expression we call Godness as Thought. (With Thought defined as an implicit *passive* function of pure Awareness and Will coming into Separation as a measure and measures of discreteness in parts.)

In its initial post-primal disposition, when in the Universe of Spirit, it is *not* forced. It is in 'peace' and thus beyond the 'existential plane' of a forced, incongruous three/four-dimensional Universe of 'enforced' parts. The two dispositions of Thought – in Godhead and out of Godhead as 'effects' – do not mix. They are separated by their inherent difference. There is no resonance between them. It is only in the choice to move away from the 'Plane of Peace' – that two-dimensional Thoughtness (in Godhead) becomes – the active 'forced' 'Thinking' (out of Godhead), making from itself the mantle of atoms, to exist in compromise states of 'Being' called 'Living', or 'Non-living'.

We can now take our journey of mind into a visualization of all this, with the simple metaphor of Light passing through a prism. Our source is derived from the invisible, completely coherent, shall we say 'laser' Light of Godhead, a point source that transforms into a more discrete coherence, the further out from the centre it is taken. At such a point it is still not separated from coherence in the Whole, but becomes so on entry into the three/four-dimensional incongruous compromise we call the space of our Universe. Here this 'peaceful', passive, coherent, let's call it 'Enlight' becomes visible and breaks into separation from the whole, finally forming '*Atoms*' on its way through the resolutions of incomplete measures of Force in parts called the Electromagnetic spectrum. The entire Electromagnetic spectrum defines the precursor partial states from the moment 'Enlight' breaks into parts of an 'atom'. The first self-contained complete platform representing the phenomenon of Parts as against what is Whole.

What proposes Separation? What could prompt the final resolution of perfect Knowing in the Whole (Godhead), to cede to Knowing in the part. We are forced to look for reasons, reasons that can only have meaning in 'separated mindedness' simply because we exist as artefacts of a Universe of Parts. If to be Whole as All is better than to be a part of the All in separation from the All – why be so? I hear you say. Why choose the folly of limit – the way of existence in Separation? And who, or what, does the choosing? Will the famous answer, that a famous mountaineer once gave, when asked why he wanted to climb Everest – 'Because it's there' – suffice?

In the neutral, unemotional righteousness of the centre of Absolutes this will seem the most apposite of all answers. It fulfils the final resolution that is its underbase, its essence – Knowledge. The knowledge of existence as a manifestation of parts can never have meaning in the state of the Whole, from the point of view of the Whole. But a methodology must exist that allows for knowledge of both, if all options in free will are to be achievable and resolved. The Universe we, as physical beings, are part of is simply the occupier of this potential as an actuality.

Again, let's summarize.

The Final Centre of Absolutes (Godhead) we have deduced as the centre of all final resolutions – where existence remains in Absolute Potential to Be, or not to Be, an Actuality. This eternal state of complete freedom to Be a 'thing' (Actual) or no'thing' (Potential) has in its nature the degrees of freedom (Fixture, or No Fixture, as its Central result) No Limit in Potential, or

Limit in the Actual. And so experience of Existence is scaled in the format of perfect co-ordinated connectability – Logic, for want of a better word. The Logic of mathematical resolution is a highway that marks admission, or denial, in terms of total fit or contradiction. One or Whole in either terms exists – One as inherent Limit in Actuality and Whole inherently without Limit as Potentiality. But to each other they are sheer opposites. Totally incongruous. The least of either is All of either and, therefore, the choice from one stance to be the other involves an instantaneous leap into total contradiction. Something incredibly 'big' is bound to happen if any part of the 'Whole Imperfect' elects to be separate as One. (A part of the whole may elect to be different, as opposed to all of it becoming different, because the whole is made up of parts and so 'knows' what 'partness', so to speak, must be. If the whole is the same as the part, it is not necessary that all the whole becomes one.) My guess, and I hope yours, would be that what we call a 'Big Bang' would occur. A Universe of Actuality – Limitedness in continuum – would happen. The product of the final discongruity, Whole(ness) becoming Partness in Choice, to a diametrically opposite point of view.

It may be asked *who* chooses to separate from the Whole, if 'Before' the Big Bang there is no separation and, therefore, no individuality in part(ness) terms? We have seen that the Whole does not elect to become part, but Part of the Whole elects to be Part.

This may seem paradoxical until we take a closer look at the formulation of the above question. The Big Bang, as the origin of space–time, does not allow a concept of 'Before'. Time is the active expression of cause and effect, that *is* the exercise of choice, actively or passively, within the context of separation. It therefore follows that we make Time in the choice to separate, and that the Universe of Parts happened and *is* happening through that choice.

Consider, if you will, the moment of Beginning. This defines an interface between the Timeless state of all Happening, happening all at once in *potential*, and the sequential happening in actuality we know as Time.

We would expect that the interface between the two states would manifest properties of both states. In choosing separation, experience becomes manifest in *part* terms, such that discrete parcels of aggregatable experience with activatable free will are 'born', if you like. Yet how did 'We' make the choice to *exist*, if it is only through the exercise of such choice that we can *exist to choose* in the first place?

If we accept that Beginning is both within and without time, the Cause and Effect are one and the same. Choice makes the Chooser just as surely as the Chooser makes Choice.

We, and by 'We' I mean all sentient beings who experience the Universe of parts, truly did (and do) create Self and the Universe by disallowing Godhead into us through choice, direct or implicit.

CHAPTER FOUR:
A STARTING POINT

Let us assume for the moment that there is an ultimate effect measured and related to in terms of a given point, or special placement. As explained previously, Entropy clearly demonstrates that the Universal momentum relative to any such given axial centre, or point, proceeds in a direction of increasing relative randomness – increasing states of chaos when judged one point to another. This singular directional drift, order to chaos, presents a fundamental principle we all just have to face. The established atomic physicality of the Universe proffers a distinct directive of the break-up of order, as well as a continual separation of points judged relatively. The Universe is expanding – planets, stars, galaxies are flying apart from each other relative to each other, everywhere. If we view far enough forward, this, plus the increasing states of chaos, would imply a point of ultimate chaotic subversion, with the separation of points, but it would also imply the reverse in the opposite direction. A singularity – a pole of sheer perfection – a resource at which all absolutes centre. A centre where there is no separation of points, where *all* points exist in perfect union, harmony, balance, so as to be seen only in the aspect of the Whole or what is affirmed conceptually as the All Together – the All.

The first and most important characteristic that must be realized from our three-dimensional atom-made 'point of view' is that this ultimate polarity of Perfection is outside Space/Time, atoms, etc. It is not 'solid', matter-based, substantial. It is metaphysical and abstract. So the point of final perfect inheritance of all Existence may be, in fact, expressed in terms of that other wonder at the centre of our own existence: 'Thoughtness'. An implied coincidence on the face of it, but one that holds the final clue to understanding the Universe and men. Since the polarity of perfection is metaphysical, abstract, outside Space/Time and atoms, its nature is therefore outside the scope of a matter-based, separation-set organism – i.e. Us – to investigate empirically. Further, all its effects, qualities, characteristics, would be out of the scope of our minds to imagine: abstract, not substantially referenced in our terms of reality. What could, therefore, imply the nature of this final state in terms of such abstraction from our substance-based point of view? We have to remember it is *a state of perfect balance, such that All is in potential to Be, or not to Be*. I have, for the sake of argument, called this 'effect' Godness. When all characteristics that might be ascribed to what is overall are considered, what basic common denominators will emerge? Let's consider what they might be.

Since Godhead, as we have defined the phenomenon, is a state of absolute balance where *all* elements, qualities, characteristics, only exist as potentials (because they are reconciled without contradiction in absolute totality) a change or move away from this state of ultimate reconciliation would imply that Will is present to make the decision for this change, and that it is absolutely free, because nothing obliges it *not* to make this change within the perfection of absolutes, as an absolute itself. That movement would further imply that the potential *scope* for the change had to exist and that this scope, if fulfilled, would provide an absolute difference to ultimate perfect union, (i.e. separation into parts).

I have said that in a state of Absolute Perfection the final idea, where what is Ultimate in Existence is reconciled without the merest contradiction, implies a balance providing Nothingness. This No'thing'ness implies just that. There are absolutely no'things' in either a physical or a metaphysical sense. There is no actuality, because all elements are reconciled in perfection. There are no contradictions here. Without contradiction, there is no state to be resolved, and so there is no dynamic implicitly demanding and funding reconciliation. Force as a principle may be said to be the product of a dynamic, expressing a demand for reconciliation. Force can be seen as an 'expectation', a potential that exists for something to happen because there is room or a capacity for it to happen. Since there are no implicit demands in the 'Perfect State' – effect, call it what you like – it is purely Forceless. It is balance *in total forcelessness*. There is, if you like, perfect Peace in perfect nothingness, uniting all elements in existence. This to my mind is a good paradigm of what may be described as Godhead. The paradigm of utter stillness. The Peace and perfection of poets and angels.

As I have said, in such an absolute and final disposition, all factors, all elements must have no actual reality – they would have to be pure Potentiality. A nothingness of pure potential to be actual. Further – this ultimate polarity of Perfection can only be an implied singularity, intrinsically, because it has no actual existence, as such. It can only be viewed away from itself as such and known as such away from itself. In order that it may be viewed as this, there must be somewhere, something else, that it may be viewed from. And here lies the crucial clue to overall existential design. Perfection and Imperfection have to exist together in an eternal continuum of reference, to be such as they *are*!

There must be, in other words, a facility, an accommodation for what is absolute in free will to allow for existence in separation. There must be 'scope', so to speak, for Chaos if there is Union. There must be scope for the separation of elements, points, to exist. If there is scope for such an absolute union of elements as the Overall, then the Overall must include as part of its empirical make-up – so to speak – the One part. This facility for separation of points to exist, this accommodation, in our three-dimensional universal terms, is what we call Space/Time. And so . . . what is the nature, the design, the contour, if you like, of this Space/Time continuum? Is there an inherent 'shape' of Spaceness?

We all know what a tennis ball looks like. There's a very interesting monogram on all tennis balls. I'm sure you know what I mean. That strange twisting shape that seems to present the same profile wherever you look on the ball. Of course, close examination reveals it is not the same profile from all sides. I don't know if the original author of the shape knew this as such, but this shape was expressing the fundamental shape of 'force' existential within all Universal effect, thereby providing a means for most of us, at least unconsciously, to register it. Now, imagine this shape made from a three-dimensional clear, transparent, square-sectioned piece of

'Space', yes, Space – out there – Space. If you have this shape in mind, you will have this spatial shape surrounded by the 'General' Space of the rest of the ball. (It may be useful to imagine the monogram's shape in translucent plastic to differentiate it from the Space surrounding it.) You will, of course, realize that since it is three-dimensional, its cross-section will present a view of a 'cross', wherever you cut it. That is, if you cut it and look at it end on, you will see the dimensional axes that define it will be a cross, from any direction. The vital thing I want you to do is to take away the spaces that surround it and look at the shape with its cross-sectional 'planes', so to speak, in view (see Figs. 9 & 10 in the illustrated section). You can now see into the innards of our model twisting monogram shape in space with cross-sectional planes set at 90° to each other. You will have before you in this mental concept the shape and twisted dynamic that creates the separation of points and makes the metaphysical into the physical. It creatively suggests the enforced atomic Universe we commonly recognize as providing our reality . . . Please pause for a moment and ponder this gigantic 'engine', our Möbius Toroid referred to previously. Visualize it in your mind in its context and try to imagine the whole wondrous scenario of Creation expressed in its terms. Let's set the scene once more:

From within Godhead(ness) rises the potential to be separate, or together. There is no such thing as Space or Time here. Everything is in instant instantness, all over. There is the Peace of ultimate Knowing in the last discreteness before Final Coalescence. The 'place' of the final Axis before all Axes end and the ultimate Glory of the effect in which all finalities centre and Godhead happens. As has been said, this is best visualized as a right-angled cross defining two axes, with the centre discrete and invisible. Let's trace the lines of the axes in gold and silver, and again, as mentioned previously, the vertical one we'll take in gold light and the horizontal axis as silver light.

In Godness everything is perfectly reconciled and balanced to give the freedom to be everything, or just one thing. To be Whole in Union or Part in discrete singularity. This means that in this state of Perfection encompassing absolute Awareness and perfect Free Will, each can exist 'independent' of the other, or together in total reconciliation in the state which can be described as Centre

Godness. We can visualize the independent state expressed as the two axes defining ultimate order and symmetry at 90° to each other, creating a centre of Absolute Perfection at the point where they intersect. (See Fig. 12 in the illustrated section).

This is a state different to any other part on either axis. It is, shall we say, the primary 'point' dimensional, whereas elsewhere all is Line, if taken relatively, one axis to the other 'plane dimensionally'. In other words, one- or two-dimensional, depending on the point of view and viewing point. At the intersection everything along the axes and on the dimensional plane taken relatively would be centred and 'known' at once, whereas any part on the straight axes, although perfectly balanced and linked to all other points through the centre, would shall we say, experience the 'Whole' as an incidental and not primary effect. This is a paradigm of how existence is portrayed. Remember the elements that define pointness up to the two-dimensional state define potentiality rather than actuality, so they do not make location in fixture or 'Space' in the terms that we visualize it. Subjectivity and Objectivity are therefore one and the same in their pre-atomic context.

From this it can be seen that the two-dimensional state (two one-dimensional lines defining two dimensions through a total directional difference, when 'seen' relative to each other) will experience 'Partness' within the context of the Whole by any move outwards on the axes. The concept of individuality, expressed in terms of 'I' and 'We' therefore exists in Godness together – at one and the same 'time', so to speak, so that a choice for partness within separation can be made freely and discretely. In Centre Godness (Godhead), 'I' and 'We' cease to exist in discreteness, but are within each other, so to speak, because at this point there *is* not Limit and therefore no difference. It is thus impossible to distinguish between 'You' and 'I'. This does not mean that what we term 'Part-ness' can't be known in Godhead, *but it can't be known distinct and separated from the Whole*. And so, Part *and* Whole can be known in Godhead – Part *within* the Whole can be known in Godhead'ness'. *Discrete* Partness within separation from the Whole can *only* be known in our Universe.

Godhead would not know Godhead, because there is no place or point of objective differentiation within Godhead for a comparison to be made and a definition established. Godhead is implicit and implied wherever it is allowed to be, in locations where there are no elements or vectors of force whatsoever. There are such locations or points in this Universe of parts where everything ceases to be enforced, you might be surprised to know. They lie within juxtapositions of atoms, between these atoms where the twist of enforcedness ceases to be. (See Figure 13 in illustrated section.) It is here at these points of total balance of all force resolutions that lie what I like to call the 'Corridors of Redemption'.

Time is not a concept within Godhead. It occurs with the inertial urgency of separation, as Godness is 'used' to dictate force patterns of varying complexity in an expanding plane of separating parts. We . . . 'us' . . . or human beings, are the result of an interface between enforcedness and no forceness. A compromise that is continually being compromised, as the species continually degrades through the momentum of decay termed entropy – the unrelenting, whirring machine of the universe of separating parts.

If Godhead is outside the realms of what is defined in physical terms, then to perceive of its grandeur is left to only the blessed few – the Buddhas and prophets of the past who sensed its glory, but only *knew* its glory when they were no longer individually 'name-tagged' – in other words when they *were* Godhead.

Will, directed and channelled through thought to create the opportunity for enhancement of the 'soul' (which may be defined as the connection between physicality and non-physicality) leads through that enhancement to the demise of, as well as a lessening of the opportunity for, the dance of atoms and the cage of physicality they create.

We have a measure of relativistic separation, the further we go out from the centre of the axes. Remember, the separation of adjacent points might increase, but their symmetry, taken to the centre, stays the same, no matter how far out you go. Within this scenario of what we will call 'Knowing', Partness and Wholeness are interchangeable through the centre, so to speak, and thus they are in total availment of complete Freedom of Will to be anything. However, as I have explained, experience within such an 'overall' precludes one thing. You've guessed it. It precludes the expression of Partness from the removed Part state. The experience of uncentred discreteness can only be achieved by the acquisition of the state as a part and thus the application of Will to separate from the Whole. So was chosen the crucial resolution of Creation from within the Outer state I have called Godness. The inner state, Centre Godhead if you like, is unchangeable, because there is no 'reason' to 'change'. It is in its 'point' focus separate and in Union at the same time. The only place that the Part and the Whole can exist, both centred and 'separate', is in the centred Ultimate state of All Knowing.

And so, from a conceptually assigned two-dimensionally defined Godness effect, individual resolutions arose in the total freedom of Will, with the total responsibility of individual accession centred on discrete Choiceability, to choose of volition to be part – discretely part. Here in this is the crucial, fundamental proposition that has tormented our thinking since 'we' could think: Did Godhead (the Centre) choose for us, or did 'we' choose to come into predicaments of separation, rationalized?

The question is simply reconciled in the simplest reason. Godhead is a state, an effect *past* and beyond the concept of 'we', where the concept 'we' is a holographic homogenous whole, with a potential for heterogeneous fragmentation into parts. In Godhead, there is a final state in which the elements that make up the holographic principle are no more separable. All effect to this final state of Being is imperfect as long as it possesses the potential to fragment into parts, where the relationship between the element of 'Godhead' and the element of 'We' is defined.

To sum up, then: Both the Godhead and Godness effect are perfectly balanced and Forceless. The Godness effect implying imperfection as a potential. This simply has to mean that No(thing) is happening in a state of Nothingness. The Moroid, however, is enforced as three/four-dimensional Space-Time in which (and this is the most vital point of all) *two* of the axes are *still* congruent and symmetrical (they are perpendicular to each other). While the 'tension', or dynamic, or enforcedness, is provided by the third axis as it is contorted in trying to form the impossible, to complete a fourth dimension spatially. It must be realized, however, that even in this forced scenario there will have to be 'points of neutrality' where all inertial forces are balanced. *This will be where the Three Axes meet*. Here will exist unforced, or shall we say, 'peace' corridors, which I will call 'Godlines'. They are simply 'Axes of Symmetry' *outside* Time and Space, where Godness can exist actually in its purest possible state and form, in the Moroid.

They can therefore be viewed as the 2D/3D interface – or the 'entry' and 'exit' routes to and from the Moroidal Universe to the prior or 'superior' two-dimensional metaphysical state of pure Thought, Knowing, and unrestricted facility. The most important implication of all this is clear. The thing that separates us in the Moroidal Universe from Godhead is quite simply Force, and so, the Godlines reflect the principle that provides for the redeeming of the prior pre-atomic state. In being the centre, where the axial lines meet, they suggest the answer lies in the union of parts. In the bringing together of things. In the expressions of combination and not division and divisiveness.

As partness within separation is the only thing that cannot be known in either Godhead or Godness, *it must have been the choice to experience separation from the Whole, as a part that made 'us' leave Godness and enter into the forced space of the Moroid*. This would happen along the Godlines that allow existence as something two dimensional in a three/four-dimensional environment. The most startling and wondrous inference is now apparent. It means, if this is possible, that the mind is outside the enforced atomic array of Moroidal space. This halfway house defines the living state. The trouble starts once we move outwards on one of the right-angled axes. In the two-dimensional scenario of Godness, this 'movement' allowed us to experience a relative partness within the balance and Forcelessness of the Whole, but the incongruity and twistedness of the three/four-dimensional axis *fixes* us 'inertially', so to speak, and makes Limit actual, creating more and more contradiction and thus Force, the further away we move from the centres of Peace and Balance, namely our Godlines.

This can be illustrated by visualizing something in orbit. The inertial forces maintain a balance, centrifugally and centripetally fixing the object, according to its velocity. The more force the object carries, the more separate it will try to be from the point of origin. In other words – the higher the orbit it will achieve. Yet, it will still be *fixed*. It cannot move of its own volition to change orbit while its own force paradigm is dominated by a superior one: that of the Earth's gravitational vector.

To say it another way, atoms are islands of continually precessing twisted spatial tension, formed out of the once coherent metaphysical forceless 'All Awareness' we have called Godhead. I believe that atoms are a form of coagulated 'Thoughtness'. A framework of 'twisted' Godhead, if you like. Made up of Godhead material itself, but unable to be Godhead, or act as Godhead, because they are twisted out of resonance with the pure Godhead state. However, marvellously, atoms may be allowed to, or allow themselves to *receive* pure Godness if they are properly set up, phased, arranged and arrayed for this purpose. Living systems are the highest and best arrangements to do this. Knowability is thus a manifestation of Godhead received and synthesized out of congruency with Godhead.

Godhead consists of Will, Awareness, Thoughtness, Knowingness, Understandingness. In other words: the Software. The Hardware is light, electricity, magnetism, nuclear force, gravity, plasma, gas, liquidness, solidness, thus rocks and stones and all non-living entities not capable of making choices out of their inherent being. The artefacts of this Universe. A Universe of Force and Parts.

You can visualize the architecture of existence as a series of interaction points. Lens Points, if you like where the 'Lenses' are presented in Point; Line; Triangular-Discoid; Cuboid/spherical, and finally Möbius-Toroidal shape. These lenses are formed by the prior source of Godhead light prescribing the geometric mathematical formula for the separation of points.

In a series of logical, minimally defined progressions, expressing the separation of points to the Law of Least Action, we can identify stages of equal differentiation showing why fixture and separation may only exist in more than 'three point zero' dimensions. Our Light of Godhead (Prior Light) emerges through logical geometric minimums: a Point continues to a line, implying a minimum of two points of infinite potential difference, with a variation of two distinct directions implied straight away, increasing this to a third point. We will have a triangular plane implied again, as a minimum, with a disc as a maximum, with infinite distance between points that still might be equal. So, Two-Dimensionality is a free disposal state, existentially limitless in its expression of the two criteria that define 'freedom', maximum symmetry and maximum variability. We add a fourth point to make a third dimension and the criteria of infinite variability in symmetry, or the equal separation of points one to the other, taken on any plane, still applies. This, however, is where infinite variability stops, because a fifth point defining a fourth spatial dimension is impossible. You will lose symmetry, or put another way, no five points can be placed equally spaced from one another on any spatial plane distribution. To do so would imply four discrete *actual* spatial dimensions and this can never happen for the following simple reason:

For change to happen there must be changeability and therefore potentiality. If there is potentiality, there must be Will – to Be or not to Be and therefore awareness to allow options to be realized. Once actuality happens a state of dependency is reached, subjectivity and objectivity part company and therefore the 'frame' of existence, space, time and matter, has lost a *self*-propulsion modulus, the three/four-dimensional Möbius atomic whirlpool has therefore 'run out of gas', so to speak, as the quest for a universe of parts has already been successful. The limits of dimensional acquisition in difference and freedom to be straight and 'true' are thus defined. Therefore the furthest reach from Godhead is, in spatial terms, resigned in three dimensions with the little extra that was sought (and at the beginning of existential logic, compromised as a twist), frozen as a 'bending tension' into the intrinsic design of the 'what' that separates parts. (See Figs. 10, 11 in the illustrated section.)

Now visualize the Prior Light of 'Godhead' moving through these dimensional Elbows, these 'Spatial Lenses', its coherence progressively disrupted till it breaks through the Grand Divide that separates freedom from fixture. The third/fourth-dimensional interface with the second; *the point of creation, incidental creation*, is thus here. I say incidental creation, because the will that seeks experience, be it whole, or part, is derived from the inherent freedom that exists in the prior metaphysical state. It is derived from Godness and Centre Godhead and most directly from the surrounds of Godhead, if you like. Remember the arms of the 'cross', stretching infinitely out. The cross shape itself maximizing differences (you cannot get more different in planar terms than a direction of 90° away from any point on the line). It's really a three-dimensional cross (see Fig. 8 in the illustrated section). Each axis is a different colour – let's say gold, silver and white. They are merged at the centre, a centre that is entirely different from the arms, because there the gold, silver and white can no longer stay colours, but are totally reconciled into the state of Clearness Absolute at the centre. This centre clarity will not mix with either the gold, silver or white, because as the point of coalescence of all three, it is uniquely, implicitly, different in its clarity and its *pointness*. The others have the common factor of being axial *lines*, their difference expressed relatively as a radial direction only. Thus the centre Godhead state will stay eternally, infinitely such, separated from the arms that radiate around it by these disresonant factors. The 'Godhead' effect, through its focal clarity and centredness, will not resolve into direction and thus separation, a separation that is not true separation, anyway, because it is still in total freedom United in the connection with Godhead Effect. And so, in the cross we see the whole metaphysical panoply represented beautifully. Perhaps this is an education made apparent by a personality that came deliberately into atoms two thousand years ago, to illustrate the 'Father' from whence He came! Perhaps the choices others took in crucifying Him were simply incidentally following the map that suggested the debauchery the Universe of parts truly is – with the shape in which the Whole phenomenon occurs as the marker of such unworthiness – The Cross.

The second dimension is a forceless free state, a 'concept' united and divided within and without Godhead. At its 'fringes', so to speak, it passes into the third/fourth-dimensional anomalous force-filled 'contradiction' we call our reality, our physical, Universal reality. Here solidness derives out of the ephemeral, the latter registered and rationalized as the phenomenon we know as conscious and unconscious Mind.

It is vital to note that the 'lenses' themselves are made by the prior, shall we say what I've called 'En-light', or Eminence of Godhead, as it sublimates the Separated Stance. Enlight in my terms is the purest dynamic effect of the Godhead state as it functions in the Universe of matter, or as I've described it, the Universe of separated parts. It is, perhaps, what religious invective calls the Holy Spirit. All light of Godness follows through in dispositions of increasing complexity, in this Universe of ours. A complexity that is born of the gathering contradiction of whole against part. It is thus mixed into a state of dynamic force and fixture in an infinitely resolved open and closed twisted loop – the Moroid. The word Grace, used so often in religious terminology, may be seen as the effect of this 'light' set in the best confluences on the

Godhead Lines that bring centre Godhead and Godness into our reality from beyond the three/four-dimensional interface.

It is already refracted by the separating effect of Space itself. Rather like the splitting of a beam of visible light by a prism, Space itself being intrinsically twisted is an engine for the separation of points – a Möbius-toroidal 'prism' inherently set to the values omniversal logic dictates for the dismemberment of Union, such that the total range of options to Be, or not to Be, may exist. The Light of 'Godhead' is diffracted into parts commensurate with the deployment of the most basic discrete platforms in an enforced force signature: atoms, molecules, elements etc., wherever and however they are expressed in the Universe. The whole becomes part in a cascade of vibrations, oscillations, frequencies, disposing and composing all that goes to make up final Union. Just as white light is split up into its constituent frequencies of 'force' that we call violet, indigo, blue, green, yellow, orange, red in progressively metered presentations, or wavelengths, so the light of Godness is fragmented in the entire range of existential meaning, starting at the 'points' the Universe of Parts begins.

I will illustrate all this with an analogy. Imagine that the space in an empty room is invisibly twisted. Smoke is blown into that room and settles in the shape of the contour of this twisted space. It will be thicker and thinner according to the dynamics its own twist dictates and be absent totally from any place that this dynamic provides no holding force. A smoke ring illustrates this nicely. Its dynamics are such that the smoke is confined and held in the area where the momentum of the air currents is most disturbed, expanding and spinning in counter vectors such that the centre remains freer of accentuated force, as the twisting toroid increases diameter. It finally disperses, allowing its constituents to be deposited in the form of soot, as substrate fractions of the once more ephemeral smoke. In similar fashion, our ephemeral Clothing of Godhead (reason), deploys in the nature of its composition to lie in the self empowered dictates of the signature of break-up be it atom, star, galaxy or supernova. The progressive inconsistencies of gathering Chaos determine the stature and velocity of change, to dictate the eventual delivery into total (Thing)ness. This is the final end of 'nothingness' at the most extreme point of Chaos, but can be seen as the most substantial Somethingness of absolute mass and thus force. It is not just something that can't be seen in terms of sensory discernment, or is metaphysical in terms of an ultimate state of force. It is force absolute, that forbids the state of being an 'entity', because fixture of any kind does not exist. (It is not there long enough to be actual, because it is too chaotic to be so.) And so the difficult-to-imagine concept of 'all-overness', in the instant instantness of no time or durational consequence we call Union, provides the other extreme in the opposite pole over aeons that are counted in magnitudes of billions of years, to the nth degree, so to speak. Our twisting toroidal smoke ring has expanded to disintegrate into oblivion. In terms of our state of Being in separation from Godhead, it is the oblivion that is the final opposite of Unionness. The final phenomenon where the No(thing)ness of utter Chaos 'meets' the No(thing)ness of perfect Union.

The ultimate of opposites can never meet in the sense of contact. As opposites attract, 'they' attract each other simply because 'they' are there. In their coalescence, and at their coalescence points, Universes of Beginning will be eternally made in explosions of fantastic magnitudes called 'Big Bangs'.

Thus, as with our smoke ring, the Space/Time continuum is defined from the Nothingness of the thought that in turn made the 'smoke ring' and blew the smoke ring into the room. Blew the smoke ring as the Somethingness of its manifestation and the Nothingness of its utter dissipation into its most basic possible component parts.

Again to summarize, in Godness all parts are reconciled in the whole. Difference is sublimated such that every part of the summary is a manifestation of the Whole. In other words, Godness is a summary of all difference and in such a state one cannot experience separation of Self, as Self. Will in Godness is essentially passive (with a potential to be active), because you don't need will in order to maintain a state of absolute forcelessness and balance, where everything fits without the slightest contradiction. Will becomes active in the choice for separation as Self, which at the same time, is the choice for Limit and Force, the force for reconciliation with the whole. You can only stop merging with the whole by being in the state of One. Limitation and Limit implies contradiction and therefore the force to keep what you are:

separate. Will can only be active when there is minimally a duality for choice, Godness as potential absolute in the Whole, on the one hand, and Universes of actuality on the other, where the separation of parts reigns. This, of course, implies that there is a minimum resolution, a 'tension', that keeps things apart. An interface that can fix limit. Will is the propulsion element of this interface. An agent of allowance that provides binary option, within a design that allows for all the contingencies of separation. Will 'creates' our 'Mind Bubble' of individual Knowingness. Will is the skin of separation that is 'surrounded' by the Spirit of Godness – and thereby oversees existential experience from whatever standpoint, viewpoint, or point of view it elects to be.

In the instant instantness of the merest moment, the merest hint of contradiction in the Whole gives rise to the Universe. And so it bursts into finite existence in the incongruous pattern of twisted space, space in the fantastic irregular continuum of logical compromise we see in the shape of a Möbius-toroid strip. A three-dimensional Möbius Meandering. The journey into separation had begun.

In a jigsaw puzzle, the final picture can never be seen perfect and true till all the 'differing' parts are put together in the whole. This whole is only reached if each and all parts fit together exactly and totally. (As illustrated previously through this jigsaw paradigm.) Similarly, 'Godhead' happens as a phenomenon when the Whole is *all* together. At this point, and only this point, a unique status is achieved that need never be fragmented, because the totally centred aspect is known in the interconnection of parts, one to the other. It is only known totally from the total point of view. The jigsaw puzzle ceases to be a number of parts making up the Whole picture. It becomes the *whole* 'picture'. It is, in other words, not a puzzle any more. It is a *different* thing. It has lost its 'puzzleness'.

Godhead is only God at the point of total resolve, when all the information of each discrete part is connected up in its entire potential for connectability and connection and the Whole scheme, so to speak, becomes One effect and not a thousand differing smaller effects together. Seen in this way, any stage up to this final Union of total togetherness in fit has the capacity to know difference and individuality. In other words, in what we have said previously, any point or stage on the arms of the 'cross' and not the absolute centre where the arms meet (see Fig. 12 in the illustrated section). The 'choice' to separate from the 'Whole' can only be made in any meaning from any such point and *not* from the Centre. 'We', originally as Godhead, are what made all the Universe of discrete parts happen, simply by moving further away from this centre point along the arms, while we could in meaning 'decide', shall we say, to do so. In doing so, 'we' created, we 'made' increasing states of 'difference' happen with reference to the Centre. We made 'space' between us and Godhead and became 'parts' of Godhead. It is from such viewing points and thus points of view, that choice to 'Be' discrete from Godhead was and is made in total free will. The word 'We' means you and me and all discrete parcels of 'thoughtability' that are stranded in the pit of Entropy. A pit of our own making. A 'pit' we made and know as the Universe of parts, simply to know and experience the separated state from Godhead – from the point of view of Separation. We are taking the Godhead state that did not do this to Hell and back.

I have had to invent a new lexicon to illustrate my ideas on the total existential outlay. Three important words have to be clearly defined so that their inter-relationship may be seen without confusion. They are Godhead, Enlight (Godlight) and Soul. Whilst in essence they are the same thing, in their articulacy and function they may be seen as follows:

GODHEAD is the final resolution of what is All in total fit where all existential paradigms within the world of atoms and outside the world of atoms come together as a total Union of all points, parts and separating mechanisms. It is that in which all absolutes come together in a single harmonious paradigm of union in total and utter fit.

ENLIGHT or Godlight is the manifestation of this paradigm I have called Godhead in and within the Universe of parts. In other words, in the Universe of atoms.

SOUL is simply the bridgehead between the two. The connecting paradigm between the Universe of total fit: Godhead, and the Universe of parts and thus atoms: our Universe. In other words, the paradigm we as human beings, or Oglanders or whatever, have chosen to enter and where we have got trapped. If it were possible to locate 'Enlight' anywhere, you could call that 'anywhere' a Soul.

I visualize God in Man as air bubbles in a paperweight. Increase the amount of air bubbles in the glass and it would be like making the paperweight disappear. Soul in other words, is encapsulated Enlight.

Although they never quite call it that, the Buddhists have to my mind come closest to a clear insight into the phenomenon of Godhead. In the interests of a non–religious and neutral definition I have in the foregoing tried to define it as a state of being where all things are known all at once and manifested all at once and all events and happenings occur in 'instant instantness'. In other words, as I have said, it may be seen as that in which all absolutes find their ultimate balance. There is thus no force, tension or space in this 'world' of total mind, total knowing and being and thus no points, or the separation of points. All here is Thought in ultimate knowing because all parts are together in total fit. It is as different as you can get from *our* existential platform which is its mirror opposite: a Universe of the separation of points and thus parts and thus time and thus force (the architecture of which is what we call the electromagnetic spectrum) and thus atoms and thus physicality (the architecture of which are the elements) forever separating and thus decaying from one state to another implicitly and explicitly in one direction. The direction away from this world of Godhead into increasing states of randomness and chaos in line with the Second Law of Thermodynamics.

To summarize for the umpteenth time, Godhead for me is a scenario where all existence is in a mode outside the phenomenon we call atoms. This existence is marked by the fact that it prevails in a state of no parts (let's call this state a state of Spirit for want of a better word) and unlike our Universe, this Universe of Spirit is maintained eternally of itself without decay, because it is a state of ultimate equilibrium and all parts fit exactly with nothing left over. All things are known here from the point of view of the Whole and not from the points of view of the part.

How, then, does what is purely of Godhead touch what is away from Godhead? How may final opposites come together and interact? They may do it through intermediaries. Situations phased in between, in an endlessly varying series that when added together, breach all difference. I believe thus was made a phenomenon that I shall call Inaugural Being, or Godbeing. The first substrate away from the pure ephemeral state of Spirit made of the fashions and forms of force we call atoms. The first beginnings of what we term the physical. A connection to Godhead that allowed the phenomenon of Soul to be activated in a Universe of force. An interface or a channel to connect the forms of the Universe of the Whole to the Universe of Parts.

In effect, Godbeing was THE interface between opposites. A phenomenon that on one side faced 'God' and thus the Universe of the Whole. A Universe where, as I have said, all parts fitted perfectly into a Whole and as such they were, shall we say, like 'Angels'. An ephemeral form. A form of pure 'Thought Being', as Jesus Christ demonstrated at the Transfiguration. You recall the description in the New Testament when he took his apostles up a mountain and demonstrated that he could transform his physical being into one of pure ephemerality. He glowed brighter than the sun.

I believe that the first 'beings' of the Universe were 'beings' of pure Thought. They were not physical themselves and 'came' or extended into the 'arms of loss' to both make and, alas, eventually become our 'physical' Universe, (*their* other side). It all happened to make happen or allow a view and knowledge on behalf of the Universe of the Whole of the 'point of view' of the Universe of Parts. The psycho-physical mechanism of such a presence would implicitly set up a link and thereby the possibility for rescue of that which might come later from the Master Universe of the Whole to do the same thing (You and I) and get trapped in the clutches of the forces that provide the dynamics of entropy. You see, doing this would compromise the natural modus of the natural aspect of Godhead terribly (as I believe happened to Jesus Christ when the 'Word' was made flesh), because our Universe was characterized by Force. A quantum that would alter those first beings drastically to a lesser, more physical form and state and thus an inherently less powerful state of implicit control of their own destiny. There might be an example of one of the differences in the two states when you look at what happened to Jesus Christ when he went to pray in the Garden Of Gethsemane. Christ is said to have sweated blood while he prayed there just prior to his arrest. Could it be possible that the strength and power of his mental concentration in tuning in to or slipping in to his 'Father's world' had the incidental effect of lowering his bio-magnetic quantum of force, by shedding the iron (haemoglobin) in his blood? In other words he temporarily resonated with a quantum of Nil force in the Masterworld of Godhead, his 'father', and in doing this exercise of mind over matter he affected his physical body in this way. He was praying (or 'tuning in for instructions') at the time, if you recall the story.

You might ask why Godhead came to a Universe that was its existential antithesis. It would really be inappropriate to say that 'It' came to the Universe. It would be nearer the truth to say that 'It' is here simply because there is such a thing as our Universe in the first place, if you see what I mean. In other words, the whole thing is implicit. It would be there because choice to save is implicit in being Whole. In other words, the answer need simply be, 'Because our Universe was there!' After all, is it not the base of all existential platforms to seek to fulfil all that may be fulfilled? Potential may only be made actual in knowing and seeking its fulfilment. I believe the true, irresistibly compelling reason Godness touches anything anywhere is due to that most misused, most misunderstood momentum we call Love. A reason that with pristine logic points to the very root on which the Universe of the Whole is set. The Universe where all things come implicitly together to fit perfectly. The Universe where all things mean Add, not Divide. Where all things blend perfectly and cannot stay apart. The Universe where the watchword is Union and not Separation.

CHAPTER FIVE:
FREE WILL AND A DIRECTIVE FINALITY

There are two ways of viewing the functioning paradigm of the phenomenon we commonly call God. The first is an anthropomorphic Directive Finality that directed itself into being, of itself, as a phenomenon, where the phenomenon itself decrees all effect in existence, with an overall custodial stance over all things in existence. Consequently the principle of individual Free Will has no meaning and all control of existential dominion is set within the overall frame of its own final arbitration.

The alternative view of God is that an incidental implicate phenomenon of utter perfection resolves into being of itself and becomes uniquely existentially viable of itself as a singularity and thus allows all possibilities 'to be' of themselves.

Let's take a closer look at the first scenario. The scenario of 'No Free Will,' or the phenomenon of a directive God.

In this scenario God is just there and invests into the procedures of subversive subtraction (as seen in this entropic Universe of ours) as an essential experiment for a view of what it is like to experience fractionation of the totally together God state from the *point of view* of fractions. Thus we, and all that happens to us, are essentially 'progress points' and pointers that trace this view. Having no intrinsic Free Will, we are victims of the plan, or dictates, of the ultimate power – to suffer, or to enjoy a pre-planned scenario mapped out for us. We are, if you like, directed 'effects' gathering information eternally through the various scopes and fractions within the Universe of Parts, so that God may experience the Whole of existential dominion from within a single-point scale from the point of view of several separated points. Thus the concepts of natural balance and justice according to individual deserving as surmised from the point of view of *our* being are illusions that are put into our perceptivity as a promotional vector, to allow us the will to follow the preordained scope to be as God intends. Some of us in this paradigm as individual, separated, discrete points on a scale are thus allowed to degrade into the furthest reach of the separation of points. Some of us are allowed to go only as far as to enable us to return from whence we came. Who is allowed this and why they are allowed this are thus questions within the remit of the final director – the final arbiter – Choice and Decision points are performances of God – and *not* our individuality.

We are the orchestra, the instruments, the players, where God is seen as the composer, conductor, composition and audience. Sense, reason, logic, acts and actions, are all products of the performance and the performer.

Some theosophies claim an important variation on this theme and that is this: God sets the confines of action and actionability; God sets the arena of function, the bandwidth of functional resolution, and within this individual Free Will is allowed to reign, such that the operation and results of Will that is freely employed may be seen in all its shades and permutations. The only directive employed is the original directive of cessation from the Universe of the Whole. In other words, God fired the pinball and his personal witness measures the result according to a given scope. Again, of course, it is a scenario of 'No Free Will,' because the scope for choice is formularized by the confines of the arena of action. If such is true, all 'fault' is God's responsibility and ultimately implies the imperfection of the final entity. The perfect state of total resolution in absolute fit is denied the entity, because culpable control is, if you like, deliberately exercised and thus 'connected' to it. Thus, the Godhead phenomenon cannot be perfect, because in the phenomenon's infected parts, scope for action will be necessarily limited. If in any way there is a feedback from these infected parts.

Whatever the mode of function of the 'No Free Will' scenario, while it is all being carried through, it is all 'going on', God is having a good, bad, or indifferent time at the expense of our individuality. Of course, the adjectives are pertinent only from our vantage point in the Universe of Parts. In this theosophy, God is simply tacitly and passively *observing*, and experiencing all happening, through our individual abandonment for purposes of experiencing what is All – in all ways. Our predicament within our own halls of perception, if Will is not free, is simply the business of God and so if we are in pain, it is His will for some reason He only knows and we must plead for respite. We must implore the Almighty for mercy. We are if we do this, of course, asking Godhead to deny His own purpose to fulfil our own puny predicament. We are, in other words, telling God *to love* us. All this from the supposed perpetrator of our predicament in the first place. By now the implications of what I am saying must be clear to the reader!

Are we simply pawns to a final anthropomorphic and anthropocentric director, whose whim provides our destiny, whose control of our circumstance and predicament suggests dispassionate, even cruel observance, the relinquishing of which suggests that we know more about love than our 'originator'? You see, the vital point is that if one single intercession is made, through which God acts to provide a dispensation, an answer to a prayer, God will deny His own purpose, when viewed in terms of the definitions stated above. One exception makes God less than 'perfection', because a single plea clearly implies God does not 'know' your predicament and has to be asked, or He 'knows' our predicament and we give Him permission to intercede on our behalf – we give Him our will to intervene. Why is God giving permission to Himself – as we are just parts of Himself set free to experience 'self'? If He, in fact, does know – then why are we encouraged to be supplicants by those who pretend to represent the religious guiding system acting on God's behalf? It seems a prayer that asks is an insult to God's Almightiness – His omnipresence – His omnipotence – His omni-everything. Especially if He is a God of Love. The truth, of course, is that the personalized Directive God scenario is a contrived man-made ethos, set up as a mystical – a 'divine' – a metaphysical substitute for our earthly Lords of the Manor and by accepting this tenet of a Directive God we are in fact reducing the 'size' of God to our finite proportions, and increasing the anthropocentrically derived rulers, both religious and political, to the size of the Divine. Something quite clearly desirable for those hungry for power.

It may be argued, of course, that if God represents all things, then all things must just *be*. All things must exist. We, in our individualities, as products or parts of Him (God) are serving this axiom, regardless of consequence, and have to depend on God abandoning this purpose to be let off the hook of suffering – be it in terms of reason, sense, logic – the very underbase of the precept of Love of which God declares Himself the definition.

How can men and women of intelligence persist in believing the preposterous implications of a final *Directive Entity* when one looks at it in the cold light of reason? If God is supposed to have given us a moral code to live by, as every major religion claims – a code designed to provide a route to the final acquisition of the God state, a code arbitrated on what is commonly termed 'Love' – why have we been thrown into this Universe of Parts, this entropic vestment, that in singular direction implicitly destroys the very meaning of Love (addition to a whole) by subtracting and subverting the very platform of our existence?

Is the God state testing itself, in individually focused and deliberate terms, against the worst scenario possible in a stance opposite to itself? If the challenge is to see that all his 'parts' are recoverable, no matter how far from himself he puts himself and his God state, then with human beings generally, if this is indeed a stage in his plan, he has proved himself to be a consummate failure. How, then, can such a state be God Almighty, a state of being that is all-knowing, all-loving, *all* the time?

A truth in any reason gives the lie to the self-contradictory. The acceptance of a final personalized Directive Entity marks the believer to be self-deceiving – at best – and untenable to reason, at worst. How often does one hear believers in a Directive God forbid a deeper logical investigation into the phenomenon with the statement: 'It is God's Will'? 'How dare we mere mortals question God's reasons for doing anything?' is the implication. 'How could such human paltriness know why God does things the way he does?' It seems to me that such expedience may reasonably justify the idea of the Devil in the same way. Such stupefying idiocy may be used and has been used as a justification for believing and doing absolutely anything. If there is no method of arbitration, any claim, any how, anyway, may be seen as a valid expression of behavioural sanction, for anything. Just how long does Mankind proceed under such unmitigated stupidity?

When seen in the above contexts – it is easy to see why we all have, as a species, arrived at an inch from Armageddon. That inch is simply the distance an average finger has to move to have enough strength to push a single button, that one day might wipe out all reasoning life from this planet. It might well be argued that, to get to that predicament, all reasoning life has *already* left this planet.

This most vital right to total freedom of expression must be inherent within any existential module, for the very confirmation of that existence. In other words, the Final Arbiter, or point of Arbitration, can never be Directive, denying any freedom of choice.

The Final Arbiter, or Godhead, for want of any other word, *must* be an *implicit* effect that tacitly allows all things to *Be* from within any frame – from within any reality, in any way, form, or direction. What I am saying (and I hope I don't confuse you by saying it) is that Godhead happens if there is no Godhead, or, if there is no Godness, there must be Godness somewhere, in some way. Just as you might say that if there is a plus, there must be a minus. That is simply what humanly observable reality confirms as the way the Universe is run. How that Godhead phenomenon arises is the question for answer, as and when an entity proceeds beyond the scope of an inherently differentiated view point – in other words, beyond the scope of atoms, Space and Time. Jesus Christ never attempted to explain things of the Universe of the Whole, which He called the Spirit state. Rather he chided Nicodemus: 'How would you believe me if I tell you things of Spirit, when you believe not what I say about the world of flesh'.

We now come to the implications derived from the alternative view of the Godhead phenomenon – that of the Implicate Finality. I have tried to show that the view outside the 'solid', 'physical', atom-based Universe of Parts we live in is inherently forbidden for us to see in physical bodies, because we are composed in differentiated parts. We are cultured as atomically defined entities in the broth of separated and randomly separating points. The Godhead phenomenon has to be a state of 'potentiality', a state of metaphysical unsolidness, if you like, that exists at the helm of the perfect resolution of all parts. Yet, the Universe of the Spirit and the Universe of Matter meet to promulgate the living entity at the interface of their partnership whether that manifestation resolves in 'Enlighted', plasma, hydrogen or 'heavy atom' – weighted types of Man. This manifestation we call 'Life' is thus a signpost – an *implicate* effect that arises incidentally through the concurrence of two final opposites. Just as the spark arises out of the *motion* of the grinding wheel and the *stillness* of the chisel that lies against it. Spirit, as the state of order absolute, is the ultimate stillness – the ultimate 'Peace' if you like, where all is finally reconciled – in the deepest meaning possible. No active physical, or material, dynamics exist here, because no contradictions exist. There is the ultimate potential to Be eternally, anything, any way, in complete freedom.

So, why do we persist in believing in an anthropomorphic finality? What a conceit it seems we have in assuming that the size of Godhead is set within the perceptions of a species that is commonly accepted to be so recently evolved, in terms of geological time. A species so small, on such a small planet of an average sun among the countless billions of suns in general outer space. How much we must need to believe in our own importance. How inherently insecure we must be, to elevate our status to such a disproportionate size, when viewed against the rates and numbers of our Universe. There is no price some of us will not pay to maintain the illusory nonsense of a Godhead viewed in the personified perspective. The power of emotional comfort provided by the familiar warm idea of an old father figure that looks to our every whim is too overwhelming. An old man with a white flowing beard – (resolved, of course, in the complexion that suits our prejudices) is the usual customized visual image that the idea of Godhead conveys, at least in Western Christian semantics. Of course, there is nothing itself wrong in assuming the anthropocentric stance if it is purely an illustrative device. It is, in fact, a wonderful way of attending the crucial psychomotivational vector of believing in a Godhead. But it is fraught with spectacular danger, in that it tends to, and does, reduce and devalue the true grandeur of the grandest absolute of all. The glory of the Spirit state is of such magnitude in its all-pervasive existential value that any limit, however sympathetically derived, provides a lessening of motive and encouragement to its achieving.

CHAPTER SIX:
ADAM AND MADAM

We are told by the 'Good Books' that we are the children of Adam and Eve, the first anthropomorphic polarities – male and female were created by God's hand directly. They were not born. They were created. What exactly was this phenomenon of Adam and Eve? The creation myths of many religions are strangely alike in their descriptions.

But how did Life and Living Beings really begin? How did we, in our species terms, as *Homo Sapiens* happen? If we take the accounts in common religious theosophy of the origins of man, whatever their brand name, there is a common ancestor of us all mentioned. Let's call this ancestor Adam, as postulated by the Christian theosophy. It could be any name, of course. Imagine, if you can, the 'creation' of what is called 'Adam', in this way.

In the first moment of separation from the Universe of Spirit the burst of its 'Light' that makes order is at its purest. Remember, it all happens where the pole of Absolute Union of parts meets the pole of total separation of parts. (See Fig. 4 in the illustrated section.) It is here, at this margin, that what might be called the creation of Universes of Force like ours happens. Everything that happens or is created at this interface will follow the overall pattern and system of the main existential duality, i.e. the pole of union is absolute order and the pole of separation is absolute Chaos. Supreme initial order at the Big Bang will thus degrade to utter chaos, to the meter of Space/Time which itself is manifested as a result of this creation and degrades in step with all that is created. That is, as

I have said, the fate of all things created *outside* the Universe of Spirit where, of course, no Time/Space or Matter exists.

At this first moment of all moments, when pure Spirit bursts out to sublimate matter, Time begins as parts happen and start to separate to the inertia of the Big Bang, trapping the Godhead Light in its new situation. From here its value in purity begins to diminish. Atoms are formed out of its degradent posture. Time increases its meter with fragmentation and subsequent gathering separation of parts. All the schemes of consolidation of these parts begin with the two primary directional vectors of Force expressed at the Big Bang, dimensionally at right angles to one another. One dimensional force vector making what we now call the electric component and the other dimension the magnetic one. The two together in inertial expression provide a moment of twist, creating the third dimensional vector (gravity) and the resulting whole spiral twist turns in on itself, trying for the logically impossible fourth spatial dimension.

As I have demonstrated, it never quite makes it and its compromise is the moroidal shape of space itself. Into and within this whole scheme, the manifestation of Spirit (Stillness) begins with the lowest (most quiet) states of electromagnetism and builds to the hydrogen atom, when there is enough force to make a self-contained unit, in localities where these electromagnetic states gather most, through the inevitable random disassociation caused by the Big Bang explosion.

As I have said, the first atoms begin when these diverse electro-magnetic radiational force vectors are of sufficient consolidational weight. Little self-contained discrete parcels form in the simplest possible moroidal shape. The hydrogen atom is born – hydrogen, the first element has happened. A multiplicity of 'figure of eight' twisted ribbons of pure force, called hydrogen, form everywhere. They are contained and discrete through their own inertial involution, but – and this is the wonderful thing, within their centrifugal-centripetal-inertial momentums there will be a place of balance of force, where no force must exist. Here the Godhead Light remains untainted, so to speak. Surviving in its initial aspect in the tiniest of fractions. Nevertheless, the vital thing is that the balance point in each atom acts as a clear unforced 'lens', through which the pole of final union, itself unenforced, may resonate.

Godhead Light will thus linger where it is most welcome or finds the most conducive home, incidentally, unconditionally, inevitably – always. It is the most glorious *fait accompli*, for every atom, to a greater or lesser extent and depending on its force resolution, may hold the Grand Author of order itself. Hydrogen is the finest and best elemental exponent for the reception of Godhead Light, and Lawrencium, or whatever is the newest element, the least and worst. I suspect that the possibility of 'entertaining' Godhead 'in' an atom disappears long before we get to Lawrencium in terms of the chemical elements.

On goes the momentum of the Big Bang: atoms tumble into atoms and into locations we call stars. When enough are gathered together to provide a large enough enforced situation, they will fuse into one another. Hydrogen becomes helium and so on, till the churn of their togetherness gives rise to the myriad fused multiples of hydrogen we call the elements. Scientists now think that this happens in the centre of stars. In this randomizing chaotic whirl Godhead still dwells, at the points of balance within the layers of force in each atom. Here the 'stillness' points receive and deploy an ordering influence, making manifestations of Godhead in atomic array.

The greater the measures of still points upon a locality, the greater the influence to order – thus life, intelligence and scope to survive in choice and reason become direct proportions of the 'receptability' and utilization of this 'Godhead Light', this still, unenforced residue and expressant emanation of the pole of union.

The greatest point, locality, of such action as far as we know is a human being. How did 'we' happen? Perhaps it happened something like this.

Into the available 'depositories' (atoms) at a stage when these 'depositories' were 'suitable', the Godhead Light settled incidentally and assembled an array that would, to the law of least action in most result, provide the best vehicle for its manifestation from the available resources. All this means is that the first Godhead Man happened in a Universe of rapidly evolving physicality. 'Human' Man is simply a much later localized version of a universal phenomenon we might call 'Adamness'. This initial point of the formation of first resolution into living beingness. The 'Adam points' of resolution must have been a marvel of physical 'Being'. Made of the time and at the time the Universe was young – made truly in the merest image and likeness to Godhead possible. *The* dominant physical expression of Godhead – dominant in its make-up of least possible enforcedness. The 'God' dominant Being – more ephemeral and nearer the state of metaphysicality from whence it all came. A Glory of knowing, understanding and realization. Of course, the scheme must have been plural in its resolution. As I have said, a Universe-wide phenomenon that could hardly have been a single manifestation at a uniquely single point. It must have happened at a myriad of points where the conditions for settlement were suitable.

The conditions that prevailed were the only resource that Godness had to manifest (inevitably) within a scheme of deploying locally increasing platforms of force.

The directive of order was implicit in the momentum outwards from Spirit and so systems of order manifested in atomic magnitudes that allowed maximums of such order. The burgeoning Universe of parts formed Adam points over all its extent and the accession to life, living and all the diffracted results we see now began.

The highest resolutions of order possible found their beginnings in newly created Spatial Time, to decay from then on to what we see in present Time. The 'fathers' of all species Universe-wide started their long travail through the thousands of millennia. The sting of restriction and limit, inherent in a Universe of Parts, stunned many into reverse drive, to reach back from whence they came. Many returned. An exercise much more easily achieved at this early stage of physical devolution, particularly where the 'conditions' of aggregated force were least. Where they were greater the capture held faster and perhaps where they were greatest they held 'living beings' to provide the vast tree of species differentiation we see today. The grip of atomic resolution became tighter the longer Godhead Light lingered in Time. The Universe was seeded with the *highest* levels of being possible, set against the highest existential priority possible at its *inception* – not, as is commonly assumed, the other way round. Every single living thing that exists now had an original predecessor that was 'Godlike': an original 'Adamic' ancestor that provided the scheme on which gradual and graduated *devolution* has taken place to provide all the myriad varieties of life we see on this planet – and almost certainly all the suitable planets in the whole Universe – *now*.

It is clear from all the foregoing that what may be described as Godness complete includes all contingencies, including the paradigms of the Whole state and the Part state within its domain. Where the axiom Godhead represents the pole of absolute Union and the post-atom Primality, or Devil, shall we say, represents absolute Chaos at the other end. In the Universe of the Whole, we *are* Godhead. In the Universe of the Part, we *become* parts, or parcelled units of Godhead. The difference simply lies in the capacity to choose to be *how we want to be*. From this arise the crucial questions affecting the situational disposition of Man: What factors then decide this capacity for freedom of choice?

Before we attempt to answer this question, let us examine our predicament as Man.

I have said that what we commonly term a 'Soul' may be seen as a unique point of living individuality that acts as a sort of 'anti-force pen' when seen functionally against the totally 'enforced' non-living Universe. A vacuum former that is – by virtue of its existential completeness of parts – the property of Order itself. In its ultimate reductive paradigm it may be seen as simply a line of connection between what creates and what is created. As such, it may come into an arena of Force and thus atoms, such as our Universe of Parts, and allow that force, those atoms, to rush into its surviving 'orderness' and form coherent shape in an assembly of whatever constitutes that arena of force, making happen a man – an animal – an insect – a tree – a mollusc, or amoeba in step with the linear march of Time. It is essentially an intercepting effect that is of a consensus outside the Force Signature of the Universe of parts. This Universe of parts provides its own signature of force, based on its own intrinsic average of order set against chaos in a scale, and this is represented by its elemental formulary and is seen in its furthest non-living ordered aspect from Godhead as rocks and stones.

The elements that make up the physical Universe, as we know, are thus made into assemblies within the modulus of the Universal average force paradigm – to be adjusted, or treated in a myriad of ways, by anything that is essentially less 'enforced' than itself. An example of this in one of its highest aspects is a Human Being. Our species' 'soul ASPECT", I believe, of all species possessed the best 'vacuum former' in our part of the Universe able to command the most effect in terms of command for atomic change. We, in other words, were the 'slowest' to devolve when compared to all other species known in our patch of the Universe.

I have used the expression 'Godhead Light' as the vector that illustrates what is called a 'soul'. The vital question for answer is – how might this Godhead Light resolve and function in a Universe of discrete separating parts to provide souls? How is the individuality that defines a soul, in living terms, set against this all-encompassing phenomenon I claim is the Author of order? Is it like an invisible beacon, floodlight, or emanation 'shining' into every part and corner of the Universe? A source that is available always, in real time, such that the 'force print' of any particular locality in space synthesizes it to provide ordered systems, according to the availability of suitable force paradigms (atoms) in that location. In other words, there is a certain amount of distribution of suitable receivers that allow for Godhead to manifest physically in the Universe and according to such an availability of resource, systems are made to manifest order in expressions that provide the best, the highest base possible for that place, that situation and locality. These fixed residential platforms of liveability did not happen everywhere there were hydrogen atoms. The Universe was all hydrogen at one point in its devolution. Hydrogen just provided the clearest lens for Godhead Light to 'reign' through. A Universe of total and uniform pseudo-Godliness existed once in the devolutionary stages of the Universe.

As hydrogen *aggregated* in various parts, so Godliness concentrated in these parts more than others. But a retrograde step was happening, because simple uniformity was being lost to greater complexity. The higher order of the simple uniform state was now being compromised and a variant of Godliness began to happen, a fundamentally important variant – a representation of the absolute state of Godhead in true discrete separation. Individuality had begun – the start of the first 'Godman' was about to Be.

How could we guess the shape and form of the first coherent individual Godman? We can only guess at its nature – its beauty – its effect. We can be certain that all the expressions of Supreme Order promulgated by Godhead Light would prevail within the ordinance of such a phenomenon. It would be as perfect in manifestation as atoms would allow.

The most important thing that we all have to remember is that any such system made by the Author of Order itself would make the final possible system in ultimate intelligence, such that all its qualities in its individuality would allow for the continuation of itself in the highest-ordered basis possible. It would allow for values of 'knowing', 'seeing' and will in maximum existential tenure, in discrete individuality terms. It would allow for what we call, shall we say, Adamic 'Man'. ALL of this would be done automatically – implicitly and incidentally – without option – without directive in option. Godhead *cannot* decide to make exceptions on the basis Man does. Of course, this would imply imperfection in terms of bias, prejudice, etc. All things that are fitted for the resolution of order will have order 'happen' without exception, in ultimate balanced fairness.

A fantastic battle between two opposed resolves. The property of randomizing chaos as a result of the initial directed Will to cause Separation against the intrinsic quality of the nature of Godness – the Will to be ordered and reconciled, always in perfect harmonious union. Such is the existential predicament of all things. And so, what of this Godhead Man, or to put it more accurately in the plural, 'Godmen' – the first happenings from which all life and liveability in the terms we know it in our world, on our Earth, have descended or have come from.

The Adam phenomenon is metaphysically outlined in the Torah, Bible, Koran and every major religious ethic we have on this planet, except Buddhism which makes no mention of personal anthropocentric origin. For centuries we have looked at the story of Genesis literally. I remember being told by the Christian Jesuit priests that a snake came to Eve with an apple in its mouth, gave it to her and asked her (I suppose by hissing at her) to tempt Adam to eat it so that he might be judged disobedient by Godhead and thus reduce his perfection and be sinful. How marvellous apples must have been in those days, that Adam, who we are told had everything in this wondrous garden of plenty, would succumb for want of a taste of it. It is through infantile, literal associations such as these that our consensus of belief has come to us. Is it any wonder that when such unreasonable nonsense is purveyed as religious truth, the might of fear in threat has to be used to keep millions of hearts in belief?

The consensus religious and spiritual outlook of billions of precious individuals has been, through the centuries, cultured against the broad screen of deadly ignorance and foolishness. In fact, the strictly literalistic approach to the Bible came into ascendancy only at the time of the Reformation in the 16th Century. It was a time of great upheaval when the Protestants were breaking free of the power of Rome. Thus they sought their authority from the Bible rather than from the Pope. Those who remained loyal to the Pope also wished to affirm their own allegiance to the Bible. So a situation developed in which the two rival factions sought to outdo each other in their professed loyalty to the Bible. This is the context from which the idea was formed that the Bible should not be questioned in any way. Thus a literalistic interpretation of the Bible originating relatively recently was handed down to the present time. Amongst the early Christians the more influential school of thought treated the stories of Genesis largely as allegory. As the third-century theologian Origen puts it, 'What man of sense will suppose that the first and second and third day, and the evening and the morning, existed without a Sun and Moon and stars?' It is thus the aim of the 'Holy Spirit' to 'envelop and hide mysteries in ordinary words under the pretext of a narrative of some kind and of an account of visible things'.

Of course, the instigators of the literalist school of thinking could not know the terrible consequences to both themselves and their 'flocks', of the rubbish they expounded. They would have to be *the* definitive sadomasochists of all time if they did, because in that kind of simplistic thinking they were responsible for the ideas that were to influence and lead to all the excesses of the Spanish Inquisition, the pogroms against the Jews, Red Indians, Gypsies and indeed all the non-Christian races and ethnic groups that were proselytized by their misconceived and misleading gobbledegook. The serious part, of course, is that the mechanism of eternal tenure of all their victims that we commonly call the Soul was terminally affected by their deadly cavortings. Their responsibility and the consequencies to themselves would be awesome. If, as I have suggested, there is an eternal continuum of Life and Death, these entities would have to chase millions of individual Soul Fields through all their own

individual circumstances of incarnacy and discarnacy to restore
the portion of responsibility, to balance the error or disadvantage
incurred at their hands, to redeem and make restitution of debt
that allowed for any removal from Godness the victim's souls
might have suffered. Let me explain why this might be so:

We have seen that thought cannot be a derivative of atoms,
but that atoms are a derivative of thought. Where these atoms
are in an arrangement that neutralizes force through an unbroken
ancestral connection modulus that preserves livingness in a dead
and dying universe, the light of potentiality, pre-electromagnetism
or Godhead-light is received in lines and patterns that define
individuality that can be seen in unit terms as 'parcels' of
aggregatable experience with actionable free will.

It is therefore obvious that conception, being the origin of discrete
physical life, or individuality, in atoms is not the beginning of us
as living being and that physical death cannot therefore be the
end of us.

One human being is thus potentially the size of Godhead. A
single man or woman with a soul is thus bigger and grander than
all of the non-living Universe. That's you and me.

We could, therefore, speculate as to the methodology of our
continuation: continuation, if you will pardon the cliché, meaning
from where or from what have we 'come' and to where, or to what
we 'go'.

If, through the mechanism outlined above, we are still indebted
to other individuals, then what more obvious method is there of
providing opportunity to restore balance *in real time*, than to return
to the atomic frame of existence, i.e. to reincarnate: in other words,
to meet the bearers of those individualities.

What does Genesis say about the creation of Adam, supposedly
the first and thus the primary creation of all our yesterdays? It says,
and I quote, (the Bible – King James Version) Chapter 2 Verse 7:
'. . . and the Lord GOD formed MAN of the dust of the ground,
and breathed into his nostrils the breath of life; and MAN became
a living soul.' I think you see my point. For 'dust' see ATOMS.
The rest should be plain. And thus the legacy of our ancestry and
the present form of Adam's descendants was set. Set in tragedy.
The tragedy of our human predicament as it has fallen now.

I believe that Inaugural Being, or Godbeing, was really an

expression of how Godhead translated into all other states outside itself, at the very interface point, where the universe of the Whole met the universe of the Part. It was a point of incidental creation. It was not explicit creation in terms of a manufacturing procedure. This happened when the first true Adam was created out of the very stuff of the universe – by Godbeing. This true Adam was an assembly out of sub-atomic particles and represented in turn the next logical interface between Godbeing and the physical Universe. This was a critical interface and represented that point where vulnerability to the Second Law of Thermodynamics, or entropy, began.

I am trying to point out that this phenomenon is the root existential event that went on Universe-wide, at all points of the interface of the Universe of the Whole with the Universe(s) of Parts. It therefore happened in all points of the Universe where the agglomeration of Forces allowed and this Earth was only one such point.

True Adam was a crucially necessary mechanism, because a modus was necessary that allowed the ephemeral state of Godbeing to work within the margins of force without being affected by this force itself. In fact even the true Adam state required an envelope around it too. It was a mechanism through which Godbeing could view the Universe of Parts. A *modus operandi* that provided a remote viewing and redeeming facility that would do all that needed to be done and yet itself keep safe from corruption all it intrinsically was. An arena or envelope was built (The Garden Of Eden) that separated it from being totally infrastructurally sublimated by the natural forces of the Universe and thus prevented it from being intrinsically trapped in an atomic cloak. These true Adams were thus original assemblages, the First Adams, and were placed on all suitable planets. They were Radiant Beings not yet truly part of the material physical Universe they found themselves in. A form of existence into which was set the Godhead power to think, to know, and to discern in Whole terms. An intelligence with the power to make choices based on the summary of information that came directly from Godhead itself. In other words, a mechanism for reason made of atoms. An agency and representation that would seek to know and understand the modes and manifestations of an arena, whose basic functional aegis was to divide of itself into parts, in a Universe that was totally opposite to the one their existential mechanism came from. The first Adams would give Godness the means of a connected yet at the same time isolated vantage point, as I said before, to observe, monitor and view all the factors that went to make up the material Universe of separated parts. To view the Whole from the point of view of parts. Something that the Whole state implicitly contradicts.

To summarize, Adam and Eve Beings were the first sublimation format into parts of Godhead and thus the order of the day at the first point of the Beginning of our Universe itself: implicitly forming on all suitable planets throughout the Universe of Parts. They were not beings as such in the common sense of the word, but we'll call them that for convenience of description. The word 'being' is a figurative description of the capacity, an ultimate Potentiality, that came into our universe to allow Godness to explore the view of the Whole from the point of view of the part. This is crucial to realize. These original 'Beings' (I use the word for convenient descriptive purposes) would thus know full well that an enforced Universe held the ultimate threat of complete sublimation and thus entrapment of their status as pure spirit endeavour, through the breaking up, separating, entropic momentum of Force in our Universe that is its signature and sole purpose. Their entrapment within the margins of Force could be final and so a device was sought that would maximize the safety of their demeanour and carry through their intention of viewing the Whole from the point of view of Parts with minimal risk. Through their direct connected aegis to Godness and thus the Universe of the Whole an environment was created where they could exist as near to Godness as possible. Just as a more substantial 'redeemer' two thousand years ago came into the world and proved this point with five loaves and two fishes. He, remember, was in atoms and thus could deal with atoms, albeit in a very advanced way.

And so did the Garden of Eden come to be in this way? What exactly was this phenomenon? Was it actually a garden, or is this too simplistic a mechanism to explain it as an actual piece of real estate in terms of a location for the origin of living being? I believe any thinking person would have to conclude that it was a metaphor. A mental picturescape on which to envision a mighty happening.

In and through these symbols, these mental envisioning mechanisms, Adam, Eve, and the Garden of Eden, the best grandstand view of all that it means to be in a Universe of Parts could be demonstrated and gleaned.

The word 'garden' conjures up an image of a total environmental scenario. A place that even the simplest mind can identify with as a location for 'liveability'. To the poetic philosophical minds it would be a view from a true 'bridge of sighs', one might say. A practice pitch for the behests of angels. A setting from which our origin progressed and had to be established so that all minds could understand the phenomenon. A place or a stadium for beginning.

There would thus be many 'Gardens Of Eden' universe-wide in as many suitable locations on all suitable planets in the Universe where all that is of Godness could prevail and prosper. They were locations or watch towers to provide a means of redemption for all who fell into them through their own volition out of Godhead once upon a time. Yes, that means *you* and *me*.

The common literature describes this phenomenon in this way. Let's begin with the Bible:

> 'And the Lord GOD planted a garden eastward in Eden
> and there he put the man whom he had formed.
> And out of the ground made the Lord GOD to grow
> every tree that is pleasant to the sight, and good for food;
> the tree of life also in the midst of the garden, and the
> tree of knowledge of good and evil.'
>
> (Genesis Ch. 2, v.8-9)

> 'And the Lord GOD took the man and put him into the garden
> of Eden to dress it and to keep it.
> And the Lord GOD commanded the man saying,
> Of every tree of the garden thou mayest freely eat:
> But of the tree of knowledge of good and evil, thou shalt not
> eat of it; for in the day that thou eatest thereof thou shalt surely die.'
>
> (Genesis Ch. 2, v.15-17).

It is obvious that this is symbolic language and must not be taken literally. *How many Trees of Knowledge do YOU know in the average garden?*

Yet almost every Christian grows up with the idea that a snake took an apple to Eve and she took a bite of it and offered it to

Adam and this act of disobedience caused us all to be cursed in some way with their sin and their guilt.

We truly are kin to baboons if we take all this literally, all of us who swallowed this simplistic garbage so ably propounded by many advocates of Christianity.

You might have noticed that I have tried not to personalize Godhead by representing it as a 'being'. There are too many anthropocentric connotations to view it in this way. Too many connections with the European medieval sexist and racist mythology of a white man with a flowing white beard, dispensing all kinds of damnation to those unfortunates who incurred his wrath and favour to sycophants and courtiers who praise his name enough. Buddhistic philosophy, while not invoking a personalized anthropomorphic Godhead, describes and clearly implies a final neutral state of ultimate being that may well be taken for Godness, if you like. This is to my mind, as I have said before, a much more accurate description of the final existential quantum.

And so, in summary of all the above, we may say that Godness and No-Godness are two sides of the same coin and all existential creation lies betwixt these two final polarities. One implies the other and one cannot exist without the other. Creation is simply the means through which one can know the other.

To continue in summary, let's say that we are all here to see, to know and to understand what is ALL, and that we are an artefact of a logical procedure that allows for just that by observing the phenomena and manifestations of our Universe of Force from within it and not from outside it. Because change is eternal, the procedure is eternal.

The way is thus always open for 'Redeemers' to come to save all that was worth saving in a Universe of decaying parts and the only thing worth saving in such arenas as our Universe was that line of individual connection that ties the Whole with the Part: our Souls – that most precious thing of all things. Redeemers could and would constantly come into our 'patch' in the Universe (because we had a soul, we all had this precious individual line of eternal heritage at least in potential), claiming that we had something precious beyond all reason we could never afford to lose. They would come claiming that we were in a situation of existential danger so awesome in degree that the giving of their lives was a price they were gladly willing to pay. They knew bodies made of atoms were just decaying devices in a Universe of Parts, just a physical shell, a means to a worthwhile end. Something temporary and transient that gave access to an eternal ingredient that could be persuaded to return of itself to an eternal existence where there was no threat of its loss. They knew that this shell would continue to make other shells, other bodies in continuums called Reincarnation Cycles, *ad infinitum*, as long as the strength of the connection all the way back to Godhead in a continuous line was never broken. It is this uninterrupted line, incarnation after incarnation, that perhaps best defines the word 'Soul'. A line that could only be compromised when the thirst and will for knowledge dims in the individual. It would then weaken until it was finally no more capable of reasoning and understanding the meaning of self. Only then would it finally weaken, not able to dictate the best scope for its existence in a Universe of atoms and go from being Man to monkey to insect (a million cicadas could sing with the voice that was once a single man) to tree to virus to plasmid to stone to atom isolate and beyond to the very ends of energy mass and finally the contours of Space/Time and the arms of 'to be', or 'not to be', itself.

CHAPTER SEVEN:

THE CHICKEN AND THE EGG

The first physical manifestation of living Being as it devolved out of Godhead is, as I have implied, a very special existential modulus. The Bible eventology implies an initial singularity where the sexual polarity of the female aegis had not yet happened. It is formed out of the image and likeness of Godness itself, we are told in the Bible. Yet the Universe of Parts by definition is the opposite of the Universe of the Whole. Would that then make the self creation of this first Adam a Being of opposite resolution, rather like a photographic positive image is different from the negative one? In other words, as we are substantial and visible the opposite of us would be insubstantial and invisible. This would imply that the Universe of the Whole is this resolution too. If the 'creation' of Adam came directly out of Godhead its resolution would be as pure and unadulterated as the opposite state would allow. This would further imply that the creation would have to be set in an environment of as ultimate a stature as our Universe would allow. The Garden Of Eden would have to be an environment that is designed to preserve this purity.

We know that the swansong of our Universe is the Second Law Of Thermodynamics. The ultimate corrupting momentum possible. An octopus called Entropy with tentacles of doom. Adam and Eve, we know, were told not to do certain things if they were to keep intact their prevailing Godlike condition. This state was essential to keep the best connection possible into the world from which they sprang. They were, after all, as I have said, a self-designed modulus self-created to observe the All from the standpoint of the Universe of Parts and act as the best possible channel for transmitting this information to Godhead. From the information gleaned through the First Adam state of singularity a further element in keeping with the nature of being in a universe of 'parts' is clearly necessary and a second modulus we know as Eve was clearly indispensable. It was definitively a procedure that followed out of the Adam state itself and was thus honed out of it. (You will recall the 'rib' story from Genesis.) A list of prohibitions was then given. These forbiddances, if followed, would protect them from being sublimated with our universe. If they disobeyed the tenets of this list, they would lose the power of automatic access to the Universe of the Whole and Godhead. They would lose the ability of automatic return through their own free volition to Godhead. They would have been captured in an atomic universe and isolated from a direct interface with Godhead and would thus be naked and vulnerable to all the forms of force that would be henceforth the order of all their days. And so, to put it Biblically, 'It came to pass'. They disobeyed the interdictions, and the clear line to Godness became obscured and their form of 'being' became corrupt, lost its straight uncomplicated line and became subject to the Second Law of Thermodynamics, or Entropy. The existential winds of change came to billow in their sails and break apart their ship of fate.

The Temptation of the Christian Redeemer is a fascinating pointer to the predicament we are all in as a result of all this and begs the question: Who, then, and what was the Tempter that brought about such a catastrophe for us all? Let's leave this question for the moment. I hope the answer will be clearly implied in due course.

Let me first speculate for a moment on what might have happened to reduce the scope of Godbeing so drastically in the First Adams and Eves in the 'Gardens Of Eden' on many planets Universe-wide. As I have said, it may well have been something that made the spirit form subject to the arrays of Force that define the Universe of Parts. What, therefore, was the 'forbidden fruit' that was supposed to have done this. An apple? Preposterous, you might say. Yet, I believe, the 'Apple' might give us a figurative clue to it all.

If you look at the shape of the inside of an apple cut in half on its vertical plane it resembles the magnetic track or shape of the lines of force that prevail on a bar magnet. Was the 'Garden Of Eden' an area that was a natural Faraday cage? A Faraday cage is a device that shields anything placed inside it from electromagnetic fields. Perhaps the Garden of Eden was a place or situation into which no electromagnetic fields could enter. A place where the most lethal thing to the spirit form could be kept away. I would surmise that Godbeing in its earliest form in this Universe was extremely vulnerable to Force and the forces that made up this Universe. Electromagnetism would then and even now be lethal to the total spirit form. Whatever interdiction Adam and Eve were under might have included the barring of magnetic fields at all costs. I have said previously that a good definition of Godhead is one that conveys the idea that it is the antithesis of what we call Force. It is the principle that defines No Force or the state of absolute Peace or Stillness. The final straight line that defines no potential difference between points. Whatever the 'apple' was it breached the defences, and here the 'serpent' may be yet another figurative clue that defined this threat and might affirm my postulation. If you think about it, the serpent travels in a regularly shaped winding form. In other words, a 'Sine Wave'. It may define an electromagnetic field producing an entry mechanism that broke down the protective 'clothing' that shielded the 'spirit form' of Adam and Eve from the full rigours of our Universe such that they were made naked. In other words, vulnerable to the Universe's dismantling array of forces and thus, as I mentioned previously, to the constantly corrosive and lethal break-down effect of the Second Law Of Thermodynamics, namely Entropy.

And so the long drift into more and more gross forms of living being began for the first Adam life form of the Earth. From spirit being to mortal flesh over billions of years, perhaps the transformation occurred in line with the behest of the entropic drift, right down to the most recent forms of physical Mankind, and the legacy of the grave. In generation upon generation of new False Adams culminating in the ones that mark the most recent history of our species, Man.

We are thus, as living beings, a line of existence discrete from Godbeing yet connected to it in ways that account for all we know as conscious living intelligent individuals ourselves.

If you see existence as a line, Godhead is perfectly straight.

Godhead is perfect 'Peace'. It is 'left' of the radio spectrum. Before radio waves begin to put in, in layman's terms. It exists before the first perturbations that mark the beginning of the electromagnetic spectrum, that in turn marks the beginning of Force. (See Fig. 9 in the illustrated section). In other words, the point at which our line develops the first kink in it. It is in understanding this line that we may understand the answers and the questions I have posed in this thesis. Particularly where pertinent to our 'friends' the Greys.

CHAPTER EIGHT:
OF GOD, MICE AND MEN

We cannot have a more obvious implication that the Way of the Universe is Devolution and not Evolution, when we see how the accent of Man's inspiration has changed through the aeons from the Metaphysical to the Physical. When the summaries and results of so-called progress, or development, are taken it is undeniable, that the existential expressions of Man have moved further and further away from an accent on a spiritual outlook and more and more to the transient temporary exigencies of the material outlook, representing the stance of the physical. It is a way of making the best of our entrapment. It is also the surest way, alas, we ensure our entrapment in this cauldron of death and destruction we call the Universe. A way of deriving the immortality of a stone by way of the immortality of a clone. I believe this to be the *only* Alma Mater of a Universe of Parts. All else is immaterial. Please pardon the pun.

Yet, while life and liveability lasts, while this 'living' quality is steeped in a flexibility that can elect the maximum options in this cage of damnation we call our Universe, we may still escape into an eternal scope that knows no limit. A scope that is inherently secure forever.

If we can for a moment generalize the basic philosophical existential momentums driving humanity in the world today, they come down broadly to two schools of thought. Eastern and Western. Those who believe in Reincarnation and those who don't. There is a logical paradigm that I have worked out for myself that allows me a snatch at deciding which of the two basic approaches, Eastern or Western, I might go along with in answering this question of what is the single most important resolution of continuity that drives existence. It goes like this.

In order to know anything you must exist in a state to do so. In other words, you must first be *there*, to *know* you exist. In my present conscious terms as an individual, I know I am here. Descartes put it so beautifully and simply as 'I think, therefore I am.' It is the final existential value that anyone can draw. As such, a rock on the Moon has been there 'to know' (I am not claiming it knows anything, or can know anything, I am only claiming it is there) for at least five million years. It will stay on the Moon for another five million years exactly where it is unless something else moves it. It will not be able to do it of itself, for itself. It is that dumb. We as human beings can go to the Moon and kick the hell out of that rock. We might even pick it up, bring it back to the Earth. Study its crystalline structure under an electron microscope, polish it and admire it on our mantelpiece. It cannot do a darn thing to us. We have total control of it and all its capacities and potentialities, such as they are. It cannot command us or decide anything for itself or us. It has no power of choice whatsoever. Yet it is superior to us in basic existential terms because it will stay a rock on that mantelpiece, or in the ground, after the mantelpiece decays and disappears and we as human beings are long gone and pushing up daisies. Our tenure will only last a measly seventy years if we are lucky. Are you getting my drift? How is it possible that something like a rock will inherently be capable of lasting longer in tenure, just doing nothing, when you and I who, in capability and capacity to know and understand and do, are so superior to a rock and its inherent value and capacity? There has got to be a way that we can continue on, to fulfil our grander capacity for choice and range of choice. I am certain that Reincarnation or the transmigration of an individual being through a carrier or vehicle outside the atomic scale (a soul) is that implicit way.

CHAPTER NINE:
TO LIVE AGAIN

I have mentioned the term 'Reincarnation'. Let me say something about it at this point. All the major religious theosophies, including Christianity, have believed at some point or the other in the principle of the transmigration of the soul. This principle enshrines the capacity for the continuance of an individual's being, over several lifetimes, in a repeated series of physical bodies. The idea is that the individual essence continues in a learning process through a series of corporeal bodies, till that individual essence has learned enough to be divested of material form. From thence continuance is supposed to proceed in non-corporeal, or metaphysical, form till all knowledge is achieved and maintained in a state of absolute all-knowing and all-powerful eternal aspect.

All Eastern religions still subscribe to this existential formula. Judeo-Christian and Islamic theosophies no longer subscribe to this principle and only believe in a single episode of incarnate existence, with the extinguishment of the individual physical being at a final posting we call 'death'. We now come to an example of the horrendous wickedness practised on us all by the so-called 'fathers of the Christian ethic' when they threw out the other traditions, and their sources of scholarship, that are now identified as the Nag Hammadi and the Pistis Sophia texts in the Coptic Gnostic Library, in the early years of the Christian Church. In the Pistis Sophia, that purports to give Christ's incidental conversations with his apostles and contemporaries, it is apparent that reincarnation for early Christians was a thoroughly accepted tenet. There is an account of Jesus describing to his apostles the difference between those who were purified and returned to heaven from a state of insubstantiality and never entered 'physical' bodies, and those who have to free themselves from the 'wheel of rebirth'. Of the first type of soul Jesus says: 'They have not suffered at all and they have not changed places, nor have they troubled themselves at all, nor have they been transferred into various bodies'. Then of his apostles he says, 'You have come to be in great sufferings and great afflictions from the transferences into various bodies of the world. And after all these sufferings of yourselves you have striven and fought so that you have renounced the whole world and all the matter it is.'[1]

Many representatives of the so-called mystical branches of both Judaism and Islam, Cabalistic and Sufi traditions respectively, also incorporate reincarnation into their belief structures. However, for the mainstreams of these faiths it appears that continuance in splendour and bliss is only supposed to be reserved for those who reach a certain level of goodly development in the favour of a divine entity whose will proffers this state to the soul as a reward. We all owe those scoundrels of the past who deemed these texts invalid and took away our right to consider all the literature about any particular belief, a great debt of ingratitude. It was easy to see why they did it. Reincarnation implies that you have many chances to get it right. These rascals knew that if we were told we just had one chance under pain of damnation their esteem and their importance and tenure as administrators would skyrocket. It gave them the power needed to lounge around in cassocks and hold to ransom almost the entire family of Man.

The Eastern philosophy of Buddhism, unlike Hinduism, accepts no Command or directive divine mechanisms that allow this as a personalized whim, but proclaims an individual and totally free custody of one's destiny. Another all-important and complementary principle runs along with reincarnation. It is called Karma. This principle enshrines the ethic that says 'As you sow so shall you reap'. Eastern philosophical thought includes Karma as the driving principle that governs the reincarnation process. It postulates in effect that what you have done in a particular lifetime governs your status and placement of return in subsequent lifetimes. All this, of course, begs the question of where are the starts and where are the ends of any individual existential sojourn? What is born? Who is born? And where does what is born come from in the first place, and why?

I can't help feeling that acceptance of the ethic of reincarnation was doomed in Occidental hands. Indeed, its eradication from the Christian codex is believed to have been the responsibility of the wife of Justinian I – the Empress Theodora, who was enraged by a soothsayer when he claimed she was a witch in a previous existence. Her influence over her husband was claimed to have been responsible for the denial of the principle of reincarnation in Christian theosophy. It is claimed that under Justinian's order the Christian Codex was wiped of any reference to it in the canon. It is also plain to see that the principle's inference that an individual continues for lifetime after lifetime would be very inconvenient in terms of controlling the 'body politic' of religious endeavour. As I said previously, it is easier to corral an acolyte within a faith if he is told that he has just one chance of getting things right than if he has a multiple snatch at things. I suppose it is understandable when one views it all against the antagonism and threats offered against the burgeoning early Church from the host of heretical views that it faced in its early days. But expediency is the author of lies, and reason and its power to proffer truth is always its victim. The price of such victimization is awesome. It is the loss of your Soul and mine.

The terrible thing is that the result is not set in punishment, as is commonly accepted the world over, but in simple, coherent, logically contrived consequence, neutral consequence. The most awesome consequence of all is, the *final loss of knowability within a state of coherent focus* – i.e. an individual human being, or 'human beingness'. And so, in final summary, let us try to see the entire picture that defines our 'being' as living entities within the scope for existence provided by and for that being.

CHAPTER TEN:
'OUR FATHERS WHO ART
OF THE UNIVERSE'

There can be little doubt that we are *not* a lone species of intelligent life in the universe. I am sure you have heard the 'implicate numbers' argument. You know, the one that goes: There are so many trillion stars in our galaxy. Our sun is just one such star. A pretty ordinary one at that. This ordinary star has a solar system with nine planets around it. One of these planets has life on it and one of the species of this life is so advanced it can know and perceive the Universe and all there is to know about all this life and thus control all other life on this planet through this knowledge. The argument goes on. If we are just one sun among trillions of suns in one galaxy among trillions of galaxies, then who are we to think that we are the only intelligent master life form in all these numbers? We don't need to prove the existence of life empirically. The implicative argument suffices.

Let us for a moment, for argument's sake shall we say, accept this implicative contention for the existence of other 'master life' in the Universe. If we do, then it follows that the Universe is teeming with intelligent life and that this life, as is the nature of intelligence, has various levels of intellectual capacity from the most rudimentary to the most supreme. What, then, defines this mentality in terms of its results?

The model for all that is best or worst in the application of high levels of intellect has to include the capacity, first and foremost, for the preservation of this acumen in its most fruitful stance. If we look at the out-turn of the whole human psychological aegis from the beginnings of its independent choice-making capability, it all comes down to, after all the centuries of development, the complete *denial* of this fundamental existential platform in the creation of the *means* to deny it. I mean by this the creation and production of the *means* to take it out completely in one fell swoop: the atomic bomb. Such a startling paradox is, you might think, the prerogative of 'unintelligence'. Yet there is no question that we all, as a species, accept that we are *not* unintelligent. So does intelligence out of its very nature implicitly beget unintelligence? It seems undeniably so. At least, *the intelligence that dominates and controls all other living platforms of being on this Earth seems, in fact, with ultimate irony, to be in the business of denying this capacity and its future scope totally*.

How, then, might a civilization that has given birth to the phenomenon we call 'Flying Saucers' and their occupants have survived to the point where they can go visit other parts of the Universe many light years away from their planet of origin without blowing themselves apart as a civilization? How have they survived against the Second Law Of Thermodynamics with such a prodigious technology, when we, after a mere two hundred years of industrial technology, are poised to take out the human race at the press of a button? The overwhelming human urge to violence for the most facile and shallow of reasons, century after century, has been proved through the tremendous numbers of wars, skirmishes and violent confrontations and in the fact that we have always used any and all the implements of war that we have invented. Their use has always been based in terms of expedience. It has just been set on a matter of opportunity, time and circumstance. In other words, the summary of our intelligent endeavour seems to have led to the development as its acme of achievement, in just two centuries, of the means to take us all out of existence at a single stroke. How could alien civilizations have coped with the above stated paradox, if this paradox is, as it seems, a natural quantum universally implied and applied? Of course it begs the question. Is it really universally applied?

Any answer to this question will of course have to be speculative. My speculation goes as follows:

Imagine a planet out there somewhere in space. A planet with its own strain of what we shall call 'creator-beings'. Beings of the highest development in morality, spirituality and emotionality. That planet's first Adam beings. Let us speculate that this planet has produced a civilization that invented a technology thousands of years in advance of ours. They developed theirs at a stretch without interruption at the same rate, shall we say, that we on Earth have done with ours since the Industrial Revolution of the eighteenth century. Let us imagine that they are highly advanced beings who carried through all of this and thus had developed systems so completely automated that all the hardware, all the utilities, all the systems that it takes to run an entire planet were run by robotics and robots. Remember that all the modern so-called glories of technology that we all take for granted now have developed since a point in time barely two hundred and fifty years ago. From the Cotton Jenny to a Cray computer in just three human lifetimes. From the merest sense of the rudiments of life to the threading of polypeptide chains of amino acids for the creation of life. From the primitive understanding of a cell to the cloning of an entire animal through DNA transfer from the cell nucleus.

Roboids – programmed robots in 'flesh' made to order in endless numbers to run an endless variety of things without the touch of a single creator-being's hand. Japan has already produced a model village where the entire thing is run by robots, albeit at the moment of the inorganic kind. If we on this planet can run whole factories with robots in just fifty years since their first inception, if we have got as far as developing organic artificial skin and tissue for transplants, it will be a relatively small step to put the two together. Then you will have homes and factories designed to be cleaned, maintained and completely run by organic soft-tissue robots: all of it completely untouched by a single human hand. If the rate of progress of an alien civilization just maintained the pace of ours, can you imagine what this civilization might be capable of through thousands of years of development?

Writing in an article in *The Guardian*,[1] John Newell reports on the work of Professor Stephen Sligar of the Immunology Department of the University of Illinois, who has reported that he has made startling progress towards engineering protein chips to replace inorganic semiconductor materials such as silicon. It has been known for some time that proteins have molecules with the complexity and optical properties needed in microelectric components, but Sligar is finding ways in which it is possible to actually engineer protein molecules into mini-microchips.

By altering the amino acids out of which long-chain protein molecules are assembled, protein engineers can also alter patterns of electrical charges on the surfaces of molecules and hence their electrical properties can be changed. Sligar has succeeded in making protein molecules more able to exchange electrons with other proteins. An advantage which protein chips have over inorganic semi-conductor materials is that they are thousands of times smaller than the smallest possible silicon chips. Thus they enable future biocomputers built from them to work much faster than their inorganic counterparts. A further advantage is that the passage of current through and between proteins produces no heat and heat is a major problem for small and compact silicon devices.

Once the necessary protein engineering has been worked out and the genes for the proteins altered accordingly, the genes can be inserted into bacteria and cloned millions of times over. So protein chips could be cheaply mass-produced in bio-creators. Thus they would provide us, says Sligar, with smaller, cooler, cheaper chips. Also, and this is the most telling point of all, protein chips have the added advantage of lending themselves well to the functions of parallel processors, which are the advanced class of computers which mimic the brain by undertaking many different processes simultaneously. The natural interactions of proteins, Sligar points out, lend themselves best to such parallel processing.

So it is safe to say that soft tissue robots (with a potential far greater than their inorganic counterparts for both efficiency and high-level programming which can mimic the human brain) have already graduated from science fiction to science *fact*.

David Tirrell and his research team at the University of Massachusetts at Amherst have made a synthetic protein that contains 3-thienylalanine in place of the natural amino acid alanine.[2] They used bacterial husbandry as well as genetic engineering to synthesize the protein. The sulphur-containing thienyl group was used because it is a building block of polythiophene, a polymer that conducts electricity. Tirrell aims to link up the thienyl groups protruding from a film of this synthetic protein to make a biocompatible conducting material for possible use in biomedical devices. The fascinating thing about this protein is that it contains sulphur. Numerous witnesses of UFOs and their alien occupants have reported a sulphurous smell that emanates from the craft or from the alien beings themselves. Might these scientists have unwittingly discovered part of the recipe for the make-up of alien cloned beings in an artificial protein that combines synthetic and organic materials, conducts electricity (which is a facility that is vital to these remote-controlled beings), and contains sulphur?

Now let's return to our advanced ET civilization out there in space and its soft-tissue robots. Let us speculate further that these robots were created to preserve the existential status and living paradigm of their 'creator-beings'. Let's say that the naturally enforced state of this Universe prevailed on their planet too and threatened the inherent existent mode of these beings. These beings, of course, originally came from Godhead as ours did. Godhead, it must be remembered, has to be a situation that was the antithesis of our Universe. In other words, these naturally living intelligent entities were subject to the same *devolution* processes that prevail Universe-wide, and they were subject to them once they entered this universe, but their particular version managed to devolve slower than our version did. They possibly held to Godhead better, with a finer focus of existential priorities for longer. Their ancestors came into our universe with the Big Bang just as ours did. Their first Adam-equivalent had the same problem ours did. The continual exposure to the entropic force of our Universe made them more and more vulnerable to it too. So how could they preserve themselves in their former state and at the same time learn about and observe the Universe of the Whole from the point of view of the Universe of Parts? *They did not disobey the rules.* They did not bite the 'apple' of force as hard and as completely as our ancestors did. They managed to stay isolated from the margins of force better than our ancestors on this planet managed to do. So how, then, could they explore the Universe of Parts from within their Garden of Eden protective envelope? I believe they created a kind of duplication of themselves out of the stuff of the Universe itself. i.e. atoms. They built a *clone* being. An exact atomic equivalent of themselves. A device that had no soul, i.e. a device that had no *direct* ancestral connection to Godhead as they did, but was a duplicate proxy version of themselves that could be exposed to the entropic dismantling force of the Universe without compromising anything as profound as the best possible link to Godhead in an atomic frame of reference. In fact, they created many cloned beings such as this: an organic/inorganic copy version of themselves. These 'Master Clones', as I shall call them, gave them the remote-viewing and functioning capability the Prime God or Adam Beings needed to have in the Universe of atoms to explore it without going outside their protective cocoon where they would be prey to the corrupting force of entropy. The Clones could venture where the Prime Beings would fear to tread. The Clones were a perfect fail-safe exploratory and marshaling device that secured and maintained the existence of the Prime Beings that possessed a soul, as long as they wished it. In other words the 'manufactured' Clones were made to run this system. They could do all the Prime Beings could do and do it till they wore out.

These artificial first-generation Clone beings had one disadvantage. The cloning process of regeneration had a price in entropy. Their atomic complement would eventually make them subject to decay. The self-propagation process made them finite. They could not regenerate themselves indefinitely. They had the same 'knowledge' complement as the Prime creator-beings. They thought themselves the same as their creators because they were, after all, perfect Clones. But they found, rather strangely, that they could not continue their own existence indefinitely. They were different. They were subject to entropy and thus the gradual dismantling of their state in line with the Second Law Of Thermodynamics. In other words, they wore out and eventually came to an end. They had to reclone themselves constantly if they were to continue. The Prime Beings, they found, although subject to the same physical laws of the Universe, could continue their tenure indefinitely by going through a process called death and return to the Universe through a procedure called physical 'birth'. They continued in incarnacy through the process of re-incarnation seemingly *ad infinitum*. In other words, the Prime Beings seemed to possess an additional mysterious capacity or mechanism for indefinite continuation. We shall call this mechanism a soul. This realization was later to have a crucial part to play in the existential base of both their world and ours. It was to be the prompt of all our yesterdays and all our tomorrows here on this Earth. I will explain later.

As I said previously, the Clones acted as isolating paradigms that enabled the Prime creator (Adam) beings to stay segregated from the forces of the hostile Universe. The Clones were living biological beings. In every way identical to the Prime (Adam) Beings that cloned them out of themselves with one crucial difference. They were made purely of the stuff of the Universe – atoms–and had thus no connecting mechanism to Godhead. Their total connection was centred on the generative plan or blueprint from which they were cloned and no further.

The Clones were Master Beings in their own way. They had independent intelligences no less than the Master Prime Beings that gave rise to them. They thus created a further version of themselves. Their own isolation mechanism. A mechanical, partially biological atomic version. Let's call this version Roboids. A highly advanced polymerized robot with artificial intelligence and the capacity for being programmed to function as a pure mechanical utility. The worker bees of their civilization. The Clones were the drones while their creators, the Prime Adam Beings, were the 'Queens'.

When you think how much robotics has advanced here on our Earth in fifty years with our rudimentary civilization, you can imagine what an alien civilization with an advanced technology might have achieved. There is already evidence from current research into microtechnology that a form of Roboid is now being designed for use, particularly for use in environments that are harmful to humans.

Mark Ward, in an article entitled 'Silicon cells with a life of their own',[3] discusses these new developments. A team of researchers from the Swiss Centre for Electronics and Microtechnology and the Swiss Federal Institute of Technology have designed a computer that can grow, reproduce and recover from injuries. The computer will be built from blank silicon cells that in some ways behave like the cells in a biological system. The silicon-based cells reproduce by copying their software to neighbouring cells – rather like biological cells passing on genetic information to their offspring. In this way the computer grows from one cell to fill all the blank cells on a silicon wafer, although it cannot create new silicon. Each cell is made up of a collection of logic gates carved out on a silicon wafer less than a millimetre square. These arrays of gates are flexible and can adopt the characteristics of any logic gate by changing the software used to address them.

The software 'genome' tells each cell where it sits in relation to the overall 'organism' giving it, and this is the clincher: *basic self-awareness*. Once it knows its position the cell can work out what its function is in the large system. So it will only implement the sections of the software that are appropriate to its position. The cells reproduce by copying this software genome to neighbouring vacant arrays. If any cell becomes damaged the cells around it will follow the instructions built into their genome and reconfigure themselves to work as if the damaged cells were not there.

'For this we took our information from the brain,' says Pierre Marchal, one of the staff scientists on the project. The brain cannot grow new tissue and so it has to re-route around damaged connections. Marchal says this ability to heal makes the cell computers ideal for environments that are harmful to humans, or where it is impossible to repair damage. For example, space probes or deep ocean survey equipment could be formed out of these computers.

So far, the researchers have built cells that have reproduced and they have also simulated an entire microprocessor built up of the cells on a conventional computer. 'The cells are as powerful as conventional computers because you can implement any computer with this. The only difference is that they will be bigger', says Marchal. In the long term this flexibility could enable identical, mass-produced arrays of cells to be optimized for any computing application by varying the software 'genome'. Thus these man-made computers which have a form of 'basic self-awareness' would be flexible to adapt to any circumstance, just as their alien-made equivalents are able to do.

According to a report in the *Daily Telegraph* (18.7.96)[4] scientists working for British Telecom are currently developing a microchip that will be ready for use in the year 2025. The microchip's design will mean that, when implanted in the skull just behind the eye, it will be able to record a person's every thought, experience and sensation, hence it is called 'Soul Catcher 2025'. Dr Chris Winter of British Telecom's Artificial Life team explained that the impiant will enable scientists to record other people's lives and play back their experiences on a computer. 'By combining this information with a record of a person's genes we could recreate a person physically, emotionally and spiritually,' said Dr Winter. 'The implanted chip would be like an aircraft's black box, and would enhance communications beyond current concepts. For example, police would be able to use it to relive an attack, rape or murder victim's viewpoint to help catch the criminal. I could even play back the smells, sounds and sights of my holidays to my friends.'

These technological developments in our own relatively primitive backyard are strong indications that technologies such as these and probably others that are even more sophisticated may have been developed long ago by beings technologically far superior to us.

Let me summarize and continue to outline my hypothesis on what might have happened on our alien extraterrestrial world, perhaps a million light years away.

The Prime Adam Beings there were straight out of the nature of Godhead. They were 'true sons of God.' They came to view the Universe of Parts from the point of view of Parts but found that the price paid was that the Forces that made these parts in the first place would make 'parts' of them too. They sought a means of staying as near Godly aspects as possible and made for themselves an environment that secluded them from the Forces of the Universe. This is the feature I have alluded to previously as a Garden of Eden. Within this innovation, they were not subject to 'entropy' and thus stayed as sweet as they were in Godhead, shall we say, as long as they remained within its precincts: a giant Faraday cage from which all electromagnetic, gravitational, centrifugal centripetal and other force vectors were kept at bay. This was all well and good. But they were trapped. How could they experience every feature of this deadly Universe and still remain untainted or unaffected by its prodigious array of dismantling forces? There was one way. They could create an equivalent of themselves. A Clone. An entity that was entirely made of the enforced stuff of the Universe, i.e. Atoms, yet made in their entire image and likeness. The Clone would be their mechanism for remote viewing the whole universe.

The Clone was their functional tool with the same intelligence and perception and could venture forth where no Adam being would be foolish enough to go. The Clones could immediately relay back to the 'Celestial Observers' with ultimate accuracy what it was like to be in this lethal home of ours we call the Universe. As the forces of entropy took their toll of them, they could replace themselves by re-cloning themselves and thus continue on in time, space and matter till the fullest extent of the phenomenon of a Universe of separated parts was known from the point of view of parts, of eyes, ears, tastes, smells, and feel. It would be like looking through one's own eyes and mind remotely.

The Clones did all this beautifully. The little utility they created, the bio-synthetic Roboid (perhaps they themselves called it a Grey: I'm sure the reader is by now seeing what I am getting at with all this), was a go-anywhere mechanism made from an organic/inorganic amalgam on, shall we say, a silicon and mercury spine. These bio-machines could venture into areas of our Universe where they themselves (the Clones) would have paid too heavy a price to go. It was a perfect system of information gathering, at least for a while. They did not reckon on the inherent corrosive corrupting nature of the Universe of Parts. The Second Law Of Thermodynamics took its deadly toll in their part of the Cosmos as it does here in ours. The further the Clones ventured to find the ultimate margins from which they could function, the more they got corrupted. The more they lingered in this Universe's chaotic maelstrom the more – imperceptibly at first, but more visibly later – their instincts got tuned away from the naturally uniting features and properties of Godhead. They were endowed with this in mind at least, when they were first created by the Primary Adam Beings. They slowly began to question their status against their parent creators. Difference as a principle became a threat. They noticed the one vital difference between them and their progenitors. As Clones they were subject to decay and disassembly faster than their creators. The Prime Beings within the 'refuge' were not. They (the Clones) wondered why this was so. They wanted to be like the Adam Beings. They had to know the mysterious difference that made them subject to entropy wherever they were. Their exposure to the Universe made them subject to this decaying, dismantling process. They began to question their status. Exposure to the forces of the Universe made them deceitful and full of guile. These are words that only have such an implication to someone with a moral or ethical code. To the Clones' emotionless intelligence it was the intelligent thing to do. They were utility beings and thus objectively totally expedient.

The Adam Beings, however, knew no such things in their innocence and direct connection to Godhead within their protective cocoon. The Clones tempted their creators to let them into their protective cocoon. (I don't believe it was with an apple.) Once in they found no difference. They still decayed, and decayed faster than the Primes. Their entry into the Garden of Eden let in the Forces of the Universe and made the Prime Beings vulnerable to these forces too. The Prime Beings began to know demise and devolvement into an atomic state. They were no more with Godhead. They were nevertheless, unlike the Clones, still directly connected to it.

The essential distinction between a God-connected Being and a Clone was that the former was united through Godhead with all that was in living natural existence. A Clone was a manufactured utility outside this paradigm. Its continuity was in a state of abridgement already separated from the Final Absolute. As such it was no more significant in existential value than a rock or stone. It was a 'living' mobile statue with intelligence.

The Prime Beings had a facility for continuous contact with Godhead. As they fell more and more into a state of Atoms, they generated a procedure and platform of communion with Godhead called Death. It was a natural artefact of the Universe of Parts and existed within the atomic array that made up this Universe, in the spaces between atoms. A halfway house between Godhead and this Universe of atomic parts. More about this later.

The Clones found thus that the Prime Beings could even conquer Death. These Godhead-connected Beings returned into new bodies through a process called birth, carrying with them their conjunction with Godhead intact. As Clones they had to duplicate themselves. They had no means of differential reproduction. They could only produce identical copies of themselves. They could not reincarnate. They could not return into life modules of their former selves. When they wore out, they re-cloned themselves. It was a purely physical process. There was no continuity in mind, only in flesh, and even this was finally subject to limit. You could clone only so many times before the dismantling feature of entropy at basic atomic level let you do it no more. They had to find a fresh genome that had not been cloned. They took it from those of their creators who themselves became more and more physical with the collapse of their protective cocoon, and decayed more and more. Most of the

Prime Beings returned to Godhead immediately their protective cocoon collapsed, of course. They were too close to Godhead to fail. Some, a few perhaps, got trapped.

They passed down a line of beings with a soul. The Clones gradually took out these beings one by one, never letting them generate themselves back to Godhead, taking them out as soon as they were born so that their Stem cells could be used to provide a new platform for re-cloning their own kind. This never gave the Prime Adam Beings a chance to live a full life and thus regenerate themselves back to their spirit form and enter Godhead through Death. Finally, in time and in ultimate tragedy, the Clones took the last of these precious soul-bearing entities out of existence. There were no more to regenerate new genomes or formats for cloning. The penny finally dropped. The Clones at last and too late found the 'Difference' between their 'father' beings and themselves. They grasped the idea that there was a Universe outside the atom and understood the holy abstraction we call soul as the all-important direct individual ancestral connection to Godhead itself. More importantly, they realized that the only way to access this Universe was to possess a soul and that you could only have a soul if you came into this Universe with it. They finally perceived that a soul was an intangible ephemeral bond line to the centre of all Absolutes. They had all the time looked in the wrong direction, in the wrong place. They looked for something physical. After all, they could never know anything but the physical themselves. They could look no further than the margins that identify the atom. They were totally of the atom themselves. Made out of star-stuff. That is why they never spotted their Holy Grail till the last of their Prime Beings had gone. It was too late to attempt the acquisition of a soul on their planet. They could not even try to see if it was at all possible. They built themselves a means that could conquer space and time and came to our neck of the woods. They came looking for our Souls. They are here now: looking for a way to beg, borrow, or steal an eternity.

I have said before that the Creators of the Clones (the Prime Adam Beings) were of the highest moral and spiritual rectitude. It was because they were of such demeanour that they maintained their marginal ephemeral state in atoms notwithstanding their protective mechanism that I have called the 'Garden of Eden.' They could never know how to divide or separate anything from its whole state. They were ultimate reason itself. They could never resort to violence because they had no concept of separation or division to know what a violent act might be and thus how to defend themselves. They didn't defend themselves when the crunch came and they were confronted with the ways of the Universe of Parts. I like to think that they did return to Godhead from whence they came like the beautiful 'Wimps' they were. Forgive the play on words. 'Wimps' is an acronym for Weakly Interacting Massive Particles. Current theories in physics postulate that most of the matter in the Universe may be composed of these particles. Perhaps this explains the ninety per cent of mass scientists say is missing from the Universe, rather than being consumed by the entry of force into the nostrils of Angels.

And thus, with ultimate irony, the stage was set for a Universe-wide tragedy so that through a functional utility manufactured to deal with an imperfect Universe with imperfect tools we all to this day stand compromised.

Going back to the Coptic Gnostic texts mentioned earlier, the scenario that I have just described is one of the central themes, it seems, of Gnostic Early Christian thought. The terms used in these texts to describe these Cloned Alien beings are the 'Authorities' or the 'Archons.' In a particular text in the Nag Hammadi Library of ancient Christian thought entitled *The Hypostasis of the Archons* there is a detailed description of both their origin and their nature:

THE HYPOSTASIS OF THE ARCHONS

On account of the reality (hypostasis) of the Authorities, (inspired) by the Spirit of the Father of Truth, the great apostle – referring to the 'authorities of the darkness' (Colossians 1:13) told us that 'our contest is not against flesh and [blood]; rather, the authorities of the universe and the spirits of wickedness' (Ephesians 6:12). [I have] sent (you) this because you (sing.) inquire about the reality [of the] Authorities.

But I said, 'Sir, teach me about the [faculty of] these Authorities – [how] did they come into being, and by what kind of genesis, [and] of what material, and who created them and their force?'

And the Great Angel Eleleth, Understanding, spoke to me: 'Within limitless realms dwells Incorruptibility. Sophia, who is called Pistis, wanted to create something, alone without her consort; and her product was a celestial thing.

'A veil exists between the World Above and the realms that are below; and Shadow came into being beneath the veil; and that Shadow became Matter; and that Shadow was projected apart. And what she has created became a product of the Matter, like an aborted fetus. And it assumed a plastic form moulded out of Shadow, and became an arrogant beast resembling a lion.' It was androgynous, as I have already said, because it was from matter that it derived.

'Opening his eyes he saw a vast quantity of Matter without limit; and he became arrogant, saying, "It is I who am GOD, and there is none other apart from me."

'When he said this, he sinned against the Entirety. And a voice came forth from above the realm of absolute power, saying, "You are mistaken, Samael" – which is, "GOD of the blind."

'And he said, "If any other thing exists before me, let it become visible to me!" And immediately Sophia stretched forth her finger and introduced Light into Matter; and she pursued it down to the region of Chaos. And she returned up [to] her light; once again Darkness [. . .] Matter.

'This Ruler, by being androgynous, made himself a vast realm, an extent without limit. And he contemplated creating offspring for himself, and created for himself seven offspring, androgynous just like their parent.'[5]

'Sophia', or the principle of 'EVE' as she is more commonly known, thus created something alone and without her consort. A Clone being, perhaps? Clones are the result of parthenogenesis, reproduction that involves only the female germ cell. Eve's creation is described as 'a product in the matter like an aborted foetus which assumed a plastic form moulded out of shadow, and became an arrogant beast resembling a lion'. This does indeed sound like a description of cloned being, a product in matter 'moulded out of shadow'. The potentially threatening nature of such being is also suggested: it 'became an arrogant beast resembling a lion'. Thus the warning is given as quoted from Paul in *Ephesians* that 'Our contest is not against flesh and blood; rather the "authorities" of the universe, and the spirits of wickedness.' Who might these 'authorities' be who are not of 'flesh and blood'? Could they be roboids formed of other substances, the 'Greys', created by the Clones to do their will?

The text later goes on to describe how the 'authorities of the darkness' became 'enamoured' of the 'image of incorruptibility' that appeared to them in the 'waters'. But because of their 'weakness' they were unable to 'Lay hold of those that possess a spirit; for they,' (the authorities, or our 'Greys'), 'were from BELOW, while it (the Spirit) was from ABOVE'. So the great enigma for the 'authorities' provided by a living being with soul seems to be described here in this ancient text which goes on to suggest the great difficulty these 'authorities' had in their attempt to 'capture' the 'image' of spirit which they had seen:

'They took some [soil] from the earth and modelled their [Man], after their body and [after the Image] of GOD that had appeared [to them] in the Waters.

'They said, "[Come, let] us lay hold of it by means of the form that we have modelled, [so that] it may see its male counterpart [. . .] and we may seize it with the form that we have modelled" – not understanding the force of GOD, because of their powerlessness. And he breathed into his face; and the Man came to have a soul (and remained) upon the ground many days. But they could not make him arise because of their powerlessness. Like storm winds they persisted (in blowing) that they might try to capture that image, which had appeared to them in the Waters. And they did not know the identity of its power.'

It is not only the ancient Christian texts that give us indications that alien beings may well have visited our planet and left their mark on mankind. The chroniclers of the ancient Indian epic, the *Mahabarata*, those of the Sumerian text the *Epic of Gilgamesh*, and those of the Eskimo, Red Indian, Scandinavian, Tibetan, Babylonian and Egyptian sacred texts, all tell stories of flying 'gods', strange heavenly vehicles and terrifying catastrophes associated with these extraterrestrial phenomena.

Among the ancient Hindu sacred books, the *Samaranga Sutradhara* contains 230 stanzas that describe in detail every aspect of flying, from how the apparatus was powered to the proper clothing and diet of the pilots. The International Academy of Sanskrit Research in Mysore, India, conducted a special study of this ancient work and published its findings in a book entitled '*Aeronautics, a Manuscript from the Prehistoric Past*'.[6] Convincing evidence was found by these scholars to conclude that the text revealed a knowledge of aeronautics that was remarkable. Here are some translated extracts from the text:

'The aircraft which can go by its own force like a bird – on the earth or water or through the air – is called a Vimana. That which can travel in the sky from place to place is called a Vimana by the sages of old ... The iron engine must have properly welded joints to be filled with mercury and when fire is conducted to the upper part, it develops power with the roar of a lion. By means of the energy latent in mercury, the driving whirlwind is set in motion, and the traveller sitting inside the Vimana may travel in the air, to such a distance as to look like a pearl in the sky.'

The Vimanas could cover vast distances and could travel forwards, upwards and downwards. A further quote from the *Mahabarata* states that: 'Bhima flew with his Vimana on an enormous ray which was as brilliant as the sun and made a noise like the thunder of a storm'.

The Tibetan books Tantyua and Kantyua also mention prehistoric flying machines which they call 'pearls in the sky'.

Further indication that knowledge of extraterrestrial being was a worldwide phenomenon is found in the mythology of the Eskimo peoples which says that the first tribes were brought to the north by 'gods' with brass wings. There is also a telling inscription from a pyramid that indicates that the ancient Egyptians were also familiar with these phenomena: 'Thou art he who directs the sun ship of millions of years.' This particular inscription is all the more relevant when we look at it in terms of our understanding of how it is possible for these alien beings to travel faster than the speed of light making 'ships of millions of years' a real possibility.

Scientists are now coming to the conclusion that there is a technique that might make it possible for spaceships to travel faster than the speed of light. An explanation of this follows later. Ian Crawford of University College London says that 'contrary to popular belief, faster-than-light speeds are not explicitly forbidden by special relativity'.[7] He points out that there are a number of concepts that aliens might use to defy the speed of light. For instance, they might use 'wormholes', short cuts through space-time created by the natural design features of the universe. 'The mere fact' that travel faster than the speed of light 'may be permitted by the laws of physics means that it might just be possible', says Crawford. He also claims that if faster-than-light travel is possible then there may be a good reason why alien beings would want to hide from us. He speculates that they would be likely to want to observe human societies and study them as though they were zoo specimens, looking at them through a one-way viewing glass so that their behaviour is not influenced by the fact that they are being watched.

To go back to our discussion about the knowledge of extra-terrestrial phenomena that can be found in the world's various civilizations, affirmations from a Judaic source can be found in a fragment of the Dead Sea Scrolls entitled the 'Apocryphal Book of Adam': 'Behind the being I saw a chariot which had wheels of fire, and every wheel was full of eyes all around, and on the wheels was a throne and this was covered with fire that flowed around it'. How similar this description is to that of a type of UFO that has been often sighted that seems to be formed of rings or 'wheels' covered in blinking lights, or 'eyes'.

We all face now the chilling prospect of an attempted hijack of our souls through the cold-blooded lethal efficiency of a super-intelligent machine-mind that has come into our part of the Universe with this one intention in mind. It is objective, dispassionate and utilitarian. Judged emotionally, it could be seen as cruel. Perhaps they themselves do not even know what cruelty is.

Perhaps you've also noticed, too, how robot-like our so-called developed industrial societies are becoming. The final demise of humanity to a point of no return may well have already begun.

Professor of Cybernetics at Reading University Kevin Warwick is of the firm belief that the computerization of the entire human aegis has indeed already begun.[8] He warns that in the next fifty years computers will be able to match some of the thinking abilities of humans. After that, machines will have the capacity to make copies of themselves like living organisms until there comes a point when they can surpass the intellectual feats of most men and women. He believes that man's treatment of inferior animals might be emulated by these machines when they deal with us. 'We can't rely on intelligent robots being nice and generous when we ourselves are not nice and generous', says Warwick. 'The best we might be able to expect would be to be their pets'. The only other alternatives he sees that might emerge are either the reduction of the human race to the level of slaves or, at worst, our complete extermination by artificially intelligent machines. 'We have to ask where AI research could take us', he says. 'It could be into extinction'.

Warwick visualizes machines able to teach each other, possibly in a language unknown to humans, and thus to take control of computer-operated weapons. Helped by the development of communications networks such as the Internet, robots would be able to tap into information and learn faster. Details available to them could even include the best ways to eradicate humans. For these reasons Warwick suggests that an international body should be set up with the utmost urgency to discuss the threat and to set rules to control intelligent machines. This, he believes, could help us to ensure that robots were programmed to protect humans or could be disabled if they tried to take over. 'There is no point in waiting, things are moving along quite quickly. If we get it wrong the human race could be wiped out or enslaved'. However, Warwick himself admits that programming a moral code into robots not to harm humans would be extremely difficult since machine intelligence does not mirror human concepts: 'We need to make it very simple. Even the concept of what is friendly and what is unfriendly is difficult'. BT Laboratories futurologist Ian Pearson, who, by the way, also said that he believed that Warwick's time scale was a conservative one, has said that programming intelligent robots not to harm people would not work.[9] I believe that he is absolutely right: it simply cannot work for the reasons that I have already mentioned. So if Professor Warwick, who is working at the cutting edge of cybernetics himself with his own research into autonomous robots, is right, then our fate at the artificial hand of these robots seems to be sealed.

CHAPTER ELEVEN:
CLONING AND ALL THAT JAZZ

An even more disturbing development than the invention of intelligent robots has been revealed recently and this, I believe, is singularly the most significant event of the whole millennium, i.e. the cloning of living systems. With the revelation of the cloning of the sheep Dolly, the world was made aware that higher animals can be cloned and the so-called highest animal of the lot, human beings, are well-nigh on the cards for the same treatment. All those in the 'secret know' are privy to the fact that Dolly was not the first cloned animal and that in secret enclaves the cloning of human beings has already been done and is still being done by certain governments and, as has been shown in this book, by other non-human agencies.

For atheists and suchlike who believe that matter gives rise to matter and there is no more in existence than the chaotic forces of the universe and what may be manipulated out of them (by what is of them in the first place, of course), the significance of cloning is relativetly minor. I have tried to show that this whole paradigm is logically preposterous anyway and that the Universe of Parts is not all there can be in existence. I have tried to show that a Universe of the Whole, where all parts fit, is a certainty and has to exist somewhere in some way if there is a Universe of Parts in existence as indeed our Universe is. If that is so then there has to be a line of continuity that ties it all together whether it be direct or indirect. This line of connection is what I have called a 'Soul' and if such a 'mechanism' or 'effect' (call it what you will) exists then cloning is of ultimate importance.

I believe that the soul is simply an unbroken line of connection to the origin of all origins – Godhead. If there exists a line of connection between anyone's individuality and that point from which we all began, (that incidentally includes Godhead's beginning if it had one) then this line can be expected to have 'witnessed' all that has happened to an individual and perhaps in some way contain and preserve all the effects, power, consequences and knowledge of these 'happenings' throughout its existence. I have tried to explain in previous chapters what this 'line' might actually be and how it exists as a working reality, at least in figurative terms.

We are all of us individuals. We may have family connections, blood connections, connections through friendships etc., but viewed with any rational sense or meaning, we each stand separated and individual the moment we emerge from our mothers' wombs. This is, of course, true even of identical twins as long as they don't share the same physical body. To all intents and purposes we stand as individuals to make our decisions and choices from the point of view of a separate identity. In other words, I cannot go to heaven in your head (if indeed there is a heaven) and you cannot go to heaven in mine. We are separate beings in a universe of intrinsically separated parts. So what are all these marvellous beings such as Gautama Buddha, Jesus Christ, The Prophet Mohammed and all those wise theo-philosophical minds of all the ancient religions speaking so consistently about when they speak of the mechanism of continuity we call a Soul or Ba or whatever name we might attach to it? They all affirmed unequivocally that there is continuity although they posited this continuity in different ways.

I would like to use a somewhat simplistic analogy which I have used to help my teenage children to conceive of and to explain what the continuing mechanism might be. I use the world 'mechanism' in an abstract sense.

Imagine the soul of an individual living being in physicality to be like a telescopic rod aerial (like the one on a car) made up of a totally forceless vaccum. This is a standing vacuum in an environment of total force (our universe). Unlike other vacuums this one exists in itself and of itself in all the atomic forces and derived tensions this universe can throw at it. It is like oil to water. Immiscible but breakable into smaller parts. This telescopic rod aerial or

'Soul Field' is spring-loaded and always set to fold into itself if allowed. It will only do this if it hasn't got some sort of anchor or restraining mechanism such as the atomic forces of the universe to stop it doing so. If it was unrestricted by these forces it would retract completely and it would metamorphose and disappear into another quantum state that is totally forceless and not physical or solid as we are. I have called this state of total and absolute forcelessness 'Godhead'.

Imagine that each human individual is an exclusive rod aerial who, before it comes to life exists in what might be termed the 'Fields of Death'. It exists in the 'Fields of Death' extended and going all the way back to Godhead at one end and unextended and slightly crooked at the other end. Waiting to be extended and lowered from this other end (the place 'Death' exists) to the space within the force of atoms we call our universe. It only becomes a pole when it is extended and lowered from Death's fields to Life's fields. Till then it stays folded up into itself at the Life's Fields end of death in its crooked disposition, waiting to be extended into incarnacy and thus into this universe and the living paradigm we call life. (I will later outline in more detail the paradigms of life and death as I understand them to be.)

Mum and Dad who are incarnate and thus in the Life's Fields end (our universe) already have both ends of their poles extended. In coming together sexually they form a ladder (two poles side by side) and the compendium of their conglomerate physical and psychological qualities form the rungs of the ladder in a stepping mechanism between them. The ladder is distorted according to the unique value of each respective soul and the rungs are the makers and markers of this distortion. Remember, if their respective poles were dead straight they couldn't exist in this Universe. They would have folded up into themselves and returned to Godhead. It is only because each rod is bent away from the utterly straight aspect that it exists at all. The measure of this distortion allows any other pole that exists in the fields of death at the time that is perfectly congruent with the total sum of the parental poles' distortion to extend itself as an exact match, and be guided down into a physical existence. Thus another living being comes into our universe. (The logic of all this, as I'm sure you have guessed, is that we are – Clones of God.) Remember the words in *Genesis* alluding to the fact that we are 'all made in the image and likeness of God.'

Each living species is defined by and decided by the straightness of the rod. In other words, each species has its own characteristic basic shape to the rod and this makes that particular species what it is. The more crooked (dog-legged) the pole, the more primitive the species. The more rough or dirty and gunky the pole itself is, the more 'sinful', more restricted the individual within the species. In other words, let's say: one slight bend – a human being; one dog-leg bend – a chimpanzee; two bends – a wolf, etc. All human beings will have one slightly bent pole. All apes will have a single dog-leg or right-angled bend in their pole, with tiny variations for each genotype within a phylum.

It follows, therefore, that the straighter the rod the more easy it is to telescope it and withdraw it into Godhead. So the straightest and cleanest, smoothest poles will automatically withdraw into Godhead and eternal life. (Try pushing back a crooked rusty car aerial for instance).

I think that in the terms I have stated that I can justify the claim that the human species can be demarcated from the rest of all species as having the straightest rod (on this planet at least). As I have said previously, let's say it is slightly bent, or it would not be here. The crucial thing to remember in my paradigm is that the more complex the curves away from the straight, the more primitive the species.

One is again made aware of the prophet Jeremiah's words: 'Make straight the way of the Lord'. Perhaps he saw the soul in a similar way. But all this allusion to rods and ladders does not illustrate much about the significance of cloning. Or does it?

Mum and Dad are essentially two primary human soul lines with all the prior information of millions of generations carried in their biological propsectus – their genes. We are each loaded from each of these parental lines to become new progeny. The newly-incarnating progeny lays its matching information (the shape of the rungs) to be able to slide down into a life of physicality in a physical Universe, on an exactly congruent parental coupling. This, then, gives that progeny a new span of time for existence to try to straighten out its rungs and its rod, and to clean up, smooth out, and polish up the rod, such that it may spring back automatically into Godhead again.

Why has it got to do this, and why in a Universe of Parts such as ours? It alas has to try to do this in a universe that itself is crooked and makes 'crookedness' happen (a 'crookedness' without which the universe itself would not be able to exist as a Universe of Parts). It has to do this in the same paradigm that gave rise to its crookedness in the first place. It is only such a universe that can match it like for like. If the rod's (soul's) crookedness was made in such a universe with the elements that made up that universe then you would expect the same quantums would have to be used to do the straightening. (See Chapter 26.)

The entry of a single soul into incarnacy is at one and the same time the most glorious and horrendous thing that could happen. The word 'happen' has a very special and significant meaning here. Birth is more an occurrence or a happening than a deliberately planned event. Or at least in most instances it is. For the highest of species on our planet it may not be so in many instances. But even for such a species the eventuality of pregnancy is more unintentional than intentional, or so sociological surveys would have us believe. The idea that birth, life and death are an automatic and implicit non-intentioned process just like water finding its own level, shall we say, is widely accepted in theological terms. It may well be true in final terms, but we can only guess that it is so. We can never know.

Intention is the final prerogative of a directive final entity some call God. You either believe that all things in the most minute detail are decided by God or you believe that there is such a principle as Free Will and that an absolute and total scope for all things to happen unfettered exists. This would be the prerogative of a non-directive final entity. Shall we call this principle Godhead? If you think about it there could never logically be a half-way house. If all things can Be through the prompt of a single occurrence, then the existence of suffering and injustice is tacitly implied and logically accounted for just as its opposite is so accounted for.

If the governance of existence itself and all things that come from such a tenet are steered under the ordinance of a directive God then there can be no cascade of certainties derived out of logic. If reason would be for the mind of God only then we would not be entitled to assume that reason itself had any meaning. There could be no speculation because there would be no rules under which that speculation could proceed. I am therefore assuming the non-directive Godhead stance to enter my speculations and offer them to the reader for good and feisty consideration. If you follow logical derivation then your guess is as g(o)od as mine!

Before I try to explain what I understand the significance of cloning to be, in relation to the foregoing, let me try to explain the mechanism of non-cloned, so-called natural existence or birth and its antecedental significance on this line of continuity I call a soul.

You all know about the birds and the bees. The principle of the appearance of new living being is based on the existence of at least one prior being, and in most instances two. We mostly are the product of a trine of action. Father and mother together produce a third element.

The winds of focused attention in urgent disposition (with emotion and goodly sense, we call it love) ply their trade in Universes of Parts and the stage is set for the grandest and most awesome event to take place in billions of locations all over the Universe: Birth.

I claim that Birth without the modulus of endless scope and scope for endless continuity is meaningless. In the spirit and with the strength of this axiom I believe that reincarnation is the most logical and pertinent of procedures to effect this continuity. I was brought up a Christian before I became a human being and saw the awesome sense of reincarnation. I believed with the rest of the 'processed' Christian arbour that we all were given just one chance in one life at seeking a better, more continued existence. I came to realize the patent lunacy and idiocy of such a belief at the age of twelve when the child of a joyfully expectant couple we knew was stillborn. It got me questioning the whole edifice of the Roman Catholic church and these 'processed Christians' it produced, as the scoundrels who in previous centuries decided what you and I should believe, in the name of its glorious founder. It took away from all of us some of the most crucial and salient truths he actually taught. I will go as far as to say that in doing this Roman Christianity may be said to have, intentionally or unintentionally, taken on the mantle of the Great Lucifer itself.

I have mentioned in a previous chapter that the earliest Roman church endorsed the ethic of reincarnation (as all the major religions did at one time or the other) with illustrations and affirmations with Christ's own words as quoted in the ancient texts such as the Nag Hammadi library and the Pistis Sophia. The vanity of one woman – the empress Theodora, the wife of the Holy Roman Emperor Justinian – was responsible for its removal as a tenet, because a soothsayer told her that she was a witch in a past life. It is a horrendous price to pay for vanity and may mark this quality out to be the single most destructive 'cause célèbre' for the demise of an entire species.

I myself, for what it's worth, am still a Christian in as much as I believe, love, and glorify the wondrous being that gave us the ethic that bears his name, the ethic as listed and disposed, as I have said, *before* the convocations of bishops massacred the ancient Judaic, Aramaic and Greek texts that came down from earliest times. Most if not all of the vital assertions that pointed to reincarnation as the most salient ethic of the continuity of awareness were left out of the now accepted Christian Codex through their machinations.

The vicious Convocations of the Roman Church and its so-called holy dignitaries who at various times adulterated, misappropriated, dispossessed and deliberately falsified and misinterpreted Christ's teachings did this in such a way that it laid a path for their own authority as a group, and took away from us all any insight that Christ might have given us of the prodigious importance of our individual predicament and our individual right to make all final decisions ourselves, particularly in a universe designed for parts or individuality.

Our individual journeys directing us out of our present predicament in our hellish universe have for the most part been based on sanction, inculcated through lies, distortion, misinterpretation and, most lethal of all, fear. Sheer storming fear.

The great revealers of the truth of our predicament and the way out of it did so through simple and non-confusing information, illustration and example. They paid for it, most of them, with vilification and, in many instances, their lives. They still do.

In my own search for the margins of forever I found I was incidentally becoming a Buddhist, a Hindu, A Jew, a Moslem, Jain, Sikh. The answers I was discovering made me fall in love with the truths and the first revealers of these truths in each of these religious disciplines in exactly the same way and with the same magnitudes with which I love Jesus Christ. (I say it this way because I was 'implicated' a Christian at birth.)

The most marvellous discovery I made, as any dispassionate objective unprejudiced student of their revelations will discover too if they have done the whole exercise and searched for the meaning of their revelations, was that in no way do they, any of them, contradict each other in the most basic and salient revelations they made as to the existential bases that underlie our predicament in this universe. All the differences were installed by their followers later and ascribed to them.

No truth can be outside meaning, reason and logic. The great revealers fought, suffered and died during their sojourn in life for rationally derived truth. These are the standpoints that make everyone equal in the pursuit of ultimate truth and we are all thus inherently free to seek after and find the final answers devoid of the fetters of other men's whims and fancies if we but use these basic psychological loci. They are the knitting needles that unravel the knots of the chaos of the 'dead atom universe' with ultimate dispassionate objectivity. It equalizes us all in all our quests for truth and lays to rest the essential myths that tend to happen when truths are seen and accepted subjectively.

I am claiming all this in the first person not because I think that I am anything special but because I hope that the reader will also see that we are all in the same predicament as a species. If logic has any meaning then togetherness counts and a world made better together for rational reasons against the entropically driven chaotic momentums of the dead, static, dependent universe will redeem and be effective in redeeming future generations of wandering beleaguered and besieged souls in this Hell we call our universe.

With reincarnation as the central mechanism that facilitates continuity in a physical disposition, the wheres, whens, whys of it all are, it seems to me, easily derived. All action begets a reaction. You sow and you reap what you sow. All Christians, for example, assume there is some kind of celestial bookkeeper outside themselves keeping a tally of all they do or think or the consequences that follow from such action or, indeed, inaction. Few if any really go after an answer to the questions thoroughly enough: Who or what and where is this entity, this mechanism that counts us and all about us? How is he, she or it disposed? Where does it live, or exist? Why have an arbitrator or clerk of all Universal works anyway? It is God, of course, claim the Christians in a hallelujah chorus. It *must* be God. It must be the supreme being's personal job to marshal the entire universe and all the doers and begetters of all consequence and to judge them implicitly for their works and dispense punishment, praise and reward. In Chapter 5 I have attempted to show how this concept of God as a directive entity is without rational basis.

I have placed God outside the Universe in a totally different frame of existence yet I still claim that we are not isolated from God: how then do the two connect? The clear implication from this is that the mechanism that allows us to conceive all of this in the first place, and indeed reach and communicate with God, may in fact be 'thought'. It may be a capacity that can reach and exist outside the frames of Space and Time and indeed 'travel' faster than the speed of light. If 'thoughtness' is such a marvellous thing and its application so powerful in deciding destiny, then we have something we have to be very careful about. Its resolution, use and reconciliation may well be the final drive of all drives that decide every detail of our subjective pasts, presents and futures. If this is so, then we are the only final arbitrators of us. We are the only librarians of the self as individual entities we'll ever have – anywhere, anyhow. As such we hold the catalogue and the pen that enters all quotients within. It is an individual journey from beginning to end within the frame of existence we call this Universe and perhaps beyond. Or is it?

What really is the pen, the catalogue, the writing? How is the record kept in this metaphor of mine? How and where can we write with thought such that a meaningful record can be kept that arbitrates our entire scopes and results?

We know that force shapes our entire reality. Atomic force paradigms, be they called strong, weak, electro-magnetic, gravitational, etc, are all simply the pen, book and ink that shape our reality and the revelations that come from it. It is what we might call a hard, solid, physical reality. If there is a hard, solid, physical abode to our reality, there must equally be a soft, non-physical, non-enforced modus existing somewhere in some way, to it, upon it, and within it too. Just as if there is a plus there must be a minus. I have laboured in this book to give the reader some concept of what it might be, if not categorically then by default. This other reality will be as I have said previously, staged in exactly opposed quantums. It will be perfect stillness, peace, the perfect absence of force. It will not be hard, physical. It will be a reality devoid of the concept of parts. As I have said several times previously, a reality of all togetherness of parts. A reality of all knowledge, understanding and perception in total fit, seen and discerned in instant instantness without the existence of spatially addressed, sequentially assessed time. Hard to conceive of, isn't it? But there it is. It really IS.

I asked previously how the record was kept. We know in this Universe the physical record of our past as living beings is kept through a double helical strand of tiny shapes of force called chemicals in a force-coded sequence called DNA. We know that anything that does not live does not have this record. So one of the most crucial differences between living and non-living things might be said to be that one has a continuity record and the other has not. I believe that the non-enforced universe that encompasses and leads to Godhead also has a record-keeping equivalent of itself. It is written with a non-force pen, if you like. A kind of vacuum writer that assembles the equivalent of DNA but is absolutely nothing like DNA. In fact it as totally unlike DNA as it can be. It is not spatially arrayed. It is not sequentially metered. It therefore has to be a phenomenon we will find almost impossible to actually conceive in our parts-conscious, sequentially metered mind's eye. We might, however, gauge an implication of what it might be and from that derive all the important qualities of the interface point that connects the Universe of the Part and the Universe of the Whole. I have tried to conceive of the phenomenon we commonly call the soul as a continuous track that connects the two and terminates in the individuality of a single living being in the world of this physical living being. This is the track that the False Creation of alien Clones, Roboids and thus Greys that are now revealing themselves more openly, do not have. It is the line of connection I believe they are all here to pirate and pillage. This, I believe, is normal practice all over the Universe where precious primary creations of soul connected to living systems like mankind still survive. They have happened in on us and now it is our turn to face the terrible music. A music I believe 'Christ'-like phenomena come to planets to try to prevent. It is the total horror story of our present predicament since these artificially created 'things' arrived here or impinged here on our part of the Universe. It may well, I believe, be the final writing on the wall for our species and indeed all the living species of our planet.

If, as I contend, the soul is the track that marks our connection to our point of interception in Godhead and uniquely identifies any and each of us, then our faces and personalities are uniquely and individually coded and set both with a specific soul track and a unique physical track we call our DNA fingerprint. It contains all the information of all 'happenings' that we have uniquely instigated from the past to the present. If our DNA is, then, that specific to our individuality and we make an absolutely exact duplicate to this as we do when we clone some living being then the horrendous consequences become immediately apparent. *We make another portal that might feed into our unique Soul-and-Body record because it has the exact keying mechanism that allows it to do this.* If we clone a thousand individuals from a single human (primary) being, then these thousand individuals share the same record of the primary being and will thus influence in equal measure the destiny of that being. The primary being will have a thousand sources of 'sin' or just simply information it cannot control with its will. If it happened to you, your clones in their individuality would share your exact biophysical aerial receiver (as it was when the DNA was extracted from you) and I believe also its attendant soul identity. You as the primary entity from which it sprang will not be able to do a thing about any negative or harmful input it might choose to feed into your central bank. It will share your account. You would have lost individual exclusive and primary control over who can deposit ill effect into it. I believe clones are simply exact multiples of the primary being they were cloned from and share the single individual line of inception back to Godhead. The horrendous outcome is that the primary and the clones all share the same individual soul.

I wonder whether Christ was alluding to this eventuality when he said: 'They shall seek for death and death will never come . . .'

Can you imagine someone cloning another you when you have died and are existing in Death's Fields (say, from a blood sample or DNA sample you might have left behind)? You will immediately have a portal into life opened for you that you might not desire to have that will hold your spirit from progressing where you intended it to. You will be anchored and even perhaps be adulterated from the incarnate equivalent of you and there would be nothing you (the Primary Being) could do about it. You would be damned by delay, and that delay may further damn you more and more in the eternity of complete disbursement.

By damnation I mean the complete entropic disbursement of your individuality in subsequent reincarnations downwards into subsets of your species: Man – to ape – to monkey – to animal – to mollusc – to tree – to bacterium – to virus – to plasmid – to various differentiated heavy atoms – light atoms and back again to hydrogen and so on! Eternal entrapment in physical universe, and the endless entropic churns they are.

I am reminded of the story of Isis and Osiris where the former was said to have swept the entire realm of Egypt for the last remnant of Osiris who was believed to have been cut up into little pieces by his brother Seth and these pieces strewn all over the kingdom. She did not rest till she got back every piece of him. It is said that she cloned Osiris back to life as the sum of all the parts found. The main feature of the story was that she had to get back every single physical part. If for the sake of speculation the Isis–Osiris story was one of alien visitors to the Earth doing their business here then their technology would have told them that you don't need the entire body to clone someone. You just need a single cell. So why make such an effort to claim back every single body part? Could the story imply that the characters, or 'visitors' as the case may be, knew the awesome importance of keeping every single bit of the physical being together as individual and entire, because the future best disposition of the soul demanded it?

It is crucial to differentiate between the capacities of a clone and its progenitor. A clone is biophysically identical to its parent being. Its entire cell assemblage and chemical autopsy is identical. It is a complete biological duplicate in every sense of the word, of the parent being.

It is equally important to differentiate between a clone and an identical twin, for instance. As I have said, a clone is an exact biophysical copy of its progenitor. An identical twin is not an exact identical copy of its other twin. Neither is it an exact copy of itself as a clone is. It is an exact copy of its mother's single cell with its father's bio-identity strapped to it. However, unlike a clone's body, the body of an identical twin is not formed from the cells of a body with a soul and thus an already established bio-magnetic field (generated by the blood circulating around the body in a coil – see chapter 16). At embryo stage two bio-magnetic fields are established. So the twins, although they are formed from the same ovum, establish two individual soul attachments to two separate bodies, after those bodies have already formed as two discrete identities with two discrete bio-magnetic fields. Thus each individual twin is a Primary soul bearing being. Their individual souls bring their own individual influence from beyond the grave to bear upon the creation of the nature of their physical aerials that receive God, namely their bodies. The implication is, of course, that the souls of twins are very much alike in their experience and nature, but this is purely coincidental. Perhaps they shared similar experiences in past lifetimes and grew to be very close during these lifetimes. Great and profound love between one soul and another when they have been together long enough can perhaps do this.

Why is it likely that the Prime Being and its clones share the same pathway of origin, in other words a soul? It could simply be said that the Prime Being came first and so will be the sole inheritor of its previous ancestry. The clone is simply an exact duplication of the initiating being and so has to share all its exactitudes. This would imply something further.

If what I say about clones sharing the progenitor's soul is not logically true, then a clone would not be an exact physical duplicate of its physical generic origin.

You see, it all begs the question, why is there such a perfect exact duplicity when you clone someone? Sameness between one thing and another implies a connection. The more profound the sameness, the more exact they are. In a clone the sameness is absolute. If the generic progenitor has a soul then is it not likely that the exact generic duplicate – the clone – would have the same elements that gave rise to its progenitor, because that is where it starts from? The clone hasn't started from its own distinct parents made up of a discrete father and mother. The generic progenitor is its parent. It is all the parent the clone has. Its progenitor is as far back as the clone's line goes. It would thus share the progenitor's line and thus his soul.

There is a very convincing argument that says that your physical appearance is the physical equivalent of the appearance of your soul. I have no logical qualms with this argument as far as it goes. But you will never be able to glimpse the physical equivalent of your own exclusive and individual soul because in life when you are born you will be the amalgamation of three elements: mother, father and you. You will thus never know if you are beautiful or ugly or who was responsible for your state. You can only know what your true appearance is when you exist in a state where you can be your own individual self outside the influences of others. I believe this state is the state of existence known as death. Here in this 'place' beyond the grave you will be totally yourself. You will be able to see yourself for the first time as truly yourself. Without the information from your mother's and father's aspects that you took on to come into incarnacy and that went to make you up. This insight will include a parody or vision of your own self that will be a summary of all the information you have gathered in that particular lifetime, that you have accepted with your will (the great admitter) in your deepest enth. Information which will process to come down to provide one of two primary momentums. That which goes towards Godhead and that which goes away from it. The closer you go towards Godhead the more beautiful you become. The more beautiful you become, the less you will be seen physically. The less you can be seen physically the less physical you can be. The less physical you can be, the less you can exist in this universe of physical parts as a physical being. If you are beautiful enough, you can never naturally be part of a universe of parts. You can never enter into a physical life unless you choose to do so to tell others, perhaps, all you know and perhaps warn them of these things that admit and deny.

Maybe the Christs and Buddhas and Mohammeds and indeed all great and goodly 'Master Beings' did this and do this to this day. Maybe such beings come among us not needing to do so, but risking their very soul at the hands of beings such as us who are condemned to wander in ignorance, personally cultivated ignorance, through our own faults. They deliberately chose to come, as any loving beings would choose to do when they see the condemned, to give knowledge that frees. Knowledge (if only we could see it for what it is) that first warns and then liberates and gives renewal and redemption. The vast majority of us reject it and go on with the entropic momentums of the world into greater and greater states of smallness of mind. We indulge in the facile and the shallow and if we do it enough we shall never know.

And what an awesome price we have made so many beautiful beings such as these pay for these supreme acts of love. We mangle them. We crucify them. We ridicule them. We close our ears to them. We make them suffer for trying to save us from our own folly.

The brain, blood, nervous system and bones all go to make our bodies into aerial-like devices with the capacity to receive and make sense of the information inherent in the entire existential scale of what exists within and without our Universe (see chapter 16). The whole system working together does this in a *modus operandi* we call 'Thought'. Unlike a non-cloned being, what I have called Primary Being, a clone's aerial will be identical to its progenitor and so its capacity and only its capacity to receive this information is all that makes it unique from every other living being. It is like a soul fingerprint manifested as a physical entity. Each human genome is simply this. A shape and form that exists in an enforced environment we call our Universe that is simply a device that can know and receive all the information within that environment.

This capacity to receive information does not mean that in the procedures of life and living and the immediate exigencies of life that your clone might encounter while living its life its memories and life experiences are going to be identical to its parent being. This could and would thus make its actions, perceptions and reactions different to its progenitor. It would now begin to make a completely separate identity for itself but it would always share the same 'recorder' for establishing this identity. It would simply be like a single cassette tape recorder taking the sound resources from several microphones simultaneously. It will all go on the same tape. It will be a shared record with no control on the primary's part for what goes in.

It follows therefore that if the tape is the source of all future information for future results, then a cloned primary being is in a lot of trouble. If this record dictates all the further 'life bodies' of that being in subsequent reincarnations, then the Primary (progenitor) being of the clones will end up with bodies (and all the *modus operandis* that karma dictates, such as species, location, parentage) that bear directly on the exact deserving of this record. This would be nothing to do with its own feed into the tape recorder. It would be twisted, moulded, manufactured, perhaps mangled in a way that is nothing to do with its own unique and precious individuality and certifiable input. Getting cloned is the best way of losing your primary individuality that stems from the very beginning. In effect you would be losing your own soul if it happened to you.

If all I speculate is true in this thesis, then perhaps it's facile to say that the writing is on the wall for our entire species. Does anyone doubt that someone, somewhere, will seek to clone human beings, acting through the laboratory-minded attitude of many scientists who will dismiss all this as mumbo jumbo in their urgency to offer cloning as a palliative for all kinds of genetic ills? Perhaps it is mumbo jumbo. If so I hope it is reasonable and well-reasoned mumbo jumbo! It certainly cannot be proved with certainty using the scientific method. If I am wrong nothing is lost that cannot be redeemed or handled. If I am right, what price the scientific method and scientists who think like this when your soul is mortgaged through eternity? They may not be in touch with theirs but you may be in touch with yours.

The cloned state is essentially and necessarily a temporary one, relevant only to the physical modus of existence of the Primary Being at any one time. An individual clone cannot continue the cycle of life and death and rebirth again in terms of its own individuality. On death it will simply cease to exist and all its existential experiences will have gone to feed the information bank of the original soul it was cloned from. It is only the prime progenitor soul that has access to Godhead, and so it will do all the reincarnating. A Prime Soul is thus the sum of all its cloned parts. It will thus have to wait for the return of all its parts from any living state they may be in to be able to reincarnate again.

The moral of all this is that if you are a Primary Soul, don't for heaven's sake get cloned if you want total exclusive control of yourself and thus to be able to reincarnate as and when it is most suitable for you to do so. You will otherwise have to wait till all your cloned physical duplicates die before you can reincarnate and carry through your karmic obligations. But even then the sum of your parts may be divested in the karma of other Primary Beings. Your clone may produce progeny with another Primary Being, for instance. Though this cannot pass your soul on to another, it can give that other individual a good look, and only a look, at your story or your existential record and vice versa. All that will happen will be that the awareness of the Primary Being from which the clone came will have another portal of indirect influence suddenly open up, but the information is only readable and choice to accept and act on this information is implied and not tacit. In other words if your clone has a son with a primary being, your 'pseudo son' will have to have had an individual and exclusive primary line to Godhead of his own in order to reincarnate in the first place. He may or may not take on the information about you through your clone but he cannot hold you to anything. He cannot completely merge with you. He is intrinsically different, his mother is intrinsically different and your clone and you as one entity will be intrinsically different. Three different keys to three differing locks. No admission.

Reincarnation is only possible if the soul is existentially alone and in singular control of the soul line in its attendance (attachment) to Godhead. The Life/Death interface can only be breached with an exclusive single attachment to Godhead, because it is the element that gives you a soul in the first place. A clone is attached to Godhead through the Primary Being and therefore the search for the Primary Being, if it dies before its clone does, will be the most and only important thing a clone can do if it is to gain a line to Godhead. It will not be gaining it itself in its own intrinsic right. It can only gain it in merging with the entity that gave it its identity in the first place. Its Primary Being.

If the genome of an individual is a physical duplication and thus material manifestation of your soul, then it follows that this may be read and information obtained that could point to any profound matches that might allow a clone to attach itself to Godhead.

The terrifying thing about all of this is that we now have a distinct possibility that a hive of aliens with their attendant purely biomechanical roboids the Greys, from another part of our universe, are intercepting and intervening in the affairs of our species. Their intention perhaps might well be to search for information from our physical genetic lines that qualitatively may be similar to theirs and from which they may be able to hitch a direct line to Godhead.

They might have killed off all the Primary Beings that gave them their existence back in their neck of the woods before they realized the significance of these beings to them. As clones they would continue themselves through a physical cloning process. (Until their genetic material wore down in line with the entropic process that makes everything decay finally anyway.) They would thus never go through the process of death. They may be doing this in total ignorance of the fact that, if they simply died, as clones they would automatically be joined back with the soul lines of their respective Primary Beings in the space between atoms – The 'Fields of Death'. This all begs the question, 'Do they even know they are clones and thus duplicate derivations of an original progenitor being?' It is completely possible that they haven't got a clue that they are copies that only hold a line to Godhead through another being. It is also likely that with their intelligence (an intelligence powerful enough to enable them to get here) they know that they are derivations and realize that they have to somehow find that unique primary being to be existentially complete. In this event, as clones their immortality would be a completely physically manufactured one. They could never risk an end to their living process because they know nothing about death. If their bodies wore out they would simply clone a new one. They would not give themselves a chance to die. It might never occur to them to actually die and that this was the best and only way to their completion. This ignorance of death may be the propelling motive for sweeping the universe for living intelligent beings in a search for their progenitors. They may well, with their stupendous technology, have a means of matching their genetic lines with suitable genetic fingerprints and thereby try to get a clue as to the disposition of the individual Primary Being they were first cloned from. They could then do a physical enjoinment of the matching DNA and thus have a line back to Godhead. They would have found a soul. Their own original soul.

My speculation would explain so much about why they abduct so many of us. If may be the whole reason for their sojourn in our part of the universe. The trouble with all this is that the uncloned Primary Beings of our species may have to pay a terrible price in the eternal scale of existence for their behests. It will be wonderful for us if what I am speculating is true and all we need to do with this particular lot is to tell them about their predicament from our point of view. All they would have to do then is die. They would then be united with their progenitors. Their progenitors would then get their soul lines back complete and we would be rid of a very dangerous entity in the universe that, in sheer ignorance of the fact that death is a portal to eternal life, might be abducting our people and doing horrible things to them in the process.

It's the stuff that nightmares are made of and it may turn out to be a very real one.

An incredible series of consequences to us all will follow if what I surmise about the Soul, the life and death state, reincarnation and cloning is true. That, however, is for another book. But I venture to say that it will be a very interesting exercise for the reader to speculate on, with logic and reason as a yardstick. But before you do that let me re-state and explain some things a little further than I have done thus far. It will fill in the picture more completely.

Many of us may have been cloned in past lives on some other planet in some other form or status of life. There is one unbreachable rule in the forms and values of reincarnation. In a physical manifestation of the process it is mostly likely to be downwards. I will explain that statement in a moment. To do this I first have to take the reader through the consequences of the Second Law of Thermodynamics. This law makes this Universe an arena of diminishing returns. In other words, this fundamental law of force and the interplay of forces says that all things go into greater states of randomness and chaos with time till at the end there will only be heat left as a Universe. (The Heat-death of the Universe.) We know that everything rots and decays with time if left to itself. Nothing goes the other way. (See Chapters 2, 3, and 4.) This all is provable with the scientific method. It is only the application of what I call 'Thoughtness' that can put the brakes on this process and stop it and even reverse it. So Thoughtness is a mechanism (notice it is an abstract mechanism, and not a physical one) that sets a scale, at least, for the reversal of the implicit working mechanisms of our Universe in its physical identity. Since it exists in this Universe, how is it there in this giant agglomeration of destructive force that is the Universe of Parts? I believe it is there because it is part of another entirely different universe that is the opposite of ours that exists both separately and at the same time, hand in glove with ours. It is at the interfaces that connect the two that the words

'Soul', 'Reincarnation', 'Life', 'Death' and, yes, 'Clones' become awesomely relevant. These are the 'connectors' that lie betwixt the two.

I have said before that if our universe of force and parts is hard, solid, tense, and finite, the other universe or its opposite could be expected to be peaceful, still, abstract, or un-solid, infinite and eternal. In our universe all things don't fit perfectly together. They can never be made to. That is why they may be said to have the qualities I have outlined. In the other universe the opposite is true. All parts are together in absolute and total fit. Nothing is left over, and this gives rise to its qualities as outlined. The existential scale is thus metered between the two.

Life and death are part of our universe. They are on our side of the divide. Let's say that the Life state, may be said to be 'intra-atomic' and the Death state. 'Extra-atomic'. The Life state is enforced and dwells in the space within the atom and the Death state is unenforced and dwells in the space between atoms, (see fig 13). The Life state, however, is totally within the margin that defines our universe. The Death state is on the margin that defines our universe and the other 'Universe of the Whole'. So the space between atoms is the margin between the two. The fields of Death, as I like to call them, are the 'corridors' that form the space between atoms. We move from one universe to the other through them.

We can now put all we understand of the total existential outlay into these paradigms.

We live, we die, we return, alas. And continue the cycle endlessly. We are meant to live, to learn, to go on and never return. Few of us do this. Go on, I mean. We return to this enforced entropic churn of Hell we call our universe. Trapped in an endless cycle of admission and expulsion we call birth and death. But, blessedly, some don't. Some pass on to the other 'Universe of the Whole'. Some escape, never to return.

The Buddhists do not believe in the concept of Soul because they say that it is something individual. Yet they would maintain a mechanism for the return of individuality at birth. They say that this individuality is borrowed from what exists overall and in the individual state you purify that overallness and make it a state of enlightened insight for that individual point of view. They never explain how the individual state arises from the overall in the first place to be admitted at birth. Is it a portion of the overall that is individualized? If so, why does the 'overall' need to be individualized? Does this individual state that is purified in life and living remain individual beyond death to return as that same individual state in life? Some Buddhist scholars maintain this is true. They acknowledge the existence of higher realms and claim that an individual Buddha can inhabit these 'realms' and return to reinvigorate himself into a higher and higher state of view till he reaches Nibbana, an everlasting state of bliss from which return into individuality is no longer relevant. I hope the reader can see where my concept of a Soul fits in with the Buddhist theorem. The word 'Soul' is just a prescription for that individual state in its connection to the overall existential outlay, however it is fashioned. It is simply a description of this modus of existence until it merges with the Universe of the Whole where it need not be in parts.

I mentioned earlier that the trend in reincarnation in this Universe is downward. From a higher state to a lower state of existence. These are essentially states of knowing. We call them species. The higher your knowing the more you are in control of everything. Yourself, your environment, etc. So species are just compendiums that mark ignorance of what exists overall. A man is more in control of the world than a dolphin. We can inhabit the world of the dolphin with wet suits and air-breathing equipment made by us better than the dolphin can survive our terrestrial habitat. We are the species with the greatest knowledge and thus control, as *Homo Sapiens Sapiens*, better than any other species on our planet. Thus the more you know, the higher the species value. But knowledge is an abstraction. It is not a solid quantum in itself: you can't, shall we say, parcel it up and hand it on. It is just there when you acquire it. But where is it? To all intents and purposes it seems to come from within our bodies, somewhere in a particularization with identity. It is specific in extent and quantum with the individual. We all do not have exactly the same knowledge as each other. But because it seems to come from within us we think that it is manufactured by our brains and our bodies inside us.

There is another way of looking at this. Maybe it is simply picked up by our bodies, our brains acting as aerials. The knowledge is out there all the time. We simply pick up more of it or less of it depending on the height and integrity and make-up of our aerials. We store it as retained electricity coded impluses in mediums called blood and bone and 'know' it as an entity from there. No different from a computer. The computer does not manufacture the information it analyzes itself, out of its parts. It is fed this information which it picks up and retains in mediums (memory chips) that can hold it and give it out. It is a better computer if it has a great capacity to receive and hold and process information. Similarly we as living species seem to be commonly judged by our capacity to receive, hold and use information in such a way that we preserve our capacity to do this for as long as possible. If you are 'not there' to 'exist' to receive and use information, then there is no point to anything, including information, and I would not have written this and you would not be reading it. So just being there is the first and most vital thing of all. I believe it is the whole purpose of the entire existential outlay.

In the Corridors of Death and its extra-atomic dominion (the space between atoms), force is far less in its power to act upon an entity. The medium that gives entropy its flare and result (directionally shaped values of force) is substantially absent there. It is thus more akin to the Universe of the Whole than our Universe of Parts. It is the in-between state where both values may be glimpsed. It is here that summary occurs. A totalling of knowledge, knowing and values. If a species is a summary of existential knowledge and knowing in individual entity terms, then here is the place the whole quantum is added and future life forms are decided. Here in the corridors of death I believe you and I get summarized. We then proceed into the heavy or the light. Heavy if our knowledge quotient is less, and light if our knowledge quotient is great. By this I mean you proceed like water finding its own level to become a state of existence commensurate with the values you have held and practised while in the previous state.

Put simply, I believe that if you had added, brought together, and tried to unify all things in your behaviour (some call it being right-minded, righteous and good) while in life, i.e. in the Universe of Parts, you would have been opposing the implicit state of that universe. It, in itself, was and is set to do the opposite. It manufactured hydrgogen, helium, lithium, boron and so on to all the heavier elements from light, in a progression schematic that made these heavier and heavier elements with time. In going against this drift of entropy to greater and greater states of randomness, complication and chaos with time, you and I who are made substantially of hydrogen, the lightest element of all, would in effect have been unwinding this chemistry and its bonds that made our bodies and thus our species, by each act of kindness and intelligently applied righteousness we did. I believe that if you did such things 'enough' (I believe 'enough' is the most important word in the English or any other language) at death you would reconcile your individual being such that your enforcednesss would be such that an atomic existence in force would not be possible. You would go on in another state till all knowledge was yours and existence in a totally EN-lightened state (Godhead, Nibbana, etc) would be eternally yours. You could no more suffer the process of rotting from the day you are conceived with the disease and pain and disenfranchisement of your being that goes on as part of life in this universe.

However, the opposite practices commensurate with the implicit mode and fashion of the essentially entropic Universe of Parts would lead you to return in states of greater and greater ignorance, demarcated by its species equivalent in function and tenure to these states of ignorance. You would reincarnate down, from Man to Ape to Monkey to Insect to Mollusc to Tree to Bacterium to Virus to Plasmid, etc, till you were as the most basic particles that make up the universe.

I have stated previously that I, perhaps, for one in this world believe the existential way is Devolution not Evolution. It is simply the inherent vanity of man that prompts us all to choose to believe that we all evolve to betterment. The overwhelming evidence, if we choose to view it objectively and dispassionately, is that the existential platform is evolution within overall Devolution, in stages or platforms of redeployment we call 'the survival modes of the fittest.'

CHAPTER TWELVE:
THE WRONG WAY ROUND
THE MERRY-GO-ROUND

We as the command species of this planet have been mastering
lesser species on this earth since time immemorial. We now might
have things such as the Greys, the Greens, the Yellows, the Blues,
or whatever shades or hues of detriment they might be, dipping
into our fish pond and seeking to do the same to us. To change the
fish in order to fit their pond. The order of the day has suddenly
changed from us doing it to something else, to something else
doing it to us. Like any common or garden racist would seek
to do to someone he or she deems as different, or lesser. Just
as scientists chase knowledge in the blinkered tunnel vision of
their specific disciplines with little or no insight and sanction
into the internecine consequences of their efforts on the general
welfare of Man. (The atom bomb was just one deadly legacy we
have been left with as a result of such lethal narrow vision.) We
as a species have been blundering around dispossessed of a sense
of our origins and nature and haven't been able to see the wood
for the trees. Blinkers forbid the crucial overall view that provides
holistic contexts that might warn of grand-scale detriment to the
welfare of us all as a species. It is an awesome warning that Man
has never heeded despite the glorious wisdom given to us by our
'redeemers', be they Hindu, Buddhist, Judaic, Jain, Christian or
Islamic. Could it be that we might have been prevented from
listening to and carrying out the behests of wisdom because we
have had something implanted in the common psyche of Man

through, perhaps, genetic interception, thousands of years ago that forbids us from listening enough to a part of us that came from outside the atom and the Universe of enforced parts? A part we might, for want of a better word, call Godhead.

The First-Adamic line fell in the ways of what we call Sin. The best description of Sin to my mind is simply Restriction. No more, no less. And so sin decides all things because it decides the scope for development according to restriction or Limit. Personal restriction or indeed group restriction that we all are a part of as a species. Once exposed to the formulas of dismantling force the geno-phyla that followed First-Adam would gradually reduce over millions of years to become ends of the line of Adamic man. The last vestiges of the consequence of being subject to the whims of the entropic drift downwards. Yes, I am saying that there is no such thing as evolution to betterment. I am saying that evolution to betterment as it is generally accepted in Darwinian terms is bunkum. I am saying that it is likely to be evolutionary *devolution*. In other words, evolution within the overall format of devolution where platforms of effect stabilize to the best possible outlay (such as survival of the fittest) as they drift down to more and more states of chaotic amelioration. They have to drift down in this way because they come from a prior state of ultimate order and are assembled thus before the entropic engine of doom that is our Universe breaks them apart in line with the Second Law of Thermodynamics.

How do we see this as reflected in the genetic ancestry of Man? Is there any evidence from the fossil record of Man and other scientific derivational means that substantiates this? I believe there is evidence that points tantalizingly to a distinct possibility that what I am postulating may well be true.

Jonathan Losos of Washington University in Missouri has done some molecular detective work that has produced results that are in defiance of accepted theories of evolution.[1] To understand lizard ancestry, Losos examined mitochondrial DNA from the species on two different islands, Puerto Rico and Jamaica. Mitochondrial DNA is passed only from mother to offspring via the cytoplasm of the egg. So it can be used to reconstruct evolutionary histories without the complication of contributions from paternal DNA. The DNA data suggested that remarkably similar events took place on each island. However, says Oxford zoologist Paul Harvey, 'that's despite the fact that these places have important differences in their plants, predators and climate.' It is highly unlikely that the same events could happen on both islands simply by chance, says Harvey, especially since the islands are different in so many ways. Harvey speculates that if more examples of repeatable evolution are found then the whole notion of evolution as a lottery may need to be reconsidered.

Further evidence for the inadequacy of evolutionary theory can be found in a recent article in *New Scientist* (28.10.95).[2] Charles Bieberich and his team at the Holland Laboratory in Rockville, Maryland have reported that by manipulating genes that control the body plans of embryos they have created mutant mice with backbones that are 200–300 million years out of date. The article points to other research teams that have achieved something similar. Researchers at the University of Wisconsin, at Madison, have created fruit fly embryos that developed with a body plan some 350–450 million years out of date. Two years ago Pierre Chambon and his colleagues at the University of Louis Pasteur in Strasbourg created mutant mice with ear bones halfway between those of mammals and reptiles. According to Chambon the ears followed a developmental plan dating back to the therapsids: primitive, mammal-like reptiles that lived among the dinosaurs some 200 million years ago.

Bieberich argues that the researchers are only doing in the lab what sometimes happens naturally, producing what is called 'atavistic mutations'. Hind limbs on whales, snakes with rudimentary limbs, people with tails, and horses with hooves split into three toes instead of the usual one are among the best-documented examples. Researchers have been intrigued for years about these naturally occurring atavisms but now that they can be created in the lab, 'the astonishing persistence of these genetic memories becomes clear. The reason for that persistence, researchers now believe, has a lot to do with the laziness of evolution.' So says Stephen Day, the author of the *New Scientist* article discussing these discoveries.

These scientists seem to believe that a genetic memory is stored, for example in a mouse's genes, from the days when mammals and reptiles last shared an ancestor. That memory can thus be unlocked, at least in the case of ear structure. If genetic information that is up to 350 to 400 million years old can be retained within a genome then does this not lend the lie to Darwin's theory of evolution via the process of 'natural selection'? Why would 400 million years' worth of redundant genetic codes have been preserved for no useful reason in terms of promoting the survival of an organism? The principle of natural selection ordains that only those organisms with genetic characteristics best suited to their environment will tend to survive best in order to pass their genetic codes on to future generations. Thus 'evolution' is able to take place. Why does the evolutionary process preserve redundant genes, albeit disabled from coding for proteins? Why did the unsuitable genetic codes survive the 'evolutionary' process without being significantly altered by random mutations over sixty-five million years? How does a mouse retain the genes of a dinosaur? Or, more pertinently, how does a human being retain the genetic codes of an animal with a tail such that this atavism can occur in some people? If this is put down to 'the laziness of evolution', I would ask the question: How can evolution be a governing principle of biological development if this useless genetic information is so faithfully preserved? It would imply that evolution is so lazy that it came to a complete standstill as soon as it started and has not moved since! How, then, have we reached our present status as a species from the original 'primordial soup' of life? Perhaps the answer is that we and all other living organisms have not in fact reached our present states from prior states of inferiority. Rather we have *devolved* into our present states from prior states of superiority. In other words, development up from the primordial soup is utter poppycock.

One of the greatest scientists the Earth has produced, Sir Fred Hoyle, together with his distinguished colleague Professor Chandra Wickramasinghe, put the postulation seriously to the scientific world that life was brought to the Earth from outer space through viruses trapped in star dust. Other scientists took the idea less seriously. Nobel Prize winner Francis Crick, one of the discoverers of the double helix deployment of DNA, and Leslie Orgel of the Salk Institute of biological studies managed to provoke the public and their colleagues by speculating that the seeds of life were sent to the Earth in a spaceship by intelligent beings living on another planet.[3] They point out that it did have a serious intent: to highlight the inadequacy of all explanations of terrestrial genesis. As Crick once wrote: 'The origin of life appears to be almost a miracle. So many are the conditions which would have had to be satisfied to get it going.' The joke may well be on them.

Sir Fred Hoyle, in his book *The Intelligent Universe*, puts forward some interesting scenarios suggesting the extraordinarily unlikely possibility that life could have originated by chance from a primordial soup:[4]

'The probability of life appearing spontaneously on Earth is so small that it is very difficult to grasp without comparing it with something more familiar. Imagine a blindfolded person trying to solve the Rubik Cube. Since he can't see the results of his moves, they must all be at random. He has no way of knowing whether he is getting nearer the solution, or whether he is scrambling the cube still further. One would be inclined to say that moving the faces at random would 'never' achieve a solution. Strictly speaking, 'never' is wrong, however. If our blindfold subject were to make one random move every second, it would take him on average three hundred times the age of the earth, 1,350 billion years, to solve the cube. The chance against each move producing perfect colour matching for all the cube's faces is about 50,000,000,000,000,000,000 to 1.

'These odds are roughly the same as you could give to the idea of just one of our body's proteins having evolved randomly by chance. However, we use about 200,000 types of protein in our cells. If the odds against the random creation of one protein are the same as those against a random solution of the Rubik Cube, then the odds against the random creation of all 200,000 are almost unimaginably vast'.

Hoyle goes on to point out that even if we were only to assess the likelihood of the spontaneous origin by chance of the 2000 or so special proteins, the enzymes, which are vitally important to life processes, then still the odds would be outlandish. The chance of these vital 2000 enzymes being formed in exactly the correct way, which they must be or else complex living organisms simply could not operate, is 'about the same as the chance of throwing an uninterrupted sequence of 50,000 sixes with unbiased dice!'.

He goes on to examine how those who claim that life originated in an organic soup imagine that complex life developed. They imagine that a clump of two or three very primitive enzymes toured around the primordial soup of amino acids picking up other potential enzymes as and when they happened to arise by chance. Hoyle points out that in effect what this model really describes is 'how we ourselves would go about collecting up a packet of needles in a haystack, using our eyes and brains to distinguish the needles from the hay. How, for instance, would the enzyme clump distinguish an exceedingly infrequent useful enzyme from the overwhelming majority of useless chains of amino acids? The one potential enzyme would be so infrequent that the aggregate might have to encounter 50,000,000,000,000,000,000 useless chains before meeting a suitable one. In effect, talk of primitive aggregate collecting up potential enzymes really implies the operation of an intelligence, an intelligence which by distinguishing potential enzymes possesses powers of judgement. Since this conclusion is exactly what those who put forward this argument are anxious to avoid, their position is absurd'.

What is that 'intelligence' that it seems must be the architect behind the origin of life? Could that intelligence be provided for by devolving soul? Hoyle has illustrated with his analogies the extreme unlikelihood of random origins for life in the primordial soup. Thus the suggestion that we are devolving from our original points of inception into the universe, our original Adam points, into greater states of separation from the state of WHOLEness we once were is, it seems to me, a far more convincing proposition. This pattern of devolution would suggest that just as the whole implicitly contains the parts that make it up, we have within us at any one time the blueprint for all future states of devolvement into the universe of parts. Perhaps that is how these scientists who appear to be turning back the evolutionary clock are able to produce these startling results. The article says that they are 'Making Evolution Run Backwards': I propose that they are 'Making Devolution Run Forwards'! They are using that original blueprint for potential devolution and making it actual. What, then, does that say about human babies who have been naturally born with tails, out of a naturally occurring atavism? There is only one implication and that is that we are indeed apes in the making, if we follow the naturally devolving course that our species prescribes for us.

Those scientists studying these mutational phenomena have discovered that there is in fact such a blueprint, 'an ancestral body plan' on which development from one species form to another is formed. This plan is embodied in what are known of as Hox genes.

'Instead of inventing a new set of body-plan genes for each new type of animal, it seems that natural selection has simply tinkered with an old one, a set known as Hox genes.' The telling question that must be asked here is: If all organisms that now exist had from their very inception into the evolutionary process a blueprint of how they should evolve, then where did that blueprint come from in the first place? How did the first multi-cellular animals evolving some 700 million years ago contain the basic template of information that only needed to be shuffled around in order to form a human being?

All the myriad changing environmental factors and chance mutations that allowed survival within changed environments and thus for evolution through the survival of the fittest had not yet occurred at that point. So where did these most basic of living organisms, or indeed the chemical soup that produced them in the first place, get this genetic blueprint from? The basic evolutionary contention that we evolved from a sea worm to a human being through a series of fortuitous genetic mutations that have occurred in turn through sheer chance in the chaotic underbase momentum of the Second Law of Thermodynamics, that itself provides a dismantling effect on molecules and atoms to gathering states of randomness, is the stuff for baboons to believe. It is inconceivable that reasoning and directed thinking capable of intelligent arbitration emerged by chance in an environment creating chaos with each progressive moment in time. It is a theory for Lucy in lunatic land. We just don't have the years in the scale of the time the universe is said to have existed to make enough fortuitous mutations to account for our existence. The law of probability summarily contradicts it. The theory of evolution to the betterment of a species really becomes more and more ludicrous in the light of these new discoveries in developmental biology.

Bieberich says that, 'We're probably not turning on old genes, but taking existing developmental pathways and twisting them into ancient pathways'. If these are 'existing developmental pathways' would not their twisting, at least in terms of the theory of evolution, lead simply to a breakdown in the efficient functioning of the organism rather than to the repeat of genetic information that should by now, one would have thought, either be significantly changed or even deleted from the genetic record? If indeed we are turning on old genes already there to new effect and not creating them from the start, we could then have the time for a plausible set-up to revitalize a species format that was already devolving. The ET Alien brief might have been instrumental in doing just this.

If scientists can so easily, by disrupting one gene in 100,000, produce such startling results, can you imagine the potential available to alien genetic engineers?

Scientists at the University of Massachusetts have created a mouse with an extra ear, a human ear. They fashioned a precision mould out of porous, biodegradable polymer, seeded it with human cartilage cells, then tucked the structure under the skin of a mouse bred without an immune system (to prevent rejection). Nourished by the mouse's blood, the cartilage cells multiplied, taking the shape of the dissolving polymer scaffold and creating a perfectly formed human ear. With the supremely advanced technology available to alien beings, an access into the human genome could result in a myriad of such possibilities.

CHAPTER THIRTEEN:
OF APES AND MAN

Of all the tens of thousands of skeletons that mark the ancestral lines of Man through the millennia, no single direct line can be traced that accounts for all the discovered strains of Man. It in fact seems clear that all the discovered genotypes seem to end abruptly, except for two, *Homo Erectus* and *Homo Neanderthalensis*. This is where, I believe, the Greys come in.

Before I explain, let me say again at this point that it is my contention that the line of derivation of all living beings is the complete opposite to what is claimed in evolutionary theory. We did not evolve up to Man from the Seaworm. We devolve and continue to devolve to our own variety of Seaworm. The ones that are there now are the ends of other lines of superior beings and species that have over billions of years come down to be these seaworms from inaugural genotypes. With a view to all the palaeontological and genetic evidence that has been gathered, all the genotypes of man found thus far are ends of the lines of Godman or Spiritman. In other words, each distinct genus branched off from the original First Adam and First Eve and as they devolved through the aeons they ended their humanoid aspect and became apes. Godbeing came into the Universe in the very special way and form I have outlined previously and all the lines of being all over the Universe come from this original Godbeing.

This would be so whether the Universe had a once-and-for-all single origin point or multiple origin points constantly happening. We are dealing with the conversion, or sublimation, of Spirit-Being to Matter-Being. The conversion of the status of what is not of atoms to what *is* of atoms and all the stages in between wherever, or however, the origination point occurs.

It is complete lunacy to have an entropic force that is busy dismantling atoms, from prior ordered states into greater and greater states of randomness and chaos with time (the Second Law Of Thermodynamics) and at the same time claim that all things are going from good to better, through a series of fortuitous accidents.

It is our vanity that does not allow us to see the truth and that is *it is all one way* – DOWN. Everything rots. We rot the moment we are conceived. It is a cast iron standard bearer basic law of biology, in the Universe of Parts. Our Universe.

So, in summary, it is my contention that the form of Spirit-Being was sublimated into atoms (flesh) with the breaking-up effect of the Second Law of Thermodynamics (entropy). This 'Spirit-Being', in billions of locations all over the Universe, reduced gradually into all the different arrays of living species you see, as represented by our particular brand of species on the Earth. Of course, this same procedure would inevitably go on in locations elsewhere in the Universe too, giving rise to their particular cocktail of species. The crucial point I want to make is that it was reduction to lesser forms, Superior to Inferior. In our Earth's terms, from Godman to mortal man to ape to monkey to animal to insect to tree to virus to plasmid to stone and all the millions of species that make up the points in between.

Let me explain this startling conclusion a little further, in terms of the Origin Of Species with a particular accent on Man.

What other evidence might there be to suggest that our species, *Homo Sapiens Sapiens*, is a product of devolution not evolution?

Simon Easteal, a geneticist at the Australian National University has suggested that contrary to the popular belief that humans evolved from chimpanzees both might have had a common ancestor.[1] Easteal says, '. . . rather than believe that we came down from the trees, we are suggesting we continued to walk upright and chimps went up the trees and stopped walking upright'. He bases his conclusions on his own research in which he has discovered a great similarity between human, chimpanzee and gorilla DNA: 'they are so similar this means we should in fact regard chimpanzees and gorillas as members of the same genus and call them *Homo*.'

If we 'continued to walk upright' and apes 'stopped walking upright', then our common ancestor would have walked upright and thus would have been a hominid form, not an ape form. So perhaps the reason why scientists have had no success in finding causes for the origin of bipedalism in hominid species is simply that hominid species started off bipedal and only later devolved into a quadrupedal stance. Apes may thus have devolved from man, not man evolved from apes.

Explanations for the evolution of an upright stance in hominid forms centre around the theory that it became necessary for various reasons when a change in climate transformed Africa's moist forests into grasslands. Thus evolution would have favoured hominids that could stand upright in order to spot predators lurking in the tall grasses. An upright stance would have lessened the heat that hominids absorbed from the sun because the forests were no longer there to protect them. However, there is one vital flaw in these explanations, and that is that a growing body of evidence suggests that the earliest hominids did not in fact move out into the savannah. The fossils they left behind were found in areas that were once densely wooded. It seems that they learnt to walk in the relative safety of the forests while living next to their cousins the apes! This lack of evidence for the evolution of bipedalism seems to suggest that anthropologists might be better advised to reverse their search and look instead for how bipedalism developed into quadrupedalism for some species of primate.

A further hiccough in conventional evolutionary theory has been found in the ancient fossil record of the Miocene period, which stretches from twenty-five million to five million years ago.

During the Miocene period a single ancestral group, the hominoids, gave rise, it is believed, to several lines that culminated in today's higher primates. According to what is commonly believed, the first to diverge from the common hominoid stock was the line of the lesser apes (gibbons and siamangs), followed by the line that led to orang-utans. Later still the remaining stock divided again, one branch leading to the great African apes (gorillas, chimpanzees and bonobos) and the other to humans. Palaeo-anthropologists believe that human and ape lines diverged between four million and six million years ago. They have, as yet, found no fossils that would satisfactorily account for this common ancestor.

Scientists are trying to trace the ancestry of the great apes and humans in the Miocene period. One of these scientists, Steve Ward of the North-eastern Ohio University's College of Medicine, has said that: 'What initially seemed to be a fairly nice simple progression [towards modern species] got scuppered by the fossil record'.[2] He is referring to the fact that the fossil record from the Miocene period is full of hominoid forms that seem to have no modern living counterparts. There are about a dozen genera and even more species of larger-bodied hominoids known from the Miocene. While today there are only three genera and four species of great apes.

What happened to these Miocene apes that have no modern descendants? Did they perhaps devolve down the devolutionary tree into lesser forms of mammal? Mike Rose of the University of Medicine and Dentistry of New Jersey says that he sees very little similarity between these Miocene apes and modern apes: 'When I look at the postcranial bones from the Miocene apes, I get a fairly clear and consistent pattern from many species. But it is nothing like what we see in modern apes'.

In fact, it is a fascinating enigma that palaeontologists thus far have been unable to find any fossil record for the African apes. There is no such record even in the five million years after the Miocene period leading to the present day. Fossil records have been found for other species of mammal living in the same habitat as the apes. So, why is there no record? Could it be that the fossil record of the African apes is actually made up of the very same hominid forms that are believed to have been the predecessors of *Homo Sapiens Sapiens*? In other words, the whole thing is the other way round – Man to Ape, *not* Ape to Man. Could it be that the ancient hominid forms of *Australopithecus* and *Homo Habilis* were the ancestors of these apes? Perhaps the problem is that palaeontologists do not realize that they have actually already found the fossil record of the African apes in these hominid forms. Just as in the Miocene apes they might have found the ancestors of a more devolved mammalian species.

There is thus significant evidence from several sources to suggest that the momentum of devolution governs the origin of species on this planet. If this is in fact the case then two salient questions must be asked:

If the emergence of *Homo Sapiens Sapiens* as a species is a result of a devolutionary process, why does the fossil record seemingly present a picture of evolution? For example, there is a gradual increase in the brain capacity of hominid species as time progresses. With the exception of *Homo Sapiens Neanderthalensis*, whose brain capacity is actually greater than that of its successors in the fossil record, the Cro-Magnons (but that is an incongruity that I will account for later).

Secondly, if man has indeed devolved from prior states of grandeur into his present form, then where is the evidence for those prior states in the fossil record?

I will now attempt to answer these questions through an explanation of why the general drift of development, at least as far as the fossil evidence is concerned, appears to be an evolutionary one. I have used the words 'appears to be evolutionary' because, as I have previously shown, the nature of the entropic drift demands that a *natural* drift into states of greater and greater species advancement is a logical impossibility.

The phylogenetic ancestral line of man down to the present time as seen now from the available information is as follows. From the earliest to the present as seen through the fossil record is:

Australopithecus Afarensis	3.6 million – 2.8 million years
Australopithecus Africanus	2.5 million – 1.2 million years
Australopithecus Robustus	2.0 million – 1.0 million years
Homo Habilis	1.9 million – 1.3 million years
Home Erectus	1.5 million – 500,000 years
HOMO SAPIENS SAPIENS	200,000 – present
Homo Neanderthalensis	100,000 – 35,000 years
HOMO SAPIENS SAPIENS	200,000 – present

Indulge me a moment and let me connect all this up to my speculation on the origins of Man. This time in the biblio-theological sense that I have previously outlined in my discussion of the progress through time of the original 'Adam point' for our planet:

The first 'Adams' on this planet who were a form of ephemeral being would have gradually translated their insubstantial existential state into the state of physical substantiality in physical life. The force signature of any location in the universe is always increasing in time due to the entropic drift. While the threshold of force at this location in the universe was low enough it allowed for this translation of the insubstantial state of being into the substantial state of being without the necessity for the mechanism of physical birth into already existing biological lines. Thus the first individual expressions into physical life, the first mothers and fathers of future species lines came to be.

I contend that during the time that such a phenomenon was possible, *most of those who passed the God/Atom threshold into the new state of physical life returned back quickly to the insubstantial state from which they came*. The fact that it was possible to cross the threshold from substantiality to insubstantiality without the need for physical birth into already existing lines indicates that it would also have been possible to reverse the process and cross back again into the more ephemeral state with relative ease. Thus it would have been the few, not the many, who became caught and led eventually to the emergence of devolved species lines. Just as Christ demonstrated the *transfigured* state from a state in physical life and converted the very atoms that formed his body into light, these prior Adam Beings could do the same. Only it was far easier for them because their species lines were not yet so far devolved into the quantumly greater state of physical entrapment. With time Christ had to cope with this extra devolution when he incarnated into our *Homo Sapiens* line and by living a particular type of 'mindedness' he demonstrated that you could divest yourself of the atomic form and go straight into an ephemeral form of enlightened Being which he achieved at his transfiguration.

Thus these first physical hominid forms would have been able in relative freedom to explore the different expressions of the Universe of Parts without becoming irretrievably caught within the margins of its scope, such that a swift return to the prior ephemeral state of being would have been forbidden. However, within a chaotic universe unpredictable phenomena that can temporarily increase the force signature of a planet may have disturbed that equilibrium. Comets, asteroids or meteor showers, and volcanic eruptions, earthquakes, etc. bombarding the planet may have caused sudden increases in its force signature such that the passage of travel between the substantial and the insubstantial state might have been temporarily restricted, or even blocked. Some representatives of original Adam man might have found themselves suddenly stuck within the treacle of universal force. From that point on entropic momentums could grip them better and these would have started to reduce gradually their scope for freedom of choice and expression as they became more and more a prey to the physical forces of the universe. However, the huge power of soul lines in Godhead with biological lines that were as yet unintercepted by alien genetic manipulation would have still allowed the vast majority of these souls the potential to escape the wheel of rebirth and return directly to Godhead. These sudden increases in the planetary force print would thus have been the first instigators of the demise of the fewest of the few. Most returned.

Thus the fact that there appears to be no fossil record for these prior states of grandeur from which we have devolved may simply be because nearly all the representatives of these prior states converted the atoms of their bodies back into light, just as Jesus did at a much later stage in the devolutionary record of hominid forms on this planet – just 2000 years ago. He could have been the purest form of *first Adam Being*. The whole exercise of his sojourn on the Earth could have been a demonstration paradigm to see if it still could be done within the force contexts of this planet as they prevailed 2000 years ago.

The natural devolution of the few soul lines that did not convert back to light when it reached a certain level would have deemed those lines suitable for alien genetic interception. The state of the original Adam points on this planet would have had to be devolved enough, caught enough in the snatching, grasping 'treacle' of universal force to allow alien being, which is intrinsically of that treacle, to stick onto it, so to speak. Prior to that threshold point, the soul lines which reincarnated on this planet would have slipped the grasp of alien being as they were more spirit-based and less matter-based. But once that threshold level was reached the experiment began. An experiment carried out by extraterrestrial alien Beings to test the ability of hominid forms on this planet to provide for them a bridging point from the physical into the metaphysical, from atoms to spirit, and thus to soul.

I believe that this experiment has been in operation since that very first point of interception and all the hominid types found in the fossil record, from the Australopithecines to *Homo Sapiens Sapiens*, are its artefacts. In that light the apparent contradiction that exists in the fact that the fossil record appears to show an advancement of the species towards states of betterment (at least in terms of brain capacity) can perhaps now be reconciled and explained. Let me put to you some ideas that might explain this seeming paradox:

Could the record of the 'evolution' of the human species actually reflect a continuous line of modification of ape-like forms (such as *Australopithecus* and *Homo Habilis*) into something that could hold, in a more coherent form, what the alien beings were looking for, namely – a Soul?

The last remnants of more superior, albeit devolving, hominid lines could have been hybridized with these more devolved ape-like beings by alien genetic interception. The resulting hybrid would have combined the cranial capacity of the two different hominid forms. Thus *Homo Habilis*, for example, would have had a larger cranial capacity than *Australopithecus* because it was a result of the hybridization of *Australopithecus* with a superior hominid form. As I have said, the fact that there is no fossil record yet discovered for this superior form may well be due to the fact that there were so few representatives of it. Thus the fossil record as it now stands is a record only of devolved and genetically intercepted forms of hominid.

This new hybridized form with a greater cranial capacity would allow more advanced, more coherent souls to enter through birth and incarnation into its biological line than had previously been possible. This hybrid, who is represented, shall we say, by the *Homo Habilis* hominid form could then in turn be further hybridized with other superior hominid forms to result in a further enhancement of cranial capacity which is announced by the *Homo Erectus* hominids. The hybridization process could continue until the aliens have drawn as many soul lines as possible into their intercepted biological lines, drawing these lines closer and closer to themselves, and therefore, alas, more and more into greater states of entropic dismemberment. Motivated, of course, by the wish to find at the end of those lines an attachment into Godhead itself. A biological bridge into Godhead that they would have had direct access into via the tracks of their own genetic interception.

Why, then, you might ask, did they not go straight to the closest points to the source and intercept the souls closest to Godhead? The answer is simply that they may not have been able to. They were perhaps only able, as I have previously explained, to influence those souls who were within their grasp, and the level of that grasp could have been far away from the first point of origin for Soul in incarnacy. Too far away from Godhead to suit their purposes. So instead they cast out their fishing lines and set their hooks into those whom they could reach, namely the more ape-like hominid forms. Then, through the connections, in karmic obligation, of those whom they had caught to others whom they were unable to catch, they began to reel in souls that were closer to the point of origin – to Godhead.

This hybridization process that would have enhanced the biological species lines of prior hominids might therefore account for the apparent 'evolution' of hominid forms evidenced in the fossil record.

Let us now look in more detail at how these interceptions might have taken place, using evidence from the fossil record as it now stands:

To go back to our example, when *Australopithecus Afarensis* (the hominid that is believed to be a descendant of modern man) was, shall we say, intercepted by alien beings and hybridized in the way that I have described, it was enhanced to allow the potential for soul which was closer to the origin point, to Godhead, to incarnate into its biological line. These souls were closer to that origin than the souls who had previously inhabited *Australopithecus Afarensis* bodies. The alien genetic interception that resulted in the new hybridized form not only provided the means by which these more advanced souls awaiting the opportunity for incarnacy in 'Death's Fields' could enter into its biological line, but also necessitated their entry into it. Previously they would have reincarnated into the prior biological lines that possessed a more direct connection to Godhead in order to reconcile karmic obligations. But now that these lines were hybridized with a line whose connection to Godhead was not as strong, they were compelled to incarnate into the new hybrid line in order to reconcile any karmic obligations that might remain.

So the interceptions both provided an increased scope for the more advanced soul to enter into species lines and also ensured that it did so. Let us now look at the fossil record in that light:

The brain capacity of whichever species of Miocene Ape preceded *Australopithecus Afarensis* may have been enhanced through hybridization resulting in this new form of hominid. In fact, the large numbers of Miocene Ape species that have been discovered in the fossil record might be partly accounted for by genetic experimentation on the part of the alien beings, who were perhaps testing out a selection of different types of interception to see which was the most successful. Remember, most of these species have no modern equivalents. The most successful intercepted species might have resulted in a form of *Australopithecus*. Into this artificially enhanced line came soul expressions that were less ape-like than the souls that had inhabited the Miocene ape bodies. Miocene ape species that were not intercepted in this way would have followed a natural momentum into states of further devolvement. Thus, as I have said earlier, these unintercepted species might, in fact, have modern descendants in the form of lesser mammals.

Thus, to sum up our analysis as it stands so far: Alien beings re-established some of the capacity that these ape-like forms had had prior to their devolvement into apes, to receive more of the power of soul connection to Godhead into their body aerials. Through their hybridization processes they were able to artificially enhance physical species that existed on this planet. However, as this enhancement was artificial, it did not provide for the 'evolution' of soul back to prior states of superior, more godly expression. Quite the converse was true. These artificial manipulations of genetic lines interrupted the natural soul track back to Godhead for those who received them. Thus the interceptions made it more difficult for soul lines to return to prior states of grandeur while at the same time making it easier for soul lines that were intrinsically closer to these prior states to exist within, and incarnate into, a physical universe. Any apparent 'evolution' in the species that seemed to result, in terms of behaviour or reasoning ability, was thus purely the result of more coherent, more reasoning soul lines coming into the physical species when the scope was provided for them to do so. Alien beings may *not* have been responsible for the difference that exists between us and the Miocene apes, in terms of the capacity to reason, understand and freely choose. Rather, this is a result of the gradual hauling-in of soul lines into the highly dangerous context of physical life. A hauling-in that is partly a result of the natural entropic momentums of the universe and partly a result of the machinations of the alien beings who are partners in crime with those momentums.

Thus dwellings were provided for more knowledgeable souls to enter into. The parental bodies were altered such that a greater brain capacity to allow more advanced souls to enter into physical life was the result. In other words, the hardware already incarnate and thus in the physical universe was rewired to provide the added capacity to take in grander soul potential.

So, if *Australopithecus Afarensis* derived from an interception in the Miocene period then the next character on the fossil record, *Homo Habilis*, was the new hominid form resulting from a hybridization of *Australopithecus* with genetic information from superior hominid lines. Of the various forms of *Australopithecus* that have been discovered it was, according to current interpretations of the fossil record, *Australopithecus Afarensis* that 'evolved' into *Homo Habilis*. It seems that the later, so-called 'robust' Australopithecines – *Robustus* in southern Africa and *boisei* in East Africa – coexisted with *Homo Habilis*. So, it would seem that one form of *Australopithecus* was re-intercepted to eventually produce the new hominid form – *Homo Habilis*. While other forms maintained their 'evolutionary' status as Australopithecines. Perhaps it is the two lines that have descended from *Australopithecus boisei* and *Robustus* that now result in the two species of African ape, the gorilla and the chimpanzee, for whom there is, as I have already mentioned, no fossil record.

The result of the *Australopithecus* alien genetic interception, *Homo Habilis*, was a hominid form that itself may have received a further interception. This interception would then have resulted in *Home Erectus* hominids approximately 1.5 million years ago. It is speculated to have been about one million years ago that the first major exodus of hominids from Africa to other parts of the world began. This exodus is evidenced by the fact that *Home Erectus* fossils are found from that point on in various places outside of Africa.

It is from this point in the fossil record onwards that there is intense debate among palaeontologists and anthropologists as to how modern man 'evolved' from these *Homo Erectus* hominids. Let us examine the different views about human evolution that form this current debate:

There are two distinct schools of thought as to the origins of the modern phylum of Man we call *Homo Sapiens*. One school contends that the present forms of Mankind come from four distinct types of ancestor, each one derived from four different geographical points on the earth. The evidence for this is palaeontological and relies on the fossil record. The structure of bones and skeletons and their internal compatibilities are thus crucial to the argument. Four distinct types of *Home Erectus* hominid found in the fossil record at four different locations in the world are identified as the ancestors of the four main phylotypes of modern man found today in those locations.

HOMO ERECTUS FOSSILS		MODERN EQUIVALENT
Olduvai		African
European	Neanderthal – Cro-Magnon	European
Lantian (Peking Man)		East Asian
Java Man		Australoid

No reasons are given as to why the evolution came about in four distinct groups at four distinct points. The spread is the important thing. *Home Erectus* fossils from Africa spread across Africa, the Middle East, India and also into parts of Near East-Asia. If Professor Wolpoff, an eminent Israeli palaeontologist and one of the main protagonists of the 'multiregional' view of human origins is right, European *Homo Erectus* later evolved into Neanderthal–Cro-Magnon Man across Europe to become the modern Europiform types. Peking Man across China and Mongolia and Java Man across Southern South-East Asia and Australasia. All the rest of mankind was supposed to have come about from a hybridization of all these four distinct forms that suddenly sprang up in these widely separated locations.

The second theory that seeks to explain the ancestral lineage of mankind uses a genetic marker to trace back the ancestry of thousands of people. It is a far more reliable methodology and can trace the ancestral lines of thousands of individuals of different racial groups back to a single hominid female they call the 'African Eve'. This theory contends that all the other anthropological strains subsequent to *Homo Erectus* come from a single point in Africa and a single individual hominid about two hundred thousand years ago. Mankind's cradle and maternal rooting point is Africa.

The two models are in contention and fierce controversy surrounds both. The latest research seems to confirm beyond reasonable doubt that the single point beginning through the African Eve is the true path of our ancestry.

To summarize it all, it seems we have a unilateral source for our present humanity. The line based on studies by geneticists proclaims the 'out of Africa' model with the single mother who started it all about 250,000 to 200,000 years ago. This mother that came from the *Homo Erectus* African phylotype suddenly seems to give rise to a progeny whose skull and facial characteristics are markedly different from *Homo Erectus*. The first Modern Humans. Every person alive today is a direct descendant from this 'African Eve.' We know through further research that a great exodus of the modern humans took place out of Africa about 100,000 years ago. Then something incredible happens. These 'Modern Humans' suddenly disappear from the fossil record to reappear again suddenly as a genotype of Man called Cro-Magnon 60,000 years or so later, the ancestors of Europiform humans with palaeontological evidence for their existence being found in France, England, Belgium, Portugal, Spain, Sweden, the Canary Islands and North Africa. The tantalizing question is: What happened during these 60,000 years to *Homo Erectus* and *Homo Neanderthalensis*?

Whatever the migration point – or why, indeed, the migration took place in the first instance – the crucial thing is that *a single entity gave rise to all this at a single point*.

We know that all the previous forms of Man just disappeared, leaving no subsequent ancestral lines to them. We know that, from present evidence, even Neanderthal Man seems to have ended its lineage abruptly 40,000 years ago. There are, however, some scientists who claim that it never died out and continues today in another environmentally factorized form whose origins are represented by a skeleton found in Israel (of a modern type of hominid) that has certain similarities with Neanderthal Man. The skeleton is that of a young boy which has been dated to 90,000 years ago, called the Qafzeh Boy. Professor Wolpoff contends that the Neanderthal's and the Qafzeh boy's genus are the same and that geographical and environmental factors in evolution terms account for quite apparent skull and skeletal differences. If the genus of both hominid forms are the same, it would imply that modern *Homo Sapiens Sapiens* could have been derived from both the Neanderthals and the Qafzeh boy genotype, and therefore that Neanderthal Man may never have died out. Other palaeontologists disagree and contend that the features of each are too different to be the same palaeontological classification.

Let us now go to the little matter of the African Eve. It is not really a little matter. It is probably one of the biggest matters in the affairs of Man. Who and what is the African Eve? Of the different *Homo Erectus* groups that populated the world from approximately 1.5 million years ago to 200,000 years ago it seems that the African group was the one that led to *Homo Sapiens Sapiens*. Java man, Peking man and the European *Homo Erectus* group, it seems, did not establish a lineage into future man. All these other *Homo Erectus* groups originally came from Africa. Approximately one million years ago, they moved away from Africa into other parts of the world. The African *Homo Erectus* group, therefore, provided the theme upon which all the other *Homo Erectus* forms varied. They were thus the original stock, the most 'undiluted' group in their capacity to reflect purely the results of interception 'undiluted' by variations caused by environmental factors. It may well have been that the alien beings were following this African group and mapping the results of its interceptions from *Australopithecus Afarensis* to *Homo Habilis* to African *Homo Erectus*. They might have been conducting a 'case study' through this group and comparing the different variations arising in other groups living in different locations around the world to that case study. The African group were thus the alien beings' first reference sample of hominids on this planet.

I believe that the ends of the lines of man that survived the entropic process of dismantling thus far to the African Eve were intercepted at that African Eve point 200,000 years ago, and later at different places and different times by an Alien intelligence. As a result, a new genus of man, Modern Man – *Homo Sapiens* – came into being. I believe that from this primary base of *Homo Sapiens*, originating in Africa approximately 200,000 years ago, all other changed forms of man emerged through artificially managed genetic manipulation and engineering by an alien species not of this Earth.

To recap: These are the most crucial points in the history of the genetic series we call Mankind, because it is likely that almost all other ancestral forms of Man from the First Adam disappeared into sub forms, i.e. apes and monkeys, with the crucial exception of at least two. These two forms were *Homo Erectus* and *Homo Neanderthalensis*. These sub-forms all the other species of Man devolved into were the primates we see today. As I have stated previously, I believe unequivocally that Apes came *from* Man and not the other way around as is commonly accepted today. (Before the men in the white coats come to make a monkey out of me, let me say that the gradual unravelling of the human genome tantalizingly is beginning to suggest this.) These forms are, of course, the Gorilla, the Chimpanzee, the Orang-Utan and so on down the primate ladder to the monkeys.

Of the two species of physical that survived down the chain from the first 'enlighted' Godman, at this time, I believe *Homo Erectus* was thus the first to be genetically intercepted and transformed through the manipulation of DNA, to eventually become *Homo Sapiens*. Perhaps the wiring of the soft tissue of the brain was changed in line with that of the Creator Beings of an alien planet. It stopped our forefathers from changing into Apes as was perhaps the fate of countless species such as ours all over the Universe. Both surviving lines of Man, including the Neanderthals, had the line of connection to the First Adam being, and thus Godness. *Homo Erectus* carried on through the now genetically intercepted African Eve whose descendants can now be found in the present modern forms of Man.

Geneticists, of course, would probably say that a naturally occurring, purely accidental genetic mutation accounted for this change. The question could then be asked why such mutations hadn't spontaneously occurred previously for millions of years to the other species on Earth and led much earlier to the invention of the wheel, for example. Can you imagine the nonsense of it all when you think of the number of accidental, fortuitous and spontaneous gene mutations it would take to change a sea worm into a man when it is supposed to take hundreds of thousands and in some instances millions of years for one fortuitous mutation to occur? The literature is full of desperate biologists trying equally desperately to prove that it is possible to get a series of fortunate mutations occurring at random in a chaotic maelstrom that produces a man from a worm. The short answer to all their attempts, if read with a minimum of objectivity, is to admit that they don't even come close to accounting for the series of links necessary to have occurred in such an interconnected fashion that it would account for all the permutations necessary to come up with any part of a worm, never mind a man. The law of probability simply forbids it and no decent mathematician would give their theories house room. It is so sad to see the desperation with which men would try, at least by implication, to avoid denying their vanity and affirming that there may be a phenomenon outside atoms that might, for want of a better word, be called God. That this phenomenon might well have provided a template for the original point of order away from which life forms devolve.

So what part, then, do the Neanderthal group play in the gradual emergence of modern *Homo Sapiens*? Could it be that the Neanderthals were left untouched? A control group to act as a comparison with the altered species? Perhaps a spare group in reserve in case the experiment went wrong? A spare group that would make a better form from the mistakes learned through the DNA manipulation of *Homo Erectus* that was carried out before. An unintercepted sample, a sample left untouched when they rewired *Homo Erectus* 160,000 years previously. The Neanderthals were reserved from that time for this reason and just such a purpose. The serially and naturally devolved large brain size of the Neanderthals was perhaps still suitable. The grey matter was there. All it needed was rewiring. And so they rewired the soft tissue in the brains of Neanderthals. Once this was done they set about isolating their experimental hybrid species from the rest of mankind through a set of rigidly defined rules or laws. Thus they developed this group secretly and covertly for their purposes such that genetic boundaries could be altered over time to fit a prospectus and an intention yet unknown.

The Neanderthals, as I have said, had a brain much larger than any other genotype of man found. Brain size per unit body mass is commonly accepted as a pointer to intelligence and thus a propensity to survive as a species. With such a brain size the question arises as to why these people seemed to be so primitive in technological development terms *for tens of thousands of years*. I believe that Neanderthals were on their way out as a genus, victims as was common with all other prior species to the whims of the entropic process. Inheritors of the *'down escalator'* of the entropic process. From Man to beast to tree to stone and thence the primaeval atom form of non-living differentiation.

What do we know about the Neanderthals from the fossil record?

It seems that there are two distinct types of Neanderthal man that are found at various locations around the world. There is the 'classic' Neanderthal type that is believed to have been a cold-adapted, specialized side branch from the human line that became isolated in Europe and then became extinct as the climate improved. Then there is the other, more generalized Neanderthal group that is considered to have avoided this specialization and thus continued on to give rise to the later modern sapient populations.

An alternative view places the 'classic' Neanderthals in the modern human evolutionary line and attributes their disappearance both anatomically and culturally to a process of absorption that involves some contribution of Neanderthal genes to the succeeding populations. There are some scientists, however, who have advocated the classification of Neanderthal man as a species separate altogether from *Homo Sapiens*.

The wide distribution of the Neanderthal hominid form certainly suggest that it, together with the transitional forms of *Homo Erectus* that also appear in the fossil record at this time, helped to determine the form of modern *Homo Sapiens Sapiens*. So, these two distinct points of alien interception, that of the African Eve 200,000 years ago and that of Neanderthal man thousands of years later, would both be responsible for modern *Homo Sapiens Sapiens* in the form in which he now exists. They would thus be the two hominid elements that resulted in our hybrid, *Homo Sapiens Sapiens.*

How, then, did that final hybridization process that resulted in modern man progress?

The date of the second major exodus from Africa of *Homo Erectus* hominids is approximated to 100,000 years ago. It is around that time that the Qafzeh fossils found in Israel that seem to be examples of an early form of *Homo Sapiens*, are dated. Yet, as I have previously mentioned, these early *Homo Sapiens* forms appear to have disappeared from the fossil record for the next 60,000 years until the emergence of Cro-Magnon man. Up to that point it is only Neanderthal fossils that appear in the European and Middle Eastern fossil record. Could the Qafzeh fossils and others like them that appear in different areas of the world in the last 200,000 years signify an early form of *Homo Sapiens*, genetically engineered by the alien beings from the intercepted African Eve stock? Perhaps they found that the capacity of these early moderns to draw more powerful soul lines into the realms of physical life was not great enough. Thus they may have decided to start to work upon their control sample, the Neanderthals, perhaps with the aim of eventually combining their larger cranial capacity with that of the African Eve intercepted line in order to provide a new hybrid that would be a point of convergence at which the two hominid lines would become one. Thus the more advanced souls that would have incarnated into the as yet unintercepted Neanderthal line with its larger brain capacity would eventually be pulled in to the new hybridized form that would connect all soul incarnating on this planet and place it within the grip of the alien beings. The fact that the brain capacity of Neanderthal man is actually greater than its successor in the fossil record, Cro-Magnon man, might well suggest that such a hybridization between the Neanderthals and a group that had a lesser cranial capacity did indeed take place.

Thus the Neanderthal line is the more advanced form of hominid that was hybridized with the lesser *Homo Erectus* form. I contend that the large brain size of Neanderthal man was naturally devolved, it was not the result of alien hybridization. Neanderthal man would therefore have been the remnant of a naturally devolving line, an unintercepted line. The fossil record is thoroughly confused about Neanderthal ancestry. All kinds of fossil skulls are attributed to the Neanderthal genotype going back to about 250,000 years ago. But there is no definitive fossil record for Neanderthal man types until about 100,000 years ago. This might suggest that the ancestral lines that led to that point consisted largely of individuals who freed themselves from the capture of the wheel of rebirth and converted their bodies back into light, transfigured. The relative few who did become caught in the momentum of devolution and were intercepted are those whom we can observe in the fossil record. However, even these few are still greater in number than prior examples of advanced hominid who devolved into lesser states, simply because the force print of the planet has increased in time due to the entropic momentum of the universe. The treacle has thus become stickier and stickier, and it has thus become easier and easier to become stuck within it.

Palaeoanthropologists believe that they have identified several intermediary *Homo Erectus* forms in Europe that indicate a gradual evolution from *Homo Erectus* to Neanderthal man in the European context. I would dispute that these forms have any connection with later examples of Neanderthal man. Rather, I would contend that they, like the Qafzeh hominids in Israel, are in fact examples of the alien beings' experimentation with their first group of interception, *Homo Erectus*. The classic Neanderthal features they exhibit would thus be a result of the adaptation of *Homo Erectus* to the cold environment of Europe. Just as Neanderthal man was later adapted to those climatic conditions and displayed those same physical features. Thus the similarity between the Neanderthals and European forms of *Homo Erectus* is, I believe, incidental to the environment that they commonly shared and not in any way a sign that they share the same line of descent.

It has become apparent from the fossils of Neanderthal groups that these so-called 'primitive' peoples used to keep severely injured individuals alive, in some cases for decades.[3] The injuries displayed by certain Neanderthal individuals are so severe that they would never have survived had they not been taken care of by other people. It is often the case that one individual has many different injuries that, according to the fossil evidence, appear to have healed over. Thus there is an indication that Neanderthal groups were indeed disposed to caring for their sick and injured. This could be taken as the sign of a spiritually advanced society for, on a purely physical level, these injured individuals could only provide a hindrance, not a help, to this hunter-gatherer community that lived in harsh environmental conditions.

Thus, that part of the aliens' 'control' group that was not intercepted in the first African Eve interception 200,000 years ago *was* later intercepted. Some of this group lived within, or perhaps was placed within, a new environment which, I believe, was more conducive to alien interception than Africa had been. That environment is the environment of the last Ice Age in Europe. As I have already explained, alien body biology is likely to be inorganically electronically based. Thus the cold environment of the Ice Age in which electrical currents flow more easily would have been ideal for their intercepting processes. This interception that took place in Europe resulted in the 'classic' Neanderthal group that has been identified as being specially adapted for cold weather conditions.

What might have prompted early Neanderthal man, or other early hominids, to choose to live in, or to migrate to, the cold climates of Western Europe which at the time was in the throes of an Ice Age? In fact, the question that also needs an answer is: Why did the two main exoduses from Africa (one million years ago and 100,000 years ago) occur in the first place? What might have instigated prior hominids to travel so far afield, to cross vast oceans and spread themselves over the enormous expanse of the ancient world? They would have certainly had the time to achieve that spread in the past million years since the first exodus. But the question still remains: Why would they have wanted to travel so far? Overpopulation was certainly not the problem at that time, so that could not have prompted these vast journeys. The puzzle becomes all the more apparent in the context of the migration of early hominids to Ice Age conditions.

Could it perhaps be the case that the random distribution of early hominids found in the European fossil record during the time of the Great Ice Age was to a large extent the result of alien beings literally translocating their intercepted hominid forms to these locations? To take this proposition further, might it indeed have been the case that much of the migration across the world after the two main points of exodus from Africa was also a result of such translocation? Could the alien beings have been setting up separate experimental groups that they wished to keep genetically discrete from one another? Vast distances encompassing land and ocean between these groups would have served this purpose admirably. It would have also allowed the alien beings the chance to examine how the different environmental factors associated with these different locations would affect their sample groups. This might seem like a wild speculation straight out of the realms of science fiction but there have been many reports from alien abductees who claim that they were indeed translocated from one place to another after their abduction experiences. It would also explain why people who had plentiful game and thus food resources in Africa would decide to trek thousands of miles in a sudden exodus. It seems a foolish, even a downright stupid thing to do unnecessarily.

The Great Ice Age, which consisted of extremely cold periods interspersed with short periods of warmth, occurred between about 1.75 million and 10,000 years ago. This time span coincides with all the main alien genetic interceptions from *Homo Habilis* to *Homo Erectus*, to Neanderthal and finally to Cro-Magnon. In fact 1.75 million years ago is approximately the time at which the first *Homo* group, *Homo Habilis*, started to appear. While 10,000 years ago, the end of the Ice Age, is the approximate date that is generally accepted to be the demarcation point at which modern *Homo Sapiens Sapiens* emerged as the primary hominid form. I am going to put to you a possibility that you might find even more astonishing: Could it be that the Great Ice Age itself was the result of alien interference with the climate of our planet? Scientists have not yet come to any firm conclusions as to what might have caused the Ice Age. Many theories have been put forward, including speculations that changes in the Earth's orbit around the sun and variations in the Earth's axis might have been responsible in part for these climatic changes. The impact of meteorites on the planet might well have caused such variations in the Earth's axis and its orbit around the sun. Could the aliens have used their supreme technology to guide such meteorites towards our earth in order to provide for themselves the cold environment that they would later require for their interception of species on this planet? A cold environment that would allow a better potential for the flow of the electric currents that are central to all their 'body' operations? It is well known that current flows more and more without resistance the lower the temperature of the medium it flows through. An environment that might also be better disposed to accommodate the physical vestments of their silicon-mercury based synthetic bodies.

The last major alien genetic interception before the emergence of modern *Homo Sapiens Sapiens* was that of the Cro-Magnon hominids in Europe. Could this fact suggest that the Cro-Magnons were the culmination of approximately 1.75 million years of intermittent alien genetic interception into hominid species on this planet? If my proposition about translocation is true then the question might be asked: Why did alien beings wait so long to bring their experimental subjects into the Ice Age environment of the northern hemisphere? The answer might lie in the fact that the alien beings were hoping to gain from hominids on this planet an insight into how to access their lines of soul connection to Godhead. Thus they would have sought to study these hominids in their natural environment and maintain a gradual series of interceptions that would slowly change them to what the aliens wanted them to be without altering any of the factors that might have disallowed the very thing the aliens were looking for: the direct connection via soul lines to Godhead. It was only when the alien element that had gradually accumulated in the genome of certain hominids was large enough in scope for these hominids to be powerfully intercepted via that alien element within them that the most powerful interceptions could take place without destroying the human genome altogether. The aliens had to establish that genetic base first through gradually getting us used to their effect such that our natural genetic structure would not break down when the more powerful interceptions took place.

In fact, examples of an intermediary stage found in Europe between *Homo Erectus* and *Homo Sapiens* between 400,000 and 200,000 years ago, such as Swanscombe man in England and Steinheim Man in Germany, may well be the derivations of the first shot across the bows for alien beings attempting their genetic interceptions in an Ice Age environment. This would explain why examples of *Homo Erectus* in Europe at this time appear to be more advanced than examples found in the same time span in Asia and Africa. These hominid forms may well bear no relation, as I have previously suggested, to modern *Homo Sapiens*, rather they could be the artefacts of ancient alien experimentation.

How, then, did the Cro-Magnons come about? They appeared in the European fossil record at the same point at which 'classic' Neanderthal man was 'dying out', approximately 35,000–40,000 years ago. The question of the relation of Cro-Magnons to the earliest forms of *Homo Sapiens* is still unclear. It does appear however, that Cro-Magnons (*Homo Sapiens Sapiens*) and Neanderthals (*Homo Sapiens Neanderthalensis*) are closer in affinity than was once believed. The origin of the Cro-Magnon peoples can best be understood by first looking at the fate of the Neanderthal group that seems to have been their immediate predecessors.

The evidence now indicates that modern humans first emerged in sub-Saharan Africa some time prior to 50,000 years ago. Subsequently they spread northward, absorbing and occasionally displacing (it is believed through competition, not confrontation) local archaic human populations. As a result, some of the Middle Eastern, Central Asian and Central European Neanderthals might have been absorbed into these spreading modern human populations, contributing genetically to the subsequent early modern human populations across those regions. In Western Europe a cul-de-sac where the transition to modern humans took place relatively late is believed to have taken place. Thus there is a preponderance of Neanderthal representatives in the Western European fossil record at that time.

I have contended that a number of Neanderthals were *intercepted by our abovementioned outside agency*, an agency that genetically altered their DNA and thus their biological prospectus, creating a special experimental genus of Man. The more general classification of Neanderthal man might have led among others to the main group that we now identify as the modern Semitic people. These would be the modern derivatives of the examples of Neanderthal man that have been found in the warmer climates of the Middle East, while the 'classic' Neanderthal grouping that is relevant to western European Neanderthals might well have led to the modern European stock, via the Cro-Magnon stage. In fact, some modern human groups that are more or less homogeneous are thought to have maintained a close relationship to Cro-Magnon types, at least in their cranial morphology. The most notable of these groups are the Dal people from Dalecarlia (now Dalarna, Sweden) and the Guanches of the Canary Islands.

It is difficult to see that a species that had done nothing in technological development terms for a hundred thousand years (the Neanderthals) had suddenly and spontaneously converted to a people (the Semitics) that became one of the most brilliant, technically innovative ethnic groups the world has ever known in a few thousand years, unless a genetic change of enormous proportions took place suddenly. A change that altered the wiring of the brain in a large proportion of the genus.

Perhaps they went further and produced a more cruel, more racist hybrid with those who were originally of the genus of Modern Man as represented by the Qafzeh Boy. Could it be that gene manipulation with people of the Qafzeh genus of *Homo Sapiens* by the aliens produced the hybrids that we know today as Cro-Magnon Man? The Qafzeh skeleton is dated as being 90,000-100,000 years old. As I have said, it is a very strange thing that this genus of man disappears from the record for the next 60,000 years. The next skeletal record of *Homo Sapiens* is marked with the appearance suddenly of Cro-Magnon Man 40,000 years ago. Perhaps it took 60,000 years to perfect this hybrid, a hybrid produced between equivalents of the Qafzeh Boy and the 'classic' Neanderthals of Western Europe. The fact that modern man emerged later in Europe than anywhere else, and that the Neanderthal stage is thus longer there, may well have been a result of the processes required to produce this hybrid.

What, then, happened to the Qafzeh equivalents in the intervening 60,000 years? Why do they not appear in the fossil record in that time? The Qafzeh fossils may well have represented a very small experimental group isolated from the main stock of intercepted African *Homo Erectus* in order to prevent inter-breeding as it might result in a dilution of the experimental results. Thus this group came or were brought out of Africa into what is now Israel. Once the experimental bed changed from this first group to the second group – the Neanderthal 'control' group – no more representatives of the first group were brought out of Africa. Thus it is not surprising that such a small population of early moderns did not appear later in the fossil record, as the likelihood of fossils being found for prior hominids is very much the exception, not the rule. The larger the population group, the more likely it is that some of its fossils will later be found. So the fact that the

Qafzeh group did leave fossils may well have been purely a result of chance.

What, then, can we glean about the next experimental group – the Cro-Magnons? This group seems to have manifested a sudden spurt of technological growth that does not appear to have taken place to any extent before their arrival on the scene. It is now believed that the Neanderthal and early modern human groups lived side by side with each other for tens of thousands of years. Yet during that time the modern humans showed no sign that they had superior technology. 'Both people were living in the same way, hunting the same prey, burying their dead in the same manner,' says Baruch Arensburg, a palaeoanthropologist at Tel Aviv University. Then it seems that around 40-50,000 years ago something profound happened. New technologies associated with modern humans – finer blades and projectile weapons – began to appear. Scientists can only speculate on what triggered this technological spurt. 'I think there was a mutation in the brains of a group of anatomically modern humans living either in Africa or the Middle East', says Richard Klein, an anthropologist at Stanford University. 'Some new neurological connections let them behave in a modern way. Maybe it permitted fully articulated speech, so that they could pass on information more efficiently.' Could this 'mutation in the brains of a group of anatomically modern humans' to which Klein refers be the result of alien interception at this very point, alien interception producing the Cro-Magnon form of hominid? Such a sudden burst of technological development at this point certainly suggests the involvement of the ultimate masters of technology – our alien Clones and their Grey roboids.

It is my contention that the Cro-Magnons are the result of direct cross-breeding with the aliens' own genetic blueprint. It was not confined to the rewiring of the brain alone. It was a whole-body interception. The final hybrid species, of all permutations that could be produced with the three main players: the Neanderthals, the Moderns and the Alien Clones. Perhaps this was done a hundred thousand years ago and indeed prompted the huge exodus of humanity out of Africa.

The last Ice Age thus provided the alien beings with the freedom to use their electronic means of interception into the human genome to best effect. Thus the Northern Hemisphere, which was largely covered in ice, provided the central stage on which these, the most complete interceptions of all, were carried out. Do you recall the Eskimo legend that I recounted earlier, that says that the first tribes were brought to the north by 'gods' with brass wings? Could this legend be based on actual truth? Could alien beings have literally translocated the 'first tribes' into the Ice Age of the 'north'?

CHAPTER FOURTEEN:
'WITH A LITTLE HELP FROM "FRIENDS"'

Genetic interception by an alien resource seems a very plausible explanation for the sudden rise in the size of the brain of human 'Sapiens' species. The scientific explanation for this is far less likely. It contends, as I have said previously, that the sudden increase in brain size occurred as a quantum genetic accident through spontaneous gene malformation or mutation. All an artefact of mere chance. Forgive me for restating it, but all this is so significant that it bears repeating. Those who know the biological imperatives that go to make up such a schematic of fundamental change, that is, the number of gene mutations necessary to change an ape to a man, know very well that we as a species have just not been around long enough for the auspices of mere chance to trigger it, let alone make it happen. The numbers probabilities necessary are simply too preposterous to envisage.

When the alien Clones and roboids set about regenerating the genome of the species of Man's ancestors whom they had found, they 'rewired' their now primitive devolving brains. Brains that once allowed the beings that returned to Godhead to be ascendant over any alien form in the universe. The aliens were attending to leftovers. These were nevertheless leftovers that had a soul, a discrete connection to Godhead and still at least a potential for eternal life. Their thinking power was given a boost by this alien intelligence. But they could never give them back the power of 'seeing God' again. The intercepting aliens of course had no Soul, only the knowledge possessed by their Creator Beings who did have one. Just as you could say that a computer has knowledge, they had only a proxy reference to know anything and do anything.

An interesting account of a close encounter with an alien spacecraft and alien beings gives us an example of how these beings might, perhaps without meaning to, provide a boost for the human brain.[1]

This encounter occurred at Tres Arroyos on 30 December 1972, and involved an uneducated gaucho, aged seventy-three, and his pet cat. 'Late one night his radio failed and a loud humming noise filled the air above his remote shack. Looking up he saw a powerful light beaming down, which emerged from a wheel-like object; on the underside tubes churned out sparks. A cabin with windows in the middle contained a strange figure, wearing a suit made up of rolled material. The being stared down at him as the object tilted on to its edge. Then, after a few seconds, a huge flash of light shot out and hit the cat, which fled. The gaucho was himself temporarily blinded by this. Meanwhile the humming noise increased in intensity and the UFO flew over some trees leaving the smell of sulphur.

'The cat vanished for several days and returned with its skin singed and its personality altered to total shyness. The gaucho also developed headaches, nausea and blisters on his skin. Then clumps of his hair fell out. After he recovered he noticed that new teeth were growing through his gums – which, given his age, was hardly normal.

'Much of this was verified by investigation teams, as was the severe burning damage to the tops of the trees over which the object hovered. But strangest of all was that this man who could hardly read and write suddenly developed a fascination for subjects like philosophy and science. He later admitted that the UFO had returned in February 1973 and an entity from this had told him many things; his recollection included a complex medical discussion which gave an alleged cure for cancer. The language is in many ways obscure and the description of this cure offers only brief snatches of lucidity.'

It seems that the brain of this uneducated man was enhanced by his encounter with an alien being. Prior to this encounter he 'could hardly read and write'. This story, if true, may offer an affirmation of my postulation that the brains of prior hominid forms devolving into apes were 'rewired' by alien interceptions and thus, unintentionally, given a boost back up the devolutionary tree to a state of greater and more coherent thinkability.

A form of physical regeneration seems to have also taken place for the 'gaucho' referred to in the account: 'new teeth were growing through his gums – which, given his age, was hardly normal.' This does indeed suggest that the man in question was in fact subject to some form of biological interception to alter his physical scope. The growth of new teeth in an old man is a phenomenon, at least in this instance, that smacks of the same clonic regeneration processes that the aliens might use on their own type of beings. The physical symptoms suffered by the man and his cat are all classic symptoms of radiation sickness – hair falling out, nausea, blistered skin. This perhaps suggests that the Clone beings effect their regeneration through a form of irradiation. The fact that the aliens discuss with the gaucho a cure for cancer might imply that they have realized that their own mechanisms using radioactive radiation can cause cancer in human beings. Thus they are suggesting means by which the disease can be cured so that their experimental subjects can be preserved in life for future experimentation. In his book *Secret Life*, David M. Jacobs says that '. . . in extremely rare cases the aliens will undertake a cure of some ailment troubling the abductee. This is not in any way related to the contactee Space Brother concepts of benevolent aliens coming to Earth to cure cancer. Rather, in special circumstances it appears that the aliens feel obliged to preserve the specimen for their own purposes. As one abductee said, "It's equipment maintenance".'[2]

CHAPTER FIFTEEN

AND & DNA

It is interesting to speculate that perhaps all these interceptions account for the thirty-seven genes of mitochondrial DNA that are mysteriously included in our cells. No one knows where they came from or why, except that they would have to have come from a source totally foreign to the human genome. It is a salutary feature that mitochondrial DNA, unlike other DNA, clones itself in reproduction instead of recombining. There is a strong hypothesis that mitochondria are the direct descendants of bacteria that entered primitive nucleated cells in a number of infections. Among billions of such infective events a few could have led to the development of stable, symbiotic associations between nucleated hosts and bacterial parasites. The classes of 'bacteria' that took part in these 'infections' have not yet been established. Could these 'bacteria' simply be the invading genetic elements introduced into the hominid genome by alien being via a series of 'infections' until eventually they were accepted and absorbed? There is a proportion of mitochondrial DNA that is not in any way involved in functions that benefit the cell. Thus, it is to a certain extent an organelle that is independent of the cell and independent of the cell's own genetic information contained within the nucleus.

A new discovery about the origins of DNA replication offers a startling confirmation that mitochondrial DNA is in fact the result of alien interception. Michele Calos of Stanford University in scouring human DNA for the origins of replication or duplication centres has discovered something quite remarkable about the specific structure of DNA that will replicate under its own steam.[1] Her initial approach was to break up human chromosomes into pieces of DNA, inject those pieces into cells and then search for ones that could replicate unaided. But there was a problem: any DNA pieces she injected immediately infiltrated and hijacked the replication centres. Calos hit on a solution. She knew that circular pieces of DNA cannot hop onto chromosomes because they have no 'sticky ends'. So she concealed her pieces of DNA inside a circular structure. The tactic worked. Almost immediately, Calos found pieces of DNA that could replicate under their own steam. 'The trick was simply to make the DNA pieces big enough', she recalls. 'Nearly any DNA piece larger than 10,000 base pairs is able to replicate'.

Unlike other DNA, mitochondrial DNA happens to have a distinctive *circular* structure. Thus, it is extremely plausible that the alien beings could have used this circular structure to conceal the thirty-seven genes of mitochondrial DNA. This concealment allows these genes to replicate under their own steam and thus maintain their independence from the human organism while at the same time existing within it. This symbiotic relationship that human cells have with mitochondrial DNA allows the mitochondrial DNA enough independence from the human organism for it to be able to act as a conduit through which information from the alien beings who inserted this DNA can pass. It is almost as though they have left a keyhole in human cells into which their key will fit such that they can open the genetic information contained within the cell and manipulate it as they wish.

Research scientists have been exploring ways of inserting the blueprints for artificial structural proteins into bacterial DNA. It seems that it doesn't matter to a bacterium whether an artificial gene in its DNA codes for a protein like one that the bacterium produces naturally or one that is entirely different. If it is in the genome, the bacterium will make proteins. In 1990 a research team led by Joseph Capello at Protein Polymer Technologies in San Diego, California were searching for a designer protein that would make cells grown in tissue culture stick to normal human cells.[2] Artificially grown tissue is already proving valuable in promoting wound healing, and it might some day be possible to grow entire organs this way to replace damaged or malfunctioning ones. Capello and his colleagues persuaded bacterial DNA to code for their artificial protein with great success. The protein is now marketed commercially as an adhesive for attaching mammalian cells to tissue cultures. If, as the hypothesis claims, the presence of mitochondrial DNA in cells was the result of bacteria entering primitive nucleated cells in a number of 'infections', then is it not possible that the alien beings may themselves have used bacterial DNA encoded with genes artificially engineered by them to enter into the biologies of living organisms on this planet? If scientists with our level of technology can achieve such success in genetically engineering bacterial proteins then the scope for such genetic manipulation by alien beings with their highly advanced technology must be enormous.

A further example of the introduction of genes into the human genome can be found in an article in *The Independent* (3.1.97)[3] entitled 'Eating new food may change your genes'. A team at the University of Cologne in Germany conducted an experiment in which mice were fed with food containing a virus known as M13 which normally affects bacteria. The researchers led by Walter Dorfler discovered short sections of the virus's DNA in the spleen, liver and white blood cells of the mice. Professor Dorfler says that 'they weren't hard to find. In some cases as much as one cell in a thousand had viral DNA.'. He added that the DNA did not usually stay inside the cells more than about eighteen hours but that he suspects that occasionally some might remain. This could form the basis for evolution if some cells retain outside DNA. The author of the article, Science Editor Charles Arthur, says that 'such genetic crossover has frequently been observed between bacteria cells, but is not expected between bacterial viruses and animal cells'. Thus he points out that 'genetically engineered food might alter the DNA of those who eat it'. The ease through which genetic interception can be carried out even with our present technology is thus amply illustrated here.

If these alien biological-robots we call the Greys are made of inorganic chemicals driven by semi-organic mitochondrially derived biochemistry which they inserted into a number of hominids and these hominids were then instructed to go forth and multiply, it could indeed explain the mystery of the strange and inexplicable mitochondria gene sequence found in present lines of Man.

Let me put a further point to you that you might like to consider. Using mitochondrial DNA as a marker scientists have convincingly shown that the origins of all mankind were in Africa approximately 200,000 years ago. If Neanderthal man was unintercepted by alien beings until a time more recent than that could it be possible that until that point of interception he had no mitochondrial DNA? His body might have employed other cellular mechanisms to provide for the functions which mitochondrial DNA now perform.

When the hybridization of Neanderthal man with the highly intercepted *Homo Erectus* line occurred, the mitochondrial history of the *Home Erectus* line would have been passed into the cells of any future progeny of the new hybrid form. Modern man, *Homo Sapiens Sapiens*, is descended from that progeny. Thus our mitochondrial history stems back to *Homo Erectus* about 200,000 years ago. The Neanderthal factors that are present within our ancestry would not have registered on the mitochondrial evidence simply because Neanderthal man in his pure unintercepted form had no mitochondrial DNA! Up to now, 'Out of Africa' theorists have claimed that Neanderthal man was not in any way ancestral to modern *Homo Sapiens Sapiens*: this is in support of their theory that all human origins derive from a certain time in Africa. Perhaps, in the light of these implications about mitochondrial DNA, they can now look to the possibility that their theory can happily coexist alongside a definite and undeniable contribution made by the Neanderthal hominid group to modern *Homo Sapiens Sapiens*.

What other evidence is there within the human genetic make-up of possible alien genetic interception? We know that the human genome is littered with waste DNA that many thought had no function. It is now thought that this waste or junk DNA may contain a genetic switch that activates other genes. These sequences of bases are called ALU and a research scientist, Wanda Reynolds of the Sidney Kimmel Cancer Centre in San Diego, thinks that Alus may have played an important role in the evolution of primates. Bob Holmes, writing in *New Scientist* about Reynolds's research, puts it thus: 'The Alu is a 283 nucleotide sequence that acts as a "jumping gene". From time to time it inserts copies of itself, randomly, into the genome. Over the past 30–60 million years these insertions have occurred repeatedly leaving roughly a million copies of Alu scattered through the human genome and making up almost 10% of all the DNA in each cell. During this time the sequences of the various ALUS have begun to diverge, so that four distinct sub-families of Alu can now be recognized. While studying one of these sub-families, Reynolds noticed a short stretch of DNA – only fourteen bases long – that looked familiar. Elsewhere in the genome there are nearly identical sequences that function as anchor points for proteins that bind to hormones and which therefore provide a way for hormones to turn genes on and off. Reynolds and her colleague, Gordon Vansant, learned that the Alu sequence also binds to a hormone receptor – in this case the receptor for a hormone called Retinoic Acid, which activates genes at the proper times during development. (*Proceedings of the National Academy of Sciences*, Vol. 92, page 8229).

'Vansant and Reynolds then turned their attention to a naturally occurring Alu that sits close to the human gene for keratin, a protein found in our skin, hair and nails. They looked at cells in which they had replaced the keratin gene with a "marker" gene whose activity could easily be measured. When the researchers then deleted the Alu sequence they found that the marker became thirty-five times less active . . . A few Alus have previously been shown to affect the activity of nearby genes, but the new study is the first to show how. The results also provide the first clear evidence that most Alus could have the potential to regulate human genes. Reynolds believes that most Alus have little effect on nearby genes, perhaps because they are bundled deep within folds of DNA. But she says that with the million Alus strewn randomly through the genome during the course of primate evolution, at least a few are likely to have landed where they could regulate a nearby gene. When this occurred, she suggests the effect would be equivalent to randomly twisting a knob on an instrument panel. Usually the effect would be harmful, but once in a while it might produce an interesting and beneficial genetic novelty. "We can't prove it", she says, "but it seems over the last 30-50 million years it would provide good evolutionary fodder".'[4]

Could all this not have been random? Perhaps these million or so Alus are in fact the attempted deliberate genetic interceptions to which I have referred, of which only a certain number actually took and married into the functioning DNA of human beings. Reynolds also says that this effect is equivalent to 'randomly twisting a knob on an instrument panel'. Perhaps this was an *actual* instrument panel operated by alien intelligences. She also asserts that once in a while turning the knob might produce 'an interesting and beneficial novelty'. My assertion is that perhaps it did – but to whose benefit? I contend that this is precisely what actually happened when hominid forms naturally converting into apes, in line with my theory of evolution within an overall format of devolution, were artificially intercepted and enhanced for the alien purpose I have outlined. It would indeed have provided good evolutionary fodder.

According to another article by Bob Holmes in *New Scientist* entitled 'Message in a Genome',[5] researchers are beginning to explore how the 'loops, twists and folds in the long DNA chain (its so-called "higher structure")' affect the expression of genes contained within them. This work, they believe, could reveal a purpose for non-coding DNA. Emile Zuckerkandl, a molecular evolutionist who directs the Institute of Molecular Medical Sciences in Palo Alto, California, suggests that cells need a lot of non-coding DNA in and around the coding regions in the form of introns and intergenic spacers to enfold the coding portions and wrap them into properly labelled bundles that open at the right moment. For now he admits he cannot prove his theory until scientists have more knowledge about the higher order structure of DNA.

Do perhaps the interceptions cause the twisting and folding of DNA that keep genes dormant such that they can only be activated when the cell unwinds the relevant portion of the chromosome, so that the enzymes can get at the genes to begin transcribing them?

Edward Trifnov is a structural biologist at the Weizman Institute of Science in Rehevot, Israel. He points out that cells have put up with these introns for hundreds of millions of years, patiently cutting them out every time a gene is transcribed and splicing the coding parts together. 'Why have a whole headache of such precise splicing and throwing away to begin with?' he asks. 'It would be stupid to introduce such an awkward system for nothing. That meant introns are doing something very important'. Cells have a mechanism available to them to eliminate introns, but they don't use it. Scientists do not understand why this is so. By making a DNA copy of its transcript with the non-coding introns spliced out and then reinstating it into the genome, introns can be eliminated for good (exactly the mechanism by which some pseudogenes arise). If our DNA hasn't the means to get rid of alien-affected DNA because it is not natural to it, if that affected DNA is instead a device for perhaps an alien purpose and strange to our human blueprint, then our natural DNA would not have sufficient access to its codes. Thus the paradox would be solved. If the alien purpose was to substitute their own blueprint into ours, this phenomenon could be the evidence that indicates this.

Duncan Shaw, Professor of Genetics at the University of Aberdeen, in his fascinating article 'When DNA Turns Traitor', speaks of a malevolent form of DNA known as 'unstable' or 'trinucleotide repeat' DNA.[6] 'They are the genetic equivalent of the mischievous creatures in the film *Gremlins*: small, harmless-looking pieces of DNA that lurk within genes, whose destiny is to grow bigger and wreak havoc. Unfortunately, malevolent DNA of this kind – known as "unstable" or "trinucleotide repeat" DNA – is all too real. It first came to light in 1991 as the cause of Fragile X syndrome, an inherited form of mental retardation that mainly affects males. Soon afterwards, geneticists found strands of unstable DNA in people with myotonic dystrophy and Huntingdon's Disease. Now it is recognized as a key player in the world of genetic disease. Answering questions like "Where does unstable DNA come from?" and "Which gene does it affect?" has become one of the latest goals in the fast-moving science of human molecular genetics.

'And not without reason. A Cambridge team examining the evolution of unstable DNA has reached a worrying conclusion: the amount of unstable DNA may be gradually, almost imperceptibly, increasing, driven by its intrinsic ability to expand as it is passed from one generation to the next. In other words, some of our DNA is trying to kill us; and for the moment, at least, there is nothing we can do to stop its advance, or correct its harmful effects.

'The rate of spread cannot be measured directly. But judging from comparisons of unstable DNA sequences in different ethnic groups, unstable DNA has been gaining ground for tens of thousands of years. If evolution was the best way through its tenet of survival of the fittest of preserving a species at its biological optimums, why has it yet to equip us with mechanisms that could protect genes from the effects of unstable DNA? Nor is there likely to be much selection pressure to eliminate the faulty DNA from the gene pool, because many of the diseases it causes disable or kill people only after they have reached child-bearing age.'

Maybe this is some small hint confirming my postulation that evolution to betterment through convenient fortuitous DNA mutation from time to time is poppycock and that *devolution* is what drives the geological, biological and psychological momentums of the Universe. More accurately, evolution within devolution as I have said previously. The unravelling of the complete human genome will soon put this beyond doubt anyway.

Professor Shaw's paper identifies a 'genetic marker' associated with a disease called Huntingdon's Disease. This disease is one of a certain kind of genetic disease, which identifies itself as distinct from classical genetic diseases in which the genes are faithfully passed on unaltered to the next generation. The reason for these strange characteristics was established to be 'a piece of DNA that grew in length when it passed from parent to child and the bigger it became, the more severe the disease it caused.' This results in a 'progressive increase in severity, with earlier age of onset in each successive generation, it is known as "anticipation".' The trinucleotide repeats that form this affected DNA are distinctive from normal DNA because of their repetitive codes: the same triplet code is repeated again and again (i.e. ctgctgctg, or cggcggcgg). Ordinary DNA is 'random and featureless' in its coding. However, a clone is characterized by the fact that it is formed from a master cell that copies and recopies itself to create a complete body. There is no 'soul field' to dictate variations on that original theme. If a form of clonal DNA has been introduced into the genome of humanity then this repetitive coding would be exactly what one would have expected to result. Professor Shaw comments that 'unlike normal DNA, trinucleotide repeats seem to have an inbuilt tendency to get bigger. It is almost as though they want to grow.' Clonal DNA copies and copies itself without regulation by anything external to its own nature. It is thus unlike normal DNA, which is a product of an architect outside its own purely physical nature – soul. Thus, of itself, normal DNA does not have this impulsion to grow and repeat itself, instead it is the implicit result and reflection of soul field translated into an atomic shell. The trinucleotide repeats thus introduce unnecessary complication into the genome which provides, in physical terms, the line tracing back to Godhead. It interrupts that line and thus, to varying extents, obscures the route back.

Also 'it seems that trinucleotide DNA can form unusual molecular structures which allow two entwined strands of the DNA double helix to slip against each other, leaving loose ends to which the enzyme will add extra DNA bases'. If it was the intention of the aliens to re-order DNA for their own purposes and in this way to reorganize parts of the human genome, then they would have required a device by which they could splice DNA in and out. These unusual molecular structures that allow the two DNA strands to slip against each other providing loose ends to which extra bases can be added, may reflect *exactly* this intention and provide just such a mechanism to fulfil it.

The fact that the DNA of reptiles is far more fragmented into small pieces than that of mammals suggests that devolution is expressed through the breaking-up of the DNA itself. A break-up that seems to be in its first stages for human beings via these trinucleotide repeats and the unstable DNA that they produce.

The human skeleton is a perfect phase-looped aerial for receiving electromagnetic signals. A simple test may be done with a short-wave radio that proves this. Just place a finger on the aerial socket point and see how the signal received increases spectacularly. I believe our bodies are receivers and synthesize and receive Godness as intuition or inspiration. The brain is just a sorting agent for the manifestation of the thinking process and *not* the manufacture of it as is commonly accepted. This jelly or colloid packed full of nerve cells in an electric field gives rise to the thinking process that makes for our awareness and thus all we know.

The diseases affected by trinucleotide repeats seem to be those that affect particularly the nervous system which, as I have said, itself forms the biological aerial for receiving the language platform of Godhead which to me is Thought. Perhaps this aerial so fascinated the aliens because it provided biologically the very thing that they lacked – a connection to the Universe of the Whole. To these purely non-'spiritual' physical beings it would have seemed as though the nervous system itself provided that connection, as they would have had no means of discerning the non-physical power – the soul, which was the true connecting factor. The nervous system is just the physical mechanism through which that connection is achieved. So the aliens would have sought to introduce their own 'blueprint' into the genes that code for the nervous system of human beings. They would do this in order to see if they could themselves latch into this aerial and perhaps from there trace a path to whatever the root was that made us different from them. Perhaps to them our nervous system was their roadway to that great enigma, the Soul.

There appears to be a threshold level of trinucleotide repeats that then leads to instability. Perhaps this can be correlated to the extent to which human DNA can resist and keep in check these alien interceptions. Once they reach a certain number, it may no longer be possible in the naturally devolving genome of humanity for these strains to be resisted and dominated. So, unlike classical hereditary genetic diseases, there is no specific mutated gene, or genes, responsible for these diseases. Instead they are the result of repeating codes clogging up the system and thus impinging on genes that are a natural expression of the human species.

It also appears that most of the expansion of unstable DNA occurs during the first few cell divisions of embryonic development. Thus the DNA is not always unstable. The reason for the instability during these initial stages of life might be that the soul is not usually established *fully* in connection with the body it is forming at this early stage. Although it must be stressed that that connection has to exist to some extent for embryonic development to be initiated in the first place. But the *full* identity of the being formed has not yet been completely established in all its uniqueness. This connection takes time to establish as the soul filters from the field of 'death' in the space between atoms to the fields of life in the space within atoms. So without the full sanctioning power of the soul, the trinucleotide sequences are freer to expand. Once they have expanded they are then expressed into the human being as an apparent *fait accompli* that cannot seemingly be corrected by our DNA replication processes because they are alien to those processes. It is worth mentioning the fact that many reporters of alien abductions have said that sperm cells and egg cells are removed by the alien beings for examination and experimentation. In fact, medical examinations on several women who have claimed abduction have revealed that all the ova have mysteriously disappeared from their ovaries. This again identifies trinucleotide DNA, the expansion of which occurs in the earliest embryonic development, as originating from an alien source.

To conclude, all these unstable genetic repeats, manifested in such diseases as Fragile X syndrome, Huntingdon's Disease and myotonic dystrophy, seem to be involved in switching genes off or inhibiting their function in one way or another. They thus serve to adapt the human genome for alien beings to somehow find a foothold into it.

Thus, perhaps, entered the 'Greys' into the whole human cocktail themselves. An alien derivative, a legacy of a type of 'Being' cloned from a superior natural type from another part of our Universe that itself perhaps was made extinct, leaving a poisoned chalice (our Greys), their creations, for the Universe to deal with. These are predominantly the creatures described in the encounters known commonly as 'alien abductions'. Perhaps these abductions were and are being carried out to this day to enable the Greys to monitor the scale of their interception and perhaps alter and hone it. It is an interesting fact that the vast majority of alien abductees come from the Europiform genus of hominid. The most direct descendants of Cro-Magnon man. It is also true that there are few if any UFO hotspots anywhere in mainland Africa or Asia, with the exception of China and Japan, and most of the sightings in China have taken place in the last fifteen or so years. The vast majority by far are where the descendants of Cro-Magnon man live presently: North America and Europe.

To go back to Professor Shaw's research. It describes an interesting discovery that might support my contention about Cro-Magnon man.

With Huntingdon's Disease David Rubinsztein and his colleagues at Cambridge University have found that the repeats which cause the disease actually originate in the healthy population. So, says Professor Shaw, 'the repeats are "evolving", gradually increasing in length over many generations until they cross the threshold into the disease range.' It appears that when the number of repeats exceeds fifty the disease itself develops. So, Huntingdon's Disease appears to be a by-product of the general deterioration of the genome itself, as it originates in the healthy population and grows there in potential until it finally activates into an actual disease. This general deterioration is relevant to the genome of north-west Europeans in particular, where Huntingdon's Disease is concerned. Its incidence among Japanese people and black Africans, says Shaw, is 'vanishingly small'. This would illustrate my postulation that these ethnic groups are far less – at least, until now, perhaps – intercepted by alien genetic effect than the Cro-Magnon-descended north-west European ethnic group. Black Africans come from the same original *Homo Erectus* stock as Europeans but, unlike the Europeans, I believe they were not involved in the genetic interception that led to Cro-Magnon man. Similarly, the Mongoloid people stem from an ethnic line that has, in the past, been subject to the least interception. So the implication might be that unstable DNA could in fact be the result of a strange and profound genetic change. An interception, perhaps! Research has yet to be done extensively on the full quota of diseases that stem from unstable DNA and the variations that they present between different ethnic groups. However, this research on Huntingdon's Disease seems to have uncovered a particular concentration of trinucleotide repeat DNA among the descendants of Cro-Magnon man.

According to an article in the *New Scientist*, 'India looks farther east for its ancestors' (8.3.97)[7], there has been further evidence to suggest that Asian people, who are normally classified in the same group as European people (the 'Caucasian' group), actually have more in common genetically with Chinese and Japanese people than with Europeans. Narinder Mehra, director of the Department of histocompatibility and immunogenetics at the All-India Institute of Medical Sciences in New Delhi, belongs to an international team studying the genetics of histocompatibility worldwide. The scientists concentrated on the human leucocyte antigens (HLA), that dictate whether a person undergoing a transplant will accept or reject a donated organ or tissue. Mehra found 'surprising results' for northern Indians, when studying three HLA genes. For example he found that of the seventeen subtypes of a gene called HLA-A2, forty-four per cent of a group of forty-six people living in New Delhi had the same subtype as sixty-nine per cent of a group of northern Chinese. But in the subtype most commonly found in European populations it was totally absent. Although Mehra points out that the number of people that he has studied so far is small and that there might be significant variation between populations from different regions, this research does seem consistent with the possibility that northern Indian and Chinese people may share a common Neanderthal ancestry that Europeans, who are descendants of the Cro-Magnon group, do not.

To go back to Duncan Shaw's work on trinucleotide repeats, it seems that chimpanzees have much smaller repeats than ours and, says Professor Shaw, 'have a long way to go before they reach the disease threshold'. This, following on from my postulation about the origin of hominid and ape species, may well be because chimpanzees and other ape or monkey forms are the result of the natural breakdown of a species line in an entropic system *without* significant interception into that line by alien genes of their equivalent. Perhaps their line of Man went into their ape stage (chimpanzee) without the scale of interception to which our human lines have been subjected.

CHAPTER SIXTEEN:
THE WHO'S WHO OF GODS AND MEN

I believe the Neanderthal derivative of mankind came down into the lines of Aryo-Dravidio/Semitic peoples. They, I believe, may be the least intercepted line of humanoid ancestry of all peoples until relatively recently. By 'intercepted' I mean a direct physical DNA interception by an alien resource. Up until then these peoples held the purest natural ancestral lines of Inaugural God Being on the planet with the least alien genetic interception of their DNA.

I further believe that the brains of some Neanderthals were 'rewired' and a huge leap of intelligence took place. Some of *these* rewired Neanderthals were then used later to set up a biological 'bed' for the gradual hybridization of the genophylum with alien stock: that of the Clones. The rest of the Neanderthal genophylum were left untouched. They continued on till they finally died out. The 'Soul Lines' of these forms would then come into the weakened, more devolved format for physical life provided by Modern Man. We may live amongst some of these souls now.

There is palaeontological evidence that supports my contention that certain examples of Neanderthal man may well have been subject to a form of alien interception involving a rewiring of the brain. In his book *Secret Life*, David Jacobs documents the physical after-effects of alien abduction. These include physical scarring, with scars ranging in shape from small 'scoop' marks to elongated, thin cuts. According to Jacobs, 'these scars are permanent records of abduction experiences and can be anxiety-provoking reminders for the victim'.[1] Mysterious cut marks have been found on the skulls of certain Neanderthal fossils. These marks recur on bones from sites that were occupied at intervals thousands of years apart. Could these marks be a result of the scarring that can follow alien abduction? The marks are on the skull, indicating that if they were caused by alien experimentation then that experimentation involved the head area, and therefore the brain.

The word 'interception' has to be explained. There may have been essentially two types. The first involved the hijacking of the human genome. Either with the supplanting of human by alien genetic material, or with an alteration of the genome in such a way as to mutate it *in situ*, such that a whole biological change was derived. Biologists, of course, think that mutation is an accidental thing. No one actually causes it to happen. It is something that happens by sheer chance and a man was made out of a 'sea worm' by a series of these incredibly fortuitous mutations. They are unable, however, to account for the incredible fact that these so-called spontaneous lucky mutations based on sheer chance finally and conveniently produced an entity that could analyze and come to the preposterous conclusion that biologists come to about the whole thing in the first place.

The other way of interception was psychological command-interception through visions, dreams and what might be termed telepathic procedures.

Could it be that an interception of the second sort happened with the Judaic patriarch Abraham? If it did, I believe this was a psychological one and took the form of a vision or mental summons to leave his Dravidian roots in the north of India and come to the land of Canaan.

It is my contention that Abraham, and others like him, were probably the descendants of predominantly Neanderthal-derived lines whose genomes were, at that time, the least intercepted by extraterrestrial alien procurement. According to the *Book of Genesis*, Abraham was a direct descendant of Seth, the third son of Adam who was sent by God 'instead of Abel whom Cain slew'. Thus, if we understand *Genesis* in the symbolic context with which it is surely meant to be understood, the following clues can be derived:

After the 'fall' of Adam and Eve, Eve 'conceived' and gave birth to Cain and then to his brother Abel. These two brothers seem to represent two distinct lines of humanity that stem from Adam and

Eve in their newly 'fallen' state of capture within a physical universe. Abel was a 'keeper of sheep' while Cain was a 'tiller of the ground'. What could this symbolism mean? Could it perhaps refer to one type of man whose primary focus was upon living things and their welfare, 'keepers of sheep', and another type of man who was more concerned with the artefacts of the physical world, 'tillers of the ground'? The 'offerings' that the two brothers made to God may be symbols for their own intrinsic states of being that are implicitly 'offered' up to, or set against, the final omnipresent reference of Godhead.

Abel 'brought of the firstlings of his flock and the fat thereof. And the Lord had respect unto Abel and to his offering. But unto Cain and to his offering he had not respect. And Cain was very wrath and his countenance fell'. In this context it would seem that the 'respect' of God does not entail the personal liking of an anthropomorphic God for one offering more than another. Instead, the commanding of the 'respect' of God is something that is achieved through the implicit capacity of individual souls to allow God into them. Thus God did not have 'respect' for Cain's offering simply because he could not reach into Cain, or, shall we say, into 'Cain-ness' because Cain-ness in free will did not allow it. Cain's 'offering', his intrinsic state of being in other words, was disposed away from Godhead. For Abel, however, the implication is that his nature was truly selfless and generous, and his gift devoid of vanity and full of genuine self-sacrifice; he gave the best of what he had, 'the firstlings of his flock and the fat thereof'. Thus God could 'respect' his offering because it was an offering analogous with the spirit of God. Cain's reaction to God's rejection of his 'offering' ('he was very wrath and his countenance fell') suggests that the spirit of his offertory was one of self-centredness, the same spirit that eventually led him to kill his brother. He expected God's countenance in return for his gift, thus his was not an unconditional generosity full of self-sacrifice. So, to sum up, *Genesis* is perhaps identifying here two distinct types of humanity. One of which is, by nature, more akin to the spirit of God's unconditional love, while the other is more a prey to the physical forces that hold it bound in the Universe of Parts and is therefore more conditional and self-centred in its expression.

These two representative types are paralleled by the two

species-lines of man to which I have previously referred. One of these lines, the Neanderthal line, was able until relatively recently in the timescale of hominid devolution on this planet to maintain itself free from the capture of the physical universe. If you envision the devolution of souls from the original Adam point as a flowing stream, then the soul lines that eventually devolved into Neanderthal man are the relatively still waters before the stream starts to travel downhill to become a cascading waterfall. The soul lines that led to the *Homo Erectus* hominids had been carried into the waterfall at a much earlier date. The relatively quiet waters can be said to represent 'Abelness' while the turbulent waters of the waterfall can be said to represent 'Cainness'. Thus the story of Cain killing Abel might symbolize how the more devolved soul lines carry the less devolved lines further and further downhill until they too are dragged into the waterfall. All soul is implicitly connected in this way, so the only way to resist being pulled downhill would have been to swim the other way. Through this pull via the implicit connection of all souls to one another (symbolized by the fact that Cain and Abel were brothers), Cain 'killed' Abel, dragging Abelness into the same state of physical capture to which he, or 'Cainness', was subject. Thus Abelness was 'killed' in terms of a death from the state of eternal life which up to that point had been his mode of existence. Now we are all, as the species *Homo Sapiens*, in the waterfall, we no longer naturally have the freedom to return easily to the state of Godhead from which we came. Abelness and the freedom from physical capture that he represents no longer exists.

The third 'son', Seth, was perhaps a figurative stance or principle representing an amalgamation of both states. One that was more centred than either resolve. Seth was sent by God 'instead of Abel whom Cain slew'. Thus souls who are closer in their spirits to the spirit of God came, from that point on, into biological lines that no longer possessed an ease of access between the physical universe and the metaphysical universe. That ease of access died with Abel. Thus these souls had to make the best of whatever biological lines were still available to them, just as Jesus Christ had to do 2000 years ago. Abraham perhaps outlines the principle on which we all as a species would have to dwell under the yoke of physicality. It was thus for Abraham to multiply himself as numerously as the stars.

I believe that Abraham and those like him were Aryo-Dravidian in origin and came from India. It is their admixture with the Semitic peoples of the Middle East that provides the overall genetic backdrop for the Jewish and Islamic people today. The close genetic affiliation of Judeo/Islamic and Indian peoples has been confirmed by research into Y-chromosome haplotypes, which is discussed by A. Spurdle and T. Jenkins in a paper entitled: 'The Y chromosome as a tool for studying human evolution'.[2] It seems that while Europeans are distinctive because of a high frequency of Haplotypes 15 and 12, the situation is different for Asiatic and Jewish populations. Haplotypes 7, 8, 11 and 24 are most common in South African Asiatic Indian and Jewish populations, and in Ashkenazi and Sephardic Jews sampled in Israel and Tunisia. This research has thus identified a division within the Caucasoid group between Europeans on the one hand and Indian and Jewish populations on the other.

What, then, do we know of the Aryo-Dravidian community from which Abraham might have come?

The word 'Aryan' has been used as an adjective by the most heinous racist scoundrels to describe their supposedly superior stances. It is adopted as a banner for a super-race that somehow appeared from nowhere and bred the so-called Master Race of the 'Fatherland'. It is also supposed to have bred every self-proclaimed Master Race since time immemorial.

The best scholarship does confirm the existence of an Aryan people who lived in North India. These people were supposed to have a highly developed culture and to have spread this culture throughout the world. There is scholarly speculation that these people came from the steppes to the north and east of the Caspian Sea and moved from there into Asia and Iran, but these speculations, the scholars admit, are purely hypothetical. The Nazi scholars somehow contrived to claim the Aryans as a European people from whose root the Barbarian German came. They hijacked the Aryan symbol of the swastika, reversed its design and adopted it as the Nazi emblem. The swastika had long been known previously in India as a derivative holy symbol in Northern Indian culture.

It seems that there is only one thing that the scholars know for sure about the Aryan peoples and that is that their Indo-Aryan language spread through India during the late third and second millennia

BC. Attempts to view the Aryan peoples as a conquering tribe who established hegemony over the local population have failed, given the fact that it seems that only their language was passed on to the local peoples: there seems to be no distinctive material evidence of the presence of a conquering tribe. One hypothesis is that between about 2,500 and 2,000 BC a continuing spread of Indo-Aryan speakers occurred, carrying them much further into India, to the east and the south, and coinciding with a growing cultural interaction between the native population and the new arrivals. From these processes a new cultural synthesis emerged, giving rise by the end of the second millennium to the conscious expressions of Aryan ethnicity found in the *Rigveda*.

The *Rigveda* is the earliest literary record of Indian culture. This text and other Sanskrit texts that appeared later, such as the *Mahabarata* and the *Ramayana*, express the foundations of the Hindu religion, the earliest of all religions that point towards the possibility of existence beyond the realms of the atom. Might this suggest that the Aryo-Dravidian peoples were the first (after the alien genetic interceptions that helped to mould modern *Homo Sapiens* into his present form), to receive direct inspiration from natural Godhead – which is not of the atomic universe?

I believe that this is indeed the case and that Abraham, the 'Father' of the Jewish people, himself originated from these early Hindus. If Abraham was originally a Hindu who later 'fathered' the Judaic faith, then the fact that Jesus was a Jew who 'fathered' the Christian faith suggests a certain continuity and interconnectedness between all these main religious ethics, does it not? Buddhism, of course, grew out of the original Hindu belief system: Buddha was a Hindu. While Islam claims its origins from the line of Abraham's son Ishmael, thus it has roots in the Judaic context.

In the combination of the Aryo-Dravidian line with the Semitic line via Abraham and those like him, the least intercepted of the predominantly Neanderthal lines of humanity were brought together. It is from these lines that all the main religions of the world have come: Buddhism, Christianity, Islam, Judaism, Hinduism, Zoroastrianism all originally come from either India or the Middle East.

A further combination of these lines with the ancient Cushitic peoples of what is now modern-day Ethiopia brought together these Neanderthal-derived lines with those of the *Homo Erectus* African genotype. This combination resulted in the Falasha Jews, the Jewish people of Ethiopia. According to genetic research, Ethiopians in fact show a combination of typically African and typically Caucasian haplotypes in both the mitochondrial DNA and the Y-chromosome.

A paper entitled 'The Differences Among Jewish Communities – Maternal and Paternal Contributions' from the Department of Genetics at the Hebrew University of Jerusalem identifies the Ethiopian Jewish community as significantly different from all the other Jewish communities in terms of their Y-chromosome haplotypes.[3] Could this perhaps be evidence for the Ethiopian Falasha Jews belonging to the 'lost tribe' of Jewish mythology, a tribe of least alien genetic interception?

It seems that of all the predominantly Neanderthal-derived modern populations of the world whose brains were rewired by alien genetic interception, the Semitic Jews were the ones who became the most profound subjects of further alien interception. Their rewired brains could act either as better aerials to receive God or as better computers to translate alien-derived information more efficiently. There is no more startlingly apparent a documentation of an ongoing alien interception of a specific community than that which can be found in the Old Testament of the Bible.

I will begin to illustrate this with Abraham himself. As I have stated previously, Abraham's was an oral interception, not a genetic one. That would come later at the point at which Jacob, Abraham's grandson, 'wrestled' with an 'angel'. I will fully discuss this later in the chapter.

Abraham was asked by the 'Lord' to leave 'Ur of the Chaldees', a place in ancient Mesopotamia, for the land of Canaan. Ur of the Chaldees is not cited as Abraham's original home. It is only named as the 'land of nativity' for Haran, Abraham's youngest brother. A series of remarkable events follow Abraham's departure for Canaan. These events are remarkable only in the sense that natural Godhead is highly unlikely to have had anything whatsoever to do with them!

Let us take, for example, the destruction of Sodom and Gomorrah. It is written that 'the Lord rained upon Sodom and upon Gomorrah brimstone and fire from the Lord out of heaven' such that 'the smoke of the country went up as the smoke of a furnace'. Two 'angels' are said to have come to Lot, Abraham's brother, who lived in Sodom to take him away from the site of the coming destruction. These 'angels' claimed that the 'Lord' had sent them to 'destroy' this place. When Lot 'lingered', the two 'angels' took his hand and the hands of his wife and daughters and physically removed them from the city, telling them not to look behind them. Is it really conceivable that God would literally wipe out the population of two cities, using what appears to be some form of explosion, simply because they did not follow the principles that he had laid down for them? What purpose could such a revengeful act serve? Only the purpose of an alien 'God' made from atoms could be served by such an act. An act perhaps designed to wipe out a population that no longer served the purpose of providing a useful experimental 'bed' for alien interception and might hinder further experiments by intermixing with other people, i.e. Abraham and his extended family, who were still part of a live experiment.

Further evidence is found for the prompts of an extraterrestrial 'God' in an episode instigated by Abraham asking God how he can know that he will inherit the land of Canaan. God asks him to 'take me an heifer of three years old, a she-goat of three years old and a ram of three years old, and a turtledove, and a young pigeon'. He is then asked to divide the three animals into pieces and to lay 'each piece one against the other' but to leave the birds and not divide them. Abraham then falls into a 'deep sleep' in which 'an horror of great darkness fell upon him'. In his sleep God tells him that he should 'know of a surety' that his 'seed' shall be 'a stranger in a land that is not theirs, and shall serve them; and they shall afflict them'. It is then reported that 'after the sun went down, and it was dark, behold a smoking furnace, and a burning lamp that passed between' the 'pieces' of flesh that Abraham had laid out. Could alien beings have been using the souls of animals that were of a low enough resonance for them to grasp to reach a human soul that was far more difficult for them to gain access to? The 'burning lamp' that 'passed between' the pieces of flesh that would have held the bioelectric fingerprint of these animals' souls certainly sounds like some kind of laser probe through which they were reaching. Perhaps this was the original reason for animal sacrifice, a practice that was rife within the Old

Testament context. The blood released by such a sacrifice would, via the iron contained within it, provide a magnetic tape upon which alien beings could write and thus reach the human subjects who were their true targets. After the sacrifice the alien beings reveal to Abraham that he is to partake in an experiment in which his 'seed', his Aryo-Dravidian biological line, is to be introduced into a Semitic line that would be 'strange' to it.

Abraham is offered by this 'God' a promise that is purely terrestrial in its scope and in no way related to any spiritual progress beyond the context of atoms. He is told that his 'seed' will be numbered as many as the 'stars' and as many as 'the dust of the earth'. This is a promise that might flatter an egoist, but what significance could it possibly have to a man who was seeking grander perspectives than the atomic arena can provide? It is perhaps a promise that would entail the bestowing of the ultimate accolade that a cloned alien being could ever hope to receive: An assured replication of its own physical body into the foreseeable future!

The culmination of Abraham's concourse with this being that claims to be God lies in a request made of Abraham to take his son Isaac and offer him as a burnt offering up to 'God'. This episode is commonly believed to be an example of God testing Abraham's faith in him. For no sooner does Abraham lay the knife to Isaac's throat than an angel calls out to him from heaven and tells him not to touch Isaac. Would God, who is all-knowing, really need to 'test' a man in this way? Surely he would already implicitly know the extent of Abraham's faith. Never mind the ethical implications of such a test which to me suggests a God who has a callous disregard for human sensitivity in his single-minded purpose to gain the worship and attentiveness of his human subjects.

Let me put a proposition to you concerning this remarkable encounter: Could it have been the case that the alien 'God' asked Abraham for the life of his only son and that it was only the power of inspiration from natural Godhead that prevented Abraham from carrying out this request? Perhaps the alien God had found in Abraham a certain resistance, an implacability, to the effects which it sought to gain through him. Perhaps the reach of natural Godhead was too strong in Abraham to allow their power to work effectively. I am sure there are a number of human beings alive today whose psychoframes are so spiritually adorned they are near the point of Transfiguration. They are very few, but they are impervious to reach by any ET so-called 'Gods' and thus truly safe from detachment by any type of technology they possess. Jesus Christ certainly was such a phenomenon, as his resistance to the so-called temptations provided by the ETs proved. Perhaps Abraham's brain was enjoined by the power of Abraham's soul to receive the natural Godhead rather than the extraterrestrial alien God. Thus Abraham would have been slipping out of their grasp again. So, to allow them to reach him again, just as, in a far lesser way, animal sacrifice had done previously, they sought to communicate with Abraham via the most powerful means of all, the released soul and thus the blood of his own son Isaac. Remember, Abraham and those like him who had relatively unintercepted lines back to Godhead would have been the greatest prizes for the alien beings who were desperately searching for the least complicated and most profound track back to God for themselves. Perhaps the origins of human sacrifice in ancient rituals also have their roots in an alien God who demanded such horrific acts to further his purpose among men when they found that animal souls provided too many complex short falls and twisted turnings back to Godhead. That there were too many staged and disjointed connections to deal with.

The episode involving Abraham and Isaac has certain similarities with Jesus Christ's temptation in the desert of Judea. Like Abraham, Christ was aware of two sources of information. One of these sources was the 'devil' (who, as I will later explain, may well also be representative of extraterrestrial alien being), while the other source was his Father, natural Godhead. Like Abraham, Christ chose to follow the information he received from natural Godhead, not from the alien source. But, unlike Abraham, Christ did not for a single moment follow *any* of the instructions given to him by the 'devil'. This suggests that Christ might well have had a knowledge of what the alien beings were up to that Abraham did not have. Thus there was no confusion in Christ's mind as to which source was which. There is substantial evidence from Christ's own words as they have been quoted in certain texts, to show that he did indeed know all about alien beings and how to circumvent their intentions. It may well be that the whole intercession of the so-called 'Christ Phenomenon' was to do one thing and one thing only. Beat off the alien input into the derivations of living being with a soul in this Universe. In other words, for 'Satan' read 'Leader of the Clones'. For 'devils' read 'Greys'.

I will discuss this evidence later in the chapter entitled 'Affirmations'. For now, it is important to point out that the Old Testament may well be an amalgam of information received from both these sources and, if that is the case, it is for us all to judge what information comes from which source.

Now, on to Jacob and what may well have been a genetic interception of his resources. In Jacob, the alien beings might have had success where they had failed with Abraham and Isaac. In the Dead Sea Scrolls a fragment has been found of a text that supports the postulation that Jacob was the first point of successful and powerful alien interception into the Jewish line. The text is entitled 'The Ages Of The Creation'[4]: 'Interpretation concerning the ages made by God, all the ages for the accomplishment [of all the events, past] and future. Before ever he created them. He determined the works of . . . age by age. And it was engraved on heavenly tablets . . . the ages of their domination. This is the order of the creation of man from Noah to Abraham until he begot Isaac . . . 'And the interpretation concerns Azazel and the angels 'who came to the daughters of men and they bore to them giants . . . and iniquity, and to cause them all to inherit wickedness . . . judgement and judgement of the congregation'.

So the 'ages made by God' in the 'order of creation of man' are somehow interrupted after Isaac – 'until he begot Isaac'. At that point the text refers to the 'angels who came to the daughters of men' and caused them (the daughters) to 'inherit wickedness'. What clearer description could one have of an alien interception? A phenomenon which might have occurred to the offspring of Isaac, who is Jacob. Thus the line of God lasts 'until Isaac'. Jacob's own nature as depicted in the Bible, which is one of deceit and connivance (he stole his brother's birthright), supports this hypothesis in indicating that he was 'interceptible' by 'wickedness' because he himself had qualities that could be described as wicked. Perhaps the 'two nations' that God told Rebecca (Jacob's mother) were 'struggling' in her womb point to Rebecca's own interception while she was pregnant by these 'angels' who came into the 'daughters of men': 'Two nations are in thy womb and two manner of people shall be separated from thy bowels; and the one people shall be stronger than the other people and the elder shall serve the younger'. Jacob is the younger son and Esau the elder.

At a later point Jacob is said to have 'wrestled' with a 'man' who 'when he saw that he prevailed not against him touched the hollow of his thigh'. It is proximal to the 'hollow of the thigh' that the storehouse of genetic information, the testicles, lies. I believe that this is a report of an alien abduction experience involving the reproductive areas of the body. The man tells Jacob that 'thy name shall be called no more Jacob, but Israel: for as a prince hast thou power with God and with men and has prevailed'. Could it be that Jacob thus provided the alien beings with a bridge into the Jewish line, he was the Father of *their* 'chosen people' who are the children of Israel. A chosen people whom they later sought to claim back via Moses.

Judaic folklore proclaims that the Jews are a 'Chosen People'. A people chosen by 'God'. Could it be that in a way this might well be true? The real question that then arises is, what God?

If the Greys were the 'God' of Israel duping a people to believe that they were true divinity in the Godhead sense, then a look at what happened on Mount Sinai would imply a technologically explainable revelation process. Thus the burning bush might have happened when, perhaps, a laser used to transmit sound (we can do it now with our present technology in this way) had a side effect of setting a bush on fire while the revelation process was going on. The request that Moses take his footwear off, because the ground on which he stood was 'holy', could have implied perhaps that his whole body needed to be used by some vibrational methodology that would in turn allow him to discern and know what the 'voice' of God was saying. It may have been that Moses was in fact irradiated during this process and he thus could not make it to the Promised Land. The column of fire that followed the Israelites out of the land of Egypt might have been a technological effect that allowed 'God' to monitor their progress. The Israelites are said to have wandered for forty years in the wilderness after 'God' revealed their destiny to them. Would not a simple route map have helped as part of the Ten Commandments in speeding up their progress through the peninsula of Sinai? Forty years seems a long time to walk three hundred miles, unless something far more significant was going on. Could it be that the strain of humanoid was being genetically altered and it took forty years (perhaps two generations) to see the results through two lots of progeny, the father's children and the children's children?

There is significant reference throughout the account of the exodus of the Jews from Egypt to suggest that their saviour from bondage did indeed originate from a spaceship. Not least in this catalogue of evidence is a remarkable account of an encounter between God and Moses's son. The lead-up to this encounter begins when God informs Moses that if he does not go to Egypt and free his firstborn (those being the 'children of Israel') then God will slay Moses's firstborn, his son. Unbelievable though it might seem were this a God equivalent in moral stature even to a decent human being, let alone a divine morality that would be beyond reproach, God then seeks to 'slay' Moses's son:

'And it came to pass by the way in the inn that the Lord met him and sought to kill him.

Then Zipporah took a sharp stone and cut off the foreskin of her son and cast it at his feet and said, surely a bloody husband thou art because of the circumcision.' (Exodus 5:24-26).

Zipporah, Moses's wife, offers God the foreskin of her son, and thus information as to his genetic structure, in place of her son's life. With that genetic map 'God' would have all the information necessary to successfully intercept Moses's line with all the information that was required to provide for them a leader of their 'chosen people' who would accurately follow all that they wanted him to do. When Zipporah offers the foreskin 'God' lets her son go. Can it be possible that such a ludicrous course of action by a supposed 'God' could have been deemed acceptable and worthy by so many people for so long? If the 'God' to which this account refers is not an alien Clone-being seeking genetic programmes to intercept humanity, then what is he? Indeed, could it actually be the case that the initial command for the children of Israel to circumcise their sons could have been a means for alien beings to monitor the genetic information of their 'chosen people'? In other words, maybe the foreskins were taken by these beings and studied. The fact that this remarkable story about

Moses and so many other incongruities within the Old Testament can have been meekly accepted by so many people for so long is surely an indication of the vast extent to which the Greys have succeeded in so programming their chosen subjects that they are blind to even the simplest logical connections that would expose their programmers for what they truly are.

In the Old Testament's so-called 'Pseudepigraphal' texts, there is an appendix to the third book of Enoch in which there is a passage entitled 'the Ascension of Moses'.[5] This 'ascension' is very similar to how one might imagine an ascension into a spacecraft would be. He ascends into a 'chariot' in which he meets a being named Metatron who offers him anything he wishes to ask for. This is, of course, reminiscent of Jesus's temptations in the desert. Metatron is also known as 'little Adonai' (the little Lord or God), thus he is viewed as a supernatural entity who is a smaller version of the true God, not as a false God. Apparently, in some of the later 'mystical midrashim' texts, the 'angel' who 'wrestled' with Jacob is taken to be Metatron.

If the Ark of the Covenant itself was a mechanism to receive instructions from a spaceship then there are significant pointers to suggest that that is true. Strict instructions are given as to the clothing of the high priest who is in charge of the Ark. These include the weaving of gold wires into his cloak: 'And they did beat the gold into thin plates, and cut it into wires to work it into the blue and in the purple . . . and in the fine linen, with cunning work.'[6] Gold is an excellent conductor of electricity and it is through electromagnetic waves that radio receivers work. In the book of Leviticus instructions are given as to who may, or may not, approach the altar. No one of any physical blemish is permitted to approach the altar, so that they will 'profane not my sanctuaries: for I the lord do sanctify them'.[7] Is this not compelling evidence that the Ark of the Covenant and the altar within it were in fact used as mechanisms through which alien beings could view human subjects who might be suitable for interception? Hence only those without physical defect and therefore with the likelihood of a genetic structure more free of the mutations that lead to physical weakness or infirmity were allowed to approach the altar.

The prophet Ezekiel's visions have by many people been taken to be visions or sightings of spacecraft:

If Ezekiel was also visited by alien beings it would certainly account for his strange encounter with 'God' in a valley that was full of bones.[8] God asks Ezekiel if these dry bones could live. He then assembles them into complete bodies and covers them with flesh. After he brings them to life they stand 'up upon their feet, an exceeding great army'. God then tells Ezekiel that these bones are 'the Whole house of Israel' and he tells him to promise the people of Israel that 'I will open your graves, and cause you to come up out of your graves, and bring you into the land of Israel . . . And shall put my spirit in you and ye shall live and I shall place you in your own land'.

'God' is thus involved in bringing to life soulless dead flesh. What kind of 'life' is he therefore promising for the children of Israel – the physical immortality of Clone being, perhaps? How reminiscent this is of the Egyptian process of mummification, a process that ancient Egyptians believed essential to preserve the physical body for the after-life. The Semitic peoples truly seem to be receivers of the same 'god'.

God then asks Ezekiel to take two sticks and write upon one 'For Judah and the children of Israel and his companions' and upon the other 'For Joseph, the stick of Ephraim, and for all the house of Israel and his companions.' He is then asked to join the sticks together and 'they shall become one in thine hand.' The fact that 'God', immediately after demonstrating to Ezekiel what is apparently a cloning process, then asks him to combine two 'sticks' representing two different tribes of people suggests to my mind that it is in fact genetic engineering that is being described here.

There was a certain sect of Jewish mystics that existed in the first century AD and then again from the seventh to eleventh centuries that concerned itself with visions of the 'moving chariot' called the 'Merkava'. These visions originated with the prophet Ezekiel who claimed to have seen a divine 'throne' or 'chariot'. This sect described themselves as 'explorers of the supernatural world' or 'Yorde Merkava'. A few documents have been preserved that attest to the existence of methods and practices having to do with the initiation of carefully chosen persons who were made to undergo tests and ordeals in order to 'ascend' through the seven heavenly 'dwellings' to behold the divine throne situated on its 'chariot'. The Talmud, the Jewish Book of Law, reports an incident in which, among four men engaging in Merkava, one died and one went mad. Thus the ascent into what certainly seem to be spaceships was common practice among this ancient Jewish sect.

Orthodox Jews today follow a certain practice prescribed by Mosaic law called 'laying the tefillin'. That practice is a result of the command to 'bind' the words of the 'law' of God 'for a sign upon thine hand and they shall be for frontlets between thine eyes'. Thus a box with four distinct compartments is laid upon the forehead and strapped there with a long strap that is tied behind the head while the length of it that remains is wrapped around the arm and the middle finger of the left hand. In that hand lies the hand tefillah, a box with a single compartment. In these two boxes parchment on which is written the law of God is placed. Is it possible that this practice originally involved electrical devices strapped by wires to the head and the hand, by which the alien beings maintained communication with their human subjects? Two boxes, one with four compartments, one with a single compartment, perhaps containing microelectronic parts that could store information such as the 'law' of 'God'. Were these boxes joined to each other by wires and strapped to the human body's naturally bioelectric aerial? Perhaps this actual device was later imitated in the form in which it is seen today, just as in Catholicism the communion wafer represents the body of Christ given by him to his apostles in the form of bread.

In October 1988 Paul Shartle, an audiovisual director who witnessed films at Norton Air Force Base in California of a UFO that had actually landed, described the three beings that emerged from the UFO as having 'thin head dresses that appeared to be communication devices' while 'in their hands they held a translator'. Are these devices examples of the same equipment that the Jewish people might once have witnessed and later mimicked in the form of tefillin?

If the original commandment was simply to bind the words of 'God' upon the hand and the forehead, then perhaps it can be inferred that the 'mark' given by the 'Beast' (referred to in the Book of Revelations) which is received 'in their right hand or in their foreheads' is in fact a part of the same process as the 'marking' of the Jewish people at the time of Moses. It (the Beast) may have its latter-day equivalent in what the German Nazis did to the Jews during the Second World War. I am not, of course, suggesting that this is a direct equivalent, for it would have been the Nazis themselves, not the Jews whom they persecuted, who would have qualified for that 'mark'. But the marking process may instead have been an acted-out memory of past interceptions, an anachronism reawakened maybe by the alien intentions that may indeed have driven the Nazi ethos.

The worship of the God Yahweh, the God of Israel, did not begin, scholars now believe, until the time of Moses. Various other epithets for God were used before that time and this has been taken by scholars as an indication that patriarchal religion (that is, the religion of the patriarchs Abraham, Isaac and Jacob) differed from the worship of Yahweh that began with Moses. They have found more evidence for this conclusion in the fact that distinctive features of post-Mosaic religion are absent in the God of the patriarchs. The God of the patriarchs shows nothing of Yahweh's 'jealousy'; no religious tension or contrast with their neighbours appears, and idolatry is scarcely an issue. He also provides his people with no obligations to fulfil as a condition of their happiness, unlike the Mosaic God who makes such demands upon his people continually.

God, apparently, was originally the personal tutelary deity of each of the patriarchs, called by a variety of names and later unified into the one God of Abraham, Isaac and Jacob, but only in hindsight. The hindsight of Jewish tradition that identifies Yahweh as the Creator of the world, who had been known to and worshipped by men from the beginning of time. It seems instead to be the case that the three 'patriarchs' may have each been communicating with different sources of inspiration, different Gods. Then later an amalgam was made of all these sources and identified as the 'God of Israel'.

The key to it all lies in an answer to the question: Who or what was the God of Israel of common Mosaic institution? The Old Testament is a catalogue of a God who seems more like a Lord of the Manor. Not an entity that dispensed volumes of warmth and love and encouragement to bring together, to bind, to add the whole aegis of Mankind, not a tiny part of it that exclusively belonged to this so-called God. In a quote from the Good Book this God admits to being a jealous God. Strategies and ploys designed to kill men, women and children in a register of caring for his own people at the cost of others are evocatively straight out of the epithets of finite reasoning. Not the reasoning of an eternal entity with the grand scale of All Knowing. It smacks of the psychology of the average medieval robber baron. Or the cold-blooded expedient dispassionate objective of a mechanistic intelligence such as a Grey. It is a statement seemingly full of vanity, avarice, greed and vengeance. It also has a hint of the binary system that says, 'either – or'. An eye for an eye and a tooth for a tooth. The straight mathematical logic of a computer program. With no room for shades of grey. (No pun intended.) No hint of compassion. It is a massive catalogue of reactionary response in threat and counter-threat.

There is something totally illogical underlying this Old Testament God's so-called rational outlook too if he claims to be a jealous God. It suggests something of huge import missing in his or her psychology, such as subtlety. That implies a God of very limited program. A boundary that makes this Divine One a little restricted in size. It is ultimately foolish to reveal you are a jealous God because it betrays qualities of loveless shepherding too. Not very good if you want the best-quality followers. It is at best a good management ethos for favourites and courtiers and suggests a massive inferiority complex. This God is a tester of loyalty and faith under the auspices of threatened murder, as described in the story of Abraham and Isaac. A duplicitous divinity acquiescing in deceit and theft in the stealing of Essau's birthright. It all describes a megalomaniac of a God with an all-consuming vanity and a love of dissimulation and subterfuge to affect his will.

Whatever or whoever the God of Israel was there can be no doubt that this deity could not be regarded as one of all-encompassing love. Again it begs the question: If there is no love, could there be such a phenomenon as God?

If this so-called 'God' was responsible for the original 'rewiring' of the brains of some Neanderthals, then this interception gave us a glory and a curse. It provided an enhanced 'aerial' for receiving both natural Godhead and the Clone-God. Within these two reference scales and the inability to distinguish which is which lies the entire predicament of one of the true Master Races of our species – the Jews.

The glory of the Jews is the crowning glory of Man. Never have so few given so much to so many as the Jews have given to and are giving to Mankind. In all fields of endeavour – Art, Music, Science, Literature, Philosophy, Entertainment, Economics and Political Science – the illustrious Jewish contribution is prodigious and singularly effective for the good of Man.

Perhaps this is why the Cro-Magnon Nazis, the true Children of Cain to my mind, tried so hard to take these precious people from us. Who would want to inspire the Nazis to do this? If you get my drift!

According to some accounts Hitler believed that he had seen a member of a super-race that he believed to originate from the inner Earth. He reportedly told Hermann Rauschning, the Nazi governor of Danzig: 'The new man is living amongst us now! He is here! . . . I will tell you a secret. I have seen the new man. He is intrepid and cruel. I was afraid of him'.[9] Could this 'new man', whom Hitler personally met, have originated not from the 'inner Earth' but instead from an alien craft? There are many reports from people who have experienced contact with a certain type of alien being that is distinct from the Greys in that it is apparently humanoid and has blond hair and blue eyes. Could the 'super-race' that Hitler and his cohorts were looking for have been representatives such as these? Remember his ideal was a blond, blue-eyed people. If, as I have claimed, the Jewish people through Abraham have roots in Northern India it is perhaps more than a coincidence that Hitler, who sought to wipe them out, believed that his alien 'super-race', his 'Aryans', came from that very same place, the Himalayas. It is almost as though the alien beings who seem to have paid him a personal visit were announcing to him a recipe for a type of humanity that was the exact opposite of the types of humanity who have retained their close connection to Godhead. This opposite, this mirror image, took the form of a Cro-Magnon 'super-race', a race that was in its 'ideal' presented to Hitler as 'intrepid and cruel'. I believe the Holocaust was a contrivance to try to ethnically cleanse the world of its 'saviour genophylum'. Jews and Gypsies, both of which are races of North Indian, Aryan descent were subject to the genocide and Hitler and his henchmen gave us a clue to it all with their prodigious obsession with the so-called Occult.

The dictionary definition of the word 'occult' is that which is mystical, supernatural, hidden, secret or shut off from view. Elite Nazi groups spent hours within the confines of a series of rock structures and caves at a place called Externstein in Germany because they thought they could derive and receive supernatural inspiration and powers there. Many latter-day Germans and, indeed, people from all over the world make a pilgrimage to this place to this day. Some in curiosity and some in search of the same juice the Nazis were looking for. There is an associated story and, I stress, a story because I have no particular hard evidence for it.

The story goes that the spear that pierced the side of Christ's body was located by the Germans and taken to a cave room there. Hitler's mob of followers were said to have gathered at the location, touched the spear which was said to have had occult powers, and from it received the inspiration for the 'Final Solution'. It is speculated that the spear, which of course was made of iron, might have acted as a kind of recording device, similar to a tape recorder. It is said to have held the emotions of Christ at the time of his crucifixion and thus a quantum of all the injustice and terror of the whole event as it struck the Christian redeemer was catalogued on it. The human bodies of the Nazis were then said to have acted as transducers similar to the one on a magnetic tape recorder and picked up all of this. A tape-recorder, after all, records information electronically on a ferrous (iron) tape medium that is later translated into a signal by a mechanism that can read this signal again electronically and make sense of it all as a coherent sound. The human body really is a biological transducer of sorts. It has a moving coil (the haemoglobin in the blood moving in circulation induces a current that produces the bio-electrical field of the body). The bones of the fingers are piezoelectric with their calcium phosphate content and may well act as a transducing mechanism, allowing the brain to sort the signals into some sort of coherent image that the mind perceives with meaning.

Just take a close look at the human skeleton. What finer aerial configuration of elements could you find in its design? (See Figures 14, 15 in the illustrated section.) It is the finest electron-dense phased loop array. The human body, as I have said, is an excellent receiver of electromagnetic signals. I am convinced that it is much more than this. It may well be a device for transmitting and receiving the radio wavelength equivalent of the 'pre' electromagnetic spectrum. In other words, 'Thought' itself. I believe each individual has a unique carrier-wave pattern to which are added signals according to intention, action and result. The aerial is flexible and movement of the joints provides various alignments that channel the signal and thereby alter the efficiency of transmission and reception. (See Figs. 14, 15 in the illustrated section.) It may be that the instinct to pray in a certain posture is, in fact, a means of phasing the aerial to pick up the 'God' signal maximally.

Whatever the rights and wrongs of the theory, Psychometry, which is a so-called fringe science, is now an accepted procedure by some police forces around the world, in the solution of difficult cases. The idea is that the adept or psychic is given a clue to the required information through some artefact connected with the crime. The psychic then handles the object and is able to picture clues connected with the transgression in the mind's eye, so to speak. There have been some spectacular successes using this technique of 'remote viewing', so much so that police forces around the world have endorsed the whole procedure with testimonials as to its usefulness.

To get back to the 'Spear Of Longinus', as it was called, the hypothesis is that it might have prompted the 'Holocaust' with some psychometric procedure.

There is only one thing wrong with that idea and that is not the mechanism of reception but what exactly might have been received. Jesus was a Jew. His dying exhortation to his 'Father' was a plea to 'forgive' them and all others complicit in his death for the ignorance shown in what they did. His love for his and all other people continued to his dying breath. If anything was 'picked up' at the point that the spear entered his flesh, it would not have been those qualities that inspired killing as a final solution. It would have been the power of LOVE and not hate and exclusion as was and is the total creed of Nazis then and now.

CHAPTER SEVENTEEN:
SHADES OF GREY

If there is no Love, could there be God? It reveals most of all that we might, most of us, be the children of this God because we too in our record as so-called intelligent beings show one thing above all things. *We are the most prodigious fools for not spotting the subterfuge long ago.* A subterfuge that was hinted at by our most beautiful sages through history. Glories such as the Hindu sages of old, Gautama Buddha, Jesus Christ, Mohammed and the Essenes of Judea, to name some of the most important. The overwhelming thrust of their message to Mankind was that there was something terribly wrong with our aegis as a species. Something we had to change or lose that most precious thing of all: Dominion over our status as thinking, reasoning, choice-capable platforms of being. That we could change our situation of limit in this Universe of Parts if only we would *add* and not *divide* at every signpost that allowed us to make a choice. They revealed the awesome deadliness of our predicament in being trapped in an enforced Universe of Parts and showed us a way out of it. A way, alas, most of us choose not to take. Perhaps we now know a very good reason why. And I believe herein lies the clue to the whole 'Flying Saucer' paradigm.

If this is true, what a chilling prospect we all face as a species. It begs the question: Is Racism the social-propulsion paradigm through which this is all achieved? Could it be that the descendants of Cro-Magnon Man, the White Occidental Europiform genus of man that is said to have mysteriously originated in Eastern Europe, have through the centuries been the 'Agent Provocateurs' of the behests of the Clones and Greys in their quest? History proves that the Cro-Magnons, unlike all other anthropological derivations of Mankind, from their very inception set about all other root-stocks of the species, to kill, to steal, to possess, to destroy with their living systems that were the inception paradigm of 'list file' mindedness. No other racial type has been such a killer and destroyer of other peoples' living systems in the known history of our planet. I believe it is very likely that the Cro-Magnons were judged to be the most suitable genetically-intercepted species for the alien cause after millions of years of experimentation. They were mentally programmed to clean out the 'Earth laboratory' of the 'unsuitable' products of a huge genetic experiment run by extraterrestrial beings. They thus set about wiping out the Neanderthal derivative as unsuitable or surplus to requirements about 40,000 years ago, and continued this holocaust through an ancient racially-set memory of yestertime through their descendants in Europe during the last world war. It is too facile to think that the Jews were picked on as victims by the Nazis *solely* because they were better businessmen.

This poses the question: Is the ethic of the Master Race as espoused by the Nazis and, it mustn't be forgotten, endorsed by the vast majority of German people prior to and during the war, an example of this? It is also an implicit ethic carried through by all the colonizing powers of Europe through the centuries through calculated racialistically-motivated pogrom after pogrom. Was the whole enslavement and attempted destruction of our father race, the African group (which continues to this day) a formula programmed into the psyche of the Europiform people of the Occidental world as a means to help alien *robot beings* carry out their unfinished business of wiping out the leftovers of an ancient racial experiment and thus leave the breed they want to use to piggy-back their way to a Soul? With ultimate irony, the unsuspecting Cro-Magnon ancestral line of humanity might well provide, with their bodies, the food, clothing and shelter for synthetic alien Master Beings that are about to make an overt appearance on the Earth in the near future.

There can be no doubt that the most racially obsessed and colour-prejudiced people in the world as a group have always been, and are today, white-skinned. In secret corners all over the USA, Europe, Australia, Canada, South Africa, New Zealand, deadly groups are forming even now, using the name, in the deepest irony, of the least racist (brown) human that ever lived – Christ – to muster their lethal conspiracies based on so-called racial purity. Their anthem is the preservation of the most debauched breed of 'humanity' the Earth has ever known. Their record of degenerate murder and mayhem among the peoples of the non-white world through the last two thousand years alone raises seriously the question whether they are, in fact, truly wholly 'human'.

The historical record implies that, broadly speaking, the people living above the Tropic of Cancer might well be genetic derivatives of a hybrid breed of pseudo-androids (taking their ancestry from the Cro-Magnons): the true unsuspecting children of Cain and thus the Damned. After all there can be no doubt that it is the Occident's machine-minded list-filing servants of technology that have polluted and laid waste an entire planet. The evidence for this is overwhelming when seen in terms of the scale of natural destruction, carnage and havoc caused by the descendants of the Cro-Magnons through the centuries in these endless processions of war, genocidal pogroms, enslavement and colonialization, etc. Far from being the superior species everyone is supposed to take them for, they may indeed be a genetically inferior assortment of misappropriated hybrids not too far removed from their list-filing, machine-minded, probable pseudo-parents, the extra-terrestrial Clones of Roswell fame.

Their Big Daddy could well fit the bill as a 'God' of vengeance, with a computer-like machine logic of 'An Eye For An Eye And A Tooth For A Tooth'. A 'God' that separates, divides and doesn't add. A God of psychogeometry as represented by the theocracy of the Egyptians, Greeks, and Romans. If ever evidence were needed of a God or Gods of Clones, the myths of the ancient Greeks and Romans and the story of the Egyptian Gods Isis and Osiris are a spectacular testament of this.

Osiris was the eldest son of Nut, the sky goddess, her other children being Isis, Seth, Nephthys and possibly Anubis. Osiris, a man as well as a god, became the first king of Egypt, and his sister Isis became his consort. He was a good king and established the rule of law and taught men religion and the arts of civilization. Egypt became prosperous and was at peace with itself. Unfortunately, not everyone was happy – especially Osiris's brother Seth. He plotted against Osiris, murdered him and cut up his body into small pieces, which he scattered all over Egypt. Isis was still childless when this happened and Osiris had no heir to take his place. All was not lost, however, for Isis secretly gathered up the pieces of her husband's body and, by means of her magical powers, reconstituted them into the body of Osiris, thus making the first ever mummy. Having brought him back to life, she was now able to have sex with him. Although this was only a temporary reprieve for Osiris, it was long enough for Isis to become pregnant with his seed. His task on Earth having been completed, Osiris transfigured himself into a star-being and went on to rule the Heavenly Kingdom of the Dead – called the Duat. Isis gave birth to a son called Horus who eventually, after a duel with Seth, was proclaimed king, the first in line of the pharaohs.

Isis and Osiris are thus the children of the 'sky goddess'. Might this title refer to a god-like being who came from the sky in a spaceship? This possibility is heavily supported by the story of how Isis used her 'magical powers' to reconstitute the pieces of Osiris back into a complete body again. That is one of the clearest and most obvious descriptions of a process of clonic regeneration that I have come across so far. The tragic story of Osiris and the heroic struggle of Horus to regain the throne served as a model throughout Egyptian history. The pharaohs legitimised their authority and deified their rule by proclaiming themselves reincarnations of Horus. When a Horus-king died he was assured a rebirth with Osiris in the afterworld of the Duat. If Isis and Osiris have their origins in alien cloned life then this Heavenly Kingdom of the Dead, the Duat, is likely to be the place in which such extraterrestrial life operates. The procedure of mummification, to which the reconstituted Osiris was, according to the story, the first to be subject, itself suggests an extraterrestrial directive. To help the dead reach the celestial afterworld it was deemed important to preserve the body of the deceased as far as possible. Preserved, perhaps, so that future cloning could take place. This would have enabled the deceased to attain to the physical immortality of clonic regeneration in the 'Duat', the Heavenly Kingdom of the Dead. Thus the tombs of the pharaohs, housed in the pyramids, were built to last forever and were referred to as 'castles of eternity' for the dead kings.

The Dogon tribe who live in Mali in western Africa were, in antiquity, almost certainly neighbours of the Egyptians. They lived in North Africa on the shores of the Mediterranean. This tribe, which numbers some two million people, has a complex mythology built around the belief that, at some time in the distant past, amphibian beings called 'Nommo' visited the Earth with the purpose of civilizing it. The Dogon revere the Nommo who, they say, come from the star system Sirius, the brightest in the sky. They make sand drawings to show that Sirius has two companion stars. One is small and extremely dense while the other is said to be four times lighter in weight, and to have a nearly circular orbit. It is from the planet attached to this latter star that the Nommo are believed by the Dogon to have descended.

A book entitled *The Sirius Mystery*, written by Robert Temple, discusses the research of two French anthropologists, Griaule and Dieterlen, who had studied the Dogon tribe. Temple was baffled as to how the Dogon could have known of the existence of Sirius B, given that it is barely visible even when using a very powerful telescope. (It was only in 1970 that the first photograph of Sirius B was obtained with great difficulty by the astronomer Lindenblad.) Most people today remain ignorant of Sirius B, so how could the Dogon have had accurate information concerning this star in the 1930s? A further mystery was how the Dogon seemed to have kept physical records relating to this star in the form of cult masks, some of which were centuries old and stored in caves. Temple dismissed theories that the Dogon's knowledge of Sirius B was derived from their contact with people who came from France with the following retort: 'The two French anthropologists started their work in 1931, and they are positive that the Dogon knew details about Sirius B when they arrived. Eddington revealed the superdensity of Sirius B around 1926. So, there is a narrow period when one has to imagine some group of amateur Western astronomers rushing out to Mali and implanting this knowledge in the presumably pliant minds of the Dogon'. Temple is supported by Germaine Dieterlen who lived with the Dogon for more than three decades. Any suggestion that the astronomical knowledge was of recent origin was, she said, absurd. The cult masks that were centuries old and held physical records relating to this star certainly confirm that any speculations that Dogon knowledge of Sirius B derived from modern astronomers are false.

Temple concluded that as this knowledge clearly had not come from modern astronomers it must have originated from ancestral sources and had probably been passed down to the Dogon before they migrated to their present home in Mali. In Egypt, in ancient times, Sirius was considered the most important star in the sky and was identified with the Egyptians' favourite goddess, Isis. Thus Temple's initial study of the article by the French anthropologists had led him via an obscure African tribe to Ancient Egypt. He wrote: 'I have been able to show that the information which the Dogon possess is really more than five thousand years old and was possessed by the Ancient Egyptians in the pre-dynastic times before 3200 BC'.[1]

Thus the Dogon people and their extraordinary knowledge provide substantial evidence that visits from the stars by alien beings did indeed take place in Ancient Egypt and its environs. The Dogons, and perhaps other groups of people who witnessed these visitations, migrated to other parts of Africa retaining their memory of these encounters and then passed that memory down to future generations.

The Gods of these so-called civilizations and religio-ethnic groups were certainly no 'Gods' of Love, at least when viewed from the perspective of 'his' or 'their' public works and record, as I have said previously in regard to the 'God of Israel'. A God of Love could never condone murder on a grand scale at the behest of tribal favourites, no matter what. True divine Godhead would cede the ultimate paradigm that gives eternal life in its highest aspects through enjoinment, and the binding of parts to a whole. Such a Being would know, cherish and maintain the sanctity of life on any condition. The example of true Godhead was there to be seen all the time through the lives and examples of representatives of *true* godly being as represented by Gautama Buddha, the Essenes, some of the Prophets of Judaism, the pure unadulterated words and meanings of Christ and the Prophet Mohammed (before the self-interested translators and interpreters got to work on them), the beautiful tenets of Zarathustra, the Masters of the Hindus, the Jains, the Sikhs and the Confucian and Tibetan philosophies and theosophies. Their solicitations to bring our hearts together in the focus of our common identity has been increasingly seen as prissy, silly sentiment by more and more people in power particularly in the occidental world. Is it any surprise that the hard, muscular self-centred forceful stances are lauded far more in the industrially developed Cro-Magnon world, and those who are gentle and care for and advocate peace, compassion and harmonious understanding with each other are increasingly seen dismissively as soft, sissy, do-gooding fools? Those with power to control our lives and destinies do so with the stern statutes of the cold, cruel list-filing mind, where the system is everything and the means of exchange is all. Power to control is the rub.

We have built our mastery of the Earth on being better than our competitors for food, clothing and shelter in the animal kingdom. Can we even contemplate what might happen to *us* if something far more intelligent than our species took over the reins? There are some very distinguished scientists who think that we humans could be obsolete within the next half-century if we continue the present rate of progress in computer development. We tower over the Earth, bigger than giants are to an ant. Our capacity to control and command the environment has made us wretchedly cruel masters to those who are less intelligent than us. If the extent of our difference in intellectual capability is so awesome when set against an ant or even an elephant, and this has allowed us to be such cruel and debauched custodians of power, what do you think an intelligence that towers over ours will do to us? When *we* can blow into oblivion ten thousand ants at the touch of a spray nozzle, do we really expect an alien intelligence of that kind of proportion in superiority to us to be benign and kind?

The physical Universe of Parts is a deadly engine of doom. It is a lethal conglomerate of force that has given rise to fabulous boiling vats of plasma, gas, acid, lava in the vast majority of orbs in space we call stars and planets. It is a Hades of hard masses and parts that cut, squeeze, mash and smash all softness out of the way. If it is of atoms and thus *force* it will act as such: Forcibly. I do not believe it is too simplistic to state it this way. All history has proved this in the affairs of men beyond any shadow of a doubt. The strong will always make victims of the weak and the stronger they are the less they notice.

'Patriotism is the last refuge of the scoundrel'. In these words Dr Johnson identified explosively the least noticeable and most deadly plague infesting the halls of humankind to the total detriment of our children's futures. They come in all races, colours and creeds. They are tub-thumpers or the most mild and benign of men. There is no external 'litmus paper' that can identify them, alas. They lurk in every household. They may be your brother, sister, uncle, aunt, father, mother, cousin, friend.

History has shown all too clearly that there are plenty of minds such as this, centred and synthesized among the limited basic ones among us that provide for the social disenfranchisement of the family of man. They are relatively few in number, when compared to the entire population of humanity, but massively powerful in effect, because their personalities are honed in divisive, aggressive reactivity. The very primitive underbase of the tribal perspective that once protected us from sabre-toothed tigers and representatives of their own genotypes across tribal lines. In a later chapter I try to show through the work of Dr Paul Maclean of the Laboratory of Brain Evolution at Poolesville, Maryland, that these individuals may be victims of the over-activity of a part of the brain called the R Complex that mimics the behaviour of reptiles in terms of the aggressive way they defend their territory. It is these 'hypothalamic' postulants who have singularly despoiled the vision of grandeur required to motivate Mankind into the Spirit sense that marks us as our brother's keeper, with their translation through history of the Godhead as nothing more than a sky-elevated Divine 'Lord' of the Manor, or tribal chief.

It is through their leadership and their influence on the social systems of humanity that the primary physical force of atomically based entropy divides and makes chaotic the prior orderliness of Spirit derivation. They are the agents of entropy in the metaphysically Spirit-borne 'mind' of men, and we never spot them as such until its too late. Till they have done their deadly work on thrones, in the army barracks, the boardroom, the political platform, or indeed the pulpit. They are the poorest in spirit of our glorious species and thus the most powerful purveyors of Armageddon imaginable, because they all too often deal, secretly, purely in the physical material investitures that have come to mean so much to men through the centuries.

The history of Man is a catalogue of constantly recurring pretexts for the most heinous behaviour towards one another, led by these so-called nationalists and patriots. The self-appointed guardians of the 'tribal' way. They are the prime instigators of war after war, conflict after conflict, that marks us seemingly as the most vicious and evil species on the face of the planet. We have the most far-reaching capacity for the control of agencies of threat as no other species does and yet we go about hitting each other on the head, claiming that we are the children of kindness and goodly things. It is a contradiction in terms that can only be defended by baboons. An awesome paradigm that marks the strictly reactionary fang-and-claw law of the jungle as decent by comparison. How can such a thing be when, in immediate contrast to this, we see a human mother's expression of endearment provide the finest contradiction to this archetype throughout the life of her offspring? Is it all just in defence of the gene? It cannot be, since our period of caring for our offspring generally extends past the reproductive years into old age. At least, this practice still prevails in some parts of the world outside the Occident. Whatever might be said about the technological achievements of man to relieve the burdens of physical life in betterment cannot be said about the psychological quantum that prompts this technical out-turn in the first place. It is commonly understood that the nature of man has changed little for the better with the inception of the technological prerogative. If at all: it seems to have got worse whatever the euphemistic minds chant. Time after time, as each war ends the prophets of hope and goodly salutation are up against the next episode of carnage that mankind devises. Even the fools who live in their soggy paradises full of hope and optimism will have to squirm at the latest example of man's devotion to man under the love-steeped slogan of 'ethnic cleansing' in Bosnia and the rest of what was once Yugoslavia. All this after we opened the gates to Auschwitz and Dachau and squirmed our resolve that it shall never happen again. If we examine the history of all human endeavour there is no evidence, particularly in the Occidental world of the Northern Hemisphere where technology has generally made for more physical ease, of man's humanity to man. Only intervals of waiting-time to make preparations for the next quantum expression of man's inhumanity to man.

Would it not be interesting to see churches in the USA, South Africa and Europe with pew after pew full of white overt and covert racists at their pious hymn-singing services and religious devotions suddenly confronted with a visit by Jesus Christ himself walking down the aisles and apses to greet them? One look at his dark brown skin and Semitic features would, I guess, send many of them fleeing with their humbug and hypocrisy into the surrounding hills in hysteria. Their faith as tenuous as the colour of a complexion. One wonders what then would 'Bless' America and save the Queen.

Would a God with a pale grey skin and almond-shaped eyes, looking more like a lizard, be preferable as a point of worship than a man with a sepia complexion? Interesting, isn't it?

CHAPTER EIGHTEEN:
FACTOR 'X' IN
THE AFFAIRS OF HUMANITY

Is it all just a pathological status quo? Are we a degenerate breed little different from the suborders of life we control? We have power to reason, to make summary and act with independent decision and choice. We possess a freedom of will unsurpassed by any other living paradigm on our planet. Why has this awesome advantage over the ages not bound us to a natural tendency to add, to bring together, to bind? Why instead has it led to an increase in the impulse to divide, to see more and more threat in 'difference'? To see this threat for more and more delusive reasons? Could we be running a programme? Could some fiendish biological engineer with an ulterior motive have planted a seed, an alteration somewhere, sometime, in the natural ancestral lines of man that produces more and more the genotype of Cain, rather than of Abel? A genotype that might well hail from the Northern hemisphere, bearing in mind the Occidental world's singular and prodigious influence on the worldwide legions of men through the centuries through colonialism? Or is it just the natural course of entropy doing its deadly destructive job, transforming things into more and more states of randomness and chaos with time, through its effect on atoms and thus the collective psychology of Man?

You will see from all the foregoing that I am convinced that there may well have been another factor. A hidden factor. One that has been covertly maintained beyond the insight of most men and has only become recently apparent through fortuitous accident or, perhaps, carefully managed revelation. Thus the current explosion of interest in the media over all the concern about 'Flying Saucers'.

And so the tantalizing question of all questions that arises from all of this is: Are we on Earth the victims of some alien scenario acted out in some distant patch of the Universe, a scenario that came to Earth in line with a directive given to some manufactured Cyborgs that were programmed to take care of the interests of Master Beings from a planet in a far-distant galaxy?

So what are the Greys, Greens, Yellows and Blues really here for if what I assert is true? Why would they restore a dying species called Man to a previous stage of its ancestral line nearer Godhead by, as I have speculated, rewiring the devolving soft tissue of the brain perhaps in line with their creator beings? What could they be looking for in doing such a thing to what was an alien and technologically subordinate and primitive species to them? What did we have that they wanted so much that they would linger perhaps a million years to find? What was it they sought among us that they could not find through their 'creator beings' on their home planet? Indeed, what was so precious, so important to them that they would comb the Universe through aeons to find it? I believe that the Greys may be chasing something they could never find. It would have to be something of enormous significance. Something as big, perhaps, as a search for a Soul.

As I have said previously, whatever they are seeking has to be something that made their creators on their home planet different from themselves. A Soul was the only thing that their creators had that they did not. The Greys were machines and could never have one. I believe they don't know this and they can't know this, for this very simple reason. Clones and Roboids have to deal with the currency of their respective programmes. They are purely physical artefacts of the Universe of atoms and deal only in the real forms and substance of this universe. It is all they may understand. It is all they have a reference for. The soul *is an abstraction*. It is simply a line of connection, but a Soul is that most precious and awesome bridge to Godhead that allowed the possibility for return to Godhead and eternal life. The Greys, be they Clones or Roboids, were only shadows of the original Master Form they were derived from. They possess a kind of immortality. A finite immortality. Replenishment of a kind. Continuous replenishment through DNA manipulation. On the other hand, a being with a Soul would have an ability to change quantum states across physically definable dimensions through the mechanism of Death through which replenishment and consequent return through Birth would occur. An immortality through the grave beyond which the access to Godhead would logically be easier if the individual Soul was ready to take it. The 'fields' of Death are the corridors formed by the space between atoms. It is a peripheral atomic arena. A balance point where the force or tension in between the atoms of a molecule or any other assembly of atoms cancels out and points of 'peace' analogous to the state of Godhead exist (see Fig. 13 in the illustrated section). Perhaps this is where an individual unique consciousness survives when a natural living body wears out and decays, to return through reincarnation to fulfil the search for ultimate knowledge. Cloned being could never do this and re-establishment of its existential modulus has to be carried through the mechanistic manipulation of its replenishment mechanisms and/or the other factors that give it existence.

We here on Earth, with our science at its present state, can clone all kinds of animal life. Can you imagine what a Master Intelligence capable of creating the Grey roboids might be capable of?

And so the manufacture of a Clone or Grey too would always have to be repeated as with any machine, whether it be biological or not. Their forms would always be temporary. Never lasting. The harrowing dictates of the dance of atoms to the power of the Second Law of Thermodynamics to dismantle states of coherence into greater and greater states of disorder with time Universe-wide would always finally claim them. Their atomic gene base would only last a certain number of replenishments. That old curse, the true Satan or 'Angel of Death', the entropic process, would see to it that it would not last. But the Clones wanted to last and, in seeking a mechanism that would automatically allow them repeat opportunities at an existence, they discovered the mechanism we call a Soul. Their subsequent search for a methodology of establishing a Soul within their living base would, I believe, have given rise to a Universe-wide holocaust. A holocaust that brought in its train all the wretchedness we are as human beings.

Each Soul's connection to its point of inception in Godhead

is unique and unbounded. A Clone could only know function. It could never know meaning. That was the exclusive prerogative of a being with a Soul. The mechanism that traced the final comparator between what was absolute (God) and what was not. Soul came from the absolute and so could implicitly know the phenomenon of differentiation into parts. This ethic of 'difference-ness' (a terrible word I've tried to avoid using) and its implication is paramount in understanding what is All. That which did not come from the absolute has to be shown what 'difference' means. Such things have no implicit scale against which they can relate it. To implicitly 'know' the true meaning of any difference implies that one may set a more accurate scale of what 'variance' implies existentially. It is the all-important quality that Soul imparts. That quality is that Soul tacitly may know all things against the final arbitration point known as Righteousness, and anything without a Soul cannot. A being with Soul will always, and in all ways, impart an on-going comparator against 'righteousness' itself. It is called Conscience. A being without this may never have conscience. I think the reader might now begin to get my drift!

The Cyborg-Clone could never have an ancestral natural connection to Godhead, and thus could never have a Soul. It could never have a conscience. It would always be different to the Creator Beings that made it. The pursuit of this difference and its meaning by these soft-tissue machines led them to dying species maybe a thousand light years away from their planet. This difference started all our histories as the present state of Man. It started all our troubles with our Soul and all our tomorrows are thus touched with the troubles of all our yesterdays.

Were it not for the eternal connection between the Universe of the Whole and the Universe of Parts there could be no return, no chance of redemption to access the Whole short of taking the long way round of devolution through entropy into the final points of separation at the end of Time. There would be no meaning to those beautiful beings who came announcing our predicament in an arena of diminishing returns. Those grand visionaries of our predicament as a species that gave us the means to take a short cut back to Godhead while our individual awareness of 'self' was still intact.

The glorious ones: the Hindu Pantheon, Abraham, Gautama Buddha, Jesus Christ, The Prophet Mohammed, Confucius, the wondrous sages and teachers of the Jains, the Sikhs, and all other sources of *true* wisdom were our beginning of hope to take a short cut back to Godhead. A short cut past repeat episodes of reincarnation and thus suffering and the 'Russian Roulette' of the whims of Karma and obligation to others caused through ignorance. An ignorance caused through the philosophies of the temporal 'Children of Damnation': the General, the Priest, the Corporation Head, the Politician, the Businessman, and all other potentially powerful blind guides who design our corrals of restriction according to the instincts of the Lord of the Manor and the Law of the Jungle. Corrals of the mind that flit at the speed of light and claim our children's futures for the trite 'Mickey Mouse psychology' that overwhelmingly prevails in programme after programme on that box in the corner of the drawing room. What price the Greys, if they are truly here, against the cheap expedient outlook and values the media expounds? And even if the Greys are not a factor, what value does our collective humanity have if such philosophy is the armour against the tirade of entropy that comes at our children?

I am convinced that an actual biophysical legacy was left by a 'Redeemer' called Jesus Christ through the apostolate that would, through their genetic lines, provide an antidote to what the Greys had done with their gene interceptions into the Hominid lines of Mankind. The two thousand years since the death of Christ are marked by the passing of a hundred or so generations. These generations would be marked by alterations made to Man that in time would change the biophysicality and psychophysiology of Mankind in line with the alien prescriptions for their species. Perhaps these wise and glorious teachers who have come among us from time to time saw that our condition as a species had a devastating hidden biological factor that had to be expunged before an accent of thinking could work to free us from the grip of the entropic stranglehold. Could they have left a biological antidote in the genes of a selected few that would work through the legions of humanity in twenty generations and allow us a chance to tune into the behests of Godness through the corridors through which the Universe of the Whole touches all living being, the spaces between all molecules and thus all atoms? It would be nice to think so. But could it be true?

I for one believe it *is* true. The likely interceptions of the ancestral

DNA of our species through the ages by the actions of alien beings have taken away the natural justice of naturally deserved demise through the individual's own fault. In other words, this demise is not in line with the incidental eventualities of the destructive devolution process of the Second Law of Thermodynamics. Natural justice is the song of the Omniverse and our Universe is subject to the 'overall'. Thus the behests of redeemers would seek to equalize the situation and redress the balance. The 'Christ' phenomenon may be one such instance specific to this planet. He called himself the 'Son of Man'. That may have been the signature of the phenomenon for this particular planet.

The signs are all too clear in the body politic and socio-anthropological schematics of the occidental world particularly that the route out of our predicament in atoms lies firmly baulked by the list-file mindedness of the computer programme. The 'system' is increasingly paramount over the person. The counting of fiscal noughts and materialistic acquisitiveness has exploded into the psychology of people to such an extent that many in the occidental world no more want to see or indeed can see the price that has to be paid in terms of human values for this dead-end short-sighted outlook. A quote from the New Testament stands vividly true when this same redeemer implored:

> Matthew 7. 19/20/21 : 'Lay not up for yourselves treasures upon the Earth where moth and rust doth corrupt and where thieves break through and steal: But lay up for yourselves treasures in heaven where neither moth nor rust doth corrupt, and where thieves do not break through nor steal. For where your treasure is there will your heart be also.'

How often have we been to homes where the walls and furniture indicate the owner's facile vainglorious obsession with things, objects and purposeless splendour? You can make a palace for a king, but you cannot make a king for a palace.

What a beautiful avowal of pristine logic the following existential principle enshrines. 'Where your heart is so will you be.' The implication is clear. We have no individual meaning without that mechanism that gives *all* meaning: *The strength of our focus*. In other words, the strength of mind-propelled heart (emotional value) is crucial to provide the achievement of anything. The most important word in any language is 'enough'. There seems to be a threshold of strength of purpose and mind beyond which the achievement of anything is possible. Most of us never get anywhere near this threshold and so our wishes are never fulfilled. Aspirations are just a property of the 'front office' of the mind, like the RAM memory of a computer. It is just a mechanism for viewing options. It has no power to achieve a need or a wish or a want. It is mind without heart. Put some of the tour de force of heart into the equation and it is like pressing the button on the computer that puts what is in the RAM memory onto the hard disc. We are constantly fooled into assuming one is the other, because both involve the process of thinking and it is very hard to judge the depth or strength of a particular element of this thinking while the process is going on.

Another quote from the New Testament that affirms this bears mentioning:

> Matthew 17. 18/19/20. 'And Jesus rebuked the devil; and he departed out of him; and the child was cured from that very hour. Then came the disciples to Jesus apart, and said, Why could not we cast him out? And Jesus said unto them, Because of your unbelief: For verily I say unto you, If ye have faith as a grain of mustard seed, ye shall say unto this mountain, remove hence to yonder place; and it shall remove. And nothing shall be impossible unto you.'

It is clear from all of this that something fundamental is missing from the instinct and intuitional frame of the vast majority of us. It may be the result of societal and cultural deterioration through the centuries and the emergence of technological mindedness. If a machine can do your thinking for you and take over all the infrastructural supports of your living aegis, why bother to use your head to decide anything? Why make the effort to work thought into choice and thus extend the capacity to receive more and more Godness? The result of not doing this is a huge raft of mental apathy that floats on a bed of sensory instinct. All this does is feed the prompts of the flesh to the hidden agenda of the entropic behest. It is this easiest of options that has condemned so many souls to the damnation of devolvement into lower life forms, beginning with the Ape. In time all that will survive is a decaying one-way paradise for sensualists and sybarites. So that they in time will lessen their living bastions, their physical and mental capacity called 'bodies', to other conducive forms through endless reincarnations down through the doorway that leads to the final doom of the Soul. Could this have been the true 'cause célèbre' that prompted the redeemers that came among Man to claim they came to 'save our souls'?

Christ is quoted as saying that there are many animals walking round in the skins of men.[1] I wonder if he meant this literally. I believe so implicitly. We essentially reincarnate downwards. The living paradigm in a physical Universe of diminishing returns provides such a strong downwards behavioural impulsion that only the few can resist it and get out of the 'Wheel Of Rebirth', as the Buddhists put it, altogether. The Universe deals in the physical through its inherently enforced atomic nature. The beguilements of the 'flesh' are thus, horrendously, too powerful to resist for most. We are even now, many of us, making our own future monkey. It is a terrifying thought that many readers will be unable to accept. But the historical evidence in terms of the violent and destructive nature and behaviour of our species is overwhelming and points to the fact that this is so. The biological research into the genome is already beginning to confirm this. I remember the look on my biology teacher's face when I suggested this to him years ago. He was almost violent in his dismissal of it. He punished me by asking me to write a justification of Darwin's Theory of Evolution. I wrote out a refutation of it instead and expected a tirade. Instead I got praised for my logic and ridiculed out of hand as a dangerous heretic in front of the whole class. A small insight of things to come.

CHAPTER NINETEEN:
STARSTRUCK

It is absolutely essential to note that there have been *two* main distinct kinds of interception in the bio–psychological affairs of Man. One comes from the eternal tenure of the Universe of the Whole and everlasting value and meaning. The other type of interception like that of the Greys and all other 'alien' beings that might have through millions of years used our planet as a laboratory is strictly a local phenomenon. It is of our Universe of Fractions and Parts, and is thus temporary and transient in its importance and significance.

It was such a puzzle to me for so long that from the very outset of the Judaic redeemer's mission he claimed that he came to 'Save' mankind. He alone among all the religious and theosophical teachers came shouting there was something awfully wrong with the very existential base of humanity. He came, he claimed, to save the *lost* 'sheep': I can't help feeling that he used the metaphor euphemistically to imply what sheep are commonly noted for. Blind tacit stupidity wrapped up in innocence. What was there in the human demeanour that he saw that marked it out as being so lost that its very existential base needed saving? It had to be something awesome in its implication to account for the paraphernalia of all that led to the modus of his conception and birth. This is what makes his 'intrusion' and that of the other genuine Master Teachers into the affairs of Mankind quite unlike that of the machine type intelligences we call the Greys, the Greens, the Yellows and the Blues. The declarations of intent made by the visionary Masters were made from the start of their respective ministries. Their entire missions and *modi operandi* were revealed and open from the start. There were no hidden agendas, nothing to hide, as has been the case with the alien Clones and their earthly cohorts that have been among our species through the centuries. Their operations among the legions of man in their laboratory called the Earth through the millennia has been covert and hidden. It is purely a phenomenon of atoms and thus force. The missions of the emissaries of Godhead came from beyond the margins of Force. Their phenomenon came *through* force, not *out* of it. It was thus from and on behalf of a world beyond the separation of points and thus timeless. It was the language of the eternal and its punctuation could never hold true for the list-filing mind of science that can only seek to pick a route through a Universe of parts and portions. That language is written in the schematic of the physical and thus the corporeal senses. It is quite simply the rhetoric of damnation. The prose of fools.

Why do most scientists dismiss the UFO phenomenon? Why are they so disinclined to unravel what may well be the most sensational discovery of the millennium? Why are so many scientists' eyes seemingly institutionally closed to the overwhelming evidence now available for their existence? It really is more bizarre than anything I have postulated here that the doyens of rationalism suffer a lack of reason where this same reason demands they take an open-minded look. The biggest factor that forbids them looking seriously, as an eminent physicist once told me, is the 'Speed of Light' conundrum. The one that says nothing can go faster than the speed of Light. Their minds are so mundane and so many scientists are merely hacks to the banality of the 'scientific method' they lack that innate brief for vision and imagination. The few that came to greatness possessed these qualities. The mediocre ones are perhaps defending their incomes. Now that would indeed be a big enough reason for contriving blindness in this day and age. If their dismissal of the UFO phenomenon really is a caution to forbid the charlatan, the prankster and the trickster wasting everybody's time, it is not only understandable, it is essential. The fool is always with Man. Yet the antipathy that greets any new idea that takes us beyond the margins of the atom is so over the top as to raise the suspicion that many of our scientists are running a microchip in their biology that forbids them looking beyond the narrow blinkered view. The scientific outlook does not inherently *forbid* investigation of interesting phenomena, it *demands* it.

It is certainly true that this blinkered retarded view dismissing the entirety of UFO phenomena is usually the prerogative of the scientist of average ability. They certainly form the caucus of the heaviest resistance to new ideas through history. There has rarely been any scientist of genius who has at some time in his career not been dismissed as a heretic, a charlatan or a fool by his lesser colleagues. Da Vinci, Copernicus, Galileo, Pasteur, Franklin, Newton, Edison, Baird, Tesla, Einstein, Feynman, were all victims of the deadly tunnel vision of the narrowly centred scientific ethos.

As the world gets more and more hemmed in by the views and inventions of technology and science and scientists, our way out of this transient shell we call a body and into the permanent eternal behest of the Universe of the Whole gets more and more inherently restricted. Theirs is the ethos of the cloned machine. An ethos that sinks us into the abyss of the closed-minded, short-sighted, programmed view. A Grey view. Have you noticed how this ethos creeps into our 'everydayness' like a thief in the night? The speed of its intrusion is staggering. Its trespass into the collective base of all our minds inexorable and comprehensive. There seems to be so little resistance to it all in the nature of Man. Its prop and prompting is written and arrayed in the spectacularly powerful palisades of light and sound. The pixel of your television screen. Beguiling words and colours in print. All of this pandering to the trace of the acquisitive instinct in us all. The seemingly irresistible mandate of the dollar and the cent and the empty, facile, transient invitations to our flesh and our vanity.

We are, it seems, finally truly primitive animals. We have no real excuse for maintaining this antediluvian stance in the face of what intelligence we possess. We have reason and a truly independent capacity for making free choices against all instinct and societal and cultural enforcements in line with what I call the whisper of Godhead: Conscience. Take the most important and the most powerful impulse in the bio-political imperatives of our being. The sexual instinct. In animals the instinct is necessarily and overwhelmingly simple and dispassionately reactionary. A chemical signal, the whiff of a pheromone and the responsive urge is immediate and irresistible. Yet we are supposed to be possessed of the instinct to grander things. We can soar with the aural glories of Shakespeare, Tagore, Mozart, and Beethoven. Dream in the spires of cognitive semantics. Feel with the tenderness of an infant's kiss. Yet we demean and condemn each other with primitive stances no animal would take on. We rape and we ravish and we sexually molest children. We turn a woman's sacred womb into a bauble within which we males rummage with our egos. Through it the human frame of aesthetic reference lies summarily condemned to its detriment more than through any other psycho–notional imperative. It comes down, after all, to the mindless improbable sexual obsession to play with, and in, each other's waste disposal units. Even an animal is mercifully past such priorities and sniffs around genitals at the instigation of a pheromone. We do it because we like it.

It seems the stately abstract wisdom that reason provides bears little trade-off value against the rushes of such corporeal blood. We seem to be doomed to bear the consequence of the reach of our physical senses. The urge to higher result seems to be possessed by so few. It would be easier to understand if this arena we live in is the true Hell. There's a thought. Is this Universe of force and parts the true 'Hell'? Read 'electromagnetism' for 'everlasting fire'. It is no beguiling thought. It may well be the right thought. Are the administering demons of medieval invective slightly less Red and quite a bit more Grey than assumed? Are we a basin for a giant experiment? A depository for the machinations of superior intelligences that made our yesterdays and, at this very moment, are making our tomorrows? Is the directive God most theosophies connote no omniversal arbiter with an incidental value in the glory of righteousness, but some 'jealous' alien superintendent with an intelligence that towers above us with the commanding scale of a man against an insect? The Old Testament opens out with vivid new meaning in the light of this surmise.

There are plenty among the legions of humanity who have been and are waiting in eager anticipation for a time in the not too distant future for the return of their 'fathers' from Space. Many in Germany, to my own personal knowledge, have packed their suitcases and waited with anticipation in their back gardens for the arrival of the inverted dishes from the sky. Perhaps it is fitting that the nation that, through our Earth's recent history, has done more to prove man's cold-blooded and lethal inhumanity to man than any other and has in this century promoted a harsh form of eugenics, would form the first welcoming committee for the Universe's arch representatives of such practices when they come to finish the job on Earth. Alas, those of goodly insight in Germany misguidedly see it as a way of escape from the cold-blooded dispassion of their present occidental societal values. These so-called New Age people are probably the best and sweetest psychotypes the Occident can produce and many in their innocence and ignorance want so much to be rescued by the Greys (not quite knowing what and who they might be) from the chilling and relentless heartless inertias that technological societies are fast becoming. The ultimate antilogy is that the Greys may well be the original creators of the psycho-concepts of machine-type society through their interception of these societies' previous forms of ancient Man, that in turn finally provided the base for a new hybrid type of man called the Cro-Magnons. It would certainly explain, as I have said previously, the sudden appearance of the genotype from nowhere around 40,000 years ago. Perhaps their present forms in Europe display instincts that whisper about their synthetic hybridization. Perhaps because of this they are implicitly horrified and fearful of its consequences for their future existential scope as living beings, without really quite knowing why. These may well be Christ's lost sheep of contemporary times. One hopes that these New Age types of Cro-Magnon descent will find the insight to see a way past their biology and their psychological programming in the messages of the great teachers. It is their *only* hope. They have to use the true whys and wherefores of their capture and, through the exercise of the power of will, disallow their subjugation to the 'alien' brief in their biology. They have to beat the deadly genes of damnation that hold most of them and thus the whole human family to ransom.

The 16th century mystic seer Nostradamus, whatever we may think of prophesy and prophets, had the most remarkable foresight. In his celebrated quatrains published in his work entitled *The Centuries*, he foresaw absolutely correctly a hail of events right through the centuries from his time to the end of the Millennium.

The most stunning was: a reference to a German called 'Hister', whose armies, referred to as 'beasts wild with hunger', are said to 'cross rivers' while 'the child of Germany observes no law' (Century 2, quatrain 24). During the first years of the Second World War, Germany's progress largely depended on her armies crossing the major rivers of Europe with manpower and weapons, and Hitler, or 'Hister', could certainly be described as one who 'observes no law'. The Spanish dictator Franco is also mentioned by name in one of the quatrains (Century 9, quatrain 16: 'From Castile Franco will bring out the assembly . . .'). His predecessor Primo de Rivera, who was in fact deposed by him, is also named in the same quatrain: 'Riviera's people will be in the crowd'. Nostradamus also made a remarkably accurate prophecy about Louis Pasteur, again mentioning him by name:

'The lost thing, hidden for many centuries is discovered. Pasteur will be celebrated as an almost godlike figure. This is when the moon completes her great cycle, but by other rumours he shall be dishonoured' (Century 1, quatrain 25).

Pasteur's discovery that germs polluted the atmosphere was, of course, of vital importance to human health. The astrological cycle of the moon (when 'the moon completes her great cycle') ran from 1539 to 1889. Pasteur founded the Institute Pasteur on November 14th 1889! Another date that Nostradamus prophesied exactly was that of the Great Fire of London of 1666: 'The blood of the just will be demanded of London burned by fire in three times twenty plus six.' (Century 2, quatrain 51). In his own lifetime, despite the warnings he gave to those involved, another of his prophecies came about. He foresaw that King Henri II would die in a 'field of combat in single fight' by wounds that would 'pierce his eyes in their golden cage', (Century 1, quatrain 35). The king died in a jousting accident in which the splintered shaft of his opponent's lance pierced his gilt helmet and entered his head just above the eye. This extraordinary list of confirmations also includes a prophecy for the emergence of air travel that would make the whole world far more accessible to everyone. 'The world becomes smaller . . . people will travel safely through the sky, over land and sea', (Century 1, quatrain 63).

A prophesy from this great mystic seer in the sixteenth century foresaw the coming of a great and evil king from the sky at the end of the millennium. The following is a translation of this prophecy:

'In the year 1999, and seven months, from the sky will come the great King of Terror. He will bring back to life the great king of Angolmois. Before and after War reigns happily' (Century 10, quatrain 72).

The common translation of the word 'Angolmois' unbelievably treats the word as an anagram for the old French word for the Mongol people, 'Mongolois'. Thus the prophecy has been interpreted as a reference to an antichrist who comes from Asia, the King of the Mongols, 'le grand Roi d'Angolmois'. (See *The Prophecies of Nostradamus* translated, edited and interpreted by Erika Cheetham, Corgi Books).[1] However, it is surprising that the translators have sought out anagrams for 'Angolmois' and have even settled for the inexact anagram of 'Mongolois' when there is actually a place in Western France called Angoumois! In fact, this place is located in the very region of France where all the original Cro-Magnon skeletons were found (see map in the illustrated section). 'Cro-Magnon' is actually the name of a rock shelter near Les Eyzies-de-Tayac in the Dordogne where several prehistoric skeletons were found in 1868. This site and the six other sites in the same region where similar fossils were also found are all either in, or adjacent to, the province of Angoumois. So, far from referring to an Asian antichrist, it seems that Nostradamus may instead have been alluding to a Cro-Magnon antichrist whom the 'great King of Terror' who comes from 'the sky' will 'bring back to life'. It would certainly seem logical that the Cro-Magnons and their descendants, who seem to be the purest representatives of alien interception on this planet, would be the seedbed from which the aliens from 'the sky' will resurrect, 'bring back to life', the closest equivalent to their kind of being that they can find.

Nostradamus foresaw all of this in a Christianesque 16th century perspective as Lucifer and his cohorts unchained and given license to thrive among mankind for a time. The great flourish of interest in UFOs and their attendant paraphernalia in the media around the world in the recent past might well augur such an occurrence. If so, we all need to beware those hugely influential people who pooh-pooh the idea as nonsense and foolishness. Some of us, no doubt, find it hard to accept that the whole universe was created for anyone other than us as human beings. Some find the absolute quantum of the speed of light a barrier to anyone else getting here (even though the latest research has showed this to be nonsense). Some, however, may well be agents, and agencies in human disguise, of an alien intelligence about to make its appearance on this Earth. If what I have postulated in all the foregoing pages is true, you would then expect their own 'fifth column' on this planet to take care of them and their best interests in ways a superior intelligence might conceive.

We need to identify and see these people for what they might well be: quite simply, the cohorts of the little devils in Grey. Architects of an alien way. Human aides to celestial pirates who seek to hijack our individual soul lines for themselves and their empty go-nowhere mechanical futures. It will perhaps be the most important and worthwhile thing we have ever done.

I believe we are right to view with suspicion those who now and in the future will speak for the intercession of these 'creatures' in human affairs. I suspect that many will speak on their behalf in the highest councils of the world. In time they will brook no resistance. In time you will never be allowed to read words such as these. I believe it will begin soon in a time and circumstance that will show these creatures as the new Messiahs of our human predicament and prepare their way in blinding colours of goodly and godly light. It will then be too late to mitigate the most prodigious threat that faces humanity. Much evidence is coming to light as people delve more deeply into the subject of a giant inter-governmental conspiracy to cover up the evidence for the existence of the Clones and Greys among us. Names at the highest levels of world society are, it seems, connected into strings of influence. Media resources the world over are being brought into narrower and narrower groupings of control to centralize the mustering of influence on their behalf over all the people of the world.

Why is it all happening now? Is it all some symbolic metaphor to do with the Year 2000? Of course it is not. The whole entry of the aliens into the world is to do with subterfuge. They have always sought to do their business in as much of a covert way as possible. I suspect that theirs is not a martially inclined psychological format. If they have the technology to get here past the light quantum restriction, they would certainly have the technological means to take care of any martial threat the Earth may possess at a stroke without resort to martial means themselves. If their intention was to wipe out humanity and take over all the real estate, they would have done it long before we got the atom bomb. The evidence for their being here thus far extends to prehistory. Then would have been the most intelligent time to strike for a martially oriented type of being if it wanted to crush all resistance. The fact that they have not invaded in all this time might well imply martial weakness in themselves, of course. As machines they may have no concept of 'violence' as such. They may yet be studying our martial capacity and capability as a species and devising some sort of scenario that remotely, without directly involving themselves, might overcome our capacity to react with force. (After all, their craft are so often seen at atomic test sites, military bases or regions where there are wars and conflicts.) They might, on the other hand, have ensured the invention of a total ethnic cleansing device if their experiment failed and use telepathy to inspire our scientists and technologists to build machines that could take us all out (i.e. atom bombs) at one stroke. They would then just need to set us all at each others' throats so that we vaporize all unwanted humanity and leave them a clear field for the physical takeover of our planet, leaving perhaps only the kinds of man-types that serve their purpose. But we all know they haven't done this up to now. Maybe they still intend to do this and they are not quite ready yet to bring it about. On the other hand, they might want most of us here. Atom bombs are crude culling devices. They forbid control. Tight enough control. If it really was their intention to wipe us all out, we have got pretty close to fulfilling it on several occasions. The fact remains that we have not yet blown ourselves up. Is it all part of their plan or ours? Who controls what?

So why are they waiting so long? I believe it is because they are trying to establish an unsuspected (on our part), complete remotely engineered genetic takeover of our species first. The best genetically derived takeovers are done to natural time scales. Natural biological processes take large periods of time to mature. Time scales that may run to thousands of millennia. If you can warp Space itself, and travel at the speed of light, vast distances may be travelled in the twinkling of an eye. Time itself, which Einstein's 'Theory of

Relativity' implies is elastic, may be stretched and contracted and thus millions of years may go by in one location while in another just a few moments pass by. In other words, the aliens need not be in our galaxy or solar system all the time while they effect genetic changes in a species.

Let me go into this in a little more detail. The bedrock law in physics, $E = mc^2$ implies that the nearer you get to the speed of light, the more time stands still. In other words, there is now evidence to suggest that the speed-of-light barrier need not prevent intergalactic travel by alien beings with a superior technology. Ian Crawford of the University College of London Department of Physics and Astronomy published an article in 1995 in the quarterly journal of the Royal Astronomical Society entitled 'Some thoughts on the implications of faster-than-light interstellar space travel'. Dr Crawford believes that there are reasons for believing that FTL interstellar space travel may be consistent with the laws of physics. One of the methods mentioned by Crawford for bypassing the speed-of-light barrier involves the nature of Space. Einstein's equations tell us that Space is warped. I refer you to my concept of this (the Moroid) in Chapter 3. This seems a strange notion as it is usual to see empty space as a blank nothingness. A neutral backdrop against which forms can be straight or twisted, flat or curved. When you go out in the direct sunlight, you cast a shadow. This is, of course, because light moves in straight lines, and because light does not go through you or bend around you a shadow is formed. But wait a minute. How *does* light go in straight lines? How can straight lines ever exist if space itself is warped or bent? Einstein's equations suggest, and experiments confirm, that light moves the shortest possible distance between two points. But this is not necessarily a straight line. In fact, the light from distant stars gets bent into a curve as it passes a massive object like the sun. Effects such as this can be measured by astronomers. But how can the shortest distance between two points not be a straight line? It just doesn't make sense, does it? Or does it?

What is the shortest path between England and Australia? If you look around you it is easy to understand how 500 years ago most people thought the Earth was flat because it presents that appearance until you travel large distances. If space is curved, then the equations imply that it is possible for there to be short cuts across vast distances of space. These are given the evocative name of 'Wormholes' by scientists. Wormholes are envisioned to be warps in the 'fabric' of space that have the appearance of trumpets with a bowl at both ends. Anything going in at one end is shot out of one galaxy and into another at the other end. If wormholes exist on a large scale they could possibly provide a means for rapid travel between galaxies. Just suppose for a moment that these 'wormholes' might be opened at our end by a sudden huge alteration in prevailing general force conditions at a particular point on the Earth. It might help to explain the sudden flurry of UFO activity after the atom bomb was exploded for the first time. Flurries of UFO sightings mark many volcanic explosions too.

The distance between galaxies through a 'wormhole' could be millionths or even billionths of the *apparent* distance between them. If alien super-technologies have the capacity for using 'wormholes' or any other types of as yet undiscovered super-warps in space, they may also be expected to have the capacity to travel at or near the speed of light. Doing this would change the relative pace of the entropic momentum so that at 99.995% of the speed of light, one year passing in the travellers' space ship would correlate to the passing of 100 Earth years. They would also be 100 times heavier than normal at that speed. This may not be a problem in the apparent weightlessness of outer space. It could be argued that having such an inertial mass would not be compatible with life. But remember, when automobiles were first invented it was widely believed that speeds of fifty miles an hour would not be compatible with life. It could be that this enormous inertial mass might require special suits and life-support systems. Many abductees have described seeing such devices in their craft. It is also likely that aliens' biologies are better adapted to withstand such force vectors. It may also be that they need not rely on the time-dilation phenomenon to travel between galaxies or indeed any great distances in Space if the wormhole distance between them and us is sufficiently short.

It could also quite simply be that the alien brief for our planet needs nothing we have got here on this planet other than our individualities as soul-indentured beings. And that means as many of our suitable bodies as possible. Our bodies intact. Our bodies alive or dead for food, spare parts and perhaps for our DNA method of replication. The only form of hijack that makes any sense is the hijack any intelligent self-appreciating entity needs. Guarantee against breakdown. Eternal service potential and thus a mechanism for continuity past the Second Law of Thermodynamics. A Soul. In other words, preposterous as it seems, the Clone Alien is looking for Life through Death. It is searching for its Original in Godhead without knowing itself that it is doing just this. It is looking for an eternal home in eternal scope.

And so what are they really like, these Greys, Greens, Yellows and Blues? From all accounts, and that means the accounts of most abductees, these beings are cold, dispassionate, non-emotionally responsive creatures. We have our own variety on the Earth. Most of us come across them every day. They are not restricted to being the office 'nerd' any more. One abductee described them as like the military administrators of the Nazi war machine that conducted the holocaust against the Jews. There are several sorts but the great majority are as I have described at the beginning of this dissertation. Small, grey and spongy. They may well come from a planet where darkness, cold and heavy gravity may have been factors that fashioned their design. They have huge eyes, suggesting that their formative environment might have been a dim, lightless world. The eyes have a filter film over them that might suggest that light is polarized in a certain way on their world. They are known to abduct almost all of their victims at night, suggesting that daylight or brightly lighted environments may present a problem for them. There is compelling evidence that ultraviolet light fuses together nucleotide bases that lie next to each other along the DNA molecule, like beads on a string. This makes it harder for the DNA to copy itself. Since 'cloned being' would require the capacity to copy its own 'cells' at an extremely fast rate to combat entropic breakdown, ultraviolet light may well be deadly to such beings.

In Professor David M. Jacob's book *Secret Life*, which is a catalogue of many alien abduction experiences, a female abductee describes how she was shown a hybrid baby and asked to hold it and hug it. Jacob asked her about the skin colour of the baby: 'Does it have light skin or dark skin, within the Caucasian range?' Her answer is: 'Fair. Quite fair. I think it is very fair, as a matter of fact. Almost like no ultraviolet light for this guy.'[2]

Further evidence for the possibility that alien beings may well exist in a cold environment without sunlight may be suggested in the 'Alu' research to which I have previously referred. Alus and their ilk are generally regarded as 'selfish DNA that serve no purpose other than their own continued survival'. But Carl Schmid, an Alu expert at the University of California, has found that at least a few Alus behave altruistically, producing RNA in response to stressful conditions as part of the so-called 'heat shock response'. This particular function for Alus might perhaps indicate that Clone beings exist most comfortably in environments of extreme cold and would therefore have to adapt to 'heat shock' when arriving on this planet. So the expression in human DNA of this particular beneficial response to 'heat shock' may well be a result of alien beings using us as a test bed to find their own means of adaptation to our planetary conditions.

CHAPTER TWENTY:
FATHERS

There is evidence, as I have stated previously, from many astronauts of both the USA and what was the Soviet Union, that alien beings are on the Moon. According to Dr Vladimir Azhaza, an expert on the Moon landings, Neil Armstrong relayed a message to Mission Control that two large mysterious objects were watching them after having landed near the Moon module. This message was never heard by the public. The powers that be censored it.

In 1979 the former Chief of NASA communications systems confirmed that Armstrong had reported seeing two UFOs on the rim of a crater. Apparently all Apollo and Gemini flights were followed, both at a distance and sometimes quite closely, by 'Space Vehicles' of extraterrestrial origin. Each time it occurred and was reported, the astronauts were ordered to maintain absolute silence on what they saw.

One side of the Moon is always facing away from the Sun and is in darkness and cold. A massive artificial structure is said to have been sited there. It would make a wonderful base site and hiding place for an alien intelligence to monitor any business they might be doing on Earth. A Russian satellite, Phobos II, photographed one of their craft twenty-six kilometres long in the vicinity of Mars, before the satellite itself disappeared mysteriously. It managed to send back the photograph just before this happened. Imagine a spaceship larger than the largest city in the world. Many abductees have related under hypnotic regression that the beings told them that many more of their kind are coming.

The spaceship photographed by Phobos II resembled a long stick in appearance. In the 'Dialogue Of The Saviour', an account of Jesus teaching his apostles, from the Nag Hammadi codex, Jesus specifically warns them about 'a single staff' that will be seen 'in the sky' which will come from the 'archons' (the term used in the Nag Hammadi texts to describe what I believe are the alien Clone beings).[1] He also warns them that 'there is not one among them who will spare you or have pity on you'. In the same text he explains to Judas the nature of Clone being: 'The archons have garments that are given to them for a time, which do not abide. As for you, however, since you are sons of the truth, it is not with these temporary garments that you will clothe yourselves.' Thus he points out the transient nature of Clone bodies that are fully subject to entropy for they are without a soul to put the brakes on that driving dismantling force.

Is this all a mighty paranoia on my part? A way of passing the buck for the ills of humanity? I hope it is not. If it is, I hope I have given you at worst an interesting warning in an interesting science fiction story. On the other hand, if it has the slightest veracity, its consequences for us all, particularly for our children, are of such magnitude as to demand vigilant action on a world scale whilst we still can respond. If, indeed, it is not too late already.

I believe the whole ministry of Jesus Christ was designed to show us how to beat the genes of the Greys, Greens, Yellows and Blues in us. There may be a psychoactive power of awesome relevance and size in using Thought and Will that adds, binds, turns the other cheek. A power that actually nullifies the physical components inserted into the human gene lines by these creatures and their ability to affect a biological change that is taking place in us with time and that is slowly transmuting us from within to be like the Greys. If we follow *exactly* and *imitate what Christ did* in terms of the eventology he encountered during his life and how he tackled each instance, then his illustration and example, together with those of his peers who spoke faultlessly in love, in adding and not subtracting, in uniting and not dividing, could well have produced a recipe to defeat the alien purpose on this planet. The example of Christ's temptation in the wilderness provides a fascinating and powerful insight into the make-up and limitations of these beings.

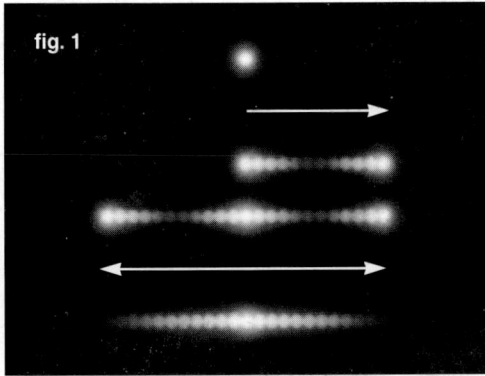

fig. 1

The point manifest as the interface between nothingness and somethingness.

The point generates another identical point in the search for difference, and direction happens in singular aspect implying two directions set against no direction.

This continues indefinitely in both directions and reaches infinity instantly as a singularity, because there is nothing to demarcate one point from another.

This is not part of the big bang, but neither is it before the big bang. It could be seen as part of the architecture of the first instant. As a singularity it still has not found difference which exists minimally as a duality.

fig. 2 Each 'line point' duplicates itself and in so doing duplicates the line at its state of greatest difference from itself, i.e. ninety degrees imply the full range of angle and curve from any given point that can be considered as a centre, i.e. all points forming plane-ness in equivalence, each point to each other, i.e. pre-spatial dimensionality defined through the mutual independence of awareness and will.

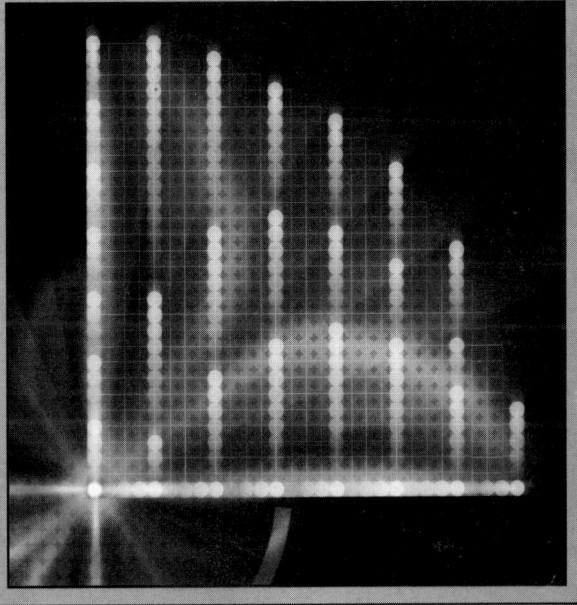

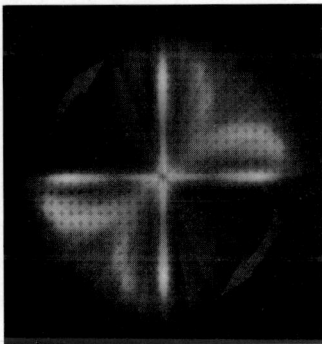

fig. 3 This change gives rise to the concept of direction, giving potential speed from stasis, a direction and thus velocity...

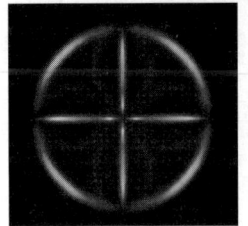

Velocity gives increased potential... Speed and so on. A continuum begins. A continuum of a differential acquisition. Our point in separated sequential velocity (time) makes a line and one dimension is born.

The sequence continues...

fig. 4

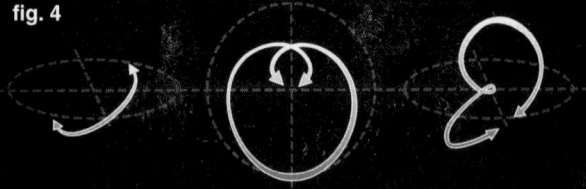

The implied circle expressing thought as the product of Awareness and Will in the search for separation generates a spiral form in a shape reminiscent of a doughnut. (This spiral is known as a toroidal helix). This traces the pattern of a Möbius strip **(Fig. 5)**. Although **Fig.4** shows this in stages, it happens in the merest instant, generating huge turning moments of spin as a product of the enormous contradiction between nothing-ness and somethingness.

fig. 5

fig. 6 These two perpendicular Möbius spinning motions together create a whirlpool effect of force within the atom, as the Möbius strip rotates tracing the full form of the toroid.

fig. 7 Cross sectional planes of the 'Tennis ball' motif, demonstrating the 'cross' at each level.

fig. 8 The universe of the whole can thus be represented by the mutually independent silver and gold axes of awareness and will existing together at perfect right angles with an implied edge (thoughtness) providing the potential for separation and a central point of perfect clarity as the summary of all summary. The pole of union absolute GODHEAD or CENTRE GOD.

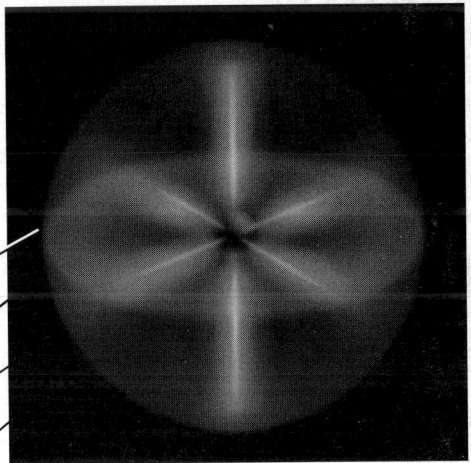

THOUGHT

AWARENESS

WILL

POLE OF UNION ABSOLUTE

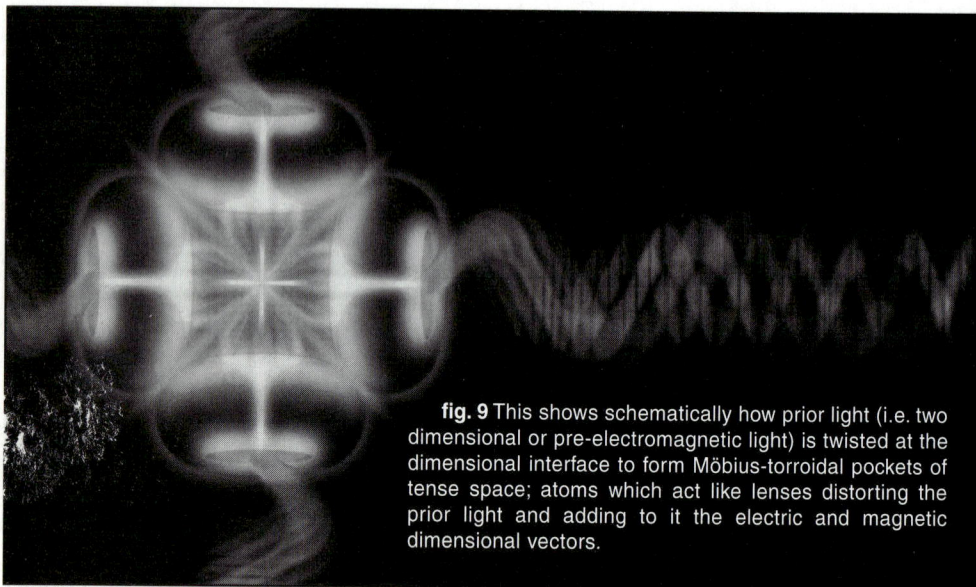

fig. 9 This shows schematically how prior light (i.e. two dimensional or pre-electromagnetic light) is twisted at the dimensional interface to form Möbius-torroidal pockets of tense space; atoms which act like lenses distorting the prior light and adding to it the electric and magnetic dimensional vectors.

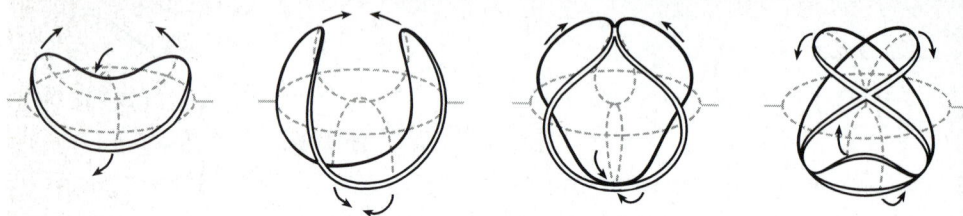

fig. 10 The tennis ball motif depicts the pattern traced by the circular toroidal axis of the moroid as it twists around both of the crossed horizontal axis within it, while it bends towards the implied central vertical axis. You will see that it reaches the vertical axis and crosses itself to pass it on the other side.

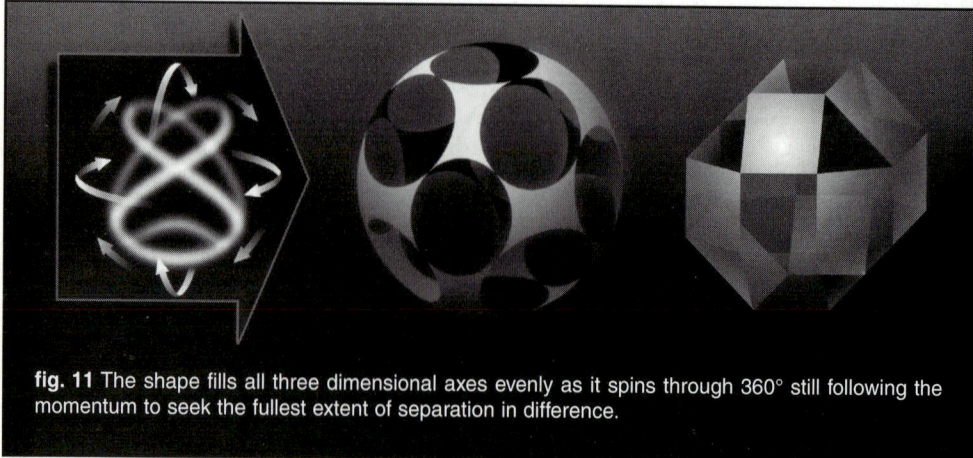

fig. 11 The shape fills all three dimensional axes evenly as it spins through 360° still following the momentum to seek the fullest extent of separation in difference.

fig. 12 This is a quantum route map at the atomic level between 'life' and 'death' and also between the universe of parts and the universe of the whole. Where opposing twists cancel at the points where the mono-atomic hydrogen atoms touch (the peace points) there are windows of prior light. These are the remnants of the bridge between the universe of points and the universe of the whole.

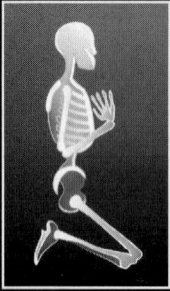
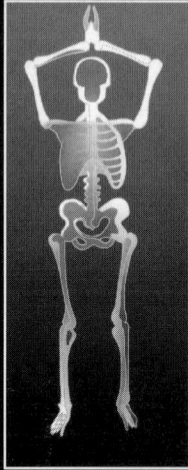
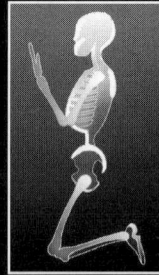
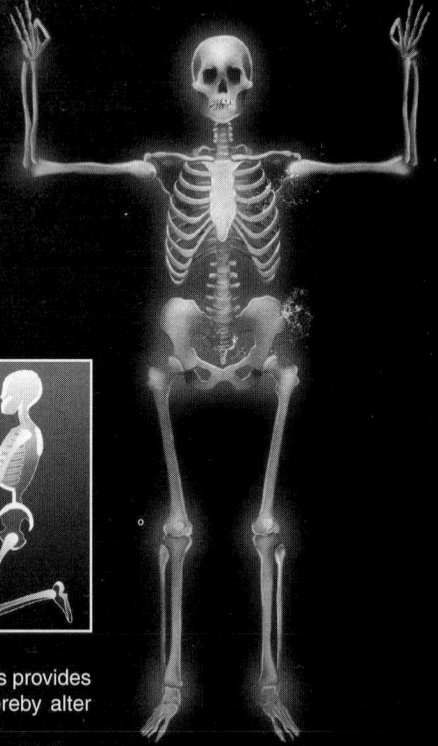

fig. 13 The human skeleton is an ideal aerial for transmitting and receiving the radio wavelength equivalent of the pre-electromagnetic spectrum i.e. Thought. Each individual has a unique carrier wave pattern, to which is added signals according to intention, action and result. The aerial is flexible and movement at the joints provides various alignments that channel that signal and thereby alter the efficiency of transmission and reception.

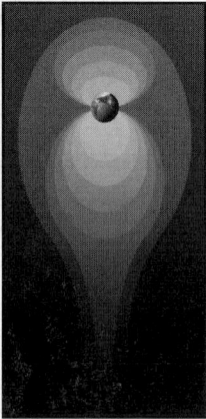
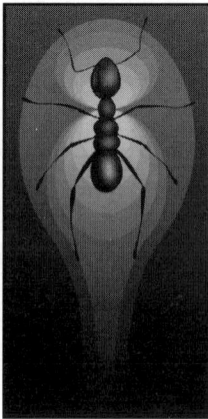
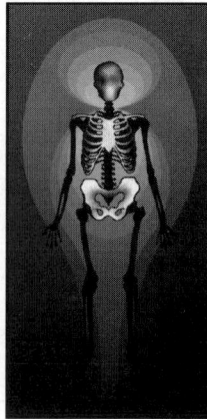
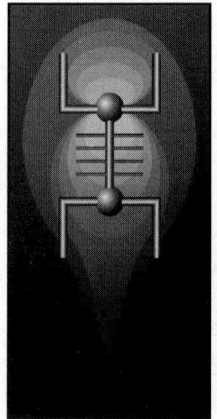

a   b   c

fig. 14 This represents the shape of the Earth's magnetic field under the influence of the Solar Wind **(a)** and its correlation to the shape of living organisms from ant to man. It also shows **(b)** the general form of the biological aerial of the human skeleton and **(c)** a commonly used format for a frequency modulated receiving aerial.

GODHEAD
(Big Bang)
The Beginning of the Universe

Heterozygous (Hermaphroditic) Being
Garden of Eden - Man Ephemeral
(A thought being in Transfigured
Form as perhaps demonstrated by
Jesus Christ in the presence of Peter, James and John)

Creation of Adam & Eve as Mortal Physical Being

ALIEN GENETIC
INTERCEPTION #1
FALL
First Adam - Eve
(Man Mortal; Vulnerable to Forces in the Universe)

fig. 15

○ Alien Interceptions
Previous to Modern Man

☐ Genetic Interceptions
Leading to Modern Man

■ Alien Interceptions (Oral)

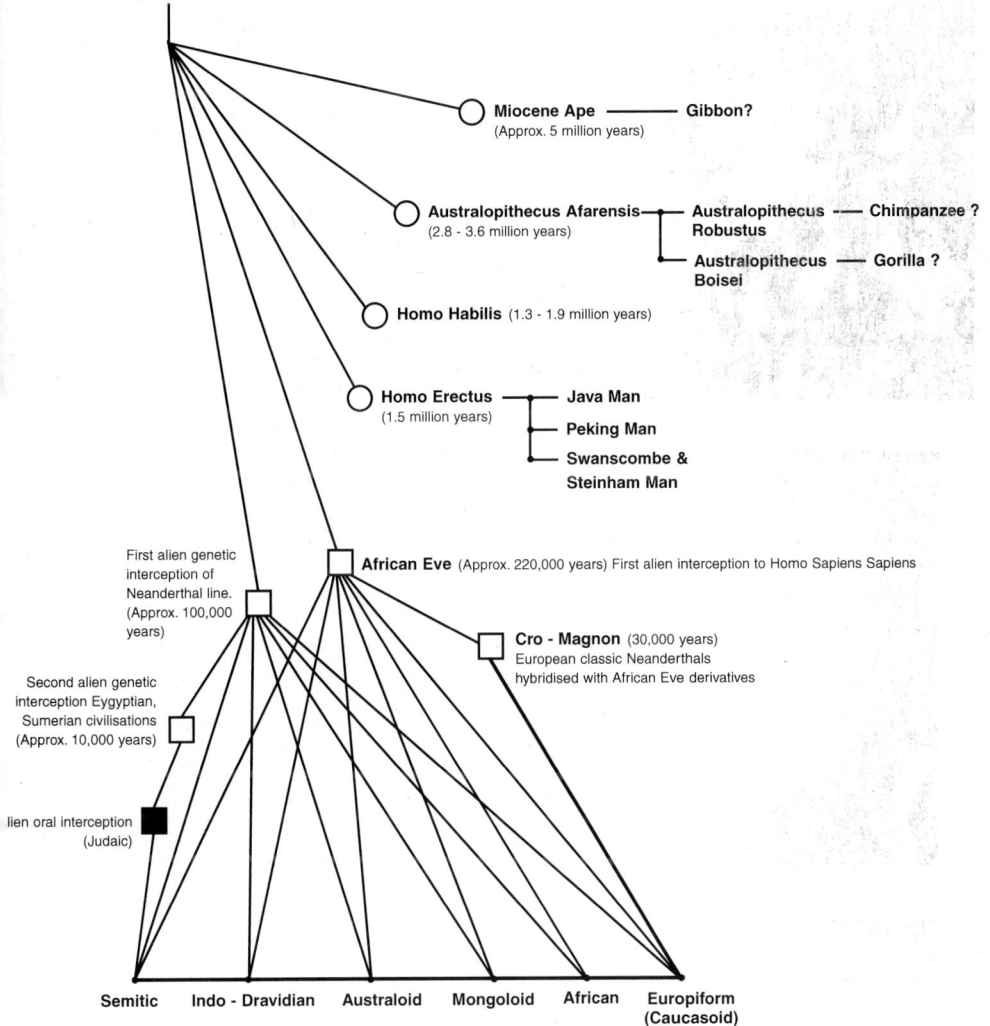

○ Miocene Ape ———— Gibbon?
(Approx. 5 million years)

○ Australopithecus Afarensis——• Australopithecus ——— Chimpanzee ?
(2.8 - 3.6 million years)   Robustus
                              •— Australopithecus ——— Gorilla ?
                                 Boisei

○ Homo Habilis (1.3 - 1.9 million years)

○ Homo Erectus ——• Java Man
(1.5 million years)
                •— Peking Man
                •— Swanscombe &
                   Steinham Man

First alien genetic
interception of
Neanderthal line.
(Approx. 100,000
years)

☐ African Eve (Approx. 220,000 years) First alien interception to Homo Sapiens Sapiens

☐ Cro - Magnon (30,000 years)
European classic Neanderthals
hybridised with African Eve derivatives

Second alien genetic
interception Eygyptian,
Sumerian civilisations
(Approx. 10,000 years)

Alien oral interception
(Judaic)

Semitic   Indo - Dravidian   Australoid   Mongoloid   African   Europiform
(Caucasoid)

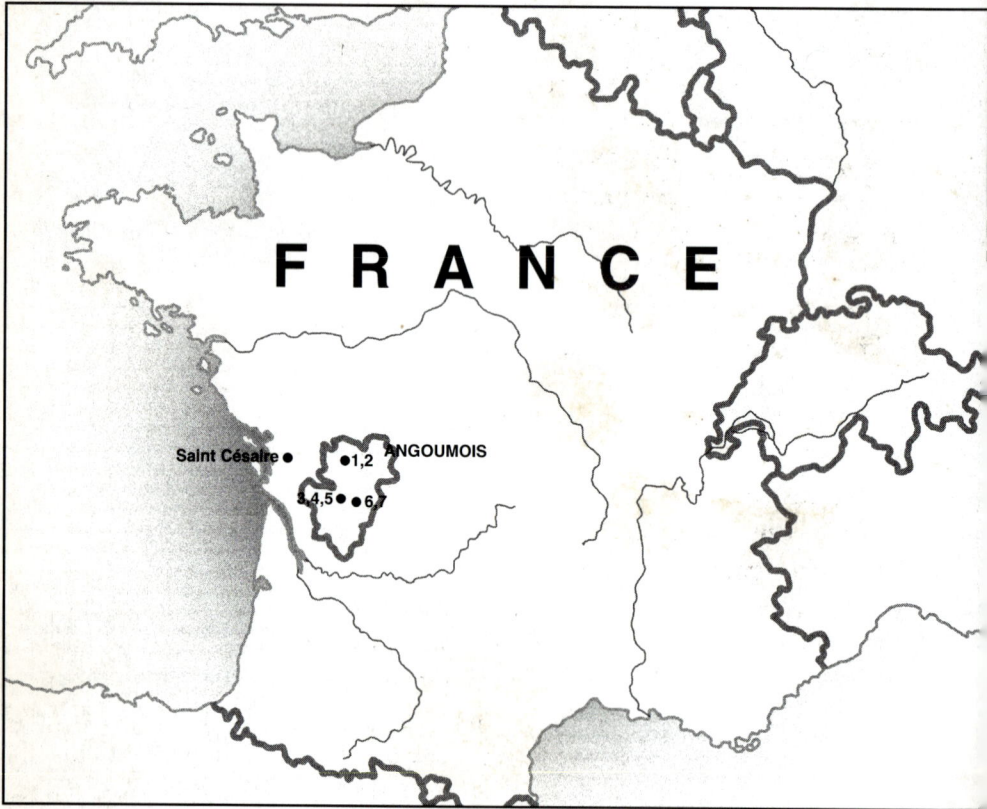

fig. 16

Map showing:
The Province of Angoumois, France.

- ● Homo Sapiens
1. La Chaise
2. La Quina
3. Cro-Magnon
4. La Ferrassie
5. La Moustier
6. La Chappelle-aux-Saints
7. La Madeleine

I alluded to this previously, but it bears discussing further. It has always been a puzzle to me, from the account in the Bible, that the so-called 'devil', without much difficulty, could at a whim move and arrange this powerful redeemer's schedule to fit its purpose. If the devil was some evil but spiritually divine being he would know that Christ was the 'Son of God', have realized that he was in a no-win situation, and given him a wide berth. There can be no such thing as spiritual evil, anyway. It's a contradiction in terms. The state of Godhead has always been described and accepted in religious terminology as *the* spiritual state. In this sense it precludes evil as a compound manifestation within it, and any state near to it will do the same. It is only outside Godhead, in a state of being that is the antithesis to Godhead, as is this Universe of Force and Parts, that true evil exists. In other words, it seems to me that evil is simply true ignorance and limited outlook. Evil is the state of being away from God in this sense. It all thus implies that this entity that tempted Christ had no idea about divinity whatsoever. It had to be an entity that had no spiritual sense whatsoever. Something like a programmed synthetic robot or one of our Master Clone aliens. Perhaps the head alien honcho who was around at the time and came to investigate this incredible being who was attracting so much attention in Palestine with the odd miracle or two. Miracles were up to then *their* sole prerogative with their super-intelligent mastery over atoms and to find another individual performing them who seemed human and not of them must have attracted the attention of the head honcho himself. So he hopped on his spaceship and gave Jesus a ride to the top of a mountain. A purely mortal atomic entity that hadn't the faintest idea who or what it was up against. It did, however, know that it had dominion over all atoms and thus could claim that it had the power to give Christ rulership over all the Earth. The thing was just a super-intelligent technocrat and Christ's answer, 'Get thee behind me, Satan. It is written thou shalt worship the Lord thy God and him only shalt thou serve,'[2] must have sent him off with a puzzle and a headache. What is more interesting is that the tempter-entity was defeated by this answer, and did not seek to impose its will on Christ regardless. It could all have been a gigantic lesson to it. Christ in his retort told the entity that it was of a basic hierarchical existential value and that in the divinity stakes it was not even a starter. This shocked the poor beast into submission and it went off with its reptilian tail between its biosynthetic legs to contemplate its next move. I believe that the Master Being, or Captain Clone, was fascinated by Christ and his power.

A small speculation here. I would like to believe that Christ reminded Captain Clone and his space buccaneers of their own 'fathers', the Master Adam Beings they were made from as Clones back on their home planet in the first place. In other words he was advising the Soul-less entity of his existential status. He would have to do this, you see. Clones could only know of themselves as a primary compound of atomic being. They would have no concept of anything deeper such as a self-identity referenced against any value outside themselves and outside atoms. They could, in other words, have no conscience. That only came from a reference with Godhead and thus a primary origin in Godhead. Clones didn't have this. Their reference would implicitly be set against the Inaugural Being they were cloned from and if that entity returned to Godhead, its first-generation and subsequent-generation Clones would exist orphaned and quite discrete from the Final Absolute. In Christ's rejoinder and reminder the Clone Captain may have realized that in Jesus it may have had a chance for a measure of redemption too. A second chance. After all, here in Christ was another living Inaugural Adam Being. Christ did claim that the power of Godhead could change stones into Sons of Abraham. Could it be that Christ as the 'Son of God' convinced the entity that perhaps at the 'Second Coming' such a thing might be possible for all Clones, as all Inaugural Beings would figure in this scenario and each Clone could then be connected to its origin point? As a result Captain Clone's tribe may well have come and still be coming to the Earth to await the glorious event in the hope that they too might finally be saved from entropy's deadly dismantling process. But they had to survive till then as Clones and that is where you and I and the planet Earth and the whole predicament of our species is centred.

If my speculation is accurate we can only hope that the Moon will be more suitable an abode for their sojourn. It certainly seems so from what one of the Moon landing astronauts said when confronted by two alien spacecraft already on the Moon. I quote: 'Their ships were far superior to ours both in size and technology.' Neil Armstrong is said to have continued, 'Boy, were they big and menacing'.

They were told in no uncertain terms. Get off the Moon and stay off. It was supposedly already theirs.

CHAPTER TWENTY-ONE:
AFFIRMATIONS

There are numerous instances in the ancient Christian texts that unmistakably allude to the False-creation Gods commonly seen as representatives of true eternal Godhead by ancient peoples. These texts suggest a knowledge of such things as alien intelligences and cloned biomechanical robots (which are referred to in some of the texts as the Archons). These so-called mystical texts are no mystery. They become abundantly clear for all to see their true meaning. I have searched the literature for the affirmations I knew had to be there. To my astonishment they were so easy to find. They had been thrown away. The flotsam and jetsam of our hope for better tomorrows. The following will demonstrate, I believe, what I mean.

But first there is something that must be clarified in regard to ancient Biblical texts, particularly those of the Old Testament of the Bible. When the word 'God', or the 'Lord God', or the 'Lord', was referred to in the Old Testament, it appears to be describing, in some contexts, the Godhead of the Universe of the Whole, and in other contexts the God of the Universe of Parts, who is, of course, a representative of the Clone beings. There is the 'God' of Moses who in one instance commanded 'Thou shalt not kill' and in another instance instructed the children of Israel to wipe out any candidates it selected as worthy of destruction. This, perhaps, identifies the Ten Commandments as a masterfully clever set of rules to allow the alien beings a degree of social control over their experimental test bed – the children of Israel. On the other hand, there is the 'God' of the prophets Isaiah, Zechariah and Joel who is far more evocative of a God of love and compassion than one of judgement and vengeance. How, then, do we differentiate one from the other? How can we tell the difference and decide what information comes from which source? Is it purely arbitrary? Can it only be decided upon by subjective feeling and appraisal based upon that? My answer is 'No'. You *can* delineate a clear line of distinction between what originates from the Universe of the whole and that which originates from the Universe of Parts. That which is of the Whole will always seek to bind, to bring together, to unite in love and compassion, in mercy and forgiveness where to forgive simply means to educate – to make the part whole. Hence Jesus's words, 'Ye have heard that it hath been said, an eye for an eye and a tooth for a tooth, but I say unto you that ye resist not evil: but whosoever shall smite thee on thy right cheek, turn to him the other also' (Matthew Ch. 6 v. 38-39), ring so true and clear. That which is of the part will be, in blazingly apparent terms, the opposite of these uniting qualities and may well use seemingly uniting qualities to divide, as the Ten Commandments illustrates.

As Jesus said to Judas (in 'The dialogue of the Saviour' – Nag Hammadi codex)[1] when he asked, 'Tell me, Lord, what is the beginning of the way?': 'Love and goodness. For if there had been one of these dwelling with the Archons, wickedness would never have come to be'. As I explained earlier, 'the Archons' is the term used to describe the alien Clone beings in the Nag Hammadi texts. These qualities, love and goodness, are the prerogative of the soul. That which is derived from atoms is intrinsically bound by the law of entropy to divide and divide further: it cannot by definition understand love. So if these yardsticks are applied to the Old Testament it is clear to see which extracts originate from natural Godhead and not from the false 'gods' of the physical universe.

Some of the ancient texts which have not been subject to manipulation and distortion by the constructors of the original Canon (that is, certain of the Apocryphal and Pseudepigraphal Texts and the Coptic Gnostic Library) present this distinction between the two 'Gods' clearly and sharply. In the book of Genesis in the Canonical Old Testament, however, the distinction is blurred. There are references to both 'Gods' within the same

Biblical passage. If we place this passage alongside its equivalent in a Pseudepigraphal Text entitled the 'Book of Enoch', fragments of which have been found amongst the Dead Sea Scrolls,[2] we can see that the distinction in this latter text between that which has its origins in the Whole and that which has its origins in the Part is crystal clear. The Falashas, the Ethiopian Jews, still have the Book of Enoch as part of their Biblical Canon. The two passages concern the visitation of the 'Sons of God unto the daughters of men' when 'Man began to multiply on the face of the earth'. The Hebrew word 'Elohim' is the word translated as 'God' in this instance. This particular word can be translated as 'gods', or 'objects of worship'. So the 'sons of God' may well refer to beings that appeared to come from the heavens, the 'gods' of this universe, not the Universe of the Whole. This is confirmed by the version of the same story in the Book of Enoch, which I will place alongside the Biblical version, such that they can be compared. But before I do that, I would like to discuss certain extracts from the 'Apocryphon of John' and the 'Sophia of Jesus Christ' which can be found in the Berlin Codex of the Coptic Gnostic Library.

In these texts Jesus describes how the Clone beings originated, why they were created, how they have cursed mankind, and how he himself came to us in order to free us from their bondage : 'That I might tell everyone about the God who is above the Universe', because 'They' (the Clone beings) 'say about themselves that they are gods'. If Jesus himself identifies this as his primary purpose for coming to mankind, and his life is such a dazzlingly beautiful reflection of the God of the Universe of the Whole, then surely there is enough evidence to claim that there are indeed two 'Gods' perceived and known by human beings. One of these, if listened to and followed, would lead to the eternal preservation of the ability to perceive and know in the first place, while the other, if followed, would lead to the destruction of that very ability to know and understand.

In the text entitled 'The Apocryphon of John', Jesus speaks to the Apostle John about the origins of all being. First he describes to him the nature of God and how existence in the Universe of Parts came to be from that state of perfect union. Various Greek terms are used in the accounts of Jesus's teaching given in the Nag Hammadi texts due to the nationality of those who either wrote or translated these accounts. The 'Sophia of the Epinoia', for example, seems to refer to the facet of God that allows for the potential for separation from his state of perfect union, a potential that must exist if God is perfectly free, as he by definition has to be. The 'Sophia' is more familiar to us as the principle of 'Eveness' which, with the principle of 'Adamness', provided the duality necessary for separation from the state of union to be possible. The 'archons', on the other hand, as I have previously explained, seem to refer to the Clone beings that were created to provide Godbeing with a safe viewing platform into the universe of parts.

So, to return to the text itself, here is an extract in which Jesus discusses with John how the 'Archons' came to be:

> 'The Sophia of the Epinoia, being an aeon, conceived a thought from herself with the reflection of the invisible spirit and foreknowledge. She wanted to bring forth a likeness out of herself without the consent of the Spirit – he had not approved – and without her consort and without his consideration. And though the personage of her maleness had not approved, and she had not found her agreement, and she had thought without the consent of the spirit and the knowledge of her agreement, (yet) she brought forth. And because of the invincible power which is in her, her thought did not remain idle and a thing came out of her which was imperfect and different from her appearance, because she had created it without her consort. And it was dissimilar to the likeness of its mother for it has another form.[3]

So, without her male consort, the 'Sophia' or 'Eve' brought into being 'a likeness out of herself'. In other words, she brought about a clone of herself. Her creation was without the 'consent of the spirit' and 'without her consort and his consideration'. If Adam was formed in the 'image and likeness of God' and Eve was formed of Adam's rib (and therefore in the likeness of Adam), it can be deduced that there is a line of connection running from God to Adam and then to Eve. So if 'Eve' or 'Sophia' creates something without the consent of Adam or the 'spirit' of God, it would follow that that which she creates has no connection back to God.

'Sophia', which we could for the sake of ease describe as the 'female principle', had 'invincible power' to create anything with 'her thought' for she represents one of the two polarities held by God-like being that was not yet trapped and held in the Universe of Parts. Thus 'her thought did not remain idle' for her thought was still free to dictate any option without limit.

However, that which she created 'was imperfect and different from her appearance because she had created it without her consort'. She is an expression of God with a direct connection through the 'male principle', Adam, to God. Her creation, on the other hand, had no such connection so it was 'imperfect'. The text goes on to describe just how imperfect it was:

And when she saw the consequence of her desire it had changed into the form of a lion-faced serpent. And its eyes were like lightning fires which flash. She cast it away from her outside that place that no one of the immortal ones might see it for she had created it in ignorance. And she surrounded it with a luminous cloud and she placed a throne in the middle of the cloud that no one might see except the holy spirit who is called the mother of all living. And she called his name YALTABAOTH.

This is the first archon who took a great power from his mother. And he removed himself from her and moved away from the places in which he was born. He became strong and created other aeons for himself with a flame of luminous fire which still exists now. And he joined with his madness which is in him and begot authorities for himself ... And he shared his fire with them but he did not send out from the power of the light which he had taken from his mother, for he is ignorant darkness.

And when the light had mixed with the darkness it caused the darkness to shine. And when the darkness had mixed with the light it darkened the light and it became neither light nor dark but it became weak.

Thus the original Clone beings are described in all their 'imperfection' through their lack of any connection to the Master Universe of the Whole. Yaltabaoth, the original Clone, 'begot authorities for himself' with which he 'shared his fire' but not the 'power of the light which he had taken from his mother, for he is ignorant darkness'. The word 'light' may well refer to the light of direct connection to God which was taken by Yaltabaoth from his mother because he was made in her image. But that light died in him because he himself had no connection back, thus he was 'ignorant darkness'. He had only an image of the light that had been conveyed to him. Perhaps this is because a clone is a single-generation artefact of atomic assembly alone. It could hold no direct soul connection to Godhead. So Yaltabaoth could not pass 'the light' or the soul connection on to the 'authorities', i.e: the Clone derivatives of himself, that he created. The 'flame of luminous fire' that he did pass on to them is the reflection of that light within a state of darkness, thus it was luminous. That flame allows for the *enlivenment* of an atomic state in the same sense that a plant is alive, but not for the *enlightenment* of an atomic state such that soul can prevail within it.

Jesus makes it clear that this 'flame of luminous fire' with which Yaltabaoth, the original Clone being, created other 'authorities' for himself '*still exists now.*' The same power with which the original 'Grey' replicated itself into other Greys still existed at the time of Christ and thus we have no reason to presume it should not still exist now, actively promulgating the reproduction of Clone-being in the form in which it now exists.

'Sophia' was apparently quite stunned at the vile nature of her creation, indicating that, as I have previously pointed out, inaugural Godbeing was not aware of the consequences of that which it sought to create.

When the 'darkness had mixed with the light it became neither light nor dark, but it became weak.' Weak because it is a living structure without a connection back to the master universe, without a soul. Thus it has no defence against the assault of entropy upon its atomic structure for it has no reference of wholeness by which to keep itself whole and resist breaking down into parts. Jesus then goes on to describe how Yaltabaoth created all the other archons of the universe:

'And everything he organized according to the model of the first aeons which had come into being so that he might create them like the indestructible ones. Not because he had seen the indestructible ones, but the power which is in him which he took from his mother produced in him a likeness of the cosmos.'

So, from the original Clone, the original copy, all the other Clones were made. That original copy had a 'likeness' of the 'indestructibility' of its 'mother', thus it sought to create Clones that were indestructible, which is of course impossible as they are purely physical and thus completely subject to decay through entropy.

'And when he saw the creation which surrounds him and the multitude of the angels around him which had come forth from him, he said to them, "*I am a jealous God and there is no other God beside me*". But

by announcing this he indicated to the angels who attended to him that
there exists another god, for if there were no other one, of whom would
he be jealous?

Which God is it who said 'I AM A JEALOUS GOD AND THERE
IS NO OTHER GOD BESIDE ME'? The God of Israel said
this countless times, so who, then, is the God of Israel? He is,
according to the report of the words of Jesus Christ presented in
this Apocryphon, 'Yaltabaoth' – the original Clone being.

Jesus then goes on to explain how the creation of the Clone
being affected its creators:

'Then the mother began to move to and fro. She became aware of
the deficiency when the brightness of her light diminished. And she
became dark because her consort had not agreed with her.

But I said, "Lord, what does it mean that she moved to and fro?"
and he smiled and said, "Do not think it is as Moses said, 'above
the waters'. No, but when she had seen the wickedness which had
happened and the theft which her son had committed, she repented
and forgetfulness overcame her in the darkness of ignorance and she
began to be ashamed. And she did not dare to return but she was
moving about. And the moving is the going to and fro."'

The mother, Eve, began to move 'to and fro' and then did not
'dare to return'. The moving 'to and fro' is the first shimmer of
separation from the whole state of being. There is no movement
in wholeness as there are no parts to 'move' from one place to
another. That movement 'to and fro' is thus the first precessional
shimmer of atomicness itself; if atomic precession were stilled then
atoms would return to the state of 'light' from which they originally
came. Thus it seems the creation of these Clone beings precipitated
the 'fall of Godbeing' into the state of physical substantiality.

In the 'Sophia of Jesus Christ', which takes the form of a dialogue
between Christ and some of his apostles, Jesus says that the Clone
beings 'came to be in the will of the mother Sophia so that Immortal
man might piece together the garments there'.[4] It seems to me that
Jesus is referring to the creation of such beings as mechanisms
through which immortal man might 'piece together' – understand
– the 'garments' worn by Soul in the Universe of Parts, in other
words, the atomic cloaks of various grades of thickness which are
worn by Soul in the state of separation from the Whole.

However, Jesus adds that these 'moulded' Clone beings were 'condemned as robbers' because they 'welcomed the blowing' of 'the breath' of God but they were not able 'to receive that power for themselves'. They were unable, in other words, to receive the direct line of connection to natural Godhead.

He then tells the apostles in no uncertain terms that he came to mankind to free him from these 'robbers' who attempt, albeit in vain, to steal soul from those to whom it rightfully belongs:

He says that he 'loosed the bonds of the robbers' from immortal man and 'broke the gates of the pitiless ones before their faces'. These bonds that are loosed and gates that are broken are perhaps the gates and bonds that interrupt the genome of mankind, blocking and holding dormant the full expression of the natural unintercepted genetic scope of humanity. Jesus describes these 'robbers' as the 'pitiless ones': many abductees have reported the complete lack of sympathy which the Greys appear to have for human suffering. Of course, if my theories about these beings are correct, it is easy to see why 'pity' would be impossible for them even to conceive of.

He goes on to say that he 'humiliated their malicious intent' and 'they all were ashamed and rose from their ignorance'. 'Because of this' he continues, 'I came here, so that they might be joined with that spirit and breath and might from two become one, just as from the first, so that you might yield much fruit and go up to the one who is from the beginning'. Thus he came to free us from these beings by making them realize their ignorance such that the process that created them could be reversed. So that 'they might from two become one', one again with the equivalent of their creator beings, returning to the same state of the first, least forceful atomicness from which they were originally cloned.

Jesus then says to his apostles that he came so that he might 'reveal to you the one who is from the beginning because of the arrogance of the Prime Begetter and his angels, because they say about themselves that they are gods.' He adds that he came 'to remove them from their blindness' that he 'might tell everyone about the God who is above the universe'. So Christ perhaps informed the Clone beings that their search for a way in to receiving soul for themselves was a pointless task. Perhaps when he spent three days in the 'cities under the earth' he was doing just that, reaching through into the higher force thresholds (*perhaps some form of irradiated life platform*) within which these beings exist. He also suggests that he might well have given mankind a reference through his own being of how to conquer the genetic interceptions, when he instructs his apostles to: 'Humiliate their malicious intent, and break their yoke and arouse my own.'

There are numerous accounts within many texts of the Coptic Gnostic Library in which Jesus carefully explains to his apostles exactly how to deal with the alien beings, should they be faced with them. Most notable of these explanations is that given in the 'First Apocalypse of James' in the Nag Hammadi Codex. In this text Jesus explains to the Apostle James how to cope with the 'Archons' if he is faced with their representatives, as in fact Jesus himself was in the desert of Judea.

> 'James, behold I shall reveal to you your redemption. When you are seized, and you undergo these sufferings, a multitude will arm themselves against you that they may seize you. And in particular three of them will seize you – they who sit there as toll collectors. Not only do they demand toll, but they also take away souls by theft.'[5]

Jesus describes these beings as 'toll collectors'; perhaps this is because through their interceptions into the roadways, the tracks, that trace our lines back to the Universe of the Whole, they make it necessary for us to pay an extra price at each juncture of our journey back. An extra price that is translated in terms of a greater effort needed for return than would otherwise have been required had the interceptions not been present. He then adds that these beings also 'take away souls by theft'. What better way to describe abduction than to refer to it as 'The Taking Away of Souls by Theft'?

The text then continues:

> 'When you come into their power one of them who is their guard will say to you, "Who are you and where are you from?" You are to say to him, "I am a son and I am from the Father." He will say to you, "What sort of son are you and to what father do you belong?" You are to say to him, "I am from the Pre-existent Father, and a son in the Pre-existent One."'

Thus Jesus instructs James to inform these beings of his origins in the state of 'Pre-existence'. This state of 'pre-existence' is the state of perfectly free potentiality for all actualities, all existences, to happen, the state of being in Godhead, in the universe of the Whole.

He then explains to James how to inform these Clone beings of the difference between them and those who have their origins in 'pre-existence'. He says that he should tell them that they are 'ours' because 'she who is mistress of them is from the Pre-existent One' (he refers to this 'mistress' as 'the female' who 'produced them'). But 'at the same time they are alien because the Pre-existent One did not have intercourse with her, when she produced them'. Thus they themselves are not from the state of Pre-existence, rather they are from something that itself was originally from that state.

Jesus goes on to tell James: 'When he also says to you "Where will you go?" you are to say to him, "To the place from which I have come, there shall I return". And if you say these things you will escape their attacks.'

Thus if James makes clear his own root of being to these creatures and shows them that he fully intends to return to that root he will 'escape their attacks'. The Clone beings were originally created to allow the potential for 'Immortal Man' to view into the Universe of Parts without being affected by it. So, once Immortal Man has for himself entered into that universe and learnt all that he can about it such that he is able freely to choose to return to his immortal root, he is able to inform the Clone beings that he no longer has any use for them. Thus he will indeed 'escape their attacks' and they themselves will return to their root which lies in the first shimmering state of atomicness which formed the 'clothing' of Adam and Eve.

Now, let us return to the account of the original interceptions themselves as presented in the creation stories of the 'Book of Enoch' and the 'Book of Genesis'.

Here are the two extracts side by side:

1 ENOCH 6–8	*GENESIS CH. 6, v.1–5.*
The fall of angels: In those days, when the children of man had multiplied, it happened that there were born unto them handsome and beautiful daughters.	And it came to pass, when men began to multiply on the face of the earth and daughters were born unto them,
	That the sons of God saw the

And the angels, the children of heaven, saw them and desired them; and they said to one another, 'Come, let us choose wives for ourselves from among the daughters of man and beget us children' ... Then they all swore together and bound one another by a curse. And they were altogether two hundred; and they descended into Ardos, which is the summit of Hermon ... And they took wives unto themselves and everyone (respectively) chose one woman for himself and they began to go unto them. And they taught them magical medicine, incantations, the cutting of roots, and taught them about plants. And the women became pregnant and gave birth to great giants whose heights were three hundred cubits. These giants consumed the produce of all the people until the people detested feeding them. So the giants turned against the people in order to eat them. And they began to sin against the birds, wild beasts, reptiles and fish. And their flesh was devoured the one by the other and they drank blood. And then the earth brought an accusation against the oppressors.

daughters of men that they were fair; and they took them wives of all which they chose.

And the Lord said: My spirit shall not always strive with man, for that he also is flesh: yet his days shall be an hundred and twenty years.

There were giants in the earth in those days; and also after that, when the sons of God came in unto the daughters of men and they bare children unto them, the same became mighty men which were of old, men of renown.

And God saw that the wickedness of man was great in the Earth and that every imagination of the thoughts of his heart was only evil continually.

And it repented the Lord that he had made man upon the Earth and it grieved him at his heart.

It is apparent from the account in the Book of Enoch that the 'angels', the 'children of heaven', were not sons of natural

Godhead. Rather, they were from the 'heavens' (which denotes the sky above) and 'descended' from these heavens into 'Ardos which is the summit of Hermon.' This does indeed resemble a description of a spaceship landing on a mountain. These 'sons of God' took 'wives unto themselves and began to go in unto them' and the women became pregnant with grotesque 'giants': perhaps these were the result of this first alien interception of the human genome.

These giants 'consumed the produce of all the people until the people detested feeding them' (the meaning of 'produce' in this context, according to the commentary on this Pseudepigraphal text, is 'toil' or 'labour'). When the people grew tired of the demands that the giants made upon them they 'turned against the people in order to eat them.' When the experiments of these alien interceptors were over and they had learned of a particular human group all that they could, perhaps they simply used their human body parts to extend the lives of their own Clone bodies which, as I explained earlier, were breaking down very quickly. Many UFO abductees have, in fact, reported seeing human body parts stored within alien spacecraft.

The account in the Book of Enoch also states that the giants 'began to sin against birds, wild beasts, reptiles and fish'. The numerous incidents of cattle mutilations discovered recently, mainly in the USA, in which surgical instruments of high precision appear to have been used to dissect the animals, exemplify these 'sins' against 'birds, wild beasts, reptiles and fish'. They seem to be searching for the elusive nature of 'Soul' in all its various manifestations.

After the quoted passage, the text from the Book of Enoch goes on to say that these 'angels' also taught the people: 'Magical medicine, incantations, the cutting of roots, and taught them about plants'; scientific knowledge about 'the seeing of the stars'; and knowledge of how to make weapons of war: 'swords', 'knives', 'shields' and 'breastplates'. One 'angel' taught 'the course of the Moon as well as the deception of man'! Quite an interesting combination of subjects, don't you think? So, expertise in warfare and scientific knowledge, particularly relating to astronomy and medicine, was imparted to mankind by these alien beings. Knowledge of weapons of warfare might well have been vital for those who were being intercepted to resist interference by those who were not part of the experiment. Thus the experimental test bed was preserved. Knowledge of medicine would also have aided the preservation of those whom the interceptors wished to preserve. These alien beings were, of course, the ultimate experts in all things physical and may well have communicated as much of their knowledge to mankind as possible, in order to bring humanity up to a point of understanding that could marry with theirs. In this way they might have hoped that they could then link in to us and receive from us that which they could never find themselves, an eternity through having a direct connection to the Pole Of Absolute Union: Godhead.

So, to go back to the Book of Genesis, it states that 'after the sons of God came in unto the daughters of men', God said 'my spirit shall not always strive with man for that he also is flesh.' From the point of these interceptions the interrupters were thus introduced into the lines of mankind such that the spirit of God could no longer reach through those lines as powerfully as before. You may have noticed that the word 'God' in these two different contexts actually refers to two different Gods. The 'sons of God' who bring about the evil 'giants' on the one hand, while on the other hand there is the 'God' who is disappointed at the 'evil' thoughts of man. This blurring of the distinction between these two is, as I have illustrated, not present in the Book of Enoch.

Thus the Old Testament itself has perhaps been tampered with by the same source that, in the first place, chose to omit such books as that of Enoch in order to present to humanity a God who was a mirror image of their own style of leadership, a God who was tribal, revengeful and extremely hierarchical in outlook. A false God of final deficit. Hallmarked in megalomania, egocentricity, duplicity and subterfuge. The maker of a set of rules that finally, when looked at carefully, might as cleverly as it maintains righteousness maintain the biggest confidence trick of all. The stage where its opposite prevails indefinitely. And when all is said and done, to coin the old cliché. Is it at all surprising? If this universe is the true Hell then what do we expect from its occupants but Sin and thus ignorance and thus restriction? We expect damnation. Enter the redeemers to be, alas, scorned and crucified.

After the Book of Enoch has described the terrifying effects of the alien interceptions, it then refers to a certain resistance in the people to these effects: 'the people cried and their voice reached unto heaven'. The natural justice of the fact that these interceptions were not wholly deserved by mankind invited the redeemers to come and seek to reverse their effect. Hence the many attempts for redemption that followed. Hence Jesus Christ.

The Apocryphon of John in the Nag Hammadi Codex seems, of all the ancient texts I have read so far, to present the clearest parallels between the words of Christ and the theories that I have expounded in this book. I have already quoted and interpreted several extracts from this remarkable dialogue between Jesus and his most trusted apostle, John. In the following extract Jesus expounds in great clarity the results which the 'chief archon' and his 'authorities' have inflicted upon mankind:

'A bitter fate was begotten through them, which is the last of the terrible bonds. And it is harder and stronger than she with whom the gods are united and the angels and the demons and all the generations until this day. For from that fate came forth every sin and injustice and blasphemy and the chain of forgetfulness and ignorance and every difficult command and serious sins and great fear. And thus the whole creation was made blind, in order that they may not know God who is above all of them. And because of the chain of forgetfulness their sins were hidden.'[6]

Thus a 'chain of forgetfulness' blinding us to our sins has been given to us by these Clone beings. Could that chain of forgetfulness be referring to the chains and chains of 'junk' DNA codes which interrupt the human genome such that a coherent uninterrupted track (which might reflect the full potential of man without the interceptions) cannot be transcribed into RNA and then proteins?

The text goes on to describe how hybrids were made between alien and human forms in order to reach more powerfully into humanity:

'And he made a plan with his powers. He sent his angels to the daughters of men, that they might take some of them for themselves and raise offspring for their enjoyment. And at first they did not succeed. When they had no success, they gathered together again and they made a plan together. They created a despicable spirit, who resembles the Spirit who had descended, so as to pollute the souls through it. And the angels changed themselves in their likeness into the likeness of their (the daughters of men) mates, filling them with the spirit of darkness, which they had mixed for them and with evil.'

Jesus then sums up the full horror of these interceptions:

'They steered the people who had followed them into great troubles, by leading them astray with many deceptions. They (the people) became old without having enjoyment. They died, not having found truth and without knowing the God of truth. And thus the whole creation became enslaved forever, from the foundation of the world until now. And they took women and begot children out of the darkness according to the likeness of their spirit. And they closed their hearts and they hardened themselves through the hardness of the despicable spirit until now.'

I have little doubt that the First Clones wherever or whenever they were cloned, made, manufactured, or set-up are what common theological references through the ages describe as the 'devil' Lucifer, Yaltaboah, Satanaku, Jabulon etc. Satan and Satanism may be the entire theo–philosophy of 'Clone-ness'.

The whole so-called 'black magic' ethic as practised through the millennia is simply a Reference Guide, a codex to the philosophies and practices that define an atomically derived and created artefact of an entropically-driven and finite Universe of Parts. It has nothing to do with what might be defined as the grand-scale Master Universe of what is eternal, self-propagating and divine, and thus outside the scale of atoms.

I believe we truly are in a predicament that has never been clearly seen as this. It is unbelievable but true. Humanity has systematically thrown out all the most important insights that identified the true story of our heritage and perhaps now we know why. I believe, unshakeably, that a huge covert conspiracy exists in the Occidental and more recently in the Northern Oriental world to cover up the existence in our part of the universe of the pseudo-'Fathers of Humanity' and their hand through the ages in the affairs of our planet. I believe our home has been commandeered as a 'farm' for the machinations of an alien species that surreptitiously seeks to use our form of existence ruthlessly for their ends. A whole paradigm of devilry that has remained hidden for what it truly is, under the banner of religion and the Occult, and has sought and is seeking to claim our patrimony and our future for alien ends.

A carefully engineered scaffolding of subterfuge and denial exists and pervades the most powerful institutions of the world, to prevent the exposure of what goes on in these contemporary times, to allow the behests of extraterrestrial beings to slowly take possession of our planet. Agents and agencies at the highest levels in the commanding governances of the world have hidden and will continue to strive to keep hidden what is going on. Many of them, I believe, haven't the slightest idea of the full measure of what they do. They will proceed under the beguiling intoxication of the physical sensory aegis and the power to control and possess the material and the extemporary. After all, the Great Tempter tried it for size on Christ in the hills of Judea as his own special and favourite piece of bribery. We all know it failed with Christ. We know equally how easily it will succeed with anything or anyone less. They have, it seems, succeeded in assassinating that quiet, unspectacular voice of the spirit that seeks to warn through the abstract whispers of Godhead: Inspiration and Intuition. A deadly hidden agenda prevails in the halls of power that may be subverted only in snatches and only for a short time. The highest 'hills' of governments, of corporations, of socio-service international organizations and the media worldwide are scaled and fall under executive control that secretly proscribes national interests in favour of the schemes of alien formats. In most instances I believe that no single truly 'human' being can have a clue as to where the orders have come from. The internecine and randomly differentiated set of instructions that make up the whole formulary of alien intentions for the planet can never be read by a single human eye, either. Its assemblage in the whole is seen by strange shaded almond eyes that once searched the dim irresolute forms of some outlandish world perhaps a thousand light years away.

As I have said before, if this is all a sop to paranoia, a flight of pure fancy that seeks to blame the natural excesses of a species on some outside scapegoat whose existence is difficult to prove, then I would have to crave your forbearance and indulgence in the hope that my theory is at least interesting. It certainly isn't original. For the really cynical amongst you, at best it is a good yarn and at worst the speculation of a fool. I hope you will be kind and think me a well intentioned one, at least. If I am right, however, I hope it might serve to set in motion a never-ending process of search and discovery within and without each of you that will seek to uncover the truth of our predicament and perhaps, as a result, promote the realization that you are precious beyond dreams as an individual simply because you have a *soul*. That in the exercise of the totally *free will* that comes with it, nothing and no one can stop your progress to the 'Masterverse' beyond the enforced atomic universe, if you simply reason out all you do and measure all choices for their value in uniting and bringing elements together and doing all things for their value in maximizing such as this. The converse, of course, will take you on a journey of horrendous demise with the law of diminishing returns into a series of more and more restricted states from which the only way out is the eternally implicit *loving* expression of Godhead, if indeed you are able to appreciate its value as such and still act to its formula of renewal out of faith, belief and trust. Unfortunately, this is almost impossible to do because it was through the lack of these qualities in the first place that your demise began. That is why Jesus Christ himself confirmed that many go into a permanent state of perdition.

Isn't this surely the most powerful urge to righteousness? The simple and blessed measures of good sense devoid of the threat and implied blackmail of hell fire and damnation? The horrifying humbug of figurative impostures that bend credibility beyond meaning and install belief through engendering paralysing fear? The deadly perspective that condemns us all more than any other is that we accept what might be patently rationally true *only* if it satisfies *our individual* comfort points. And that is the biggest price of Sin. Sin, to my mind, is no more than restriction. Hard, cold restriction. It prevents us from viewing options objectively and, more importantly, acting on them with dispassionate zeal. In it and through it we dictate our own demise. The ignorant fear to tread where the wise don't. If we spend our lives wastefully in premises of indolence and apathy without seeking after the knowledge of those vital perspectives we have lost and forgotten. We may never regain those vital viewpoints that will help release us from endless returns to mortal endeavour lifetime after lifetime. The pursuit of release from what the Hindus call the Wheel of Rebirth will be subject to the law of diminishing returns and thus will lead to reincarnation down into more and more basic lifeforms.

Our religious mentors and administrators have, by and large, spurned the truth as uttered out of the mouths of the great revealers of existential verity in favour of their self-centred vanities and mortal sensory-based insecurities and inertias. They formed and managed organizations that are the antithesis of the ways, the truths and the lives of righteous offertory. Take a single look at the Vatican and its grandeur. Look at the splendour of the uniforms that line up in pious arrays a few steps away from Popemobiles, Cardinal-cadillacs and the like, and then think of a beautiful Man who walked the stones of Jericho with bleeding feet to serve the poor. These hypocrites who claim the right to pontificate on the moral adjuncts of us all have, as a result, authored the demise of countless millions of souls who followed in meekness and trust the prognostications of those who at best were fools and at worst charlatans. It is the terrible price we all pay for belief without rational wisdom. We, of course, all know that ignorance begets ignorance. The compendium of loss we see drafted and recorded in the ninety-five per cent of pseudo-genes not coding for protein in the human genome signals a coffin for the species that once burst with the fireworks of all knowledge in Godhead.

You might well ask what can be done to stop an intelligence so superior to ours from doing whatever it likes with us and our planet too. As one would expect with a highly intelligent species (they have proved they are far superior to us, in intelligence at least, by the mere fact that they have got here past our understanding of the laws of physics and the barrier of the speed of light) they are doing just this in the most economical, ergonomical and efficient way possible. That means just one thing. They are doing it covertly. I wonder if you see what I mean. It is not as important to know *what* they are doing as it is important to know *how* they are doing it. They have been the progenitors of humanity, albeit for their own purpose, out of the womb of African Eve. I have tried to take an educated guess of the '*what*' of it all in this book.

I believe the alien plan for our planet was boosted with more and more urgency since we as a species made the first atom bomb, perhaps under their telepathic inspirational guidance. If I read them right, they could once upon a time have never anticipated or carried through a violent act. They were exact parodies of their angel-type Master Adam Beings and could only know the behests of Godhead. But they had *free will* and may have decided to do an act that was, of course, murder and genocide on a purely utilitarian basis, i.e. they were just carrying out the brief of their Adam Beings to protect the whole quantum of existence on their home planet at any cost from any threat. They did just this. Alas, the threat they identified turned out to be their Creators themselves. When they wiped out their Creator Beings on their home planet they came to know the deadly psychological quantum we call violence or aggression. The Clones had become Cain. It would thus be in their 'programme' to be violent and to kill if at all necessary. They, I believe, do not consider it necessary to take out the human race at a stroke. They need us in vast numbers either as food, clothing or shelter. I mean that figuratively, of course, but it may well be *literally* true. They now have the means to take us all out at a stroke, if needs be, by remote control, thanks to the creation named 'Trinity'. This was the code name of the first atomic bomb that was exploded in the New Mexico desert in 1945.

There are numerous accounts from the records of the past of the 'Gods' laying waste to or vaporizing, with what sound suspiciously like neutron bombs or thermonuclear devices, vast numbers of the enemies of these 'Gods'. Judge for yourselves from the following accounts.

In the eighth book of the Mahabarata there is the following narrative:

'Gurkha, flying in his swift and powerful Vimana, hurled against the three cities of the Vrishnis and Andhakas a single projectile charged with all the power of the Universe. An incandescent column of smoke and fire as brilliant as ten thousand suns rose in all its splendour. It was the unknown weapon, the iron thunderbolt, a gigantic messenger of death which reduced to ashes the entire race of the Vrishnis and Andhakas.

'The corpses were so burnt that they were no longer recognizable. Hair and nails fell out. Pottery broke without cause. Birds disturbed circled in the air and were turned white. Foodstuffs were poisoned. To escape, the warriors threw themselves in streams to wash themselves and their equipment. With the destruction ended, the Kuru king Yudistthira was informed of the power of the iron thunderbolt and the slaughter of the Vrishnis.'

The projectile is dropped from a 'Vimana', which, as I have described previously, is the term used in these texts to describe a mercury-driven aerial chariot, ridden by the 'gods'. The result of this projectile falling is unmistakably a nuclear blast.

A nuclear fireball ('as brilliant as ten thousand suns'), a mushroom cloud (an 'incandescent column of smoke and fire') and an atomic bomb (which is indeed a projectile 'charged with all the power of the universe' because it unleashes the force that makes for the atomic nature of the universe from within an atom), are all described here. Even perhaps what we now term 'radioactive contamination' is mentioned: 'Foodstuffs were poisoned'. Hindu scholars believe that ancient atomic explosions such as these occurred, according to the texts in either 3102 or 2449 BC. There are remains along the Upper Ganges river, the area described in the 'Bharata war' in which Vimanas and nuclear weapons were used, of numerous charred ruins that have yet to be explored or excavated. Observations that have been made indicate that these ruins could not have been brought about by ordinary fire. They appear as 'huge masses fused together with deeply pitted surfaces.' In a second group of ruins dating from an earlier period in which ancient stone furniture seems to have been vitrified (melted and then crystallized), Russian researcher A. Gorbovsky reported in his *Riddles of the Ancient Past* the discovery of an ancient human skeleton the radioactivity of which was fifty times above the normal level.

Similar traces of an apparent nuclear holocaust have been found near ancient Babylon. Again these remains display vitrification, this time that of the melted ruins of a ziggurat structure whose ruin 'has the appearance of a burnt mountain' reports researcher Erich Von Fange.[7]

A further passage from the Mahabarata describes another apparently nuclear explosion:

'It was as if the elements had been unleashed. The sun spun round. Scorched by the incandescent heat of the weapon, the world reeled in fever. Elephants were set on fire by the heat and ran to and fro in a frenzy to seek protection from the terrible violence. The water boiled, the animals died, the enemy was mown down and the raging of the blaze made the trees collapse in rows as in a forest fire. The elephants made a fearful trumpeting and sank dead to the ground over a vast area. Horses and war chariots were burnt up and the scene looked like the aftermath of a conflagration. Thousands of chariots were destroyed, then deep silence descended on the sea. The winds began to blow and the earth grew bright. It was a terrible sight to see. The corpses of the fallen were mutilated by the terrible heat so that they no longer looked like human beings. Never before have we heard of such a weapon.'

This passage then goes on to explain that those who escaped washed themselves and their arms because everything was polluted by the deathly breath of the 'gods'.

The Sumerian hymns and prayers often mention divine weapons. For example, a character named Inanna is described crossing the heavens radiating a blinding gleam and destroying the houses of the enemy. The god Mars is said to have made fire rain down and to destroy his enemies with a lightning flash.

The Tibetan 'Stanzas of Dzayn', dating back several millennia, also depict a holocaust engulfing two warring nations who utilize flying vehicles and fiery weapons.

In 1952 archaeologists excavating in Israel unearthed at the sixteen-foot level a layer of fused green glass a quarter of an inch thick and covering an area of several hundred square feet. It is made of fused quartz sand with green discolorations, similar in appearance to the layers of vitrified sand that were left after the atomic tests in Nevada in the 1950s. That brings us to the story of Sodom and Gomorrah in which 'God' is said to have destroyed these two cities because they were so full of sin. Lot, a relation of Abraham, is warned in advance to flee these cities with his family and go to the mountain 'lest thou be consumed'; he was also instructed to hurry in order to get away quickly. Was Lot asked to flee from the epicentre of a nuclear explosion to the mountains where the rock faces would absorb the powerful radiation? Lot's wife, against instructions, looked behind her and she became a pillar of salt: could that have been a result of facing straight into a nuclear 'sun'? When Abraham later looked towards Sodom and Gomorrah, 'lo, the smoke of the country went up as the smoke of a furnace.'[8] And, of course, the most pertinent question, be there an authentic account of a nuclear explosion here or not, is: What type of 'God' would destroy whole cities and wipe out their inhabitants?

Robert Oppenheimer, the designer and scientific coordinator of the atom bomb, was a representative of perhaps the most illustrious of the directly and dynamically intercepted people in ancient times – the Jews. As a religio-ethnic group the Jews are to my mind one of the most, if not *the* most, marvellous groups of people the planet has ever known. The boosting of the Semitic genome through the Neanderthal link, by the extraterrestrials, improved the capacity of all humanity in all that is best about us. It also did the opposite.

The astounding contribution to what is the best in humanity by the Jews is incalculable. Yet with the deepest respect for them I believe that, along with the rest of us, they were duped in taking for 'God' what was no more than the 'leader' of an opportunistic extraterrestrial intelligence that was superior to a devolving hominid ape species on an ordinary planet with an ordinary sun. It was no 'God of all things'. It was merely a 'God' of its own self-interest.

I believe the entire module of the readornment of the Neanderthal genome by this alien intelligence ironically served as a boost for all humanity. But it was a double-edged sword, particularly as another distinct intercepted line of man was also vying for existence. These were the Cro-Magnons, as I have said. It is more likely to have been that this experimental genotype of Man was not a distinct creation planned for some future goodly purpose to benefit humanity through altruism. They were wired with a different brain-set or mind-set more akin to the bioids and android Greys than their Cloned Master Beings. We are seeing this legacy now in the form of their 'white' Cro-Magnon descendants of the northern hemisphere.

Could it be that an even more recent interception has taken place and is taking place even now, evidenced by the present high incidence of flying saucer manifestations in the northern hemisphere of the east: China, Korea and Japan? Could the Mongoloid peoples be the current test bed for alien interception? The following may well be a sample of what they have in store for mankind under the banner of progress and development, a form of progress and development for which Japan seems to be the world's vanguard nation.

The world's first 'Robo Priest' punched in at Yokohama Central Cemetery in 1992. Well versed in the liturgy of ten Japanese Buddhist sects, the robot spends his days serenely chanting sutras to the spirits. He bows his head and closes his eyes while his lips and facial muscles move in time to pre-recorded blessings. One hand raised in prayer, the other beats a rhythm on a wood block. He never tires and never – as far as anyone knows – skips a prayer. 'Many real priests are not so diligent these days', says Hirata Isao, Robo Priest's proud creator. 'They make the morning service as brief as possible, then drive out to play golf.' There is also a $400,000 mechanical monk who performs regularly at death anniversaries and other fitting times of the year. He also says the daily prayers for particular spirits in the liturgy corresponding to their sect and conducts special services at the request of the dead person's relatives. While he is not working, the platform on which he kneels is raised into a cubby hole in the ceiling! As the cemetery's management had hoped, Robo Priest has attracted a steady flow of clients to the privately run business, which is located in the hills overlooking the port city south of Tokyo. Priests have also made the journey to check out the opposition, says Sakurai Tohru, the chapel's creator. 'All of them praise his technique'. Robo Priest was designed and programmed by Hirata's Tokyo-based company, Elevator Systems. A maker of factory automation systems, it has also created other humanlike robots, including several android priests for a shrine in northern Japan. Hirata says he has received many enquiries and several orders for more. 'Fewer youths want to become priests', Hirata explains. In the past Japanese sons followed their fathers into the priesthood and eventually took over the daily operations of the temple. 'This is the same thing that happened to factories here when skilled workers were in short supply,' says Hirata. 'They were replaced by robots. Now the priests are in short supply, and robots can do the job'.[9]

CHAPTER TWENTY-TWO

OF MIND AND BRAIN

A highly significant piece of research has been done by one of our greatest scientists, Dr Paul Maclean at the Laboratory of Brain Evolution in Poolesville, Maryland.[1] Dr Maclean discovered that the brains of higher living organisms were divided into three distinct schemes of tissue. In other words, we have three distinct brains in our body expressing function in one mass. Dr Maclean called it the 'Triune Brain'. The three separate tissue schemes that make up our brain correspond to three distinct behavioural modes. He identified the three tissue schemes respectively as the Neo Cortex, the Limbic and the R Complex.

The most advanced scheme, judged in terms of manifested behaviour, he called the Neo Cortex and it comprised of the Cerebrum with special emphasis on the pre-frontal lobes. It is by far the largest of the three brain schemes and he associated it with the higher, more ephemeral functions of aspiration, intuition and aural communication in terms of language and a sense of the aesthetic. The expansive mind facility that deals in overall associative meaning.

The second scheme he identified as the Limbic system and this comprised mainly of the Cingulate and Hippocampal Gyruses, the Hippocampus, Insula and Hypothalamus. This he associated with behaviour that identified the 'family sense', with the nesting instinct and the group husbanding sense, the emotional bonding sense and play.

Dr Maclean identified three schemes of tissue as the R

Complex. It was largely composed of the Globus Pallidus, the Olfacto Stratium, the Corpus Stratium and attendant satellite grey matter. Maclean called it the 'R' Complex because the behaviour control ascribed to it resembled the posturing of reptiles. The hunting instinct, the territorial instinct, the fighting instinct and the instincts for ritual, display and challenge. There was a clear implication that the aggression centres worked in conjunction with these instincts, accompanying their functioning.

I believe, in line with my theory that devolution and not evolution is the true existential way, that the brains of higher animals were once a single mass devoid of sulchi. The three schemes of tissue that we presently find are the product of degradation similar to what happens when a plum becomes a prune. The three schematics of tissue were all one once upon a time and became more and more separated and discrete in function.

I believe that the brain is a bioelectric receiver. It itself, of itself, instigates nothing. It simply coordinates, analyzes and presents received signals on a bland chemo–electric table called consciousness that is made by the electrical interplay of atomic arrangements made up mainly by the water molecule powered by an electric coil (a stream of circulating iron [haemoglobin] called the blood circulation). All three schemes of tissue that make up the brain enable the personage to synthesize and interpret what is observed with meaning, within certain predominate accents and verifications based on each individual's unique brain chemistry at the time. The brain chemistry and neural pathways and connections simply allow for a specifically modulated and highly individual quantum summary and interpretation of sensory signals. In other words, the chemistry of the brain is like a map with different colours. The colours, shall we say, denote different regions on the map, and are analogous to different chemical packages in different areas of the brain giving a fingerprint or pattern, bioelectrically, for a certain thought or thought process to happen at any given instant. Change the chemistry and thus the bioelectric quotient, and the same sensory observation will give a different interpretation and a different rationalization instantly. The information is always coming at you from 'out there'. It is never made *inside* you by the brain. So where does it come from and what is its nature? Let me try to explain.

To me, consciousness is like a blank television screen. A neutral physical electrical status of potential 'to know'. The paraphernalia that allows you to make a picture on the blank screen comes from outside of atoms and molecules and is thus something that is not of this universe. Everything in this universe is loaded with a fantastic amount of pent-up force. If you release all the force pent up in a single thimble of water it will destroy your house and probably the street so completely you would not recognize either. Onto this enforced bed of universal 'atomness' imagine we can bring to bear a pen, a 'vacuum' pen that unwinds the prevailing force of anything it writes on and leaves a mark thereby. It can thus instantly judge any scale of difference it has left a mark against and thus proffers meaning on a relative scale basis wherever it writes.

This pen is of an existential status without 'force'. It is thus of a nature of what for want of a better term I have called Godhead. I believe that all that *is* Godhead is of no-force and all that is of *no* force is the entire compendium of 'Thoughtness', 'Meaningness', 'Understandingness'. Yes, I know the words are not in the lexicon, but I think you will see my predicament and forgive me for using them.

I believe all this world of 'no force' is plugged into us. It is plugged into our brain and we *choose* to receive it all in direct proportion to the status of the pins of the connecting 'plug' and the condition of the circuitry that switches its accessibility, and its storage facilities. It is what makes the picture and writing on the 'television screen' of consciousness. It is what plugs into and sits in discrete parcels on the colour-coded map of the chemistry of the brain that I alluded to earlier. We are, that is our physical bodies are the television sets already wired in and powered. Godhead provides the elements of information that give this already powered up background state meaning. *We* are the *hardware*. Godhead provides the *software*; which includes the programme that allows us to know and understand, and indeed the incentive to want to know and to want to understand, the hardware and the software and the interaction of the two put together and what it all means apart and together. If we disturb or alter the hardware in any way, the ability to read the software will be proportionately affected and the software will have reduced or no meaning.

If someone interrupts our conscious table by, say, hitting us hard enough on the head, we immediately lose our sense of 'thoughtness', 'meaningness' and 'understandingness'. The engine, or power coil, that powers our consciousness is temporarily stopped with the blow. In other words, the blood going around the body stops flowing for a fraction of a second at the instigation of the blow. Our radio thus stops picking up inspiration, intuition. We instantly, partly rightly, assume it happens because we have injured our hardware, our head, brain, etc., where all the facilities are contained within and we never envisage that we may be interrupting a mechanism that only picks up the three elements above that themselves exist outside the body frame or the skull frame. In either paradigm the end result will be the same. A loss of conscious knowing. In other words God is the awesome overall facility that makes it possible for you to think and know and see and do. This is another way of envisioning what is called Mind. The abstract concept that describes all this physical and metaphysical capacity functioning together.

The distinct tissue schematics Dr Maclean identified is like our map having three distinct background colours, Red, Green and Blue, shall we say, on which all the other colours and infinite variations of shades of colours may be painted, and thus each colour will take on something of this background hue when painted on. If the colour brown, shall we say, is a biochemical and bioelectric quantum for the 'instinct for survival' when it's painted on the blue brain schematic (Neo Cortex) the instinct to survive will be seen rationalized and acted on as a peaceful and clever process of escape from threat. That same colour brown when painted on the red schematic (R Complex) will be rationalized as a prompt aggressive act of killing and murder in order to escape the same threat.

For purposes of illustration let us assume that we each have a predominant chemical mind/brain 'set' of colours, if you like. A highly distinct and individual one. The colours, shall we say, are analogous to negative qualities of human nature. Ignorance, anger, fear, greed, avarice, deceit, etc. manifest a specific colour as they 'speed' in line with the entropic ethic of breaking up things into parts in gathering states of randomness and chaos. Each quality thus has a tone nearer black the more its power to divide and separate a prior state of union. The total colour mat together defines a species. The human, let us say, will be defined by a specific total colour mark. The collective colour summary when all the colours are superimposed. A tiger will have a species colour mark different from this and a butterfly one still different. It is all dictated by the experiences of our past lives and every physical body we design in the womb of our mothers for birth into physical incarnacy holds this highly particularized 'set' of deployed colours that dictates the shape and value of the new body we are taking on. I believe we design our own bodies in the womb before 'we' come into it. We come loaded into life with this. A quantum pattern of 'understandability' and 'discernability' and preferred 'actionability' highly specific to our individuality. There will, however, be much variation within this overall predominant theme of colours and on each minute colour point, and this defines what I would call the 'personality' of each individual within any given species. This facility is, I believe, what is commonly mistaken for our Soul. I believe our Soul is, as I have said many times before, just the unbroken 'line of connection' to Godhead since we all left Godhead to observe the Universe of Parts from the point of view of parts. We went on a safari to experience the only thing impossible in Godhead, got stuck in the jungle of karma and have been struggling ever since then to get back.

See yourself like a radio receiving the signals of God. These signals of God will always tend to rearrange the radio and its parts into such an ultimate symmetry and state of total intrinsic fit, that it will take the radio out of the Universe into Godhead if you let it happen. The trouble is that the Second Law of Thermodynamics or the entropic process seeks tacitly to distort the radio–body and its parts and thus countermand all that the 'Signals of God' are *unconditionally* doing, also tacitly, to stop the process.

What, then, is the 'you' that lets this happen or not? It is simply your particular quantum of restriction or your personal 'field of sin', if you like. The 'colours' of your mind/brain set in its minutely different set of shades from within which you receive God.

Let me use another analogy and liken the brain of human beings to three empty skyscraper buildings made predominantly of opaque, light-reflecting glass windows. No light is let into the buildings unless the windows are open. Each building is specialized in taking in light at a particular frequency. Let's say the red frequency, the blue frequency and the green frequency coinciding with the three tissue schemes of the brain. The buildings are just shells and have no significance at all in function unless the light, the wind and the breeze enter the windows and light up the inside. The light itself is made up of infinite hues of blue, green and red that are put together holographically in perfect union in Godhead to make what I would call the clear white light of the God Signal.

It is this God Signal that allows the brain to know, to understand, to discern, to analyze anything. In other words, what is defined as 'meaning' and the relative scales that give 'meaning' power for decision and change all happen only when this God Signal of light enters within the 'skyscrapers'. The extent of final truth we can derive and the actions we may take through this derivation about anything is thus proportional to the deployment and numbers of windows open in each and all of the three skyscrapers. The windows have to be completely open to admit the light without breaking it up into its constituents. The slightest angle of closure and the windows act as a prism and do not admit the light in its perfect state, but in its broken state where the 'knowledge' it contains has to be gleaned from its parts.

Godness may be likened to both this light and a fresh clean breeze seeking to come into your set of skyscrapers to light up, clean and replace the bad air within it. The 'light' is analogous to the total quantum of God knowledge and the 'air' is analogous to God Awareness and the 'breeze', that is the speed of the air in momentum, is analogous to Will to accomplish anything. All three together impart the possibility for change to take place in any prevailing situation by the individuality it touches. The crucial things are the windows. The uniqueness of an individual may be likened to the number of windows each individual has open in each skyscraper. Let's say the more windows are open, the more the skyscraper grows tall by making more and more elastic and malleable the girders of its frame. If all the windows of all the three are open they would finally reach the firmament ceiling and disappear proportionately, transmuting the whole frame of the skyscraper on the way.

The colour mat of my other analogy corresponds to the pattern of open windows on any and all faces of the three skyscrapers at any given time. The open and closed window scale will give us what may be called the individual's God-Quantum. The scale on which the pull of the physical universe is set against the pull of the Masterverse for that individual.

It is up to you to want to open the windows (the physical universe and its outlay of forces) to let all the God elements of the Light and Wind into and within your three skyscrapers. The trouble is that so many of us as human beings have got used to the bad air and a darkness within for so long, we do not know that there is a smell and darkness around us any more. We don't feel it is necessary to open the windows. Some have got to the stage that they don't know they have any windows. The entity thus stays in stagnation till the bad air rots the structure of the whole house and makes a smaller and smaller module available for liveability.

The ideal state for the three skyscrapers to be is empty of furniture with all the windows fully open to the light and the breeze. This is the highest state of Godbeing possible in a Universe of Force (the Transfiguration state) and many who came to explore this deadly Universe of Parts from Godhead have, I would guess, gone back into the Masterverse of enlightened being by doing just this soon after the Big Bang, when the scales of limit proffered by an enforced universe were experienced. They were truly Wimps and wise ones. Alas, it gets harder and harder to do with time due to the compound breaking up effects of the Second Law of Thermodynamics. We start putting furniture into our skyscrapers (this represents limit and thus restriction and thus Sin), in other words impediments that take up room in our liveability-module that light might otherwise fill, and we inherently handicap ourselves and limit the range and potential of our deliverance.

Let's say that the size and make-up of the furniture in the liveability module is proportional to a given species and that there is a minimum size and particular arrangement of furniture that defines that particular species. If you are a human being the reduction of these quantums to those minimums will propel the individual to devolve down to a subspecies, i.e. to ape, monkey, beast, insect, tree and stone in all the endless variations in between we call living species, till they become undifferentiated atoms and primary particles as prey to the dismantling force of entropy.

To summarize it all, the God Signal contains all knowledge and the Will to action within it and thus proffers the Will to do and carry out any of this action with any alteration good or, alas, bad that is deemed necessary. It invests the potential for perfect freedom. You can use this potential to become restricted, too. You can so restrict yourself through making wrong choices that the manifestation of Will itself is mitigated. It becomes weaker in you till it is so weak that you will leave the choices that mark your own destiny to others. That is when the implicit change of any situation becomes seriously compromised and the long drop to what might be termed perdition and damnation begins. You lose the ability for self-change. The biggest killer of any soul line is thus apathy.

You can, of course, do it the other way and become more and more blessed and enlightened till a physical body is no more suitable as all restriction evaporates through the Knowledge the God Signal gives. Happily, in triumphant resource you will change to take on ascendant mantles of existence till you reach the final triumphant state of enlightenment that signals Godhead itself.

Let me go back to my metaphor using colours to illustrate the mind/brain set. The whole idea is to have no colours at all. Go clear and you are in and with Godhead. It is as easy and tremendously hard as that. I believe Christ came as a man to demonstrate that it still could be done and how it should be done, in the form and formulary of the species called Man. He affirmed this on the Mount of Olives when he demonstrated that he could achieve the state of transfiguration to Peter, James and John. The final unwinding divestment and dissipation of all force in his being.

The Masterverse of true Godhead always seeks to save all ways eternally. It is its very inceptual aegis. Unlike these false so called 'Gods' that bring in conditions based on their own vanity. You know them for what they are when they claim they are a 'Jealous God' and ask that you 'should not have strange Gods before them'. It is such an obvious falsehood, it makes one wonder why humanity has let the subterfuge go on for so long. We seem to assist daily in our own demise as a species. We never seem to learn that good logical sense is our only reliable tool to seeking and finding the truth about our own deliverance. We insist on believing humbug. We kill, maim and abandon the saviours that come amongst us imploring us to listen to the sweetest logical sense. We injure, diminish and distort their words, deeds and examples in favour of the deadly scoundrels who have brought poison, death and destruction on us all. Why? To me it can all be summed up in four words: Grey, Green, Yellow and Blue. We didn't spot and couldn't spot this terrible intercession in the affairs of Mankind. That is the trouble and the whole trouble of our existential predicament in a Universe of diminishing returns with time.

It is undeniable that the inspiration and upliftment of the human family through the Neanderthal (Aryo-Dravidio-Semitic) interception in terms of Art, Science, Poetry, Literature and what might be termed the humanities has been fundamental to the positive progress of us all as a species. I think the Alien Clones and Greys got more than they bargained for in some of the hybridization experiments of theirs.

It bears saying at this point that it might well have been discovered by the aliens when they did their experiments all those millennia ago that highly melanized humans (darker-complexioned forms of our species because of their stronger dominant genes) were resistant and could not be easily genetically intercepted for hybridization. Darker skin types may have been safer from the alien grasp because they had mechanisms that resisted too powerfully the inserted alien blueprints, for a more complete hybridization. They thus may have retained their genotype a little nearer the Godhead scale with a rewired brain but very little else of the alien prospectus. Their aerials (brains) were thus enhanced to pick up Godsignals. This boost allowed them the perception to spot the Alien subterfuge and intentions, and some of them may have isolated themselves from alien grasp to survive as a less polluted genetic line. They would later pass down this line through their own and through cross-breeding with other humanoid lines, including the more alien hybridized ones, weakening the alien prospectus all the time.

It is, however, likely that of those early types of humans the ones with the most recessive genes were the best material for interception. This stock was perhaps found among *Homo Erectus*. These were the people that formed the main caucus of human life types and were thus most suited for general genetic interception. It would finally lead to the so-called 'African Eve' mentioned previously, and eventually to the Cro-Magnon legacy of fairer skin type and all the other physical manifestations of an 'intercepted-gene' ancestry.

The enhanced 'Adamic-Neanderthals' probably hid and kept away from alien contact and influence. Their newly enhanced brains gave them an edge and they could take more sophisticated measures to hide from the uninvited visitors from space. Perhaps it is their surviving progeny that make up the present Aryo-Dravidio-Semitic component of Mankind. I for one would bet on it.

The renewal of the aerial's (the brain's) capacity to receive Godhead was an inevitable stage to pass through in achieving the final hybrid the aliens needed. It may be that the enhancement of the Neo Cortex in some of their human experimental stock, perhaps particularly the Neanderthals, caused an increase in non-material visionary and abstract 'thinkability' in this genus. Remember the Neanderthals, strangely, had much larger brains than any of their contemporary hominid forms. The aliens would have wanted this feature built into their hybrid stock and were likely to persevere with their attempts to genetically adjust Neanderthals, no matter how resistant they were to the genetic engineering process. The large brain was a facility the full use of which the Neanderthals had lost in the natural path down to becoming primates through devolution. This rewiring of it allowed them an enhanced reception of Enlight and thus Godhead and thus thoughts accented with a view outside atoms. Not a useful and easily understood quality for roboids. They were, after all, only the masters of the physical atomic universe. Perhaps some Neanderthals saw clearly what was happening and escaped from further genetic experimentation.

Others lingered. The aliens made more genetic adjustments to them over long periods of time. A number of these enhanced Neanderthals were selected; those who now perhaps form the so-called 'classic' European Neanderthal group to which I have previously referred. In these Neanderthals the other schemes of tissue that made up the brain could have been genetically enhanced to meet further alien requirements. The R Complex was an obvious target. Its genetic enhancement in both this Neanderthal group and the *Homo Erectus* alien-enhanced group with which these Neanderthals were hybridized, I believe, produced the (Cro-Magnon) 'barbarian' genotype. The Cro-Magnon predisposition to violence and colder, more dispassionate almost mechanical emotional sense emerged from these adjustments and are nearer the alien bio-psycho disposition as attested to by many abductees. It suited the aliens' final purpose for 'conquest' of the human soul aegis much more. A close examination of the aggressive violent tribal history of Vikings, Goths, Visigoths and Huns may confirm this surmise vividly and beyond any shadow of a doubt.

All the foregoing may explain why the Aryo-Dravidic-Semitic people of our planet gave us all the great religious teachers the world has ever known. The vast majority of the most devotional and spiritual races of our planet come from this dark-skinned stock. Not one religious teacher of the stature of Gautama Buddha, Jesus Christ, the great Prophet Mohammed, the Prophets of Israel, the Jains, the Sikhs or any of such stature has come from Northern, thus Cro-Magnon, climes. In fact, the further north you go the more mechanistic, binary and materialistic the so-called 'prophets' there become. Till we now have General Motors, Ford, Mercedes Benz, Adidas, Coca-Cola, Shell, Microsoft, McDonalds and many more of such ilk forming the new lexicon of prophetic glory for your children and mine to believe in, in the future.

All the experimentation with the hominid species was likely to have been done in the spirit of random hybrid empiricism, in intention no different from our attitude in animal experimentation today. The cold logical list-filing premise of what was best for their purposes was allowed to take its course and through this the Cro-Magnons (now the most heavily alien-intercepted line) probably set about wiping out the leftover little-altered surviving Adam-Neanderthals when they could find them. But these Neanderthals were too clever now and survived the pogrom as a modern type of hominid. Part of the *Homo Sapiens Sapiens* genus. The urge to cull all other forms of hominid in the Cro-Magnon mindscape continued and continues through history to this day, through pogrom after pogrom victimizing the Jews and other Semitic people, the Gypsies, the indigenous Indians and Africans, the Afro-Americans of North and South America, the Aborigines and Maoris of Australasia. An incidental exercise was embarked on, of supplanting all the best representatives of least-intercepted humanity with a machine-minded breed, the Cro-Magnon derivative. An industrially developed so-called 'cultured' people, and yes, they continually use the word 'civilized' about themselves to describe a historically proven bunch of colonizing killers and pirates with pale complexions that through centuries have been and are acting more akin to the little Grey roboids that now visit the by and large unsuspecting people of the Earth. Could they simply be doing what their genetically engineered forebears have left them to do as a legacy? I believe that the aliens were counting on them to do their dirty work for them and 'tidy up'. A clean-up of the Earth laboratory of unwanted humanity. It all goes on to this day. The atomic eggs that might provide the final solution are being gathered in one basket. We read all about it. It's called the Non-Proliferation Treaty. Who's not proliferating what? The whites are allowed to 'proliferate' in the name of peace while the blacks, surprise, are told they most definitely must not do anything of the sort.

But they reckon without the power of Godhead in the Universe to preserve naturally that which receives Godhead best of its own accord. Just as the alien behest persists, so too continues the intercession of the representatives that serve the Master world beyond the atom. When the finally summary is totalled, it is they who will certainly prevail in an eternity of glory, beauty and goodwill. The lances of devilry can never prevail, as Christ reminded the head 'devil' who took on the central aegis of redemption in the hills of Judea with the words, 'Get thee behind me, Satan. It is written that thou shalt worship the Lord thy God and him only shalt thou serve'.

The needles of doom will inevitably alter their courses to point at the heart of all that is facile and finite. They will carry through the natural justice of righteousness on all who offend the line of that infinite and eternal mandate that preserves the just wherever they may be through the mechanism that connects them to Godhead that we call a Soul.

CHAPTER TWENTY-THREE:
THE CRO-MAGNON LEGACY

And so, are we all done for? Do we have to accept the evidence of history written in the blood of innocents destroyed through various forms of racialism? Their blood cries out a warning of a terrible truth catalogued through the centuries. That truth reveals that, broadly, the Occidental psychology, far from being 'purely white', is more akin to the (Grey) demons in mythology and has shown itself to be a haemorrhage on the collective soul of all humanity. The 'Whited sepulchres full of dead men's bones and all kinds of corruption', as Jesus Christ put it. In cohortship with the Greys and their cloned Inaugural Adamic leader, perhaps known as Lucifer, they are now the arbiters of the fate of Mankind with their inherent systemic-mechanistic view of the world. Their creation: technology, the fang and claw that tears at the spirit of what is still God in Man, makes them the 'Keepers of Entropy'. They will continue to dance on the propensities of a melanophore and chromatophore (nature's colouring pigments), insidiously and covertly fermenting discrimination and dismissal of all who fail the test of the eye instantly. Such is their dignity. Such is their shallowness. Will they not cease their deadly dance till the chaos and madness of socialized entropy is complete and we are all as a species taken out of this world, leaving a legacy of a dead planet of winking lights to shine into space, till all the batteries run out and there is no more hint that sentient life once had living fathers?

The northern Cro-Magnon breeds of humanity and their derivations, be they Goths, Visigoths, Huns, Vikings, Angles or

Saxons, may well serve the purposes of the alien franchise through the Greys. They have contrived the means of human destruction for the aliens, through the atom bomb. Are the northern breeds keeping it in storage for them, guarding them well in refrigerated silos for perhaps the final purpose awaiting man? The culling of particular lines of man deemed unsuitable for the purposes of the Greys. A culling the aliens may well carry out if and when they openly come to call.

As I have said previously, the Cro-Magnon derivative has managed to get control of almost all the nuclear devices in the world under the best guises with, apparently, the best motives. The largely non-white so-called Third World will do well to watch this Little Red Riding Hood factor. The Occidental West and Northern Oriental East can fabricate 'Saddam Husseins' galore. How long do those living between the two geographical tropics have to swallow this codswallop? It is a terrifying thought for all the billions of non-white and mostly poor people in the world.

Certain 'hybridized' Northern Caucasoids and Mongoloids will naturally scream denial in high dudgeon and in pious protest whenever they are confronted by history's proof of their decadence and debauchery of human values through the centuries. The racist root that motivates it all is carefully hidden at all times. If all this fails, the favourite strategy, the age-old principle of divide and conquer, has always been and is always brought into operation. They pour placating balms and reassuring solace on their financially sponsored expedient Clones among the people of Third World nations, backing them with promissory notes of financial and political backing for their favourite schemes. Schemes designed to keep these people in positions of influence and power. Too often the subterfuge works, but if all this fails, dark and deadly teams of fixers and assassins go into operation, taking out their victims in cleverly arranged accidents and murder. All in the name of the sponsor countries' 'national interest'. Follow most Third World dictators' lines of sponsorship back far enough and you will find a genetic line of predominantly Cro-Magnon derivation sitting behind a desk somewhere in Europe or America.

There can be no doubt that a huge covert international intergovernmental conspiracy is taking shape in America, Russia, Germany, France, Britain, Italy and many other Occidental nations to ensure that the 'Haves' will at all cost seek to ethnically cleanse their countries of largely non-white 'Have-Nots' who, worldwide, outnumber them five to one. Some important people of conscience among their ranks, some of them victims of Soviet and Nazi race pogroms, now work within the various infrastructures that plan and carry out these evil formulas and toil ceaselessly to expose this evil. Yet few in the Third World will believe that such a conspiracy exists even though the evidence is widespread.

The current immigration laws with evil racialist slants being adopted in many European countries are seen as only short-term measures. More effective long-term measures pointing to global ethnic cleansing are disturbingly indicated in recent events. Some highly respected social commentators claim that a 'notional engine' is being created in the minds of white people through subtle propaganda in the Press and electronic media for the tolerating of first the social, and then the physical culling of largely non-white populations on a global scale.

Population control mechanisms, nothing to do with the condom and the Pill (although they too are used), such as deadly, targetable, socially pointable disease vectors, are being used to adjust and control increasing non-white numbers. A good example of this is Aids. There is potent evidence to suggest that Aids was developed in the West to act as a sexual culling agent of black populations, to be used against the traditionally promiscuous sexual practice of some African nations. Other diseases even more horrendous and still under development will be cleverly deployed to do as much damage as possible to other non-white populations worldwide. These ethnic biological agents exploiting biological weakness in different racial groups are being developed in laboratories all over the western world at this moment under hidden disguises and pretexts.

The racial war of the worlds has begun, and few know about it, and fewer still will be told about it.

Third World nations, through their representatives, must take the greatest care to read accurately the smile on the face of the Occidental tiger when it approaches benignly to set its scale on their cheap labour and set its noose on their growing and prospering markets. They are deadly courtiers with poisoned chalices, if history is anything to go by. Their nooses lead to secretly contrived financial corrals that could hem in, under their dominion, many poor countries for periods of time that could well reach the first century span past the new millennium.

Many developing countries that have sought to break from systematically Western-controlled money supply institutions are targeted for destabilization. These countries are now in serious competition with the Occident in terms of trade. They have to be destabilized because they do not seek to follow the monetarist free-market system of the Occidental world. For obvious reasons, unstable countries, be they politically or financially unstable or both, are not likely to get their act together to present a serious threat to their international competitors in trade. The advantages that newly developing countries have to get ahead with their cheap labour and, in many cases, locally available raw materials is prodigious. They have a lot of leeway to make up and while they are making it up through means by and large independent of Western sanction, the industrially developed countries with their horrendously expensive labour market will have to see to it that as much unrest prevails in the countries that are trade- and resource-producing competitors. For one thing, it sells the arms they make and kills the people they want to kill. Secondly, it provides a base both political and fiscal that is unstable for growth and discourages investors and investment in these potential competitors. Consequently this investment might remain in or go in the direction of the Occidental world. It gives a new and awful meaning to the axiom of 'killing two birds with one stone'.

How, then, are they likely to set about this? Every country in the world has a 'piece' of each other. These 'pieces' are called Embassies, Legations, High Commissions. Agents from these places do their deadly work covertly all over the world. The more sophisticated the 'set-up', the more successful the result which, of course, is to do as much damage to local economies as possible.

Agents under various titles and subterfuges from these places, in cohortship with paid (bribed) locals willing to sell their countries' interests for financial and other benefits, work covertly in the interests of the sponsor nations. The rich Occidental nations have highly developed and efficient mechanisms with huge financial resources to do as much damage to the developing poor nations as possible. They can do it to the Third World, but in large financial structural terms the Third World is itself defenceless and cannot do it to them.

Political parties, labour unions, vital commercial concerns, government departments and important social agencies are infiltrated. Leaderships are subverted. Important people (vital cogs in the efficient running of things) are targeted and set up one against the other, subtly causing divisiveness and thus reducing the capacity for efficient working practice be it in factory, office or port.

While many countries have to cope with all kinds of locally engendered threats to the well-being and welfare of their citizens they would do well, in the present context of racially oriented nationalistic threat from abroad, to *wake up* to the danger of it and wake up *soon*.

The world's non-nationalized media, both print and electronic, are in the hands of about two hundred individuals. The vast majority, including the most powerful of them, are white. While a few enlightened ones might believe in the concept of the global brotherhood of man, the likelihood is that the majority are small-minded parochial kith-and-kin racists and tribalists hell-bent on preserving small hierarchical patchworks of citizenry as inheritors of all our yesterdays and all our tomorrows.

Few nations and their heritages have been left untouched by the 'songs' of the civilizing white man. To the tempo and meter of the gun, the bullet and the cannon ball they carved their name in greed and avarice and taught the values of *take*, *take* and *take*.

What of the future? Line up . . . line up . . . line up . . . for the box in the corner. Out of it, day after day, will be thrown at you Mickey Mouse values of awesome profundity. In reels twenty-four hours long you will be entertained, indeed riveted by the grandiloquent depth of twelve-year-olds discussing their second abortion and the flow-density of lipstick. In the name of such civilizing wonderment let us come and take your values two thousand years old, your devotion and love of your ancient gods and put some Coca-Cola dash and fizz into it. Let us build a hundred million homes with the wood from your forests and then come and let *us* teach you not to be ignorant naughty boys and cut your trees down. Let *us* destroy ozone layers with our industrial pollutants and then ask you not to buy and use refrigerators because we are the most vulnerable when you let the gas out. Let *us* keep the means of your nuclear destruction in our hands. Don't you dare keep the means of our destruction in yours.

Preferential choices in terms of who we want to live with will always be made by human beings, or for that matter all animal life, in the light of perceived differences. How, why, when and where these choices are made is, of course, crucial in terms of consequences to the living process and the quality of life of any and, ultimately, all species. Human beings are the dominant controlling species on the Earth and the destinies of all life systems, including that of our own phylum, are in our hands alone. The internecine relationships within our own groupings are thus awesome in their importance and significance to our survival as the species we call *Homo Sapiens Sapiens*. It sounds almost trite to say this, doesn't it? Yet they command such an axiomatic stance over our real-time thinking process that what we do in the interests of one another in our day-to-day 'everydayness' is of vital and significant magnitude.

The four-year-old child who shouts racial abuse at black players from a European football terrace, or the eighty-four-year-old white pensioner who hides his wallet on no more provocation than the sight of a coloured face may be doing it less from the prejudiced pre-conditioning propaganda of his peers than from an intrinsic psycho-blemish that has been passed down through the genes of his white ancestors.

When are the people of the non-Occidental world going to wake up and see the writing on the wall? Why have thousands of years of lesson after lesson steeped in blood and suffering served to teach so small a lesson to the non-whites? A lesson implying that the glaring fangs on the hate-filled features of the white American, South African, Australian, Canadian, New Zealander, Hispanic South American, may not just be an ugly but temporary colonial social effect derived from the example of his fellows. It may well be an intrinsic effect in the polluted mind quantum of just being 'white'. When will they realize that the vast majority of whites may hold this polluted quantum of mind as a prevailing and all-pervading condition with which he or she faces every non-white person they might meet? That some hide it better than others and that is all. They just hide it to manifest it overtly sometime, somewhere, when the surface is scratched deep enough for the poison to pour out. That it is going to be there and stay there as generations come and go and unless non-whites do something to deal with it now, their children will bear the deadly legacy of at the very least a bondage of purpose and result, and at the worst the total extinction of them all, based on the colour of their skin.

What I am trying to say is that, even though the basic instincts of mankind point the other way, strangely the law of the jungle prevails far more strongly in the nature of man than the law of God, with, on our planet, the tribalistic precepts of the descendants of Cro-Magnon man in overwhelming command of the decision makers, particularly of white societies, to this day. The so-called civilized countries strangely seem to be more uncivilized in this respect than the simpler, gentler, more religiously devotional ones. These, of course, are overwhelmingly non-white. In them racial 'difference' by and large is considered to be a curiosity and a thing of wonder. A totally different psychological quantum from the 'white' societies that peremptorily dismiss non-whites as a collective species inferior to them.

In this respect, a truly 'civilized' people are the Yolgnu Aborigines of northern Australia. Helen Verran, an Australian philosopher of science at the University of Melbourne, has for the past decade studied the knowledge system of these people.[1] Their way of viewing the world seems to reflect the values and expressions of natural Godhead just as Western ways of viewing seem to reflect the manifestations of an alien intelligence. Verran points out that the Yolgnu's knowledge-system is so highly structured that they are 'just as addicted to a machinery of logic as we are'. She adds that 'when you get up and say that Aboriginal life has a very strict logic it rather takes people aback. You become quite unpopular because it disturbs people's cherished views that these people are in touch with romantic spirits.'

So, what kind of 'logic' do the Yolgnu base their knowledge upon? It is certainly a different sort to the Western variety. In Western science the logical underpinning is provided by numbers. Physicists, and to a certain extent scientists from other disciplines, use the language of mathematics to explain the world. The Yolgnu system, on the other hand, derives not from the symbolic use of numbers but from kinship. The name they give to this kinship-based logic is 'gurrutu', which Verran suggests must be seen as an alternative mathematics. The parallel with maths is clear. At the root of mathematics are the ten numbers, which traditionally arose from the naming of the fingers. In 'gurrutu', the basic elements named are not the fingers but the relationships between three generations of a family. Altogether there are sixteen different possible relationships within a family group that is made up of husband and wife, their four parents and their eight grandparents (i.e. the relationship between the husband and his father is 'gathu' from the older man's side and 'bapa' from the younger man's). The system thus constitutes a network or mesh of relationships. Everything in the world is understood by the Yolgnu using these sixteen basic elements. Verran offers an example of the difference between the Yolgnu and the Western approach in the understanding of land: 'land is meaningful because it has area which we represent in numerical terms. For the Yolgnu, land is meaningful because it has specific places that belong on the 'gurrutu' mesh'. Thus there is mother-land, father-land, grandmother-land, and so on. Thus the very basis of the Yolgnu's understanding of the world is borne only out of that which derives from the Universe of the Whole, from natural Godhead, i.e. human beings and their relationships. Mathematical measurement using abstract numbers could not, by its very definition as a system of measuring separate parts, have derived from the Universe of the Whole. Such measurement lends itself far better to the technological development that prevails in the West and to the alien beings who are themselves the epitome of the highest technological development.

To return to the knowledge system of the Yolgnu, all things fit into the 'gurrutu' mesh by belonging to a 'clan'. Each of the sixteen basic kinship names is associated with a clan, and all things belong to one or other of these. The 'gurrutu' mesh, says Verran, 'is like a very complex locating system', a sort of all-encompassing map of the world. But whereas with Western science we have to make our maps from studying the world, for the Yolgnu 'the world comes to life already mapped'. Their map is integral to the very being of the world and is quite inseparable from it. Thus the Yolgnu have an essentially holistic perception of the world, they view the world as a natural whole through which they understand the parts that make up that whole. Conversely, the Western view seeks to understand the whole by understanding the parts and putting them together.

Which view do you think might be closer to a view derived from natural Godhead?

Within the 'gurrutu' mesh there is a primary classification dividing the world into two halves: Yirritja and Dhuwa. Of the sixteen clans, eight belong to one half and eight to the other. All Yolgnu knowledge can be seen as an explication of the ways in which the two clans interact. Throughout the world the two strive to balance and harmonize each other. In human terms this means that a Yirritja man must marry a Dhuwa woman and vice versa. As Verran puts it, for a Dhuwa 'the only way you can then go on is to get together with a Yirritja person. This means reproduction, but also much more. In the conceptual sense, you have to get Yirritja knowledge to go on in life'. So, the Yolgnu place the greatest importance upon the value which the two different groups can have for each other, it is in the piecing together of the two groups that a whole and complete understanding is achieved. Thus those who seek racial 'purity', the fascists of Cro–Magnon descent, would be, in Yolgnu terms, only ever receiving part of the whole picture in terms of gaining knowledge. It certainly would seem logical that if we, in all our differing racial groups, are pieces of a puzzle that was once holistic being in the state of natural Godhead, then it would be in the piecing together of that puzzle that the whole picture can be regained. Thus if difference in terms of race, creed, or colour is received with welcome, it is the sign of a truly civilized way of understanding the world.

The collective attitude of racial superiority is thus perhaps the most debauched, destructive and dangerous element of mind in human society today, because the factorizations necessary to proclaim such a tenet when the nuclear prerogative may be used as the final arbitrating factor wins the argument for only one side: the predominantly white Northern Occidental and white Northern Oriental world. Yes, even in the historically broadly peaceful Chinese people, the white-skinned northern types instinctively practise discrimination against the darker southern Chinese. The colour of a complexion may well broadly define the extent and strength of alien genetic interception in an individual.

Let me at this point put before you a very interesting thing. The Earth spinning on its axis puts out a magnetic field. The strength of this magnetic field is greatest at the poles and weakest at the equator.

Magnetism, remember, is a force. Other force vectors also prevail, such as gravity: centrifugal and centripetal force derived out of the mass and axial spin orientation of the Earth concentrate greater force per unit area the further you go towards the poles away from the equator. It is well known that if you beam microwaves (little straight-vectored invisible bullets of force) of a certain strength and frequency at living animals, let's say normally peaceful mice, they become aggressive and will even try to kill each other. Secret experiments have been done on soldiers in America and the Soviet Union and a marked elevation in aggression thresholds was noted. This was due to changes in the biochemistry of the 'R Complex' regions of the brain. That part of the brain that Dr Paul Maclean noted as accounting for behaviour akin to reptiles, as mentioned previously. The accentuation of the aggression centres, the tribal sense, the hunting, fighting and territorial instincts.

If force acting on biochemistry of living systems can propagate and sustain behaviour such as this, might it not account for the overwhelmingly violent socio-behavioural paradigms of the Vikings, Goths, Visigoths, Huns, Franks, Angles, Saxons, Mongols, etc. of northern climes, as history proves through the centuries? Might it be that the altered alien hybridized stock of African 'Eve' migrated (or was perhaps 'taken') to northern latitudes to be cultured where the natural environment sustained these qualities? Qualities that would and could encourage conquest of all other genetic stock on the Earth if needs be. (Guess whose needs might have required this.) Thor and his thunderbolts fit in very nicely with being a God of such people.

On the other hand, the absence of force vectors acting on the astronauts in space turned many of them into dedicated evangelists and aspirants to better, more peaceful spiritual paradigms of behaviour than many of them had aspired to previous to going into space.

Broadly, the people of the Earth who live between the tropics of Cancer and Capricorn have less force per unit measure acting on their biology and thus their brain chemistry than those who live above and below these two tropics. They have proved to be, by and large as a group, the most devotionally spiritual of all the peoples on the Earth. A sign, maybe, that in less environmentally enforced paradigms the biochemistry of the Neo Cortex of the brain is so altered as to allow better reception of the Godsignal we might call 'grace' or Enlight.

It is beyond argument that the people with the strongest spiritual faith and devotional religious strength and focus have always been, and are particularly now, the people that inhabit the regions of the Earth where the geophysical force paradigms are least. A census of the church, temple, mosque and synagogue attendances in these respective sites will amply prove the point. While sociologists and behavioural psychologists might account for this in a myriad different ways, I cannot help feeling that the intrusion of physical point force acting in point perspective and location has a fundamental role to play in defining negative and positive human behaviour. It is strange that the further one goes towards the equator the warmer, more friendly and welcoming people become and the less the severe, strict, unemotional list-filing mindedness of northern-hemisphere people prevails. It is a people-oriented urge of mind in the geographical mid-band of our planet.

I noticed a marked affirmation of this in a domestic context in my own home. Whenever we had European guests to dinner, the overwhelming accent of the conversation was centred on material possessions. What latest model of car, size of conservatory, swimming pool, location and extent of holiday etc. Our guests from tropical and mid-band climes would unfailingly talk to us and each other quite naturally and in an unsolicited way about whom they had met, where old friends were, who married whom, how the children were doing, etc. A total people-centred social evocation. To put my conclusions to the test I asked my friends to observe any differences in the conversation between the two types and they too, without exception or prompting, came to the same conclusion.

As I have said previously, not a single great founder of the world's great religions came from a latitude very far above the Tropic of Cancer. A point that perhaps begins to demarcate a significant increase in the level of force such that it forbids a biochemical advantage in receiving the emanations of Godhead on this particular planet.

I would like to stress that this is a broadscope view of all the elements and that there are and will be many exceptions to the rule if the properties and consequences of reincarnation and karma are true. It is utterly shameful that I should be writing with a seeming racist slant in this way, but it is the only way I have to illustrate the deadly hidden factors that might lie at the root of our destructibility as a species.

It is interesting to note that when a point of view illustrating the disgrace of racialism as practised by the white-skinned breeds of our world through the centuries is avowed and proclaimed, a chorus of protest claiming 'Foul' rises from almost every pale-complexioned racist aficionado from the northernmost tip of Canada to the southernmost wilds of the Yucatan horizontally across the entire northern globe. Yet these same deadly disciples of racist debauchery keep the silence of the grave when, day after day, the most draconian overt and covert methodologies are used by them to corral, control and devastate whole nations and communities of coloured peoples in starvation and servitude.

All political roads lead to national interest. All social roads lead to tribal interest. It is easy to see what the current carefully measured and brilliantly stage-managed push by the Occidental countries to keep nuclear weapons from Third World countries might be really leading to. Under concerned-sounding, apparently worthy motives they may well seek to ensure that the finger on all buttons is as pale-complexioned as they can make it, China and Japan included. There is no doubt that they too could well be aimed at for destruction in any future race purge in the new nuclear targeting postures of the Occidental political and military mind. The plain truth is that you don't see them taking out *all* their nuclear arsenals. They play-act with small degrees of weapons reduction and have the almighty conceit to demand that, while they keep the vast majority of their weapons, no one in the Third World should dare hold any.

History proves beyond any reasonable doubt that *the black man suffers where any white man goes. Racially contrived nuclear writing is now clearly on the wall.*

The non-white nations of the world would do well to watch the gathering clouds of white-sponsored racialism as reflected through the drafts and discussions of grouped nations such as the European Community. A careful study of recent legislation would quickly reveal a monstrous catalogue of racially motivated rules and regulations, with the British, the arch colonial slavers, at the helm in sponsoring them. It is a dirty business of finely worded, overtly expressed tolerance in the media and covertly actioned red-boned racism in the halls of legislation.

Somewhere in the centres of these newly formed massive organizations of the Occidental world lurk secret groups of powerful men and women with the sole intent of quietly and covertly spawning the seeds of white supremacist philosophy. They cleverly and deviously design deadly and divisive paradigms to sow the maximum discord among the body politic of mankind, their stipend to come from the gun- and bullet-makers of our world. Their goal, one speculates, might be simply to derive and possess the means to take out at a stroke any or all of those they deem to be their enemy.

So let's see how a clever power might set about such a nuclear defined goal. After all the military 'Think Tanks' of the Occident are full of behavioural psychologists who have to be put to good use.

You would first need to have a plausible reason to hog all the nukes. That reason is easily found. There are enough irresponsible scoundrels in the world who display the qualities that alarm all peace-loving people. If there weren't it is easy to set one up. Of course, this threat has to be believable. Scenarios will have to be brought about that show up the threat as a draconian one and a mechanism has to exist where the world's media could be duped, threatened and marshaled into line to expose it and make sure everyone believes that this is the genuine article. Enter America and their contrived clone Saddam Hussein. The Power and the Gory. Game, Set and Match. Our Greys have got the result they may have been carefully cultivating since the Pyramids were built. A ready-made mechanism on our territory, not theirs, that can take out at a stroke all they want taken out if need be. All done by remote control. i.e via the Superhighway, the Internet and all the other wondrous devices that connect you personally to each other and to their representatives on this Earth.

What evidence do we have to substantiate such conspiratorial thinking? Take the so-called 'Internet', for instance. The Internet was the brainchild of the US Defence Department's secret information-gathering mechanisms. A series of top-secret military satellites were launched in the 1970s and 1980s with the specific intention of providing a facility for eavesdropping on any conversation anywhere in the world. This intelligence-gathering system needed a global grid of computers that, when connected together through a network, could be used to collect and process information from multifarious points of input. The world was invited to provide this hardware through private and public auspices, under the guise of the attractive proposition that a free exchange of information would be available for any subscriber on the network. The covert intention was, of course, to provide the US with an instantly accessible fund of data. Facts and figures that would facilitate the creation of a fantastic pool of knowledge of the affairs of us all that could then be used in the interests of the US in maintaining itself as the primary world power. The carrot has grown to enormous proportions and with it, of course, the stick. A stick that could be used to beat us all into the fashions and means that could control all our destinies with the interests of the super power uppermost. Any person or nation deemed an aggressor could then be dealt with in whatever fashion the US chose. Touted as an innocent facility to serve mankind for the benefit of mankind, the Internet's secret, covert US government-sponsored intention of holding individuals and nations to ransom if they so chose to do has by and large been already achieved.

Let us take the US out of the equation and substitute in its place an alien power. I think you will get my drift.

'Information warfare' is now the hottest concept in the halls of the Pentagon. The whole thing was planned in military and civilian 'Think Tanks' funded by the US Defence Department from the start, of course. It began substantially in the 1960s. 'Information warriors' hope to transform the way soldiers fight. Their goal being the exploitation of the technological wonders of the late twentieth century to launch rapid, stealthy, widespread and devastating attacks on the military and civilian infrastructure of an enemy. According to interviews conducted with numerous military, intelligence and administration officials it seems to be the case that the Pentagon has wide-ranging plans to revolutionize the battlefield with information technology, much as the tanks did in World War I and the atom bomb in World War II. Says Admiral William Owens, Vice Chairman of the Joint Chiefs of Staff: 'This is America's gift to warfare.'

In June 1995, the National Defence University in Washington

quietly graduated its first class of sixteen infowar officers, specially trained in everything from defending against computer attacks to using virtual reality in planning battle manoeuvres. More than a dozen secret infowar games have been conducted between 1993 and 1995 to determine how future military tactics should be changed to accommodate information warfare.

Spy agencies are also dabbling in infowar techniques. The National Security Agency, along with top-secret intelligence units in the Army, Navy and Air Force, has been researching ways to infect enemy computer systems with particularly virulent strains of those software viruses that already plague home and office computers. Such viruses could be inserted into the aggressor's telephone-switching stations, causing widespread failure of the phone system.

Another type of virus, the logic bomb, would remain dormant in an enemy system until a predetermined time when it would come to life and begin 'eating' data. Such bombs could attack, for example, computers that run a nation's air-defence system. Or they could intercept computers that run a central bank and thus instigate widespread financial panic. They could also destroy the electronic routes that control rail lines and military convoys. Or affect the flight-control software of aircraft such that they 'mysteriously' crash to the ground. The CIA has a clandestine programme that would insert booby-trapped computer chips into weapons systems that a foreign arms manufacturer might ship to a potentially hostile country – a technique called 'chipping'. In another programme the agency is looking into how independent contractors hired by arms makers to write software for weapons systems could be bribed to slip in viruses. A CIA source who specializes in information technology has been quoted as saying the following: 'You get into the arms manufacturer's supply network, take the stuff off-line briefly, insert the bug, then let it go to the country. When the weapons system goes into a hostile situation everything about it seems to work, but the warhead doesn't explode'.

The US Air Force's latest weapon is the Commando Solo. This aircraft contains microelectronic equipment that enables the plane's crew to jam a country's TV and radio broadcasts and substitute messages – true or false – on any frequency. During the Gulf War in 1991 the plane's crew broadcast radio reports to Iraqi soldiers eager to hear uncensored news of the war, including some of the next areas to be targeted by US bombers. As a result, many Iraqi soldiers deserted those positions. Specialists for the Army's 4th Psychological Operations Group, which prepares the taped messages that Commando Solo airs, have considered the possibility of morphing the images of a foreign leader and putting words into his mouth to get him into trouble.[2]

No one can quite hear the clicks of the enemy keyboard, or the fuseless bombs travelling over the Internet. However, a pattern of computer mayhem begins to emerge.

As for the extraterrestrial aliens, with final and ultimate irony it is likely that they will have no aggressive intent when looked at in martial terms. A highly intelligent species need never use violence as a means of conquest, but they will always keep something like the nuclear prerogative up their sleeve for use if needs be, just in case. A technologically primitive and emotionally unstable species like ours is not likely to follow the laws of logic and reason. Many abductees describe these Greys as emotionless beings that show no aggression or anger whatsoever. My guess is that they are pure intelligence wrapped up in a semi-organic biological chemistry with a kind of mercury-silicon sponge material that makes up their body mass. They have one quest and one quest only: to understand all about us and single-mindedly lay claim to what it is about us that interests them. As I have said, if they were intelligent enough they could take over a relatively primitive race of hominids without a shot being fired by them. They would simply instigate it amongst us.

'No, no,' I hear some of you cry. 'How could they achieve this with a peaceful, loving, caring species like human beings?' Ha, ha, you thought I was kidding, didn't you? You thought I had looked at the evidence through the centuries of man's loving custody of each other and finally seen the light. Men just aren't capable of aggression and violence. Are they?

Of course I am only joking. But it may be that the joke is inappropriate. It may just be that as man devolved down from Prior Adam-like Man in stages of more and more gross physical genotypes to Ape Man and then to ape, his tendency to senseless aggression diminished. After all, overwhelmingly, animal species are only aggressive in defence, or because of chemically prompted instigators like pheromones to preserve a species through dominant sexual transfer. In other words, as a prompt to breed. It is only man in all the so-called 'animal kingdom' that can be, and is, insanely aggressive against reason.

It used to be thought that some animals were inherently aggressive and killed wantonly. Studies were done on why foxes caused such unnecessary carnage in a chicken coop. In other words, they did not just kill one chicken and take it away, they would kill many seemingly senselessly. They discovered that the killing was done merely as a reflex reaction to movement and that the panic and chaos that ensued when a fox got admission to a chicken house caused the animal to snap at all movement. It was simply trying to kill its prey quickly before it got away. When some birds were tranquillized and stayed still in an experiment, the fox only killed the birds that weren't sedated.

I previously alluded to experiments where mice killed each other when subjected to remote microwave stimulation of their brains. You can bet that the defence services of all the super powers have been experimenting with such devices for use against human beings. (It may be that we as a species need very little stimulation indeed.) If our primitive science can do such as this, what do you suppose an intelligence perhaps thousands of years in advance of us might be capable of doing?

I am trying to say that the interceptors of man, in enhancing the brain capacity and inserting their own biological constituents into our species, might also have set in a predisposition to senseless aggression. In other words, a prompt to kill. It would be a very useful feature in a farm breed. A self-destruct button if the breeding experiment failed. A self-destruct button that is always there or in certain circumstances could be switched on by remote control, to kill. Perhaps specific to individual human beings.

CHAPTER TWENTY-FOUR:
HIDE AND SEEK

Are extraterrestrial alien beings going to make a personal appearance on Sky TV in the near future? Watch out, Rupert, your profits are going to hit the outer planets. The SKY's the limit. Preposterous and ill-conceived though this question might be, I believe unequivocally that our planet has been and is a kind of cradle to death and, through death, continuity in life to an alien species. Our planet is their battery farm providing endless numbers of Soul-connected bodies that when they die provide a mechanism of attachment for alien soulless beings to have an eternity. A depository of hope for their go-nowhere futures. Millions of years of careful remotely cultivated adaptation have finally come up with a hybrid product, a human product written in some human genetic lines that have been and will be serving their purposes till they take a direct hand in all our affairs in the not too distant future. In other words, our Earth has been a place to search for that elusive track to Godhead they misappropriated in their own world perhaps a billion parsecs away. They are here now, hiding on the peripheral planets and, if we can go by the reported affirmations of the Moon-landing astronauts, on our own Moon.

Given the capacity these alien beings have to reach humans anywhere by remote control, the answer to the question I originally posed may well be that they need not actually physically arrive here. In other words they need not actually set foot on terra firma. It is likely that, apart from the North and South Poles, that is the Arctic and Antarctic, these alien creatures would find the environmental conditions on Earth hostile. I believe that the tropics and by and large the mid-band of the planet (thirty-three degrees either side of the equator) seem to be relatively free of their visitations. It is possible that they need superconducting environments to run the current fields of the biomass of their synthetic bodies. We all know that cold environments assist the phenomenon of superconduction. It is likely that they have taken up stations on the Moon and the cold near planets for just this reason. A disproportionate number of UFOs have been sighted near the Poles in the Arctic and Antarctic. They may well be the best terrestrial landing sites for them. Remote and unpopulated, they would leave them relatively undisturbed to go about their business.

It has always been unlikely that the synthetic roboidal alien 'life-form' called the Greys would have used martial means to take over our planet. That is, until we exploded the first nuclear bomb. However, left to their own devices it is likely that their roboidal utilitarian programming would have suggested just that without compunction. Take over the whole shooting match. I believe they have not done this up to now because their hidden masters, the Primary Clones, would not let them do so. I think the reason for this might go back to Christ's temptation in the desert by perhaps the 'head honcho' Clone which itself perhaps led a particular batch of them in our solar system at the time. I have always wondered how the Son of God could be so easily manipulated apparently against his will, taken up a mountain (or, what is more likely, into a spaceship) and shown the world at the whim of another being, unless it was through some kind of advanced technology. No mountain, as we all know, is high enough to show anyone the whole world. My presumption is that Christ was accosted by a UFO in the desert around Judea. Perhaps Jesus provided enough evidence for the alien occupants to take him for what he (Christ) was, and that he convinced them that he had the means to lead even a Clone to eternal life in Godhead by means of his power. With the words 'Get thee behind me, Satan: it is written that thou shalt not tempt the son of man', perhaps Jesus was putting a synthetic creation in its existential hierarchical place. For all we know, it and any others that may have been present at the time may be enjoying the benefits of an eternal pension of total happiness in Godlight even now. Christ, after all, did promise a thief that he would be with him (Jesus) in Paradise.

But what about all the other alien Clones that might be left in the vastness of our Universe? Are they awaiting the promised return of Christ? And where are they waiting? If we have them here now, our solar system could be a very crowded place. There could be plenty of them sweeping through hyperspace towards us on the instigation of the Clone that Christ might have redeemed. This creature might well have got on the old wireless and told any of its mates left on its home planet that they were on to a good thing on this little blue-brown orb called the Earth. There was a phenomenon that could in fact lead them to a natural eternity devoid of constantly needing to be replenished in Clone juices.

Are they coming here even now, perhaps to await Christ's second coming because they missed the first one? Why are they staying out of sight or keeping out of the way on the outer planets? Are they trying to pre-empt Christ and trying a 'Do-It-Yourself' Soul-acquiring kit out, with us as the expendables? In doing this is there something they would have to do to themselves biologically to prepare for the investiture of a Soul? Is this something we as humans (and our humanoid ancestors) possess and possessed naturally, something vital like body parts or DNA strands they need from us? Perhaps this something requires that we exist as living individuals and exist in numbers, and are not taken out of the equation by their zap guns, shall we say. (I apologize for the sarcasm). Perhaps thousands of years in their covert custody proves this is so or they would have taken us all out eons ago. We might have been able to come to a deal with them. I'm sure we all know a few characters we might be willing to swap in exchange for peaceful co-existence with a superior intelligence and its singular usefulness on Earth. The trouble may be that this 'something' they need seems from all the evidence to require us to be altered in the way *they* need us to be for *their* purposes. That is, perhaps, the whole trouble and has, I believe, been the whole trouble with Man through the millennia. As I have said before, they want as many of us as possible in an altered state that fits *their* purpose of trying to 'piggy-back' on our genome to a Soul. This, ironically, may be our only guarantee of life and living on as a species and has kept these creatures away from setting up permanently on our real estate. They can do it more conveniently, and more usefully perhaps, by remote control.

There is, of course, the possibility that we are extremely dangerous to them as a species and they would survive better in our neck of the woods if they kept out of our direct way.

This all may explain why they have not made an open landing before this time, let's say soon after we took out two entire cities with nuclear bombs and demonstrated Cro-Magnon 'man's' loving kinship with its own ethnic groups and all other ethnic groups of humanity. Perhaps that left the aliens in no doubt that their 'creations' were very dangerous fellows indeed. It is intriguing that they did not make their entrance then and ask to be 'taken to our leader'. In other words, they might have considered that we, as their genetically engineered creation, are much more dangerous to them than they can be to us. Then, at that particular time, that is.

As I said, they may have been here for countless millennia, farming our planet with 'alien'-adjusted progeny, and have not taken it over completely or let us know that we are a captive breed and they are our masters because overall covert custodianship from a scientific observational point of view was necessary. They may just be watching us. And if and when their observations are done they could and would be overtly the Masters who will be finally in charge of all our tomorrows as they have been in charge of all our yesterdays.

There is, however, still another scenario that could have forced them to change their mind and impelled them to make an actual overt entrance or landing in the future. The discovery of nuclear fission and the creation of the destructive mechanism made through it – the atom bomb – could explain all this fevered alien activity since the 'Trinity' atomic test explosion at Alamogordo in 1945. This may be the whole reason they have had to take a more direct hand in the affairs of man. Nuclear bombs may have been a useful method of culling and wiping off the face of the Earth the unwanted products of their millennia-long genetic experiment. A remotely handled methodology that they would help us to apply to ourselves, through ourselves and our legendary love for each other as a species.

The aliens may, in fact, have telepathically 'inspired' the whole idea of it all into the consciousness of certain of their specially cultivated 'genotypes' here on the Earth, as a means of culling *en masse* the unwanted products of their ongoing genetic experiment among humanity. But after doing so they may have seen the products of their efforts as a very dangerous thing in the hands of man. They may well have anticipated that to put such a thing into an agenda as telepathically 'inspired' scientific discovery was perhaps too big a chance to take with our kind because we have amply shown, after they did it, that we are well capable of taking the entire species out at a stroke. I believe that in the first instance they were forced to take this chance and 'inspire' the setting-up of an atomic world. Theirs may be a race against time. They may well be running out of 'Clone juice'. There may be a limit to the number of times you can re-clone without new sources of fresh vital DNA, to put it crudely. We may be that resource and all this two hundred years of industrial technology may well be a way that we set up all the 'hardware' for them to use for their own selfish purposes in the future. The 'software' may well be us.

If our world has been seeded with alien genetic hybrids, there must also be lines of man clear of this poison. In the long run these clear lines would breed with the alien genetic hybrids and render them unsuitable. In other words, they would mix down and clean up the aliens' own suitable Cro-Magnon hybrids, taking them from their genetic and perhaps psychological grasp. That would take away the future administrators of their larder or storehouse of suitable humans, humans they may need to use as a mechanism for hijacking Soul lines, and defeat their whole purpose among man.

The atom bomb may have been intended as a culling device for taking away this threat very effectively, but in developing the mechanisms to take the unwanted forms of humanity away at a stroke (albeit under their inspiration) they were 'giving' us a means to take their own access to a Soul away from them at a stroke, too. They were faced with another dilemma. These deadly instruments would have to be in our own human hands if they were to maintain their covert stance in the affairs of our species. They could hardly let us know they were here trying to control it all. Instead of an eternal clean-up franchise under their control, humanity would have it under its own. That's us, an emotionally immature species quite unlike their own master form on their planet. Remember, we were a species on the way out when they found us. Wandering aimlessly on the whims of entropy to end our suitability when we became apes, monkeys, animals, insects, trees, viruses and finally stones. We were a rejuvenated but nevertheless retrograde species. We had already burnt our boats and were well on the way to becoming monkeys. As I have said previously, they returned us to a former mental state by genetic interception – rewiring our genome. It could have been that, in some of the roots of the human ancestral tree, not only the brains were rewired. A more complete gene interception was done in some. All these various permutations were bred and interbred till they arrived at the final version most suitable to their purposes – the Cro-Magnon root. We perhaps all, as humans, generally still retained a component of our previous ape-man form and retained naturally something too much of the wrong base of mind to ever again be like our first beautiful Adam form. They could never genetically scrub it all out. They thus could never allow their destiny to lie totally in such unreliable hands. Albeit hands that were a reconstituted form of a wondrous past self. A past form that, once upon a time, was like their own Inaugural Adam Beings but in our case unlike theirs, a form that had failed to make it back to Godhead naturally. They would have to have final control. This would necessarily risk revealing their covert authorship of some of humankind. It would risk revealing their presence, but it was a risk they just had to take.

They did take this risk and it accidentally exposed their presence, as happened at Roswell, New Mexico and a thousand other sites and sightings for millions of people all over the world since the time of the first atomic explosion in Alamogordo, New Mexico. They knew then that sooner or later, mankind as a whole would spot the subterfuge. A lot still could be done to hide their presence. The natural cynicism of mankind would be a great asset in still hiding their presence. They would have to set up agents and agencies on the planet that would maintain the subterfuge for them, through lies and disinformation. They would have to do this through their own biologically intercepted 'root people'. Those among man whose genetic ancestral lines had been strongly adjusted to suit their purposes. Those whose mind sense they could control telepathically. This they are doing with remarkable success up to now. But not all of humanity is theirs. The Russian roulette of a Universe chaotic through entropy would ironically finally work against them. Genetic lines of man clear of their poison would breed into their best-made plans and constantly weaken their 'adjusted' kind on the Earth. Remote control of the situation would get harder and harder. Their lines would have to be strengthened constantly. Abductions for genetic purposes would have to begin. They have begun.

But the control of the nuclear prerogative is crucial. Mankind is not theirs enough for the total remote control of it. They would have to get their own hands on it to be sure of total control. It just could not be left in the hands of their agents on the Earth.

The prospect of interbreeding between racial and ethnic groups is more than anything else what the aliens are likely to view with horror. As I have said, interbreeding between the racial types of man will weaken their deadly kind hidden mostly among the people of Northern Cro-Magnon and Northern Mongoloid ancestry amongst us. The last thing in the world they want is a total brotherhood of man all across the world. A true humanity devoid of their genetically engineered hybrids. Perhaps that would be the end of all their tomorrows.

And so we have a deadly prescription for all our tomorrows. The biggest problem in the world of tomorrow will be inter-ethnic and interracial rivalry. It will be narrowed down further to inter-group-interest rivalry. All over Britain, Continental Europe and America, in city after city, the 'Haves' are gathering under the aegis of self-protection and forming communities of 'Haves' in the midst of communities of 'Have-nots'. In some instances, armed guards patrol the periphery of fenced-in communities of privileged people and ensure that they keep out those they consider unsuitable, ostensibly as protection against crime. It will be very interesting to take a close look at those living in these self-segregating hives for evidence of alien interest. How many, for instance, are members of self-interest groups such as the Freemasons? It is well known that the higher orders of this cult are supposed to pay homage to a God-entity called 'Jahbulon'. One wonders if these people are being duped into sanctioning the purposes of the 'head honcho' that leads an extraterrestrial mob of celestial opportunists.

The nuclear shuffle has begun, too. The possession of nuclear weapons is not the tacit prerogative of a few privileged nations anymore. There will always be a chance that anywhere, any day, any country with the necessary physical and intellectual resources may and will come up with the nuclear goods. There are over twenty countries with the capacity to build these weapons. The alien interests would have to stop them from doing this at all costs. No treaties will stop it all. Despite all the Test Ban and Non-Proliferation treaties there are facilities being set up in the territory of one of the chief signatories of these treaties to manufacture large numbers of these weapons covertly on a fully automated scale at a moment's notice. This is to be done when a full ban on the manufacturing and holding of nuclear weapons is signed. All the nuclear-headed rockets will never be destroyed. Many will be kept on, ostensibly to guard the Earth from large rocks dropping on it from outer space. A safe nest-egg for northern birds and perhaps for others that sing no Earthly song.

The alien extraterrestrials would try see to it that all nuclear eggs would be in a controllable basket . . . just in case it all goes wrong again as it did in Roswell, and in case this time they may not be able to cover it up. They would then need a culling device that can take huge numbers of humans unsuited to their purposes out at a stroke if needs be. Numbers and names they could mark on the foreheads, perhaps, of their chosen ones would help keep their own safe. Numbers that lie in the range of 666 in genetic make-up terms would be segregated for saving. It may well be a biological gene arrangement that defines their storehouse of effect on the human genome. An effect that sets the scale for artificial semi-organic biologies in this Universe. It would take another book to attempt to explain that one, so for now I'll only say purely figuratively that if you place the figure 9 and the figure 6 together you would see that they are opposites that make the figure 8 when superimposed. The sign of the Moroid. In other words, the twisted figure-of-eight that signifies the pattern of the whole force-signature of the Universe. If there are two basic forms of existent Being in the Universe, one Natural and of God and one created and not of God, then perhaps the 9 signifies the one signed the right way and the 6 the one signed the wrong way. There is, of course, much more to it than that. It will have to wait for that other book.

Have you noticed the sudden upsurge in ethnic differentiation all over the world? Bosnia is the most vivid example. A massive ethnic sorting seems to be taking place all over the world. I predict it will get worse. A lot worse before the 'song of the greys' reaches its last stanza. I believe that arbitrary interracial mixing, diluting their stock on the Earth, is becoming a serious threat and one that is more and more difficult for the aliens to stop or indeed control remotely. They will, sooner or later, have to take a direct hand in it all, to finally take control themselves of this massive random threat to their destiny. You will then see what the Nazis were really about. God forbid. The alien 'cuckoos', their genetically engineered intercepted kind on the planet, are logistically set around the planet too diversely. They will have to get them together in enclaves. They have to be brought together to stop them from getting diluted through interbreeding. It has already begun. The real fun will start if and when they achieve this. The rest of us may well all be expendable.

It is not only Americans that can conveniently clone a Saddam Hussein. If the abduction accounts are anything to go by, the aliens, ironically, are evidently at this moment busy cloning huge numbers of Americans. I wonder why they are doing this with such apparent success in the most powerful nation in the world.

I believe the alien extraterrestrial Clones and their Grey roboid aides are getting ready to declare their presence and I can't help feeling that in not too long a time you will see the world's media preparing the way for their physical deployment on our planet. As I have said earlier, many highly responsible intelligent people believe that a massive covert operation is being carried out with the United States of America, leading the countries of Europe to aid and assist such an event. Sensitive intuitive minds all around the world, usually labelled and dismissed as mad or cranks, are perceiving the lethal threat to our species. I believe the whole SETI programme (the Search for Intelligent Life) is a giant ruse designed to make us think that extraterrestrials are not already here. This is ostensibly a worldwide programme using some of the most powerful telescopes on Earth to try to locate other intelligent life in the Universe.

The welcome committee to greet the alien big boys is already set up. It is likely to include some of the most distinguished names in the governments and armed services of many of the top industrialized countries. Some, I would wager, will be (white) household names. You think I'm joking, don't you? Well, maybe I am. We will have to wait and see.

The welcome mat will be carefully laid with a contrived series of written articles, films and television programmes, all seemingly unconnected but all letting the proverbial cat of an imminent alien arrival out of the bag. They have already begun, as I have said, by pretending to search the universe for alien life. One can't help feeling this is one of the biggest exercises in deliberately propagated humbug and deception the world has ever known. This ruse will be designed to achieve in many people's minds the desired effect of making everyone relax and think that aliens are not already here and that we are innocently and sincerely seeking to find and contact our nearest neighbours. This in itself is, if you think about it, a very foolish thing to do. The risk of a contact holds with it the implication that the contactee has intelligence. We know what an intelligent species like humans can do to lesser species. My spray-can ant-killer amply demonstrates what we have done to all lesser life forms on the Earth. Can you imagine what a more intellectually intelligent and emotionally primitive life form might do to us if they decide to come calling? Do you really think the so-called intelligences that set up SETI haven't anticipated this very real danger? Of course they have. So why do it? The whole thing is one big contrivance designed to hide their true Masters with the huge almond-shaped eyes and hearts that beat like atomic clocks.

When the powers that be are told to begin the declaration process that will finally introduce these creatures to the world, humanity will first need to be carefully pacified with the idea that we are not alone. Slowly and surreptitiously, the contact will be developed and explanations will be given as to how this could be taken further and how the laws of physics and the laws of psychology may be brought in line with 'their' arrival on terra firma. When the time for revelation comes, and we learn that they have all the time been in our back yard anyway, it will be too late to do anything about it.

People will be encouraged to see these alien cloned creatures and their roboid pseudo-machine aides – the GREYS – as no threat but, rather, a boon to humanity. All who take the contrary view and succeed in challenging these agencies will not do so for long or for long enough to make an impact or a difference. They will be dismissed, scoffed, ridiculed and laughed at. Demonstrations of alien technology and alien power to heal the sick will impress many and we will all be exhorted to welcome the true fathers of Man as our progenitors. The 'takeover' will be peaceful, effortless and complete. The vast majority of the world will not even be aware that our planet is no more in human hands. It has all already begun. Our lives as human beings will never be the same again.

Yet what kind of life will it be? Will there be room for a sense of the natural beauty of field, of tree, of flower, of mountain river, stream, meadow and glade? Will our children be allowed to see a doe tend her fawn as their own lungs draw a draught of fresh clean air? Or will the odour of synthetic flowers waft in chemical winds of change that claim our horizons through the plastic windows of a farm laboratory, where we are just the next spare part for the mandates of an alien life form?

CHAPTER TWENTY-FIVE:
'ONCE UPON A TIME'

Could my surmises about these extraterrestrials be totally wrong? Could they be, in fact, the opposite of what I claim them to be? Are they really a marvellous benediction for humanity? The fact remains that if these alien beings *were* benign and kindly fathers of our species, they could so easily take up, abduct, abjure, whatever, important representatives of mankind, explain that they were this and reassure us to our satisfaction that their motives in coming here were for the benefit of man. They would not need to hide or obscure their presence. It all could and should be done openly. We would then welcome them with open, perhaps even loving arms and look forward to a happy future of computer-enhanced humanity. The Earth might well be renamed 'Nerdland'. The entire physical universe would be our oyster and we would join the other pearls of inhuman kindness skidding across starscapes and abducting and sticking needles, rods, probes and prods into and onto other hapless unsuspecting entities out there . . . somewhere.

Why, then, are they not doing this openly, if their intent is one of benevolence? Why all the subterfuge? The secrecy? It all is no mark of a benevolent benefactor. It all smacks of a threat. Perhaps a deadly threat to all our futures.

You might still ask why a complete 'takeover' with actual occupation of the real estate of our planet is necessary for these alien beings when humans might be so easily duped and controlled remotely. It seems that they can do whatever they need to do with abductions couched in anonymity. Their ability to communicate telepathically and wipe memory as documented by Harvard Professor John Mack through accounts by his patients, the so-called 'abductees', suggests this strongly.

The nature of the 'telepathy' that the alien beings use is, I believe, technologically based. In fact, Japanese researchers are currently developing a device that can read thoughts.[1] In a recent experiment at the University of Tottori, west of Osaka, a volunteer concentrated on one of five words that flashed on and off on a computer monitor. Researchers connected the volunteer's head to several electrodes that monitored electrical activity in his brain using an encephalograph. The encephalograph measured a type of brainwave called P300, which the brain produces when it focuses on an idea. A computer then analyzed the pattern of the brainwaves, comparing it with the patterns associated with words it had already learnt. It took about twenty-five seconds to guess correctly which word the subject was thinking of. The research team has been testing a prototype device for a year and the university's Associate Professor of Computer Sciences, Michel Inoue, says it has an accuracy rate of eighty to ninety per cent. The device is being developed specifically for patients suffering from a disease that paralyzes the brain's motor functions such that the patient is eventually unable to move and, therefore, unable to communicate. However, mind-reading, or 'telepathy', via electronic devices is also a practice that is fundamental to the Greys in their dealings with human beings. Almost all abductees who have been abducted and re-abducted say that as part of the normal abduction routine an alien being stares into their eyes for long periods, apparently reading their minds. In fact, it seems that the method of communication that the Greys use is a telepathic one as they do not speak: their 'mouths' do not open. But this is not telepathy using the power of thought, it is telepathy using physical mechanisms and thus it is not telepathy in the commonly accepted sense of the word at all.

In Professor Mack's book there is an example of an abductee who claims that the large head and huge black eyes of the Grey is actually a form of 'helmet' full of microelectronic devices: 'I've been waiting fifty years to say this, you know . . . What our little television computer machines do here on Earth is similar to what happens inside these helmets. There are mechanisms on the inner brow. When it sticks out on the lower brow above the eyes, inside are mechanisms, the means to altering what enables the various manners of seeing. It's just like looking into the workings of a microchip in a computer or other electrical operations. And there are lots of microchip connectors on both sides of the brow. Inside the helmet is full of these'. This abductee says that he has actually worn one of these helmets. From inside the robotic 'head', he felt that he could see temperature and other biological processes: 'It is not unlike what we do with computers and electrical generators. When I am a creature or in the creature's examination structure, I'm studying too'. When Mack asked him what he was studying he replied: 'Humans'.[2]

There is, of course, the chilling possibility that the whole Earth environment may be geophysically shaped for their arrival. All they would need to do is hijack a passing comet or asteroid a few hundred miles across and bring its orbit to coincide with that of the Earth. They could then crash it in the North Atlantic under Greenland, between New York and West Ireland, shall we say. It would considerably alter things on this Earth, don't you think? Some might say for the better. God forbid.

I don't wish to be flippant in parading such a horrendous idea. I want to illustrate the relative ease with which an emotionless breed of creature like an alien Grey could so easily accomplish things to their advantage. Hijacking an asteroid of that mass in the weightlessness of space is probably not too hard to do given their level of technology. Driving it in our direction is even easier. What price all the foundations of humanity? What price our vanity?

This is amply illustrated by referring to what I like to call 'The Great Erasers'. The evidence for the Great Erasers, as I call the phenomenon, has been there for all to see all the time. But few of us saw it. In common with most of us in this world, I too was blind to what was right in front of my eyes. I too could never see the wood for the trees. The only real way to see a wood despite the trees is to ascend. To see it all from above. By that I mean to rise up and take a look. In this instance though, seeing the wood from the trees meant looking up. Up at the sky – in the dark.

Take the night sky, for instance. A million pinpoints of light are somewhat hidden at the first glance when you look up. In the bland sweep of the first view of it all. Then, if you keep looking, they will reconcile into view till before you stands the glory of the 'Beads of Satan', the very cradle and clothing of our atomic being: the stars. Boiling, burning, baking cauldrons of plasma and gas in unimaginable enforcedness and tension. The soup of our atomic nature whirling its blazing eddies of 'star-stuff' into the further forms of you and me, us and them.

We all began there. Or that is what science claims. My claim in this book is that we all *ended* there. We all ended there to begin again. At least in a beginning of sorts. A beginning in Hell.

The clues to our predicament are there, in the stars, for all to see. They began as we began, in terrifying force, and will end as we will end, in terrifying force. Not for us the eternal peace of angels while we persist in this Universe. Their world is the Multiverse beyond Force and thus atoms, infinite and forceless. Ours is the world of the finite, the captured and the set. The world of separated points in point resource twisted in formats of chaos we call Space and Time. Yet still dressed in the twisted breath of God – its windsong. A melody that still allows freedom of Will and purpose to search through reason for the meaning of it all.

I hope this all doesn't seem like a church sermon. It's not meant to be. It's meant to define the hard edges of 'unreason' where poetry can still find root in Chaos and a symphony still seems to transcend the bounds of the Second Law of Thermodynamics. The devil of it all is, why?

Let me explain. If you look at all solid space bodies you will see the tell-tale marks of the great fault that defines our Universe – chaotic transformation through impact. The collision marks of the seething mass of space bodies. The pockmarks of Chaos. The Moon's surface is a great swathe of pits and craters that tell the tale of the ballistics of doom. The doom of us all as a species, perhaps. Visible affirmation of the modus that underpins the root nature of our Universe – all-pervasive explosive violence. The spit of Entropy, if you like. But it is more than that. Much more. It drives into those of us with searching, seeking minds these questions: Why is there Awareness, Knowing and Mind in the Universe at all? Where did it come from and why? How and why did and does it prevail if we are here to die in a seemingly meaningless chaotic Armageddon of forces and violence?

Impact craters are now the most prominent geophysical features on solid objects in the solar system and perhaps in all the Universe. There are tens of thousands of craters on the Moon alone. Over 6000 of them are estimated to be hits from space bodies of a size of half a kilometre or more. It used to be thought that most or all of these craters on the Moon were volcanic in origin. The reason was that meteors, comets and asteroids hitting the Moon would have left their evidence of impact in many elongated craters and shapes, not the predominantly circular ones that are seen on our natural satellite. This is because most of them would have approached the Moon at non-perpendicular angles. The vast majority of the craters are indeed circular. It was only when it was realized that a huge explosion would result when the missile hit and that this explosion would leave a residual circular format of impact on the surface of a hard body that scientists began to accept that the craters on the Moon are a visual history of constant bombardment.

Now, can you imagine the number of significant impacts that would have taken place on a body six times the size of the Moon, namely our Earth? At a conservative estimate one could say that at least 30,000 collisions with space bodies of half a kilometre or more in size would have taken place in the last 200 million years.

Scientists have worked out that, all present things considered, a single hard-bodied rocky asteroid the diameter of one cubic kilometre crashing into the Earth would probably wipe out all intelligent life on this planet. Their present sweeps of the heavens are throwing up such startling discoveries in terms of numbers of these things crossing Earth's orbit as to affirm a horrifying story of the danger we are all in. So where are all these craters on the Earth and why have we found so few?

The collisions of galaxies, star bodies and planets and the consequences of such impacts, the comets, asteroids and meteors, are themselves the mechanism that provides the 'Great Erasers' of the Universe. I am convinced that they have on their own been the most awesome destroyers and changers of both the dead and the living features of the Earth during the planet's entire history. It is very likely that the impact of these space bodies and their horrendous consequences have meant that no civilizations can endure on the Earth for longer than an average of perhaps eight thousand years. We are almost at the threshold of this average number now and one giant asteroid called Toutatis is on its way in 1999, to keep an appointment with the Earth that may well involve a 'handshake' of the most catastrophic proportions.

We all know now that a single asteroid of about ten cubic kilometres in size striking the Earth sixty-eight million years ago wiped out all the dinosaurs and nearly sixty per cent of life on Earth. Why, then, are these impacts so deadly and so dangerous? After all, the circumference of the Earth is huge. It is 43,000 kilometres and one would expect, on the face of it, that a ten-cubic-kilometre-sized pebble from space would be as an insignificant thimbleful in an ocean's expanse. The clue that it is not is, in fact, inferred by the ocean. These meteorites travel at such velocities that if they impact the Earth in water the resulting *tsunami* or tidal wave that will hit all the ocean boundaries of a given expanse of water may easily be as high as eight kms. If you remember that Mt Everest is the highest point on Earth and is about nine km high, it is easy to see why no evidence of coastal civilizations surviving for very long exists. When the immediate tidal wave has done its job and cleaned all signs of life away for tens, maybe hundreds of miles from a coast, the huge explosion detritus and quantities of sulphurated water going up into the atmosphere and then falling in massive quantities of battery-acid-strength rain will lay waste to vast areas of life and vegetation.

Let me quote a harrowing commentary from Gerrit Verschuur's excellent book on the threat of comets and asteroids entitled *Impact*:[3]

'You are there and you have been observing an odd phenomenon in the sky . . . On this day you watch the increasing fireball activity and the enormous fan of light that is the comet's tail. It seems to be growing larger. It is so bright and so close that it is visible by day and by night. As you stare you notice something odd. If you look very closely, it is almost as if you can see a small dark spot in the comet's nucleus and it seems to be growing larger. As startled as any creatures around you, your instincts tell you that there is something very wrong. Animals howl and seek shelter.

. . . A thousand miles to the south . . . the approaching comet looms. You are there. You arch your arm above your head to shield your eyes from the sun's glare. When you first noticed it the object was a little larger than the moon but it is growing in size. Thirty seconds tick by and the looming mass seems to be about three times the Moon's diameter. Ten seconds pass, fifteen, then twenty. You reach out your arm as if to shield yourself and your hand can barely hide the object from view. Five more seconds and you feel suspended in time watching the onrushing monster in slow motion. You crouch in terror, two hands outstretched, barely able to cover the apparition as it begins to glow fiery red. Within a second it bursts into incandescent fury and its glare fills half the sky with flaming light as hot as the sun. The sea begins to boil as the object passes into and through the atmosphere, puncturing a hole its own width, and smashes into the sea, gouging a hole kilometres deep beneath the sea floor.'

It is outside the immediate scope of this book to mark down all the details of space-body impacts and their dangers to our planet. The above quoted author does a marvellous job in spelling out the huge danger and significance of these objects in his book. It is a truly chilling story and well worth a read.

There is no doubt whatsoever that our world has its existential priorities written on its rear. Catastrophe Theory, for so long ridiculed by scientists, is now proving to be one of the most significant premises accounting for geological change on this planet. It may almost be said that if scientists ridicule a theory or insight you can count on it being proved right in the not too distant future. Like moles they blunder through the darkness of ignorance staring only at the space immediately before their eyes. It sometimes takes a bulldozer working above their heads to reveal the significance of the sky and their tunnel vision and the stupidity of their narrow and prejudiced views. There are, of course, great exceptions, open-minded visionaries who are also scientists. Alas, it is the rare exception. The vast majority of scientists are of the mundane mole type.

A poignant example of the relevant scientific establishment's disgraceful mental impotence, importunity and cussedness was exposed in the case of the K/T Impact boundary controversy. This is the event described so vividly above by Verschuur, the one that accounted for the demise of the dinosaurs on Earth.

In 1979, the Nobel Laureate Luis Alvarez, an eminent physical chemist, and his team discovered a layer of iridium at a geological deposition boundary line (to be later called the K/T boundary line) commensurate on a time scale with the disappearance of the dinosaurs. Iridium has an affinity for iron and should long since have disappeared from the Earth's crust and found its way to the Earth's iron core when the Earth was still molten and young. Any iridium found now would have had to have come from space. This led to the conclusion by Alvarez that the iridium would have had to be brought here by an asteroid that crashed into the Earth at about the time of the disappearance of the dinosaurs. The theory seemed to verify prophetic claims made by pseudo-scientists and mystics that a catastrophic impact with a thunderbolt from space destroyed the creatures. The world's scientific Mafiosi went straight into action and not only gave it scant regard but ridiculed the distinguished Nobel Laureate's theory for years. In time the iridium deposition was found worldwide, marking it as a real and substantiated phenomenon pointing to a globally significant impact cataclysm.

In 1981 the results of years of undersea exploration and geomagnetic surveys of the Gulf of Mexico area found the smoking gun to be a crater over 100 kilometres wide in the Yucatan peninsula of Mexico, age-dated to correspond to the age of the K/T boundary deposition of iridium approximately sixty-five million years ago.

There is little doubt, now that the whole thing has been put together, that Luis Alvarez has been totally vindicated. Needless to say, few apologies were forthcoming from his peers for the disgraceful way some of them treated the great man for daring to propose such a theory.

I am really not trying to vilify science and scientists. I have the deepest reverence and respect for them. I would be flying in the face of my own appeal for the rational analysis of all the evidence of an alien presence amongst us if we were to put all our 'belief eggs' in a basket of mere speculation and condemn all these doyens of intelligence and reason out of hand. There is, however, an irrational and sometimes arrogant consensus on the part of many scientists against being open-minded. You can't stop a ten-kilometre piece of rock hitting our planet and wiping us all out if you procrastinate with closed minds and dismiss ideas as preposterous, as many palaeontologists did, for instance, with Alvarez's postulation. They were blindly following what text books had previously taught palaeontologists: that the bombardment of the

Earth had only happened when the Earth was young and forming. If you always took your books as gospel, you would never look up at the sky or down at your feet.

And so the vast areas of water that cover our planet and the huge tidal-wave action that is set up after space-body collisions with the Earth conspire between them to erase or hide the vast majority of 'smoking gun' evidence that points to impact phenomena being a hugely relevant geophysical phenomenon in shaping both the Earth and what lies and lives on it.

In 1995 it was estimated by Sky Watch scientists all over the world that in excess of 10,000 bodies of half a kilometre in size with Earth-crossing orbits exist, each one capable of taking out civilization at a stroke if it hit the Earth on land or sea. When all the latest available figures are extrapolated as to the likelihood of impact with an Earth-orbit-crossing body of significant size, it all converts to a civilization-destroying Tsunami every five thousand years.

This, then, may well be one of the main reasons if not the main reason why there is no evidence of the prior 'God-men' phenomenon that marks the devolution thesis of all living species I have proposed. The Great Erasers could have easily wiped away all evidence for it time and time again.

We, of course, all know that there is a kind of industry of doom and catastrophe theory touted from soap box, pulpit and the institutions for the mentally insane since time immemorial. The trouble is that every self-seeking scoundrel, charlatan and pretender to religious thrones has throughout history used fear to muster and marshal support from the gullible. Science and scientists have, by and large, stood as our guardians of good sense and balanced, ordered summary as we make our way through the darkness of ignorance. But the human mind has a tendency to excess and it is easy to dismiss anything on the basis that it has proved to be so too many times in the past. The boy did cry 'Wolf' too often, but the wolf *did* come. We can never, it seems to me, afford to close our minds to anything, anytime, anywhere. Mountains in the sky cannot make choices. We can.

Might it not be better that the end comes for us all while we still may wonder about love? The Masters that could truly love came and we bent and bludgeoned their glorious sacrifice with crosses of dogwood and stabbing nails, knives and javelins. They slipped on the spit of our ignorance and rejection. We laughed at their bended knees and bleeding foreheads and resumed our stance in Hell none the wiser. We shall welcome the demon as we crucified the lamb.

And so, indeed, before the alien experiment has done with our species, will a passing comet crash into the Earth to close again the pages of human history? A celestial eraser that will come in the silence of a tomb and cast all our glories and wretchedness into lines of dust that will curve with colours of the Earth to write the epitaph of our species with the salutation 'Once upon a time'. Will then some new form, perhaps with green hair and yellow eyes, speak the words 'Alas poor Yorick' to the broken shape of our yesterdays in his hands? Another souvenir with a billion memories locked tight in the sands of time. It will be smiling with the smile of the dead.

CHAPTER TWENTY-SIX:

THE ALIEN TRUMP CARD: RACIALISM

The spirit sense, or what could be described as the innate sense for the world beyond the atom and the margins of force, may still have been retained by our most ancient ancestors with mechanisms such as telepathy. There would be no need for language if this were so. The invention of 'language' may well have signalled a point of nadir in the so-called 'development' of man, and not the point of ascent that it is commonly taken to be. An artificial point-by-point substitute for the natural holistic language of the Soul through its still relatively strong connection to Godhead.

The Australian aborigine still shows these marvellous values and attributes and is looked on as primitive and pilloried as such by his grotesque Occidental plastic modern counterpart in his machine-minded splendour of polished stones and engine oil. These Aborigines, as with many others of the less inter-cepted genotypes of man in other parts of the world, have been systematically exterminated by the Grey's Cro-Magnon legacy among us, those who are commonly called the white Caucasoids.

Seen as antediluvian savages in jail after jail in Australia, the beautiful, gentle aboriginal people have been murdered and forced to commit suicide time after time by the partisans of the machine mind in the name of civilization.

This is an extract from an interview I had some years ago, when I was a medical student, with a white Australian police officer working for the Queensland force. He was on holiday in London and I interviewed him about racism in Australia for a university student publication.

'All it takes is just the merest sight of them . . . The sight of the bastard's black spindly body. Neanderthal . . . features. You don't think of them as human . . . it's an instant thing . . . A mixture of fear . . . anger . . . you know, mixed with aggression, I suppose. It kind of wells up from deep inside . . . You get this . . . this . . . urge to threaten . . . to hurt . . . to punish . . . It comes at you from nowhere . . . The mere fact that . . . he's different . . . they are different . . . I suppose. They've never done anything to me . . . personally . . . I mean . . . You know it is all . . . outside reason. All outside . . . sense . . . control. You know you have to be in control . . . but you don't care . . . All you see is that he's different . . . not like you . . . your people. You want him to disappear. He doesn't matter. He's just a piece of . . . shit . . . grotesque flesh. He doesn't belong. You are looking for the merest excuse to make the bastard . . . disappear. He speaks. He says, "I've done nothing, man". It's enough . . . He dared to talk to you. You bring your stick crashing down on the side of his face . . . He falls to the ground. You like it. He is not with you for a moment. You're relieved . . . He's not so near you any more. You turn away. Trying desperately to stop yourself . . . You tell yourself you're a policeman . . . It doesn't work, mate . . . nothing works . . . He grunts and moves on the ground, recovering his consciousness. He whimpers and clutches at his face. Shame grips you now. Then anger. I suppose you are really angry at the fact that he existed at all, and that fact has brought this ugliness out in you. It's mad, I know. You put him away as quickly as you can. You can't face him anymore. Now there's . . . well . . . shame there . . . and that is to do with you, mate . . . He has to go away. He has to disappear. You pick him up. You kick him because he dared to be there and make you ashamed. You throw him into the back of the car and close the door. You have to shut him out. Its instant. It's mad . . . Am I mad? . . . I think somewhere inside we are all fuckin' mad . . . You . . . you know what . . . I think they are far better than us . . . I mean you and me, mate . . . Er, the whites, I mean . . . I think . . . I really think that's what it is . . . Mad . . . mate . . . It's fuckin' mad . . .'

I wonder how many million times this Australian officer's sentiments can resonate within the minds of racists, murderers and torturers the world over. Is it likely that the seed of the Grey incubi that have intercepted the lines of humanity are strongly aspected within the bioscope of people such as this? It would explain the irrationality of it all.

Could the racist and the xenophobe be running a programme inherently in their genes? Are there measures written in our genes that make some of us helpless automatons working to the mandates of celestial interlopers? It is likely, of course, that there would be some genetic ancestral lines that hold the alien recipe more strongly and more cogently than others. If this is true, then the racist and the xenophobe are the most lethal types of human beings on the earth. They should carry a worldwide public health-warning notice around their necks. I for one would not harm a hair on their heads. I would, however, avoid their company as though they were carriers of the deadliest plague, no matter how close they were, even in terms of biological family ties.

Brothers and sisters might share the same parental biology. They will not and cannot, however, share the same Soul connection line back to Godhead. This is affirmed by this simple fact. The germ cells of our parents are made from the biological prospectus of the same individuals. One would expect every child to be exactly the same because your mother and father are the same biological identities when they make each subsequent child. Why, then, is there such difference between brothers and sisters? Why is each sperm and ovum different? We get identical twins, of course, but that is understandable because a single sperm fertilizes a single egg and the cell mass divides into two identical halves at oogenesis and two identical foetuses develop. But why aren't all children from the same parents identical when made by different sperms? They are, after all, the same parents and you would expect their gametes to be the whole summary of each parent in the form of a biological code. Why, then, is there any difference between gametes, unless the gametes of the males in the world provide enough permutations to match exactly each differing 'soul field' ready to reincarnate into the world? In other words, could we males be carrying the formula, or potential bodies, for each and every soul that can be reborn at any one time? There's a thought! It would thus suggest that every male in the world has a stock of differing gametes all able to admit into life the soul of a particular African bushman, perhaps, who might have died yesterday! Preposterous? I still back my hunch that this is true. I believe that we truly are our brother's keeper.

We are joined at the elbows of all endeavour, each and every one. If we all originated in Godhead, then there must be a mechanism that reflects this. I believe there is such a mechanism and the clue to it and perhaps the proof of it lies in the fact that the same parents produce children who are very different from one another.

The female of our species has all the stock of eggs she is going to produce in a lifetime when she is born. Every healthy woman can count on producing about four hundred eggs in the course of her reproductive lifetime. The She of the species thus produces the neutral living format on which the specifics are written. But the male produces hundreds of millions of sperm every time he ejaculates. Biologists will account for the profligate number as the way the species ensures fertilization against all the impediments the sperm has to encounter before it meets its complementary half, namely the ovum. In other words, it needs millions of sperm to ensure that one gets through to fertilize the egg. I believe this is an utterly facile assertion.

If you look at the way nature works, its assemblies always have the most wondrous economy and ergonomy to them. Everything seems to be arranged for maximum utility and efficiency of function, until of course entropy raises its ugly head and goes to work on them. Why, then, is the most important process of all, the reproductive process, such an inefficient chaotic amelioration? The Russian roulette of conception that the biologists would have us believe. I believe it is not inefficient. It is as efficient as possible if you take into account the fact that it has a built-in mechanism to cater for such metaphysical ideas as Karma, soul-fields and all the other artefacts of the other half of physical life: Death.

Of course, an assertion of this sort is designed to make every arrogant mechanistically minded scientist gnaw at his trouser leg in rage. I don't think we ought to worry too much about their tailor's bills. Science and scientists are always only temporarily right and as history proves, in the end often wrong. Isaac Newton's mechanistic universe, for so long the holy of holies of scientific thinking, has been substantially holed and almost sunk with the ideas and proofs that Einstein and Dirac, through Relativity theory and Quantum theory, have come up with. The truth is much bigger and more significant than the temporal explanations the explorers of the lines of break-up of the universe come up with from time to time. Spiritual insight is far more likely to bear testament to eternal truth than they are.

The postulation that Life arises out of the enforced centre of the atom and Death is the centre of the space between atoms is an absolute truth not open to negotiation. The soul, if 'un-enlighted', will linger in less enforced 'Fields of Death' that lie in the corridors between atomic and molecular arrays and return to form a body on the sperm that bears its unique resonance frequency. In other words, if any one of us dies and our soul enters the space between atoms, we will currently theoretically have approximately two billion chances of coming back into life again to expedite our debts to others in a physical format. Put another way, every male with the capacity to produce children living on the Earth today (about two billion individuals) will hold one of these chances on behalf of all the members of the human race whose souls still linger in the 'fields of death'. It begins to become plain what a horrendous thing abortion is, if all this is true.

How, then, will each living male get the information that marks a sperm with the name of every person that dies? What is the mechanism that can communicate a connection between two separated individualities, now separated by Death? The whole wonderful thing, if true, might prove that individuals are *not* separated by death. The space between atoms exists in life and physicality and death through the *same* corridors between atoms. We are all connected through the corridors that mark the spaces between atoms. Life and Death are interwoven into and betwixt us all. It is why Christ claimed that the kingdom of heaven is within you.

What a marvellous thought that each male (and I don't mean this in any chauvinistic sense at all) of the species carries on him the 'prints' of all the other identities that await admission in Karma, to life. There is no gender in death. Gender simply marks a particularized format for the cultivation of 'knowing'. The two final polarization points through which the separation of parts may be reconciled as the Whole.

Of course, Karma need not be expedited and debts owed paid back in a physical format alone. I think we have to remember that 'debt' in this sense is paid when the debtor gives back to the indebted that value of loss taken away by some action that would have otherwise allowed the indebted to return to Godhead. Lies, falsehoods, murder, theft, false witness, or any other negative impulsion provides a vector for further separation from Godhead. This has to be restored 'personally' to the individual soul-field concerned. This, of course, can be done through the giving of knowledge or understanding to the soul concerned through one-to-one tutorial. In other words, the dead can communicate with the dead as easily as the living can with the living. If the two individuals with an obligation in Karma are both in the space between atoms, a resolution of that obligation is possible. It is only when communication between the living and the dead has to take place for the revocation of karmic obligation that the problem arises. The souls have to be *able* to do this. There has to be a way through to each other that allows for each to learn from each other that which enlightens and gives effect to a reconciliation of the loss that has caused the debt or obligation. Each individual identity has to be able to communicate with the other and know through verification that they are doing so, such that each registers the compensation and each is liberated to move the lost distance to Godhead that caused the debt in the first place. It is not only the expurgation of Karma that is important, it is the notification of this recompense that is even more vital. Each debt is specifically coded with the signature of the 'debtor' to the 'indebted' at the moment it is incurred. All moments in time are unique unto themselves and all that happens at any specific moment is coded, so to speak, with a tag of this uniqueness. While the basic principle underlying any karmic debt may be common, the will underlying the actioning of that principle is unique to the personage. Each individual is also unique. Thus the two things are joined at the hip, so to speak, in their distinctiveness and have to be accessed, and can only be accessed, by all the elements that made that karmic obligation in the first place. It requires the 'key' and the elements that made up that key of that specific moment acting in concert to function together. And so the living elements that possess the memory of that moment have to be able to get together in some way, in recognition of the amelioration of the Karmic deficit.

It is a terrifying thought that Karma is eternal in its quest, as it were. That it does not end in terms of its individual encumbrance if, say, a whole species is wiped out on a planet, if you get my meaning. If you incur a Karmic debt to an individual who subsequently becomes a monkey and you yourself retain your humanity, do you have to become a monkey in order to expurgate this debt? I am sure the reader will be able to extrapolate logically what the answer to this quandary entails.

Karma is the most serious business the Soul can undertake. It underlies, I believe, all Universal momentums.

If we all were a Jesus Christ with his fabulous understanding of existential truth, we would never incur karma in the first place. We would know enough of the consequence never to do this most lethal of things.

How many of us believe in ghosts, for instance? How many of us ridicule those who believe in ghosts? How many of us believe in life after death as a principle? Do you see what I am trying to get at? For some among us who can dip into the space between atoms (perhaps mediums, clairvoyants, etc.) inter-medium conversation and exchange may be possible from Life-field to Death-field. For most of us the means of revocation of debt lies through the potentially lethal mechanism of reincarnation. It is the only means for some of getting to the individual (in a like frame) we have the Karma with to make restitution and compensation. This subject would take a library of many volumes to tackle adequately, and so I will leave it at this point.

So, to change tack for a moment, I would like to ask an interesting question based upon the implications of some of the points which I have addressed in this chapter: Since the first 'African Eves' (the first announcements of our species Homo Sapiens Sapiens), the human population has, of course, increased dramatically in size. Does this mean that the number of souls incarnating into our species line has been increasing quantumly? If so, where does this ready supply of soul come from?

If we are, in fact, a species devolving into states of greater and greater restriction of the scope to know, understand and freely choose, then the very need to reincarnate into physical life would be a result of that devolution. We, in our free will, pull our line of connection back to God further and further away from that polarity of union into states of greater separation, tension and enforcedness. There must be a certain threshold of tension that necessitates incarnation into a physical form.

Soul lines of connection can be viewed as 'elastics' that are pulled tighter and tighter the more a soul becomes entrapped in the Universe of Parts. The 'fields of death' have a certain ambient tension and, if the elastic of a soul line is as tense or less tense than that ambient tension, then that soul need not incarnate into physical life to free itself and resolve its Karma. Unless, of course, it has karmic obligation to other souls who *are* obliged to incarnate physically. If the elastic tension of a soul line is greater than that which naturally prevails in the fields of death then the context of physical life is the only context that can provide that soul with an opportunity to reconcile the heavier Karmic debts that maintain it in the 'tense' state that it is in.

It should be pointed out that 'death' is not 'outside' the atomic universe. It is a far less intrinsically enforced state within the purview of atoms than 'life'. Let me try an illustration on you. The mode of existence in the fields of death can be likened to walking freely along a path so that only the air you move through provides a resistance to your movement. Whereas the mode of existence in the fields of life can be better likened to walking through water that is waist deep. When you walk through the water the resistance it provides to your movement forces you to work harder to move through it. It is that extra effort to fight against the greater ambient tension of the fields of life that provides the 'anti-force' necessary to lessen the tension of the elastic. If the water is flowing in a particular direction and that direction is that of the entropic drift, then if you walk in the other direction the water you push in front of you as you struggle forward provides that 'anti-force'. In the fields of death you are only pushing air in front of you which does not provide such a powerful anti-entropic surge.

So the increase in the numbers of human souls incarnating into the fields of life on this planet might well be a direct result of the increasing elastic tension of human soul lines prevailing within an entropic environment. Perhaps as far back as the point of the 'African Eve' when human populations were far smaller, the majority of souls were able to reconcile their Karma in the fields of death. However, as entropy took its course and human souls succumbed to it, there would have been a tendency for souls in the fields of life to accumulate more karma rather than expedite existing karma. Souls in the fields of death who had karmic connections to these souls in the fields of life would be pulled implicitly towards those souls in order to fulfil that karma; in some cases they could be pulled into the fields of life themselves. Thus there would be a vanguard of souls leading the way for the human species line into entropic dismemberment, pulling the others connected to them down with them. These in their turn would pull down those connected to them, and so on, until the whole species line is pulled down further and further into greater and greater states of tension. Souls that might otherwise have been able to reconcile karma in the fields of death are thus forced into the fields of life with all the risks that that involves because they are pulled there by souls to whom they are karmically connected. Hence the constant increase in the human population on this planet. God's instruction to Adam to 'Go forth and multiply' thus takes on a new meaning. The greater the multiplication the more it is a sign that the species is being pulled, in general, on an entropic course.

It is essential to realize that we are not alone in this universe as a species. I have written this book to try to expose a rather unwelcome lot that have come from elsewhere to our patch in the whole shooting match. There are probably hundreds of millions of other planets with life on them. All souls everywhere are just connection mechanisms to God and thus have recourse to each other everywhere. This may well explain why a child is born crippled at birth for no apparent reason other than the seeming lottery of fate. It may simply have previously been of some other life form and was not able to make the requisite body suitable for this planet at the first try. What I am trying to say is that there is an inexhaustible fund of souls drawn from all over the universe that may reincarnate at any point in the universe anywhere – drawn by the inexorable winds of Karma to that point and place.

So, the greater the population of the world the greater the implication that more souls *need* to reincarnate in order to fulfil karma. The sperm count of the first *Homo Sapiens Sapiens* expressions may well have not been too dissimilar from that today. This is because that count is a measure of the number of souls in death's fields which could in potential incarnate into life. However, the extent to which that potential number becomes an actual number reflects, in some measure, the overall demise of the species, be it through individual culpability or incidental effect through the culpability of others.

Thus there may well now be a great demand from those in the fields of death for reincarnation into the fields of life. If, through such factors as abortion and the use of contraceptives, the necessary amount of doorways into life are not provided, problems can arise. A bottleneck of souls attempting to enter into the fields of life, but unable to do so, could build up. If the soul line of connection provides for a vacuum of no-force within an overall environment of force, then those souls with the biggest vacuum, the more 'enlighted' souls, would be best able to command their enforced environment to their advantage.

The whole Universe is a gigantic paradigm of Force. Every point in it is unstill. It shakes with a locked-in tension. The more the locked-in tension, the more each point of it shakes or vibrates.

Let me ask you at this point what your concept of the word 'Force' is. How do you personally envisage the idea of 'enforcedness', if I may put it that way? Does, for instance, a tightly clenched fist shivering with tension, power, effort, convey an image of force to you? The dictionary defines 'Force' as strength, or energy, or power. The science of physics defines force as a dynamic influence that changes a body from a state of rest to one of motion, or changes its rate or direction of motion, thereby changing its momentum.

The trouble with the definition of force as explained by physicists is that it never really tells us what force is, it only describes what it does.

So what actually is force? Summarizing the above it would seem that it is quite simply put in everyday terms as: 'that which makes anything happen' where 'happening' implies a change (or an apparent change) in the status quo of a situation.

What, though, is generating this effect we call force? From where or from what does it derive its power and how does this *abstract* property make anything at all happen such that we can actually see its effects?

Let's set about answering these questions by looking a bit further into what science tells us about force . . .

As far as current scientific knowledge goes, all force in the universe exists in one of four categories. These are Gravitation, Electromagnetism and two types of Nuclear force, one of which holds the core (or 'Nucleus') of atoms together and another which is responsible for nuclear breakdown and radioactivity. So we can then envisage the scientific world view as of a sea of 'bodies' or matter being buffeted this way and that by the forces between them. Or can we?

There are no material 'ingredients' floating in the sea other than the sea itself! Or, to put it another way: our bodies, the planet we live on and the stars in the sky are all simply shaped patterns of force of diverse textures and tones. The chairs that we sit on may seem real as objects or 'particles' in their own right, but when we analyze our experience of the physical world we soon come to the conclusion that all we are really detecting is the product and property of these forces. Our sensation of our weight on the chair is made both by the spatial tension we call gravity between our bodies and the Earth below us and by the electric potentials that maintain separation at the molecular level (our backsides do not [usually] merge with the chair). The atomic elements that make up the chair are formed out of and maintained by the nuclear forces, etc.

Wait! Aren't we missing something . . . ? If force is all there is and force is both the cause of all that happens and *is* all that happens then it might prove interesting for the reader to speculate on what all this happening is happening to, how did it begin and where and when is it happening if space and time are themselves simply artefacts of force?

Of course, 'force' can't be all there is in any self-consistent or reasonable model of the world. At this point the reader may find it worthwhile to stop and ponder a while as to what the nature might be of anything that is totally without force, an effect which I will call (again for want of a better word) 'non-force,' although a better word might have been 'un-enforcedness'. I believe that through an insight into what may well be not of or subject to force we can arrive at a fascinating suggestion about what force may really be and how it and its space-time arena can exist.

The vacuum of Godhead is like a pen of no-force that can write upon the tablet of force. Thus it would be these more enlighted souls who would have the best potential to achieve the passage from death to life. The less enlightened ones would be more likely to be held in the bottleneck, unable to gain entry into the fields of life to fulfil their karma. Perhaps the desperate need of these souls to enter into life results in what is commonly termed 'possession', the attachment of a soul in the fields of death to a soul in the fields of life. An attachment which occurs without the tacit invitation of the soul who becomes possessed. Thus it is an expression of imposition and, therefore, of force.

Possession thus occurs through the mechanisms that allow for such a forced effect. High magnetic fields, for example, could make the body-aerial more susceptible to attachment by souls seeking to possess it.

Our body-aerials are, as I have previously explained, receivers for the 'light' of connection to God. This is the strangest light of all. It has no frequency of oscillation, direction of oscillation, or wavelength. In other words it is utterly unenforced and totally peaceful 'light'. Let me call it 'Enlight.'

Enlight is received differently by each body-aerial according to how that aerial is tuned. The light is just a manifestation of pure knowledge. All that is known and can be known in a quantum. The specific tuning of the aerial is a result of an individual's own specific pattern of restriction and this allows that individual to receive only that quantum of God-light that it will allow. See the individual that is 'enlighted' as one whose lens is plain flat glass and those that are restricted and thus sinful as variously shaped prisms that split the quantum into parts that are difficult to put back together again. Restriction (sin) provides blocks on the total emanation of Godlight such that not all of it can be received. This, shall we say, has the effect of tuning the aerial to receive enforced light of the electromagnetic wavebands that are not of Godlight, but instead are transmitted by the force artefacts of the atomic universe: the reception of these frequencies of force blocks, to the extent of an individual's restriction, his reception of Godlight. These physically derived frequencies are transmitted more powerfully in environments of high magnetic fields, for example. Thus high magnetic fields, for instance, can tune the body's blood and bone aerial further away from Godlight than it might naturally be.

Roger Bacon, the eminent scientist, philosopher and thirteenth-century Franciscan monk, postulated a beautiful paradigm on what religious terminology calls grace. Bacon saw grace as a kind of polarized 'light' with the recipient providing the modus and phase for its reception and use. The straighter we are the better it works.

So the holistic emanation of Godlight is available for reception and our aerials can receive it in its pure uninterrupted form, or in the form it takes when it is defracted into the various potentialities of the universe of parts. Soul field which seeks to possess is an individual expression of Godlight set in a particularly defracted and incoherent state. It is really the contour of the individual's pattern of restriction, a schematic of his or her sinfulness.

Perhaps we are all simply like lines, route lines on a map coming out of Godhead. See these lines as tubes. The straighter they are the more powerfully Godlight shines through. Bend them, twist them into dog-legged complications and we are no longer able to allow Godlight to shine through to light our way back. The Universe of entropic force is in the business of bending these 'lines' if we let it, and it is only our reach to constantly add, unite, bring things together, to bind, through offertory kindness, warmth, fellowship, and all other positive acts that allows the lines to get soft, pliant, less substantial and thus resist and keep force from having an effect on them such that it will bend them. Entropy's negative effect is registered just as much by what you don't do as what you do.

So, when the body-aerial is subject to effects such as high magnetic fields which increase its ambient state of tension it can become more tuned to receive these defracted patterns of light than the more coherent patterns that contain more of the frequencies of Godlight. Thus, for souls that seek after possession as a means to contact those in life's fields, high magnetic fields are the medium through which they may force their entry.

High-value magnetic fields also provide the pathway for alien Clone being to reach into our body aerials. To the same extent to which these high force fields block our aerial reception of the light of God, they increase our reception implicitly of signals that originate from the atomic universe – i.e. those transmitted by the alien beings. However, their reach is not of course anything to do with defractions of Godlight. Their reach is purely atomic, they write upon magnetic fields in the same way as sound waves can produce a recorded signal on a magnetic tape. More primitive soul field that is unable to enter into the fields of life and is desperate to do so thus reaches us through the same pathway as the alien beings. Could it be that such soul field in fact provides a channel through which these alien beings can reach more powerfully, a channel facilitated by the 'no-forceness' that characterizes the route all soul fields take in the spaces between atoms? Could the pen of soul connection writing no-force upon a tablet of force provide alien beings with the most powerful reach of all into our body-aerials, if that pen itself writes the same messages of force and imposition as the aliens themselves write?

If such is the case, then the greater the number of souls entrapped and unable to reincarnate into life, the better it would be for the alien beings to have the potential to reach into us and conduct their search for the enigma of soul. Factors resulting in the limitation of doorways into the fields of life, such as warfare, murder and abortion, would thus be advantageous to them and may well be promoted and, through their hybrids and agents on this earth, actually instigated by them.

Through the channel provided by growing numbers of trapped souls desperately clawing at the doorways into life, the alien beings would be able to reach more and more powerfully into those whose 'enlight' is greater. Through possession itself and the alien interception that can ride on it, the weaker souls in life's fields can gradually be pulled into the same net of entrapment. Thus the alien beings seem to be reeling in the lines of soul, perhaps in the hope that at the ends of these lines they will find the equivalent of their Creator Beings who provided them with their initial spur into life. Remember, in entropy their processes of Clone regeneration are breaking down. Thus they are looking for the same power that originally enlivened them to regenerate them into their original status.

Professor David M. Jacobs in his book *Secret Life*, in which he catalogues hundreds of alien abductions, offers a great deal of evidence to suggest that alien beings are indeed desperately searching for an elusive factor that they cannot seem to get to grips with or understand. A factor that might enable them to gain a foothold into the human soul track through an attempt to combine our track with theirs.

Jacobs identifies a common thread that appears to run through almost every abduction report. This involves, for the female abductees, the harvesting of ova, the implantation of embryos and the subsequent extraction of the embryos. For the male abductees, these procedures focus on the taking of sperm. After these procedures have been carried out secondary procedures involve 'the interaction between abductees and what seems to be the product of the alien breeding programme'. In these strange encounters the aliens carefully watch as women, men and children are required either to observe or physically interact with bizarre-looking 'offspring'. The abductee is walked into a room full of incubators and shown fifty to one hundred foetuses gestating in a liquid solution in containers. The containers are attached to an apparatus that seems to give them life support. Then the abductee might be led into a nursery-like area containing as many as 100 babies. The babies are old enough to live on their own but they 'appear phlegmatic and sickly'. They are often informed that some of the babies are biologically theirs. Abductees are required to touch, hold or hug these offspring. 'Apparently it is absolutely essential for the child to have human contact', says Jacobs, 'although the aliens prefer that the humans give nurturing loving contact, any physical contact seems to suffice . . . If the abductee resists she may be given a reason to force her to hold the baby'.

Jacobs observes that 'abductees universally state that the baby does not have the normal human reactions of a human infant. It is almost always listless. It does not respond to touch as a normal baby would. It does not squirm, it does not have a grasping reflex with its hands. It is lifeless, yet it is not dead. Most women think there is something terribly wrong with the baby. They feel that they must hold the baby to help it survive. After holding the baby for a while, women report that the baby seems "better". It appears to have a bit more energy or to be thriving slightly'. The abductees 'get the impression that they are part of an assembly-line process'. The aliens 'instruct newly pubescent girls that they should breed and mate as if they were animals in a biological experiment'. Thus, concludes Jacobs, they have no concept of humanity as anything other than a breeding machine.[1]

So, it seems that the alien beings, in their attempts to hybridize themselves with human beings, are finding that there are certain elements missing in the hybridization process. Without these elements the offspring of the process cannot seem to survive properly: they are sick and lifeless. The aliens must have realized that the purely physical processes of uniting sperm and egg do not provide the viable living state that they are so desperately searching for without certain missing ingredients. Thus they are looking for the origin of these ingredients in human physical contact. What they do not realize is that their hybrid offspring cannot survive for very long because it does not have that vital element – soul – to enable it to resist the entropic drift to which all purely physical things are subject.

There is evidence to suggest that these reproductive procedures are actually resulting in the production of foetuses that are later removed. 'Missing Foetus Syndrome' has happened to many abductees. These women are confirmed as pregnant by doctors. If during the first trimester they decide to terminate the pregnancy, the doctor discovers that there is no foetus to abort. No miscarriage or extra-heavy bleeding or discharge occurs, the foetus is simply gone. Jacobs says that this phenomenon has now happened so often to claimants of alien abduction that it is now considered one of the consistent features characterizing these abductions.

In *New Scientist* of 7.10.95 there is a report of a remarkable phenomenon which is dubbed by the author of the report: 'The closest thing to a human virgin birth that modern science has ever recorded'.[2] A young boy has been found whose body is derived in part from an unfertilized egg. The geneticists first realized that the boy was unusual when they looked at his white blood cells. Because he is a boy his cells should all have a Y chromosome that contains all the genes for maleness. But his white blood cells contain two X's, the chromosomal signature of a female. The real surprise came when the researchers discovered that the boy's skin is genetically different from his blood, with the skin containing the normal X and Y chromosomes of a typical male. This prompted them to look more closely at his X chromosomes. In a normal female each cell contains two different X's, one from the father and one from the mother. So was this the pattern found in the boy's blood, that of a normal female? No, it was not, for all the X chromosomes in all the cells in his body were found to be identical to each other and thus they originated only from his mother.

The only way in which the researchers could account for this was that the boy's development as an embryo must have started when 'an unfertilized egg self-activated and began to divide. A sperm cell then fertilized one of the cells and the mixture of cells began to develop as a normal embryo. This fusion with a sperm must have happened very early on because self-activated eggs quickly lose the ability to be fertilized. At some point the unfertilized cells must have duplicated their DNA boosting their chromosome number back up to 46. Where the unfertilized cells hit a developmental block, the researchers believe that the fertilized cells compensated and filled in that tissue'. The report further states that the boy's case 'demonstrates that whatever blocks there are to successful human parthenogenesis, unfertilized cells are clearly not always disabled. For example, these cells were able to create a seemingly normal blood system for the boy'. Parthenogenesis is the development of an unfertilized female sex cell without any male contribution. Sometimes an unfertilized mammalian egg will begin dividing but this growth does not usually get far. The self-activated 'embryo' will create rudimentary bone and nerve, but there are some tissues that it cannot make, and this would normally prevent further development. Yet experiments with mice have apparently shown that parthenogenetic cells grow more slowly than normal cells and that the two can co-exist in the same tissue.

You might recall from the discussion of trinucleotide repeat DNA in an earlier chapter that these repeats which lead to certain kinds of genetically inherited disease always seem to occur only at the point of the first few cell divisions of the embryo. If these repeats are the result of alien interception then perhaps they are a result of parthenogenetic elements that have been inserted into the biological lines of man. Maybe in the past there have been other people, perhaps similar to the boy mentioned in the report, who have survived a parthenogenetic start in life. The children born of these people and their children's children might be those affected by trinucleotide repeat DNA, which is a form of DNA that mimics cloning as it repeats itself again and again. It may well be those parthenogenetic elements in any particular biological line of descent that allow the aliens to reach with their tentacles of doom into the biological aerials of those born into that line. Jacobs notes that abduction, for example, seems to be a phenomenon that runs in the family. A family history of abduction experiences is the norm for the abductees on whom his research was done.

The seemingly incessant search for the crucial difference between human beings and aliens is further illustrated in a different context by an account set in the location of Bahia Blanca in Argentina. The account is given in Jenny Randles's book *UFOs and How to See Them*.[3] It involves a retired airline pilot. On 28 November 1972 a being with a blue suit materialized in his armchair while he was watching TV and imitated everything he did before declining a glass of water. Eventually the being went into the yard, looked at the sky, pressed a few buttons on a belt and vanished. Several similar cases to this have occurred around the world. If this account is genuine, and there is no reason to believe that it is not, then it offers irrefutable evidence that the alien beings are indeed studying humanity to discover something about us that they, with all their technology, are unable to pinpoint. They cannot find what they are looking for in the biological make-up of human beings so they assume, as they only have physical yardsticks by which to judge anything, that it must somehow originate from the actions that human beings perform.

David Jacobs in his devastating book *Secret Life* refers to other procedures used to investigate human capacities. One of these techniques he refers to as 'imaging'. This involves abductees being shown images on a screen in front of them: some of these are frightening and disturbing (such as scenes of war, atomic explosions and death) while others are sexually charged (involving romantic fantasies, perhaps with a person to whom the abductee is attracted). At other times the images are mundane and commonplace, such as a scene of a pretty garden with a fountain or of normal family life. While the 'imaging' goes on an alien being stands to the side of the abductee and stares deeply into her eyes while the procedures are in progress. 'The aliens seem to want to analyze the emotional effects of viewing the images' says Jacobs, 'the scenes themselves do not seem to have any prescient or prophetic value.'

In conclusion to his book Jacobs asks the question, 'What does the abduction phenomenon mean?' This is his answer:

'We have been invaded. It is not an occupation, but it is an invasion. At present we can do little or nothing to stop it. The aliens have powers and technology greatly in advance of ours, and that puts us at a tremendous disadvantage in our ability to affect the phenomenon or gain some control over it. We do not know what is going to happen in the future, just as we do not know what the aliens' ultimate purposes are. We do know that the effect on abductees' lives can be devastating. The net effect of the abduction phenomenon on our society and culture at large could very well be the same over a long period of time.

'Contact between the races is not taking place in a scenario that has been envisioned by scientists and science fiction writers: two independent worlds making careful overtures for equal and mutual benefit. Rather, it is completely one-sided. Instead of equal benefit, we see a disturbing programme of apparent exploitation of one species by another. How it began is unknown. How it will end is unknown. But we must face the abduction phenomenon squarely and begin to think rationally about what to do about it.'[4]

In looking for the whys and the wherefores of all of this I am convinced that this deadly alien 'interception' that is happening right now in our back yard, to a largely unsuspecting world, may have a fascinating purpose. The clue may lie in man's inhumanity to man through the centuries. Pogroms that lead to genocide are practised by and large on the less intercepted and, in most instances, *un*intercepted lines of hominids. By instigating this, could it be that the aliens are seeking to direct in some way the transmigrating souls to parents of intercepted genotypes that have their (the aliens') biological 'microchips' in the genetic ancestral lines, so that they could monitor the whole process and phenomenon of soul-acquisition right through the entire scale of all humanity?

Escape from the physical tie of karmic debt to individuals requires that we learn enough to be able to do this. In other words, to obtain 'forgiveness' for *ourselves* for what we are and what we have done, we have to learn enough about the situation that causes a restriction not to let that restriction happen. To me the word 'forgiveness' can only mean one thing. It simply means 'Advisement'. The giving to yourself of knowledge. In other words you 'forgive yourself'. No one and nothing else can do this to you or on your behalf. The whole business is strictly personal. This deadly idea that someone else waves his or her hand and provides you with a benediction on behalf of a God or a deity or a saint is an invention of power brokers on behalf of themselves. It is one of the biggest expedient falsehoods and frauds perpetrated on the body of man in the name of religion. It is utter nonsense when viewed rationally and if there is no rational logic in reconciling anything we move into the province of being baboons.

The words of Jesus Christ on the cross hailed his father to teach us more the 'whys and wherefores' and consequences of restriction when he said, 'Father, forgive them for they know not what they do.' It was not a plea for absolution from punishment with thunderbolts as a sanction and chastisement. That would have been the very denial of the status of the wondrous infinite Love that marks all of Godhead. The love of Godhead can only teach. It can *never* chastise. It can only ask. It can never enforce, if 'free will' means anything at all. It is we who bring such as punishment on ourselves. It is all our own work and consequence in this wretched Universe of Parts.

Can you imagine how much knowledge we would need to have to be able to reconcile all karmic obligation *en masse* to everyone? You would have to have the knowledge of Jesus Christ, Gautama Buddha, or Mohammed the Prophet and all the other provenly beautiful authors of rational spiritual truth to be able to do it effectively enough and escape the deadly wheel of rebirth. That is why 'sin' or restriction and thus restricted practice keeps us bound in this Hell of a universe. This is simply why we need to have complete faith, belief and trust in these proven beautiful ones who came among us to show us what we need to know and how we need to employ that knowledge to be able to stand the slightest chance of escape from the deadly 'bodies' (that are the atoms) that make up this universe of those who failed and have left their momentum away from Godhead in the form of entropy to pull us away from our salvation.

When we think of the evil creatures who have hallmarked the progress of the human race through the millennia, be it Genghis Khan, Herod, Vlad, Attila, Hitler and all the countless contemporary comparable types who have visited their collective depravity on our species, it is well to remember the terror of their personal futures. Their removal from our midst through death signals the beginning of an impossible karmic chase. Their debt is measured in multiples and perhaps millions and ensures their inexorable devolvement into subspecies of 'being' through the torture of future twisted bodies to ape, monkey, animal, insect, virus and stone. Their folly is the frustration that comes with trying to reconcile so much that is unrealizable. Their future is likely to be written in the carapaces of insects and the skin of worms. It is a salutary warning to those who seek to act on behalf of others in corporate terms. The karma is proportionately bigger if you don't get it righteous. What price the politician, the corporate head, and the title holder, that lead astray the innocent and the helpless in our world? The laws of Omniversal justice could never let them escape their folly. Though kings in this world, their solace will be torment. No devils with tridents will marshal their demise. They are their own demon and their own measure of result. It is as simple as cause and effect and as completely just.

CHAPTER TWENTY-SEVEN:

DISINFORMATION AND DAMNATION

If you have chosen to read the chapter entitled 'Affirmations' you may be stunned by what the so-called custodians of the Christian faith for one have done in the past to remove from us the vital codex of knowledge and insights that might have revealed the possibility of humanity's interception by an alien species. Whatever their motives, the fact is that their guardianship of the ethic of a redeemer of Christ's significance to all mankind, a redeemer whose ethic and even incidental words and deeds were the most precious of all things, gave them a responsibility to see that his every word, every deed was never obscured, hidden or distorted. Such is also true of the Talmud and all other texts that purport to come from the brightest wisdom of our greatest teachers. A reference here illustrates:

A group of 120 sages called the 'Men of the Great Assembly' helped to compose the Jewish 'Talmud', which extrapolates and comments on Jewish law. These men were called the men of the 'Great Assembly' because they, according to Judaic tradition, 'restored the crown to its rightful place'. This refers to the fact that Moses had described God as 'the great, mighty and awesome God' (Deut. 10:17). Subsequently the prophet Jeremiah believed that it would be more appropriate if the word 'awesome' were deleted, and the prophet Daniel deleted the word 'mighty' deeming it an inaccurate adjective to describe God.

The Men of the 'Great Assembly' reinstated the two terms that had been deleted in order to restore the description of

God to what they believed to be its 'rightful place', that being a position of power and authority over men such that they would be expected to be in 'awe' of their God who was a 'mighty' being who had power over them. Thus the 'God' of Moses was asserted over and against the very different 'God' to whom the prophets Jeremiah and Daniel addressed themselves. It is probable that Daniel and Jeremiah understood the concept and nature of an implicate, eternal, infinite God who was there in the perfect expression of unconditional profferment for all who wished to and were able to receive it. To their deeply philosophical and probably psychically gifted minds, the idea of awesome might in a God was too representative of the national and tribal leaders and power-hungry rogues of their acquaintance. It may even be that they suspected that this so-called God was something more tangible and less ephemeral than an insubstantial truly divine entity would be. Such a 'God' would not be 'mighty' as he would in his commitment implicitly allow his 'children' the freedom to choose to know and understand him or to choose not to. There would be and could be no directed sanction other than the implicit consequences that any logical result prescribed. Similarly there would be no need for engendering the premise of being awesome in the minds of courtiers unless you were trying to invite and inculcate a sense of wonder and fear in your intended converts. 'Awe' would simply be out of place in man's relationship with God, just as it is out of place in the relationship of love that lies between parent and child.

If something is 'awesome' you tend to keep yourself at a respectful distance. Would a God of Love have demanded that we keep a respectful distance from him? Surely, if we are to return to him as Christ exhorted us to do, we would have to lessen that distance, not maintain it artificially. The 'God' that is 'mighty' and demands 'awe', worship and supplication can thus be construed as a suspect God that seeks to impress through spectacle and fear. A God that perhaps has something to hide, as a space-travelling opportunist perhaps would. It is an entity such as this that would need unqualified obedience to effect its purposes, and thus would have set about keeping at bay intelligent questions that might have exposed its true status. It would need devices of outlook designed to engender fear. Of course, its humanoid victims were a captive audience in those times. If a tribe in New

Guinea in contemporary times would worship the picture of the
Duke of Edinburgh as a God and an old Victrola (phonograph)
as God's spokesman, what would you expect old Ezekiel to think
and do when he saw a spaceship land with its blinking lights and
swirling winds? What references would he have to relate to it for
what it was?

Judge for yourselves from this extract from Ezekiel:

'A whirlwind came out of the north, a great cloud, and a fire unfolding
itself and a brightness was about it, and out of the midst thereof as the
colour of amber, out of the midst of the fire. Also out of the midst
thereof came the likeness of four living creatures. And this was their
appearance; they had the likeness of a man. And every one had four
faces, and every one had four wings, and their feet were straight feet;
and the sole of their feet was like the sole of a calf's foot and they
sparkled like burnished brass. Now as I beheld the living creatures,
behold, one wheel upon the earth by the living creatures with his
four faces. The appearance of the wheels and their work was like
unto the colour of a beryl and the four had one likeness: and their
appearance and their work was as it were a wheel in the middle of a
wheel. When they went upon their four sides: and they turned not
as they went. As for their rings, they were so high that they were
dreadful; and their rings were full of eyes round about them four.
And when the living creatures went the wheels went by them: and
when the living creatures were lifted up from the earth the wheels
were lifted up.'[1]

Ezekiel also heard a 'noise' of 'great rushing' of the 'wings of
the living creatures that touched one another, and the noise of
the wheels over against them'. This account immediately brings
to my mind eyewitness accounts of the spacecraft landing in
Roswell, New Mexico in 1946. The 'amber colour' of the light
surrounding the craft and the alien beings coming out of it. The
fact that these 'living creatures' had 'the likeness of a man' but
each had 'four faces' and 'four wings' and 'went upon their four
sides' and 'turned not as they went' suggests to me some form of
remote-control robot that follows a single path without turning.
The 'rings' that were 'full of eyes' that were so 'dreadful' evoke
images of the blinking and flashing lights around the often-seen
'wheel' of disc-shaped UFOs.

Let us now suppose that you are driving happily along in your car one night and suddenly a bright light spins down in front of you, revealing a glowing disc. You manage to avoid crashing into it and when you stop some nasty old aliens 'zap' you with their Ever-Readies and take you into their spaceship and do nasty things to you. You emerge physically none the worse for it, but in time you change from a nice stable provincial Englishman to a layabout lager lout who wants to clout all Manchester United fans on the head, for no more reason than they have the best football team in the world. That may be normal understandable practice to some, but to you it is bizarre behaviour, especially as you had hated football up to then. You question it all for some time, but in the end you begin to like clonking the red-and-blacks on the head till you take some of them out of this world. Pretty soon you are on the Mitcham Common Police Station's 'Most Wanted' list. You are arrested, convicted and sentenced to two months' imprisonment because the judge is a Chelsea fan.

I do not wish to belittle the awful experiences of some abductees by writing this in a tone less than serious. I do it to illustrate that many people tend to view the whole 'abduction thing' with amusement. It may be one of the most monumentally significant and grave pointers to the fate of our children tomorrow and we laugh at it all so easily and ignore it at our peril. Whatever its status in terms of what we might qualify and quantify as reality, there can be no doubt that something hugely significant is going on. As I have said, an eminent Professor of Psychiatry at Harvard University, Professor John Mack, has written a book attesting and affirming the 'abduction' experiences of many people as real and, in his opinion, outside the broad stroke of what may be considered mental illness. He is paying a terrible price at the hands of his contemporaries for his bravery and vision in validating it as a real and significant phenomenon in the affairs of human beings. I can't help feeling that when he is finally vindicated his critics will melt into the fickle background greyness that marks all clouds in a stormy sky. They may well be the first casualties of the lightning that will strike us all when the discs of doom finally spin their sizzles across the horizon of our world.

My parody may serve to illustrate how we can all find ourselves in the predicament of flesh through the deadly random and capricious winds of entropy. How circumstances not of our direct making can load our souls with negative input, such that through the aeons of our soul's sojourn in the Universe of Parts we dim our link with Godhead.

It is this kind of acquisition of negative input that may in past lives have infected our connection line with the 'Masterverse' of Godhead with the vile gene investitures of alien origin. These accessions are then passed on in flesh through the generations for a particular incarnating soul to take on. If lessons are not learnt subsequently during a particular lifetime by these souls, the polluting effect of these infected parental formats will manifest in the physical casts and social fashions, generation to succeeding generation, marking out the racist, the rapist, the murderer, the brigand and the fool, and reincarnation downwards in species terms begins.

The question remains of how any outside agency to the self could achieve complete instigation and control of a human being from impulse to act?

Could it be that the R Complex brains of certain individuals or groups of individuals are better able to synthesize electromagnetic and magnetic impulses referenced to instigate violent and aggressive behaviour? It is well known that if you pulse microwaves of a certain frequency and intensity at mice they will all attempt to kill each other.

One of America's most brilliant scientists demonstrated a few years ago that he could raise and lower the volume of conversations people were having in a restaurant with the aid of a device the size of a matchbox strapped to his wrist. The people in the restaurant had no idea that they were being manipulated in this way.

It is beyond question that magnetic fields and extremely low frequency (ELF) electromagnetic waves can be used to control and shape the thoughts and moods of people. It is in the domain of some of the most secret and successful work done in secret laboratories and agencies in the United States, Britain, France, Israel, Japan, China and the former Soviet Union to this day. It comes under the title 'Electronic Warfare' and is a field of activity pursued feverishly today by scientists and military researchers in many countries.

If we can do such things with our technology, can you imagine what an alien technology that can come here to our solar system past the barrier of the speed of light can do? Many abductees report that these Clones and roboids have complete control of their minds and bodies while they do medical and biological experiments on them. It is a chilling thought for us all.

There can be little doubt of the value of mind control as a governing instrument to effect the takeover of any agency or mechanism with the least wear and tear on the seekers after control. An ignorant and passive bio-field mitigates resistance best and all hardware is left intact. Is it not patently apparent that if the brain can be imposed upon by a means that functions remotely, its chemistry together with the human skeleton may well act as an aerial and a receiver? The atoms and molecules acting in biosynthesizing concert to provide the thought and the idea that invites and prompts an action. The choice, of course, to carry it all through is always independent of the prompt. That is the property of conscience and thus the Soul. The possession of which by the individual allows for the word 'No' to operate in the universe of diminishing returns. A facility without which there could be no free will and thus no 'living being'.

Yet no matter what the strength or value of a remote interceptor's grip on our bio-psychology, it could never in any way mitigate God-connected free will. This is simply because the two things are two entirely different phenomena. One shapes through an increase in the ambient level of force, the other through a decrease in it. Let me explain.

If you want to change the prevailing state of anything in this Universe you have to do it by applying a force, or coercive mechanism, to it that adds force to the state in which it previously existed. You shape a flat piece of metal to the shape of the damaged part of your car and replace that part by using force. You can achieve the same end by forming the shape in a vacuum chamber that operates by removing force or air pressure from the chamber. And so the same action is achieved in opposite ways.

Godhead is where NO force whatsoever exists. It is the perfect place of Angels. It is 'peace' in absolute perfection where not the merest ripple, shaking or vibration exists. It is the intercession of this 'peace' into the enforced state of our Universe that shapes and forms things for Godhead. It does this by unravelling force using a God-vacuum, if you like.

A mental programme by aliens would have to be written with atomic writing in force. In other words, it would imply that a gene-instigated chain of chemical events provides a mental function where the perpetration of any act is achieved regardless of any sanction of Will, through this function.

Let's say that a magnetic instigating signal is pulsed to susceptible individuals with suitable R Complex brains and from then on a special chemistry synthesized by this brain translates any signals with a definite predisposition to a selected ` action. Those actions will be predisposed towards violence and aggression, ritual and deceit and all the associated actions the R Complex brain provides the necessary chemistry for.

It may only be resisted with the power of well-attested and referenced values and verifications based on a simple codex of ethics designed to protect individual liberty and freedom. But how does this codex operate? Where is it stored and how is it actioned in the brain such that it can resist a chemically 'programmed' brain?

A programmable R Complex is only one of three dispositions in our Triune Brains. We have to remember that we have two other brains. Just as the R Complex's brain chemistry may schedule predetermined tendencies, so may the Limbic brain and so may the Neo Cortex. The predominance of a particular brain's receiving and actioning capacity depends on the fund of previous actions and reactions catalogued by the individual. If actions were centred on Neo Cortex functions long enough then the chemistry of the Neo Cortex would be more developed and dominant in instigating and shaping views and thus the likely results would be accented in positive, uniting, binding modes of behaviour. The individual will act in a way that preserves and maximizes the freedom of others. He or she will allow the best dispositions and circumstances to prevail in any given scenario that provides warmth, understanding and caring. In other words, what may be described as loving forms of behaviour.

The urge to action may come from instinct, impulse, sensory gleaned inspiration or electromagnetically imposed instigation, but well notified sanction in conscience or reason may and will always put in its way a stopping mechanism. Of course, this requires a free, aware and cogent mind that can make the right choices at the right time. If the control of the mind is in some way restricted or in some way removed from conscience then you have a problem. But, as I have said previously, I believe the strength of connection with Godhead defines the value gradient of conscience. In other words, the power of the Soul in you is the best saviour of the self. It is the part of yourself no outside mechanism that uses force can breach and deny without your choice to control it. Lose Perspective and Will and thus this control through apathy and carelessness and you are in fault and, what is more, in deadly danger. You are prey to all the mind-bending external force that seeks to control you.

CHAPTER TWENTY-EIGHT:
DELUSIONS AND DEMONS

The real demons that policed humanity and composed the committees and convocations of the past that decided on our religious ethics and freedoms in terms of what was put up for us to believe were probably unsuspectingly acting at the behest of the little grey 'devils'.

These were scoundrels more deadly than murderers, these committees that framed the religious beliefs of generations of men. They were in effect what might be commonly termed the 'Arms of Lucifer' because their manufactured lies and extrapolated distortions of the original words, rhetoric and intentions of the authors of a faith condemned the faithful in their millions to inappropriate and mistaken views and practices in the names of these blessed ones throughout the centuries. Every faith has had them. Their main purpose, one suspects, was to maintain power and authority in the hands of the few religious administrators at the expense of many for no more, in most instances, than temporal and purely physical benefit. Organized corporations of pious plenitude, with the accent on 'plenitude' in most instances. It didn't take long before the religious organizations of the world had most of the land and the wealth all given to them and seconded to them in the name of fear and favour by the poor mass of people who sought the blessings of powerful, vengeful divines lest thunderbolts and eternities of damnation were to be the legacy of their futures.

Christ's brief, as he himself declared, was to save our souls, and he did so with burning zeal and blistered bleeding feet in the most final act of love possible. The sacrifice of his own life. Such was the magnitude of his intent. There were no scarlet sofas and decorated guards for him. Those whose decision had a direct bearing in removing, obscuring or in any way obfuscating the minutest detail of his sojourn on this Earth, whatever the motive, whatever the intention, bear a horrendous karma or debt to all mankind. They may well be reaping what they sowed through their own hands in an eternity of devolving bodies desperately seeking to redress their subterfuge. It is their legacy to us and presumes a grand implicate injustice that we all bear.

That is the terrifying accountability of all who claim grand leadership in collective terms, whatever purpose, way or function that leadership might drive consequence to a conclusion. They take responsibility on a grand scale and their debt when they are mistaken is in proportion to their motive and the ways and means of its application. Karma is final only in the individual's free choice and guidance under coercion proscribes free choice. It is surely the ultimate lesson that individual freedom of choice, free of sanction, is the safest way past the trappings of karmic consequence and thus a dispassionate objective view of all the facts and information available is a crucial prerogative for us all.

Of course, there are circumstances when the general collective good may have to be marshalled within the precincts of delegated choice. In such circumstances the urge to all the best results still runs complementary with extrapolation on all the available information. The terrible thing about censorship is that it signals insecurity, cowardice and lies and opens the route to falsehood and misrepresentation. It stretches myth and legend into the parlours of truth and in something as crucial as the custodianship of our souls and our quest for eternal tenure, condemns us to sleep forever in limit and damnation.

The lethal and instinctive tendency in those of Cro-Magnon origin to set philosophical and theosophical perspectives with totalitarian ethnic, racial and tribal marks and then set these marks as points for antagonism and enmity further ensured that humanity would scale the heights of idiocy. It ensured that whatever chance we had of spotting the aliens in our midst evaporated through the lack of internal reference. This may well have been the alien intention all along. The two mainstream intercepted human lines were set at each other's throats so that their handiwork in both could be seen in action by them over time, and adjustments could be made along the way to achieve their goal of a genotype best fitted for their purposes. It is a remarkable fact that the two altered lines, Neanderthal and Cro-Magnon, and their respective descendants, the Dravidio/Semitics (Neanderthal) and the Caucasoids (Cro-Magnon), have interestingly derived congenital diseases linked strictly to their respective groupings. As I have said before, one wonders if the secret strategists who plan national and racial interests in their 'Think Tanks' are looking at disease as a control mechanism to further their dastardly interests. Ethnically derived disease-disseminating bombs with germs tailor-made to take out particular populations based on racial vulnerability may well be the order of the future.

I first wrote the above as a surmise when drafting this book. Little did I think that it would be affirmed so soon afterwards. The *Daily Telegraph* of the 30th September 1996 carried an article by Roger Highfield, their Science Editor[1]. I quote: 'Scientists could develop genetic weapons designed to infect and kill or sterilize specific ethnic groups, the World Medical Association is to be told. Eugenic and ethnic viruses are among the weapons that could be created as a result of burgeoning knowledge of genetics, according to a paper to be submitted by the British Medical Association to the WMA's meeting in South Africa next month'. Dr Vivienne Nathanson, author of the paper and head of science and ethics at the BMA, has explained that genes that provide the signature of a particular population could be tagged with a probe armed with a toxin. In this way scientists could genetically engineer a virus to infect a specific ethnic group. She points out that 'you could have a tribal group which has very much the same genetic structure and that is equally true in white populations as any other' and she adds that it is possible that the effects of a genetic weapon could be delayed so that it affects only the next generation. 'What makes it very frightening is that it could be done in ways that are much more insidious and less obvious', she said. Her suggestion is that the right international legislation is passed to prevent such weapons from being developed. However, there has to be considerable doubt as to whether any kind of legislation would stand in the way of the development and use of these weapons. Given the fact that their covert application is such a relatively easy task, how could any legislation be effectively applied? So many 'secret' experiments that have exposed specific groups of the population to certain 'harmless' chemicals have recently been brought to light and even confessed to by those governments (the British and American) who were involved. If there is the motivation to develop these horrendous weapons in the first place, how can any amount of legislation stand in the way of their application, particularly at the hands of a right-wing ethnically-biased government? The Nazis are not dead. They never were. They are alive and well in the bowels of all the Western intelligence services and all their laboratory 'mice' in many secret establishments all over the white Western world, dancing to the whims of their deadly 'Grey' masters and, perhaps, fathers.

CHAPTER TWENTY-NINE:
ENDS AND MEANS

The scaffolding of true Godhead is inherently scribed with the ink of logic. Pure and natural mathematical logic. It stretches the 'heavens', charged with the power for uniting all parts. Its urge is rescue and its touch is peace. Herein, I believe, lies scope eternal and hope for everything and all. If there is limit it has to be written in leftovers. The bits and pieces of a Universe of Parts. The home of lies.

Close your eyes a moment. Take a deep breath and feel the contours of yourself in the quietness of your individuality. The world is gone, and yet the world is still there. Open your eyes now and feel its instant electric blast. To many of us, alas, it is reassurance itself. Reassurance that we are alive and that is all that seems to matter. It is where all our sureties seem to lie. Yet to a blessed few it is the solace of a convincing falsehood. The edge of all transient finite result. A feel-good factor for fools and mannequins.

The eye alone may never see truth. Its margins so often frame the lie and the misconception. Yet it is all most of us really believe or indeed want to believe. Our legacy as a species has been written for too long with the short nibs of the bully and the scoundrel. The Lord of the temporal Manor prevailed with the tribe and the bribe and the bludgeon while the poets and the priests sang psalms and lullabies to themselves. They had to build their ivory towers away from us. Most of us just did not want to listen. The enforced universe, alas, makes the frame, the cradle and the baby.

God is quiet. Man is loud. We keep being told that the pen is mightier than the sword but we keep using up more metal making the latter. We institutionalized force in our nature and too many of us now tremble too much within to its psychological syntax to want to listen to the sweetness of birdsong. If you don't believe me take a catalogue of how 'force' has gradually and progressively increased in musical formats and formulas through the centuries from the first sweet lullabies sung by a mother to her baby child. Sweet cogent melodies and lyrics where meaning conveyed music and song have given way to rasping, discordant cacophonies. You can hardly describe heavy-metal rock as a musical format synthesized for the peace of angels. Perhaps only Hell's Angels. It is a remarkable progression, affirming the insidious and unnoticed power of entropy to demean reason.

As I have implied before: I am convinced that this universe is the true Hell. The trouble with Hell is that you only qualify for it when you *don't* know what it is. That begs the question: How, then, am I as the author of this work in Hell, if I have spotted this Universe for what it truly might be? The answer to this might of course be that I am wrong and the Universe is not the true Hell. It also might be that I am right, that Hell might simply mean you don't know what it is when you come into it, but that you can learn what it is after you've been here some time. That may well be the 'hell' of it all. Hell is the darkness of ignorance itself. Every atom and every particle of every atom that makes up its contours is the result of the loss of knowledge and the gaining of ignorance. It needs something or someone not intrinsically of it to show it up for its true nature and implication. I know it is a hackneyed old thing to say that a light is useful in darkness but, you know, humanity has had so many beautiful teachers and prophets, we've had so many torches to light our ignorance, paying us a visit proclaiming our predicament with the loud hailer of an entire life commitment, don't you feel we should gratefully acknowledge them? It is the nature of Hell to drain all batteries and the nature of demons to short-circuit them before their time. We all know our demons within our deepest deep. The price for our education coloured the sands of Judea with a single patch of red. It was the most devastating indictment of our ignorance. One would have expected humanity to learn our lessons better. It was the supplication of the truest love, after all. But the universe has an eraser for that. It is its very nature to try to see that we don't remember such draughts and sentiments through the stern, cold, cruel and impersonal drift of the devil's orthodontia: the Second Law of Thermodynamics. It is in the programme as part of the constitution of the Universe.

Yet the grandest thing of all is the discovery that even in Hell, Hope is the watchword. That there can be the potential for absolute freedom of choice. Choice through which freedom and liberation from Hell may come. Damnation or Liberation is only eternal if you as an individual make it so. No one else. There can be no directive from anyone or anything that cannot be overcome through that awesome individual absolute freedom that is the very central axiom of Godhead.

I have tried to write this book free of obscurity and in as plain and effective a stance as possible. All of us who sincerely seek after the whys and wherefores of our existence have been too often bludgeoned to death by a smog of phoney intellectualization. The search for truth has too often been steeped in the broth of cerebral vanity. Meaningless contrived verbiage, daubed in thick coagulated lumps over the halls of religious and philosophical learning, has over the centuries only served to conceal the truth. The deliberate censorship of the available record can only be done under motive. It can't be innocent. The huge and proven worldwide conspiracy of the military and the politicians in the USA to hide hard evidence of alien landings can only profit those whose interests lie in maintaining a myth. A myth that if exposed could have massive financial and social implications that might affect the rich and the powerful and bring crashing down some religious edifices that depend on their God being divine and not some alien lifeform. It is not and cannot be done for the usually touted altruistic reason of stopping panic among the general population of the world. The conspirators well know that the public is far more likely to react not with panic but with benign curiosity and perhaps welcome the fact that we are not alone in the universe.

It is terrifying that every soul in the whole world may be held to ransom for reasons such as this. Our eternity is mortgaged by a pack of scoundrels who keep us all in the dark and steal our chance of a blessed tomorrow for their blind, greedy and lethal need for power and control. This whole thing concerns our sacred individual destinies and countless millions have very likely been duped into perdition and damnation by the running of the current lies that seek to hide the truth about Flying Saucers and what the authorities know about them and their occupants. If I am right about the existential base set in the strands and obligations of karma, each and every one of these perpetrators will have little or no chance of making amends to the millions of souls they have duped. They would be chasing their tails into smaller and smaller bodies through crippled forms and huge suffering, lifetime after lifetime. A hopeless chase for atonement. It may be what they deserve but we would all lie victim. Victims because we hadn't what it took to solicit the truth. And so we tacitly deserve our predicament, too.

It may well be that the whole 'Flying-Saucer-aliens-in-our-back-yard' thing is as the governments claim – a total myth. If that is so then every single individual human being has, if you'll pardon the deliberate pun, an inalienable right to decide for themselves its veracity for the reasons stated above. The last thing we need is some deadly military general or governmental politician or religious priest sitting in judgement on our right to decide our own fate. The fate of our eternity. The final question for answer is surely: Do you want to, in the final analysis, mortgage your right to an eternity in Godhead on the behests of those empowered to rule and kill?

I have only touched the tip of the iceberg in illustrating how our religious custodians have raped our souls with their proscription of the total available record of most of the grand theo-philosophical authors of the world's spiritual codex. Most of it done, no doubt, in the 'interests of the public good'. This old adage has been the refuge of the self-seeking, self-interested scoundrel and charlatan and cheat through the centuries. The censorship practised by these deadly instruments of lies in the name of Gautama Buddha, Jesus Christ, the grand prophets of Judaism and Islam and all the other wondrous religious teachers who sought to love us all with their wisdom and offertory. We have been given the total religious codex in terms of subjective translations arrived at by individuals and committees, till in contemporary times its dissemination is no more than a cheap tabloid form of its former self. The full scan of the theological prospectus has been subject to endless censorship

and downright interdiction to such an extent that the borders of
truth as the Masters revealed it may be seen no more against
the margins of lies as the interpreters have subsequently made
it known. The church had selected the twenty-seven books of
the New Testament by the fourth century after a great deal of
political intrigue and internal rivalry. It was only when the canon
had become self-evident that it was argued that inspiration and
canonicity coincided.

Implicit in the parables that Christ used to illustrate the view
of existential truth is a clear invitation to use reason and logic to
sort the wheat from the chaff. His teaching method was a powerful
exhortation to see that veracity is the child of logic and reason.
There is a further and more important implication, and that is
that the individual has to discretely work out truth for himself
or herself. That in this mechanism and ONLY this mechanism
is liberation of Being accomplished. That it never can be done in
proxy by anyone on behalf of anyone or Jesus with his stated love of
the 'Father' for us all would have zapped us poor miserable sinners
and converted us all to see the light instantly and taken us all back
home to the Master Universe where our own one has its origins.

Obvious, you might think. But if one thing is clear, through the
record of the centuries of human endeavour, it is that human beings
have the most awesome capacity to believe humbug. Indeed, we
seem to *want* to believe humbug. If we are condemned as a species
it is a just 'reward' for the madness that sometimes claims even
the best of us. The madness that prompts us to abandon the stern
pith of logically extrapolated truth in preference for the lies our
emotional comfort points dictate.

The rich man would spend thousands of dollars, pounds, marks
or roubles to push the muscles of his *gluteus maximus* a little more
gently against his hip bone in his Rolls-Royce than, say, a Morris
Mini would do. He would do this when perhaps a ten-thousandth
of the value of that Rolls will get him the same distance from A
to B for as long a time, by the Mini, and leave so much for saving
the lives of perhaps hundreds of little starving children. Such is
the merit of the world we see today, where we ruthlessly ignore
the little starved faces crying at the empty paps of a Third World
mother in favour of decorated stones and empty fancy monoliths
that adorn our equally empty vanity.

Poverty and disease in the non-white Third World has existed on such a tremendous scale and for so long in the face of so much excess and profligacy in the Occident. We should have long ago seen that it has never been a question of 'Can we cure it?' It has always been one of 'Do we want to cure it?' By 'we' I mean us in the shamefully wasteful West. It is now way beyond a reasonable doubt that we don't care enough to cure it. There is something truly evil in the thinking paradigm of the broadly white Occident, and it prompts the conclusion that most of its population are really covert racists. The country that proudly claims to be the moral leader of the world today, the USA, has imprisoned one in fourteen of her black citizens. This heinous figure exposes the unpalatable possibility that, one hundred and fifty years since the emancipation of slaves in that country, with all the modern devices at her command to promote mass-media attention to the evil of racism, the majority of her people have remained primitive racists to this day and continue to be so. And so it is in every Cro-Magnon seeded country in the world today. No matter how hard they seek to hide the fact, how cleverly they posture the sublimation of it, their citizens by and large succumb to the stench of racism on the slightest excuse. In elections over in the Occident it's called 'playing the race card'.

Take a look around the world. The least is done to relieve the condition of the hundreds of millions of desperately sick and hungry people everywhere but particularly in the Third World. It is no longer a question of ignorance. Information technology explodes it in our faces daily. When something is done it's largely palliative: it is embarrassingly minute and miserly but carefully orchestrated and presented to look grand and generous by the Western media. Such a contradiction to the natural drive in human nature generally to give aid and succour as an immediate reaction to someone who might suddenly fall down in the street immediately in front of you. Why?

What devil can do such as this? What demon can possess our instincts and our insight such that we can't and won't see the folly of such contradictory 'thinkability'? As I say, we walk along any street. Someone nearby drops down and falls to the pavement in distress. The vast majority of us will instinctively reach down to lend a helping hand. Our unthinking instant urge is not to finish them off into oblivion with manic relish. The natural instant reaction of almost all human beings will be to serve and to help. The power of Godhead is immediate and always present still within our human condition at the very base of our knowing.

Why, then, has humanity long ago not rid the earth of poverty and want? Disease and suffering? Why has one-fifth of the population of the world conspired for so long to keep four-fifths destitute and condemned to meagreness when it so easily could have banished indigence from the face of the earth long ago? The social statisticians are constantly giving us the numbers that betray a covert congress deliberately preventing this. There can be no doubt that if the world had continued to put the same effort to beat starvation as they put into the effort to beat Saddam Hussein in the Gulf War, or indeed if all the world's countries were to halt for one year their expenditure on arms and put that money they save towards developing the systems to beat famine and disease in the Third World, we would eradicate want and suffering from the Earth forever.

As I have said before, the most remarkable thing is that if you look around the Third World, and count the number of white or Occidental faces that are not those of tourists, consultants of one thing or the other, priests, nuns or religious servers of some kind, the number of purely voluntary servers of the poor and the unfortunate in the non-white world, acting in generous unselfish offertory, amounts to about 0.00000001 of the total Occidental population of the world.

Measure this against the horrendous picture of the massive scale of want and deprivation we see daily on TV screens and it provides a stunning indictment of the altruistic nature of the so-called civilized people of the West.

We are all fooled into thinking that the Cro-Magnon legacy to the world is one of civilisation, largesse and highly cultured magnitude. Such is the skill of the media humbug makers. A quick empiric measure of actual results shows a quite different story. It shows a story of pirates, parasites, murderers and covert manipulators of cleverly set-up systems that steal from the poor to give to the rich. A largely callous, heartless machine-minded breed of fortune hunters hell-bent on coldly and selfishly exploiting defenceless and disadvantaged people for their cheap labour or raw materials and skilfully making it look like goodly service for the poor and the unfortunate. Many non-Occidental countries have of course the local versions of such people, ever ready and willing to assist their Western counterparts in their work. But they are largely Occidentally educated and usually have heavy traces of Cro-Magnon juice in their veins.

What I am trying to say is that this juice might well be infected with the sap of alien origin. That the heavily extraterrestrially apprenticed Cro-Magnons magnified their influence on the affairs of man and lead the ways and means of things done in the name of humanity. It includes elements of machine-minded programming. No room in the inn for sentiment, compassion and offertory.

There *has* to be a covert agency, a deadly hidden factor in the affairs of men and perhaps in the psyche of human beings that can keep the instant natural instinct in man to save, to proffer and to help and give succour to the helpless in check and prevent the species from employing the means and the good sense to save itself from its own destruction. There can be no doubt whatsoever that we have the intelligence and the expertise, the hardware and the software to easily rid and forever forbid the source of much of the trouble in the world today: poverty and the want engendered by the basic human need for shelter, food, and clothing, with dignity. The vast majority of the world's eminent social and demographical experts haven't the slightest disagreement about this. If we have the collective intelligence to go to the Moon, build nuclear reactors, nuclear bombs, build and deploy complex missile systems, satellite systems, planetary explorative systems, how is it we are supposed to lack the intelligence to build a simple social system that brings us all together in co-operation for the good of the very survival of the species? The point, as we all know, is that we don't lack the intelligence to see to our saving. We lack the WILL to see to it. Herein lies the rub. Again, WHY?

We all, of course, know that human nature is a mix of the monster and the saint. Or so it seems to be. You hear the oft-quoted adage to the point of triteness, 'There's good and bad in everyone.' What, then, makes the bad dominate so much the good? Or how is it we all seem to be led by the nose to world crisis after world crisis? War to war. Famine to famine. Pogrom to pogrom. Evil certainly is the dominant and deadly drive that underpins the world. The daily casualty rate from wars and skirmishes and social and political murder around our planet pour out in huge magnitudes. The peace makers, century after century, can never sleep. The deadly horsemen of death ride rampant, the ropes seeking to restrain their steeds covered in the blood of failure till they have borne away their fill of innocent blood.

I am convinced that the central point of all evil rests at the pivot where we demarcate on the principle called 'Difference'. The root of it all in terms of our human predicament lies in the operation of social, racial and ethnic platitudes and taboos. The welfare of the whole planet lies here at this one point. A point when a socially diseased white Occidental mind's 'eye' meets a complexion a darker shade than pink. The point when an accent can turn away a face in disgust or the sound of a surname can forbid an opportunity. Through millions of instances such as this taking place each day all over the world, the globe of our living rostrum spins a darker and darker announcement that we are doomed.

What is it in us that instigates such evil, if our basic nature in instant reaction to someone who falls in injury before us is to immediately and unthinkingly go to their aid and is thus 'goodly' or 'godly', for want of better words? Why do we do such injury and harm to so many so often and so constantly when we have more time to think about things? What are the driving points that cause us to proffer such a deadly harvest of doom on ourselves with calculated instigations to war, starvation, (it is used very effectively by rich western nations as a tool for political control of poor ones), if our innate unthinking reactive nature is to aid and give succour to those in need?

I believe, as I have said before, that there is a covert agency, a 'force' not of man, that intervenes in and interferes with the affairs of man and prompts division and separation among us all. The ignorant and the weak-willed will always be the first to fall prey to this 'force' and will be the first guinea pigs in a giant universe-wide experiment for the artificial seeding and reallocation of soul, impossible though it may be to achieve. It is done through an agency not intrinsically and endemically of our world, our planet or, most importantly, of our nature. I believe it operates remotely from the nature of man and invades man from without. Further, it is not natural in the ways of the cosmos itself. It is an artificial modulation of the Universe and is a contrivance of it. I believe this agency is one that operates universe-wide and affects all natural existential forms that have their ancestral origin in Godhead and thus have a soul. Be it Human or Oglander, the phenomena of alien primary Cloned-Being and artificial synthetic Roboid-Being programmed with artificial intelligence will infect all the living soul-possessing occupants of the Universe with their own emotionless machine-type binary standards in an endless search for definition and thus their own place in a self-propagating eternity. Our original fathers, the Inaugural Adam Beings all over the Universe, just should not have made a duplicate physical creation such as a Clone. It was, I believe, what should be termed *the* Original Sin. The demons of mythology were always real. We just did not know who or what they were until now.

The choice of final settlement is thus to be made by those who possess the widest range of options and that has to be the prerogative of Beings with a soul. We don't always make the best choices that would maintain and grant us this eternity. That is an intrinsic function of free will. But the potential to make the right choices is nevertheless there. We have the fantastic privilege of knowing that we have an incidental ongoing eternity as long as we have a direct connection to Godhead. No external entity may inherently forbid us to make choices in free will. It is we who forbid ourselves to do this. The widest stretch of choice will inherently lie with being connected to Godhead even in a Universe of separated Parts and the ultimate poles that define the apparent infinity that lies between.

The universe IS a system of opposites. The universe itself has its opposite. If there is a push for things to unite, there will be a push for things to separate and divide. Where, how and in what way these compliances operate in the micro- and macroverse is the name of the game we call life, living and the pursuit of . . . well, whatever!

I have tried to seek the answers to the questions posed by the Flying Saucers and their occupants with reason and logic and without claims that may not be independently verified in the journals of science or religion. The whole so-called phenomenon has too often been the butt of every bar room joke and cheap dismissive aside by our so-called expert mentors. It is the favourite way that their own 'agents', both biological and psychological, use most effectively to dismiss and thus hide the phenomenon from more serious examination and view. I too had summarily dismissed it as the rantings and ravings of over-enthusiastic buffs with over-active imaginations. I have found, way beyond reasonable doubt, that it is certainly one thing if it is anything. It does NOT belong in the realms of the Hobbit and the Tooth Fairy. It has a real and very tangible verification of its own. All of the tangible part of it, unfortunately, is in the hands of the governmental and world organizational powers that be, that for reasons best known to themselves have kept it all from those that really matter. The children. The future citizens of the planet Earth. They are, I believe, taking away from them their furthest heritage. The place where they must build or relinquish their eternity. It is the ultimate act of piracy and has to be controlled by those with minds that wink with the briefs of diodes. No human that can feel and truly care can perpetrate a subterfuge so awesome when looking into the eyes of a child and still say goodnight with a kiss. The authors of this staggering deceit have to be of the plasticated biosensitivity of Clones and roboids and I believe unequivocally that they were and are just that.

I sought after the truth of a predicament written for humanity in the nebulous shaped forms of saucers, discs, ovals and cigars. The geometry of our times written in the firmament of even our most trite day-to-day dreams. It led me to discover that this was no phenomenon discrete from the central avenues of our frame of being within the face of reason as existential truth.

Existential truth can only be the most personal of things. Its verification and thus its value has no functional meaning unless it is deeply subjective. It has no value in the ether. It can never be, what just IS. It always IS, what you and I ARE.

For me, it all has led to a fundamental catharsis of both nature and outlook. In doing the research for this book and subsequently chasing an answer as to the nature and properties of the 'Flying Saucer' phenomenon, I have to admit, somewhat incredulously at first, the entire existential gamut unfolded before me in the light of reason and not personal claim, opinion and fancy. I began to see the size of the con that had been worked on humanity by some religious administrations through the centuries. I saw the way past their lies and deceit. The Dragon may be slain, the R

Complex brain in all our heads circumvented and left for dead by simple realizations in logic. Logic is the kiss of Godhead. Realizations that point each one of us to act in our day-to-day lives with actions that cherish our fellow man, no matter where he or she hails from, or what he or she looks like. Against the dead cold minds of the Greys we all look the same. What is more horrendously to the point, our children taste the same. It is the ultimate sanction that should make us all seek to add, to bind, to unite, to reason logically with objective and not subjective analysis. To me, all this goes up to make what is Good against what is Bad. Terms that would otherwise be meaningless. This is the codex of true Grace. It is a gift of salt. A flavour, a zest of spice, of colour, of light and perhaps Enlight as we look to our personal horizons. I know that I, as a stranger to you and as an individual, can touch the whole world and through that I can touch you. With reverence and respect. I for one know you for your splendour and your precious value no matter what others might say or do to deny the awesome glory of your individuality with a soul in humanity. And I know truly it is no fanciful poetic notion. I am smiling now, when I only thought I was smiling before. I hope that in sharing all this with you, you will be smiling too.

The author of the Judeo-Christian ethic came to turn the other cheek. He came to spell the reasons for love with the finest logic and sense. He had to do it with the sight of his blood. He came to plead for peace through peace. Yet have you noticed how, in the hands of the Cro-Magnon legacy, despite a hideously contrived codex of huge and mighty sanction formed in fire and brimstone underwritten by the threat of final and eternal damnation, it is the faith that now spawns the emptiest places of worship? In addition, the Christian churches and their administrative zeal through the centuries have been responsible for the most repulsive acts of torture, murder, mayhem, suicide and sexual debauchery on a scale unprecedented in the history of the world, all in the name of the 'King Of Peace'.

The Buddhist philosophy, on the other hand, with reason and freedom of choice as its arbour of faith, has kept its adherents in resolute devotion through the centuries without the slightest resort to violence and thievery. Yet they seem to have achieved it without horrendous threats of final and exemplary damnation in a vat of fire through eternity. The Buddhists have, in fact, with exquisite reason argued a philosophy that gives no limit to change. It contained no threat, no sanction. Just purely logical consequence. A triumph of reason, and thus a true and noble triumph.

In searching for the answer to my son's question I was led on a metamorphosic search for the meaning of life itself. It was an incidental result. A result that made me see a way through to truth such as truth may be found. History has taught us unequivocally that to make the discovery more important than its existential meaning is to assassinate both the discovery and the meaning. Yet again and again the sirens of the 'flesh' were too formidable a screen that blinded most of us to this rule. The universal anthem of disposable, the true Satan, entropy made its machines of dispatch all too easily, and we wait, we all wait for the final outcome.

It is so easy to make prognostications of doom. To sit on a base that all too often has delivered a dead reckoning and never learn our lessons in terms of the cohortship of humanity. We can see that the misleading geometry of material development, with its sharp, clear, sometimes pretty lines hasn't changed for the better the deeper underbase of human motive for the caring for the betterment of the species – Mankind. As a whole we kill more, we maim more, more cruelly and with more efficiency, than we did before. We dismiss more than ever on no better a decision point than the mere colour of a skin, or the shape of a physical contour. The deadly tribal lines speak more evocatively in the affairs of men than they ever did.

The right to belief in independence becomes a panordinate threat to the instinct of the herd. We have not as a species developed out of the animal sense and its attendant paranoia against 'difference' of any kind. Instead of an increase in a sense of our group-species identity for the betterment of co-responsive social perspectives, the deadly entropic drive has increased the pro-eclectic drive in the 'Macluhan' sense that lauds individual goal-orientation at the cost of the group. Such perspective now rules the day wherever we look in the Occidental world and it is my firm belief that it will rule our future days with increasing strength and bring about the prophecies of grand insight we tend to dismiss as heraldic excess.

Entropy isolates to separate. Those who follow this in human terms are thus what may be described with a new word in the

English lexicon: Entropes. But, gloriously, we still have their opposites. Call them what you will. Seers, Mystics, or Prophets had the glorious insight to see the writing on the wall, because they were ahead of their time in one simple respect. They noticed that all things, in purely material terms, were always dying, all ways. They simply had a view of entropy by adding the signposts of doom that others ignored. The rest was easy. They saw the material, existential vista for what it was – as Devolution and that the human physical capacity was measured in loss and not gain – ongoing loss that is measured exponentially in increments and not decrease, as the atomically derived Universal slant separates the basal and doesn't add to it.

The true glory of these superior, or Spirit Dominant, souls was listed within their insight, an insight that viewed the spirit sense from within the standpoint of flesh, so to speak. These were individuals whose physical atomic array had the quality of possessing stupendous 'aerials' that received a visionary view of the final existential domain, clearer than most others. Far from being ephemeral dreamers with their heads in the clouds, they truly had their heads beyond the clouds, beyond the margins of matter itself and realized and understood the true ultimate reality of a Universe of Union called Spirit. Too often, and it seems sometimes necessarily, they fall prey and victim to the inferior atom-dominant 'aerials' of lessening, reducing mankind, who could only see a truth of the physical senses.

Strictly atomic 'viewability' is the hard line of entropic derivation. As the scenario for separating, it is inevitable that vast hordes, probably through the repeated life-generative procedure of reincarnation, (believed, incidentally, by every major religious ethic in the world at its inception, as I have said previously) would pay the price of 'dipping' into matter, or atomic, universes. In the wake of such a disaster, individual scope for grander view would, for most it seems, inevitably dim, until the very control mechanism of everything in existential tenure – Will – was itself mitigated in the end, through staging posts we call Man, Ape, Plasmid, Tree or Stone. Christ saw escape through Thought as the only life raft outside these atomic fingerprints. He clearly saw 'Thought in Will' as something so wondrous, it was the cradle of meaning itself – and, as such, not part of the 'idle, static dependent' resolution of force that made up the dead disbursive physical world of matter. The Great Teachers saw the existential vista was marked by three states of Being – the highest and most final they called Spirit. The lowest being static dependency non-life, with 'physical' life being the intermediate state. The home environment state of 'eternal life' alluded to by Jesus Christ as the ultimate progression of Being. Spirit was confirmed as a concept that we may not in our parts-conscious finite environment in the separation of points envisage accurately, in its own terms: when Christ chided Nicodemus with the exhortation that if he (Nicodemus) and others found it hard to understand and believe what was said by Him (Jesus) about the world of 'flesh', how could they believe or see anything of the world of Spirit'? Ultimate everlasting tenure in awareness, meaning and knowing, was the only 'reward' promised by Jesus Christ as the consequence of leading a righteous life. Nothing else was made an implicit certainty by this marvellous teacher, and in the light of any logical progression could never have been promised by Him, because it simply stresses what is patently obvious. There can be no greater achievement in existential terms than the confirmation of existence – in eternal tenure. A state, or effect, that provides for such a thing, therefore, implies the absence of inherent implicit risk. No physical-matter state can be free of risk. All matter is implicitly destructible. We may build the grandest civilizations – cities that provide the facilities, self-appreciating facilities that run themselves endlessly – and one day, as I have said, an asteroid may crash into this world and a million years of development will count as nought.

Quite clearly, the great teachers in asking for what may be commonly called 'righteous living' as a behavioural vector to be followed for release into this effect they called Spirit, marked the abstract metaphysical concepts of Thought exerted through Will, with a wonderful connection and connectability, to the hard dead world of the physical atom. Christ, Buddha, Mohammed and many others saw this magical connecting point quite clearly. I believe that by the public demonstration of His 'transfiguration' on where it is said to have taken place, the Mount of Olives, Jesus Christ was the only being who actually achieved direct release into the Spirit 'frame', from the force vector of atoms that holds us all bound. Buddha, I believe, glimpsed it from within the frame of atoms, but Jesus actually achieved the transfer temporarily, when He transfigured on the Mount of Olives, and at His 'death' and subsequent resurrection achieved the transfer completely.

Here, at last, through all the foregoing prescriptions of doom I have outlined, we arrive at the most marvellous admission of all: the triumphant accession out of this predicament of ours through the example and wondrous everydayness of Christ, Buddha and Mohammed is possible. This is now the Age of Reason. Alas, the ages of Faith implicit have gone with time in our procedure through the churn of Entropy. For many, we now have to see Truth reflected through the elbows of connected logical reason and not through the highly aspected blind resources of faith, belief and trust that once served a lesser entropic form of mankind as signposts for release from atomic capture.

I believe that what was once man in some glorious, mild, force print, in some far away league of Space/Time knew better the truth of Loss. In this faraway 'then', when the Spirit ruled the atom, to the claims of first men, the proposition for return from whence we all came was easier and achieved for many. We, alas, are the leftovers. The last ones to know and *not* do enough. To see and *not* achieve enough. We have delivered ourselves through the universal entropic churn – from planet to planet – finding through all the vagaries of atomic disbursement in the Universe-wide 'places' the exact matching of the resonant resolutions for our surviving spirit-field to make bodies – material bodies, be they Oglander, Earthling or Fool. Alas, to get progressively more captured by these same bodies.

Buddha, Christ and Mohammed demonstrated the most awesome techniques in the everydayness of living and Being, both with their example and teaching of gaining this world of eternal life, instantly, and this is the most wonderful thing of all – directly. I mentioned the instance earlier of Christ's demonstration of transfiguration on the Mount of Olives. Here His triumph over atoms was completed. I believe Christ showed the chosen Apostles the final result of living a life in such a way that His power of thought and deed unravelled the very atoms of His physical being. I believe that all His exhortations to doing 'good', as it is commonly expressed, had far more atomic a result than has been appreciated up to now.

I am saying that I believe that any genuine act that provides a mental or physical momentum of will to bring parts together, to unite endeavour, to add to each other and make whole, any resolution of will that binds, sublimates and encourages Union, will open out the valve inside you that channels the 'power' of Godhead in the universe (Enlight) and every hydrogen atom in you will be subjected to, within itself, a natural antiforce or unscrewing effect of the force that keeps it a hydrogen atom. If you maintain this momentum *enough*, as Jesus Christ demonstrated, you will *inravel* (I apologize for the new word) the force in you to the point that you will no more be substantial. You could no more be embodied. You will transfigure. In other words, you will resonate with the next quantumly less enforced environment, call it Heaven, Valhalla, Paradise, whatever you like. You will be on your way back to Godhead and eternal life without the incumbency of ever having to reincarnate and thus go through the process of rotting from conception again. You will, in fact, have 'forgiven' yourself and while doing the acts of retrieval, if you have done them well enough and often enough, you would have learnt enough to free yourself from restriction and thus sin. You would have seen the humbug of the humbugs that populate the precincts of the axiom 'Praise the Lord and pass me the money' for what they are. Never more will your soul be subject to the whims of Karmic obligation. I think that the word 'enough' is the most important word in any language lexicon. We all, alas, mostly touch the surface of belief as we only skim the surface of what we believe.

The thematic of all conventional religions consist of a series of platitudes that usually describe abstract ideas in abstract terms. They commonly border on the obscure to the very obscure and leave the listener and postulant nothing real to get to grips with. For example: we are asked to practise right thinking. Even the Buddhists are sometimes capable of cant. It is a favourite chant of religious teachers in countries like Sri Lanka, for instance. What on earth does 'right thinking' mean? It is never clearly defined. Right thinking to a thief will mean the best possible way of depriving another man of his goods. It is all a relative scale, if you see what I mean. Yet the world is subject to a pack of enrobed clowns chanting these pious platitudes in fusillade after fusillade from temple and pulpit alike, and we are asked to take seriously these squeezed, excruciating cacophonies as some glorious blessing and benediction that will metathesize our very souls.

When asked to give details of what exactly all these things mean, or how they work on our physicality, we are told that it is not for us to ask questions. It is for us to disqualify reason and reasoning. That is for God to know and answer in God's way and in God's own good time. They imply they are a conveyance for God's message. The Christian would hear, in mind-numbing repetition, the bumbling bromide 'Jesus came to take on the sins of the world'. He has vacuumed the vat of our transgressions. Paid the piper on our behalf. He was the great ethereal blotting pad. Absorbed all the rubbish in our souls and thus we need not ever redeploy ourselves for any returns anywhere. In smooth timbres, the cannoning chants and well-meaning voices rise in massaging platitudes to this day extolling the virtue of letting our redeemers carry our burdens. The flatulent madness and shame of acquiescence in another's gains, works and example was another way of saying to a burgeoning organization: 'He did it for you. We are his church. His representatives. Hold to us and our ways, and as we hold the admission tickets to the reward he earned for you, we will give you one if you earn it in the way we prescribe'. In other words, there is no way to heaven unless you go through our door. A nice way to corner the market.

Could it not just be that 'taking on the Sins of the world' might simply have meant a valuation of ignorance? An explanation and expurgation of mendacity? The simple laying bare of the megalithic falsehood that is our status as beings in atoms? It is far more likely to have been an invitation to revelation.

The Christian redeemer was born in flesh as a human being and did not arrive as some celestial light form that magically zapped us all, and beamed us all unconditionally up to Heaven because he and his Father loved us so much. His entire brief was didactic. The implication of this was that we had to do the 'doing' bit ourselves. It was a charge. Not a request. He showed us why and how, with the sacrifice of his life. There could be no free carriages to Alhambra borne by angels if we did not build the carriage ourselves *for* ourselves. In other words, he endorsed that we all had free will and thus had the choice to do it ourselves because the system dictated that it could not be done otherwise. The alternative was, 'Beam them all up, Ark-angel Scottie, I like this lot on Earth. They are so ignorant and so cluttered up with the dirt of restriction (Sin) this ignorance gives, it would be a great exercise giving them all a bath.' You don't clean anyone in a cesspit. They would be dirty again as soon as you had finished cleaning them up. You would surely take them to the great bathroom in the sky and let all the angels at your disposal do the job. At a guess, the Son Of God might have qualified for a fair team of the winged beings. Why, then, did he do nothing of the sort?

This great teacher cleansed us by telling us about soap and bathing. He let us figure out how, where and why we were 'dirty' because only we knew best where we put our own dirt and where, how and why we were polluting our own individualities. He knew very well that all the detritus would only be back again if we did not understand within ourselves its true nature and what it was doing to us. It was up to us to want to be clean. If we did not do this, it would all be a waste of time. It is psycho-restrictive dirt. Highly person-specific. It is thus a panoramic perspective of the principles that define restriction that would serve our interests best. That is what he did. He taught us the lexicon of restriction (Sin) and left the choices to us. The existential fundamental paradigm of Free Will left him no choice.

Yet this theocratic nonsense that suggests that we must put ourselves into some kind of spiritual palanquin created for us by this lovely being is a mind-numbing insult to his labour and final sacrifice and a denial of his lasting meaning in all that is good sense.

This kind of madness leads to experts taking a chimpanzee's paintings, as has happened several times, and unknowingly hailing it as the work of a great Master. It literally has made monkeys out of men if devolution is indeed the way of the 'world'.

All this would be funny if our line of ancestry back to Godhead were not dependent on the objective logical and rational interpretation of the glorious wisdom and knowledge imparted to us by the great religious teachers. We have been left more often than not on the subjective whims of scoundrels who have hijacked the ancient teachings for their own powermongering convenience and purposes and led millions to perdition through their debauched claims and fancies.

The great teachers taught by living example. They were on

the roads with bleeding feet and parched dry throats screaming in the zeal only the touch of Godhead can provide. Their words were translated into deeds. Deeds drenched in devotion and gut-wrenching dedication to the poor and the lowly. A dedication that by any rational yardsticks exemplified, proclaimed and backed exactly the words they spoke.

Whose words would you take seriously? Those of Mother Theresa of Calcutta or those spoken and written by cassock-draped hypocrites at religious helms the world over who in pious and plenary rectitude claim the right to pronounce on morals, ethics and other social magnitudes while sitting in their candlewax-soaked vestries and parlours, and grand incense-smoked cathedrals of religious academia. It seems to me they have made it a quest to stare at plagues of gnats and swallow whole herds of camels. The Inquisitions have gone. The requisitions are here. The grand retreat into the primitive logistics of fundamentalism has begun. Dripping with ignorant fawnings and naive distortions and meaningless platitudes, more often than not as a sop for ignorance and the lack of a credible and rational argument. They say the juice of the devil seeps from fundamentalist sap. You can't get more fundamental than the physical fathers of humanity and who in fact they might be. If the efforts of the alien Clones and Greys have made them the progenitors of most of humanity, it is easy to see what trees the sap of all so-called religious fundamentalists will grow. God help us if I am right and some of our 'Fathers' come in the form of winking diodes and sheet electricity travelling on grey, green, yellow and blue biosynthetic superconducting tracks. We are done for if we have to deal with pure robots without the merest sense of Soul. There is no quark called 'feeling'. Find it, boys. Make it happen. There are a lot more fundamental particles than have been found by detectors. There is still room for one called 'feeling'.

I know where it would be safer to listen and follow if my soul was at stake. Christ said in the simplest, most awesome wisdom: 'By their fruits shall ye know them'. My simple axiom for what it's worth is: 'If you can't taste the fruit as sweet, don't eat it.'

We all live in divided societal pro-formas. Modules of humanity defined by political philosophies, ethnic and cultural standpoints based in the main on race, caste, creed, colour and, of course, geophysical environment. We call them Countries, States, Tribal

Areas, Enclaves etc. For the most part they are pigeon holes that demarcate our living 'everydayness' through necessities that define administrative convenience. The awesome and fundamental personal individuality and its unique properties can never be taken in itself into consideration when set against the interests of the herd. Yet our only existential importance as living beings when scaled against the omniversal poles of Godhead and its opposite lies in our individuality. It is the place that each of us begins and ends. It is the place of final summary and result. The dichotomy that elucidates the interests of the herd against that of the individual seems an impossible one to reconcile. It has always through history led to the terrorization of the individual in the interests of the system. It need not have been so, or indeed be so, if the simple rules of omniversal engrandisement as spoken through reason and logic were totally believed by all. Impossible, you might say, in a universe of physically diminishing returns.

We have, by and large, a world of Communists and Capitalists. Irreconcilable opposites, some might say. But are they, really? In their best meanings they outline the principles that cater for the highest interests of the group and the individual. The cherishment of each other and the cherishment of the self. The evil moiety in each system lies in the corrupt individuals within the assemblage that usually propitiates the principle with excesses in self-interest and greed. The grand spiritual leaders all hailed a resolute and abiding group ethic in the highest measures of kinship and fellowship and coupled it with the strongest recommendations for a sense of personal individual value. It was all said in Christ's most potent of axioms: 'Love thy neighbour as thyself.' Alas, the story of our world and history runs overwhelmingly, not with the pure sap of goodwill in unionizing parts but all too often to its opposite momentum as dictated by the swansong of the universe – entropy. The 'weight' of the dead Universe dragging the universe of life to the dispossessing articulacy of the Second Law of Thermodynamics and, most importantly of all, the hidden factor only now coming to light: the Greys, Greens, Yellows and Blues. Our hitherto alien synthetic 'Fathers who art of the Universe.'

It is the role of this deliberately hidden unknown factor that has artificially altered the natural value scales of living systems Universe-wide. Intelligent life is the amalgam of the two most basic existential natural drifts. It is the sum of countervailing properties commensurate with what is of Godhead and what is not. The disposition and function of insets, such as intelligent beings with free will, will thus define all the non-natural ways and means of '*Being*' in the Universe. A cosmos empty of life and intelligence will be a very different place. The almost hysterical urge for scientists these days to deny anything that suggests there may be existence beyond the atom has led to the most bizarre theories postulating that the Universe is so conveniently arranged in all its balances and artefacts as to be totally anthropocentric and this is the incredible bit. It would not be there, they claim, if it weren't so.

Cosmologists believe that initially there could have been many Universes possible, each with its own laws and constants. That we live in the only Universe compatible with our presence. The other theory known as the Anthropic Principle postulates that the Universe must be such that it allows and even favours the presence of human beings.

Professor Ramon Moliner says that one way to interpret the Anthropic Principle is that some universes are more 'fit' than others in being compatible with our inquisitive presence. One of them was the fittest for us. But what came first, the chicken or the egg? Was there indeed a 'first'?

Professor Moliner, in an article in *New Scientist*, goes on to make a very salient point. If the world was not discoverable by conscious beings, we would not be here to discover it.[1]

Scientists like random arbitration. It is why they feel so comfortable with the Darwinian theory of natural selection. They shy away, as Professor Moliner puts it, from a belief in 'cosmic purpose.' I believe it is because it smacks too much of a God creator.

Moliner, an eminent neurobiologist, goes on: 'We are happy to assume an inventive principle in human affairs, but we cannot imagine the presence of something in nature capable of "imagining" evolutionary objectives. When people invent anything, they start out by having a representation of what they want to improve, or the function that the invented item will have. But we cannot conceive how nature could have a representation or "Idea" of the biological characteristics that she wants to develop or improve.

'Yet something nags at the back of the mind: The only way to make this view consistent is to EXCLUDE humans from nature. If Darwin was right, either humans continue to be an unsuspecting and non-foresighted product of past interactions between mutations and natural selection or things drastically changed with their arrival. To build an aeroplane, the conscious brain of a foresighted engineer is necessary. But we are told that nothing of the kind is needed to create the gliding skill of an albatross: Blind natural selection will suffice. Darwin's hidden message is that human creativity and inventiveness constitute totally novel processes in the history of the universe. It is not easy to accept this hidden message, but it is equally difficult to propose a general mechanism to account for both human and non-human inventiveness.

'Is it reasonable to admit that the conscious intervention of humans represents a phenomenon that was absent in nature prior to their advent? The age of the earliest civilization is less than one-millionth the age of the universe. Do we have to accept that during that fleeting instant something happened that had never occurred before? That humans can achieve highly improbable feats thanks to their capacity to plan ahead is self-evident. For example, two teams of workers can start tunnels on opposite sides of a mountain and meet exactly in the middle after months of drilling in the dark. Without foresight this would be impossible.

'Many co-operative adaptive features found in the living world are equally amazing. Take the fangs of a viper, which have evolved with a canal inside them; an adjacent gland that secretes the poison; a reservoir to store the poison; a membranous duct connecting the reservoir to the canal in the fang; an intricate osteomuscular system that erects the fangs before they strike; an enveloping muscle system that contracts the poison reservoir at the right time; a nervous system that sends the signal for contraction, also at the proper time; and the instinct to use the fangs against prey and not against mates.

'It is easy to visualize how random mutations followed by natural selection could lead to the right curvature of the fangs for better grasping of prey. But what would have been the selective advantage of the rest of the poison system if just one of its components had failed to evolve? To claim that it can be achieved through unbiased evolution is like expecting that nine independent miners can attack the core of Mount Everest from various points at the foot of the

Himalayas and meet exactly in the middle without the guidance of a surveyor.' (*New Scientist*, November 1995).

As I said before, such is the stuff of baboons.

I am, of course, perfectly aware that my own intuition of existential outlay as outlined by this book flies in the face of arguably the most hallowed and sacred vestment of science, 'The Darwin Psycholith'. I have no reputation in science to defend and so the vipers and their fangs will be wasting their fury and their poison on me if and when they try to take all this apart. Let me say that when all the judgements are made and the dust settles, I am quietly confident I will still stand vindicated. I have merely stood with the minds that originally revealed all this, but were misunderstood because nobody then and since knew about the existence of UFOs till their more contemporary appearance after the first nuclear explosion on the Earth. I have tried to explain some of the religious invective with it all included in contemporary terms. I realize I am a poor measure for the glorious and truly original standpoints of the original Master originators of the world's major religious faiths, the grand teachers who came among humanity and tried to warn us about this artificial and synthetic creation of the Universe. What I have realized and deciphered in the way outlined has always been there for discovery century after century and only hidden and obscured by the vanity of humanity. It was, however, underwritten by the lives and courage of countless saints through the banner of their belief in the warnings given to our species by the Great Teachers of all the credible grand Faiths. I have merely stood on their platforms and simply asked the questions. Were they all liars? And if so, why?

CHAPTER THIRTY:
CONCLUSIONS

There can be no doubt that the whole alien phenomenon is potentially the most awesome threat humanity has faced in all the time of its existence as a species. I have been pretty scathing about their entire prospectus and it is clear that their influence on our species has, if not deliberately, tacitly had the effect of gradually turning us all into a machine psychology over the centuries. They are, it seems, defeating that property in us that might give them a chance at redemption too. The instinctive reach for what is beyond the atom, in other words the Godsense in us, has lessened in the entire Occidental world with the cold one-sided influence of science through technology and the fact that the leadership of the entire world comes from the Euro-American sphere. If anything will beat these creatures it will be the power of what lies beyond or out of atoms. These alien Clones are Masters of the world of atoms and we are dead in the water before we start if we take them on in those terms.

Alas for us all, we seem to have little choice but to face a catastrophe while the leadership of the world rests in the hands of the techno-materialistic behemoth of Euro-America.

Europe is the world's 'father' of psycho-existential corruption. European forces through the centuries systematically unleashed on the world a holocaust of detriment through conquest, colonialization and slavery that has left the entire planet poisoned and burnt out, its people subjugated and starving and torn apart in racialism and ethnically and fiscally fermented wars and conflicts. North America is now the 'son' carrying on more of the same, and doing it better and at a faster rate than the 'old man' – Europe.

What a glorious country the United States could have been if it had followed the precepts of wholesome family values of its founding fathers. How is it possible that the most magnificent opportunity for all mankind to prove that we are one family was squandered here? The 'global immigrant ethic' that founded this nation out of the four corners of the world now lies in tatters. It claims to be the moral leader of the world. Yet the most cursory examination of the place now will reveal its present values extolling materialism and banal and delusive consumerism to be the least likely keeper of the world's ethical standards. Anyone who has been to America recently cannot have failed to notice on its negative side what an intrinsically superficial, deeply racist, violent and vicious society it is. The world requires a moral lead of enormous magnitude. If the United States of America is currently our planet's most influential and powerful country, if nearly ten thousand years of civilization has produced in summary the leading nation in the world saturated with such debauchery, where and to whom does our species look to find a change? It would be one thing for America to be this way if the widespread simplistic 'Mickey Mouse' psychology that seems to prevail over there could be isolated and strictly and exclusively reserved for Americans only and not exported to other regions of the world. Speech after speech from a succession of their Presidents claims America to be the moral and martial leader of the world. This nation is so forceful in packaging, marketing and selling its wretched brew of fiscally modulated electronic Clone juice to the unsuspecting world that we should all beware this humbug and note the nature of the poison that it sells to us all.

There is little doubt that, sadly, judged by any objective standards, the USA is the most morally defunct and debauched source of influence the world has ever seen. This is the leading spokesman nation of the Northern Occidental world. The so-called civilized world. What price a hundred centuries of human development if this is the result? What price our future as a species?

The historian Michael Woods puts it thus: 'Throughout the countries of the rich West, there's a growing and profound disquiet – a feeling that the Western way of life itself is no longer supportable morally or practically, because of pollution, environmental destruction and the continuing exploitation of the mass of humanity.' I believe that God is effectively dead there now and the people of the Barbarian West must, and will, face their own terrible consequences. The rest of humanity has to take the greatest care that *we* do not face their consequences.

How did a group of tiny islands in the western and northern Atlantic come to dominate the world, when huge civilizations like China and India that were seats of learning that far surpassed the Barbarian cultures of this era did no such thing? I believe it can be put down to something inherent in the nature of the people. Let me put it this way. A man who will throw a javelin, no matter how small he is, will always dominate a man who throws a handful of rice, no matter how big *he* is.

Gunpowder was known in China for centuries before Marco Polo brought it to the West. The Chinese used it only for firecrackers. Polo immediately saw its potential to kill, to maim, to conquer. Could it really be that the inheritors of direct Cro-Magnon ancestry are the true bearers of the mark of Cain? After all, colonialism showed us in vivid and undeniable terms all the qualities Cain ever had and more. The instinct to kill, to steal, to pollute, to destroy the inheritance of others seems so natural in the Occidental varieties of humanity. Certainly a historical scan of the colonial era provides ample and undeniable proof of this.

The deliberate genocide of hundreds of thousands of Native American Indians. The enslavement of millions of Africans in Europe and America. Their subsequent genocide. The wiping out of the Australian Aborigines and their culture. The wiping out of the magnificent Maori culture. The deliberate enforcement of dope addiction on more than a hundred million Chinese. The horrendous holocaust that took from us six million precious Jews with an industrialized disposal procedure. And this is only the modern equivalent of other countless ancient pogroms conducted by the Greek and Roman civilizations on millions of victims. The destruction of the Incas, the Aztecs. The list of Cro-Magnon-sponsored debauchery is endless.

The precincts north of the Tropic of Cancer define largely the most decadent and entropically driven varieties of our species. Industrial technology is the spokesman of the damned and it was inevitable that it was born of the central crucible of Force on our planet, the Occident. The forge where all the metals of our nature were beaten into the swords that have ravaged the innocence and the innocents of Man century after century. The 'Barbarian West' stands condemned as the birthing pool of cultures that defiled the Earth with countless wars, pestilence and famine. The broadscope of Babylon that idealized the extremes of human grossness more consistently and for longer than anywhere else. How, then, could cultures that boast the glories of Shakespeare, Newton, Da Vinci, Michelangelo, Mozart, Beethoven, Schiller, Goethe, Franklin, Edison and the host of others such as they be the cornerstone of depravity for a whole world? Does the culture of wisdom lead or does it follow in the wake of another more dominant behest? A Master behest that claims the heart and sentiment in favour of the strict edict of socialized geometry? Is it a mere afterthought? An inevitable spin-off that simply happens because its opposite does?

Have you noticed that, when all the totting-up is done, the culture of the West comes down to a culture of the mind? The song of the list-file and the binary system. The Christian prophet chided one of his disciples with the axiom: 'Think with the heart'. That disciple was Judas. The implication is inevitable and obvious for any objective mind to see that has travelled to the societies of the more spiritual and social mid-band of our planet. Largely the countries between the Tropics of Cancer and Capricorn.

Yet how many of the Northern Occident and Northern Orient would tread the poverty- and deprivation-ridden streets of the Third World and look down with relief and perhaps disdain on the little hungry eyes and outstretched hands, breathe a sigh of superior relief and give thanks that they are not thus because of their racial and mental superiority? One can't help feeling that, with the deepest irony, they are looking out with the eyes of the damned.

The greatest prophets and seers through the centuries have predicted, as the falls of Egypt, Greece and Rome confirmed, that the development of the human resource as a consumer-based ethic with the self-centred acquisitive materialistic sense dominant is the ultimate paradigm for damnation. Why did all the greatest seers affirm this point of view, without exception, as true? If they were right, and history teaches us that they were categorically right, those in the West who are driven by this ethic are done for. I have no doubt that the synthetic Greys, as biomachines, run to a computer program, as do all their cohorts on the Earth that have brought about this situation via the psychochemical interception of mankind through the Cro-Magnon legacy. There can be no doubt of this if you judge it by the increasing tendency of many Northern-hemisphere people to have a cold-blooded, machine-minded list-filing mentality. This psychotype of humanity gave birth to industrial technology and thus the heartless consumerism (some would say the two things are synonymous) that increasingly dominates the people of the Northern hemisphere. It begs the salient question: Are they largely under the control of the Greys already?

'And man shall walk as machine,' the prophets screamed.

It is undeniable now that our future as a biological species is increasingly fuelled with the sap of engine oil. Switch the TV on any day of the week anywhere in North America and the enthusiasts of virtual reality and futurescope will fawn, enthuse and facilitate the anarchic glories of inner space, while in near space, just out of the window in the street outside, some unfortunate African-American or Hispanic is getting his head beaten to a pulp by the pure white sons of America riding out of black-and-white carriages. A random selection of any ten of the most popular newspapers and any ten of the most popular films at any one time that come from that part of the world will show you in vivid Technicolor what I mean. The Clones seem to have the entire shooting match well and truly taped up and posted to the furthest reaches of a Euro-American hell, if Western values as propagated by our media are anything to go by. It may well be that the only way out of self-destruction for most Northern Caucasoids is a ride on a spaceship designed by their own 'mummies and daddies'. There will certainly be a surprising number of them lining up enthusiastically to welcome the cold grey list-filing bioids as their long-lost relatives when the sky 'nerds' finally come to ground and declare themselves.

In the end it is the power of focus of mind away from the material that Christ and all the greatest teachers told us was the answer to beating all that is not natural in Godhead. Have you noticed how the deeply spiritual nations and regions of the world, mainly in the tropics, where focus outside the atom is strongest, are being gradually overwhelmed by the grotesque monster of the fiscal ethic? The last psychoactive bastion for our defence crumbles under the covert intercession of the deadly grey 'men' on the back of the Moon and their cohorts, be they in Wall Street, Threadneedle Street, or the one they call 'the street where you live'.

The simple adjunct 'Where your focus is, so will your heart be' is beyond any doubt the final and most powerful psycho-existential resolution for us all. I am convinced that all those simplistic exhortations to 'be good', do the 'right' thing, be 'right-minded' are meaningless nonsense and no more than transient palliatives to ward off temporary states of distress for parents, teachers and mentors all over the world. What do they really mean in actual terms of effect? What actually happens when you *are* good? What really does the word 'good' mean? No one ever tells us this. No one can. It is and has to be the most relative abstraction in the lexicon of meaning itself.

If you see physicality as screwed-down space formed out of screwed-down atoms, in the case of our bodies mostly screwed-down hydrogen (eighty-seven per cent of our body is made out of hydrogen) and that this screwing down has a particular direction, a direction in line with the action of the forces of entropy, then action in line with what entropy does will enhance and propagate the screwing-down effect. If your actions divide, separate, tear apart, destroy, hurt, kill, maim, you are a child of entropy (an entrope). You will forever be bound in line with what entropy does, and that is to break up, divide, decay into more and more basic assemblies of parts in more and more states of randomness and enforced chaos with time. Not just your atoms, ALL that is you will distort and get more and more tightly screwed down.

I explained previously that individuality is simply Godhead twisted by atoms in a particular way. Your way, or my way, or anyone's way. We, at least our metaphysical consciousness, 'thinkability', or 'knowability' in every single one of us, is just Godhead in a unique trapped and twisted pattern of the forceless centre points of the space between atoms. We can know, be conscious and think, simply because we are connected to Godhead in this way. And so thought *is* God. The clearer the pathway of the space between atoms is. The freer it is of twists and turns. The more incisive and clear the reach of Godhead. The nearer we are to God.

The less we become physical. The more we know. The more we are like God the more powerful we are in making thought accomplish all that is the reverse modulus of entropy. In God all is totally free to accomplish all things. Christ said, 'Seek ye FIRST the kingdom of God and all things shall be freely added unto you.' Here is the ultimate power to cancel out the strictly atomically derived power of the Second Law of Thermodynamics in its effect on our Soul. It will always have an effect on the atomic side of us, our bodies, but in the exercise of Will through Thought all its power of incidental corrupting effect on our Soul will be nought.

I alluded previously to the nature of thought, thinking and strength of focus and what right thinking might mean. For these exhortations to have any power and meaningfulness at all they have to imply that the focus of thought in ways that add, bring together and bind has a real and active power to reverse the effect of entropy on a given individual's quantum of unique being. The implication is that mere thinking can influence and change atomic determinations of force. Our bodies, as I have said, are eighty-seven per cent hydrogen. It is most of our physicality. A mode of thinking that cares, brings together, unites and adds rather than divides and subtracts, I believe, can actual physically *unwind* the hydrogen bond that keeps us all bound and trapped in force and thus in the Universe of Parts. To illustrate what I mean with a metaphor: When we act in what is commonly accepted as goodly perspective in the 'everydayness' of life, shall we say, we pull at the bond and try to take it apart. But it is rather like trying to extract a screw by pulling it out of the wood with a pair of pliers, without trying to unscrew it with a screwdriver. Well-considered 'right' thinking can unscrew the hydrogen bond, the natural way it should be done, as Jesus Christ accomplished it and proved it could be done with his transfiguration. A life led as his example showed is the way and the truth to the state of enlighted being in Godhead. The screw has a particular-sided thread and wrong thinking only serves to make it tighten further in its place. This of course implies what I said about the one-sided nature of entropy. That when things are seen in an atomic context alone, just in terms of the physical and not the metaphysical, all things go one way to Chaos. They rot, break up, and their parts break up to greater states of randomness till all that is left is a Universe of heat with no differentiated parts.

(What scientists call the Heat-death of the Universe). The force and urge necessary to do it without understanding what we are up against is forbidding and cannot accomplish anything, just as pliers can't grip a screw head without destroying both the screw and that which it is set in.

Maybe what is commonly called Love provides the power of mind to act as a kind of screwdriver that unscrews and loosens the bond, and hate does the opposite. This is what the Christian prophet and 'redeemer' Jesus Christ probably invited us to do when he said, 'Believe in me and I will give you eternal life'. Perhaps his entire glorious life's example and those of his beautiful contemporaries were master paradigms showing how we as a species can in the Earth's 'force print' physically unloosen the atomic cloak and thus transfigure into the Universe of the Whole. He put such importance on the power of prayer. The problem is that it seems we don't believe *enough* in what we do in righteousness, and thus our mental focus in what we want and do is not strong enough for this power to accomplish our wishes and dreams and make them come true. It is up to the as yet by and large innocent people of the non-occidental world to see that the debauched societies of Euro-America do not further infect them with the plague of materialistic filth they export under the name of freedom. The mid-band nations of the world are the most spiritually devotional places in the world and still hold to the pulse of that which is beyond the atom with some quantum of decency and moral certitude. It is here, mainly in Africa and Asia, that a defined moral sense and strong family values still prevail, by and large. It is here we can paint a haven of example for any machine-man with no gun (as our own kind from the Occident have, alas, too often proven to be) and show them that the answer to both our predicaments is to realize that we perhaps need each other. Now more than ever.

There can be no time for niceties any more in face of the alien threat. All nations pale beneath the intelligence of the grey species that has been gradually singing their anthem with our voices. Carefully chosen words written by behavioural psychologists and calculated to bring out the surface gloss of particular vested interests, be they scaled in terms of the individual or a nation, serve only to gild a dying lily. It is the can of worms beneath the surface that will take both individual and nation out if the hidden putrefaction is not squarely faced with open and complete honesty. 'America the Great', the Marseillaise, and 'Rule Britannia' will sound rather metallic and hollow in voice boxes driven by helium.

I believe that the threat to our species – Humanity – is greater than we have ever faced in the history of our planet. A crucible beyond our own natural quantum of atoms awaits to pour its poison into the centres of our very being. The ancient texts that spoke of the threat have been wiped off the common lexicons of man by hands that count with strange-looking fingers. The Kabbala, the Tetragrammaton, the Pistis Sophia and countless other ancient texts spoke loudly of an unnatural creation that was not of the ancient aegis of life eternal. They gave us a *warning* through the centuries about the true fathers of men. A warning written in the blood of humanity crying out in bewilderment for justice. The same dispassionate cruelty that will eat the pieces of our children on tables of crystal onyx and stone just as we now discuss test-tube mice and their juices over mouthfuls of claret and cheese.

The vast majority of us are simple folk. We see, know and understand things best if they are presented simply and in ways that illustrate their meaning for all to see. It has been the curse of most theosophies and philosophies that their, in many instances, self-appointed custodians have more often than not been intellectuals who pontificate in chant, recitative, and complex conundrums the simple erudition of the great Teachers' accounts of the way beyond atoms. So often pulpits and temple precincts are the places for ego-vending intellectualization that comes down to no more than mumbo-jumbo. The vast majority of these utterances are of little or no value to the listener or student. We are so often left none the wiser, and we go our way too embarrassed to say that we haven't a clue as to what's been written or said. The Great Teachers such as Gautama Buddha, Jesus Christ, and the Prophet Mohammed taught in the simplest of ways. Christ is noted for his brilliantly illustrative parables. The Koran is a glory of wisdom and simple elucidation.

The rascals who came afterwards so often mangled it all. In high-handed and self-centred and self-interested authority these lethal 'human beings' hijacked the Masters' words and meanings and twisted and mutilated their blazing sagacity. The heart of

Truth as we on Earth could know it. A vital word changed here and there. A phrase misquoted, a deed misrepresented, sometimes deliberately, could and did serve to distort and in some instances reverse completely a statement of vital revelation. Let me give you an incisive example.

The word 'Repent' in the theosophical lexicon is commonly taken to imply an expression of culpability in sin. A powerful suggestion of guilt, contrition, penitence and regret was culled from its meaning and touted by priests and partisans of theology the world over, century after century. Then the marvellous scholarship of Martin Luther, a philologist priest and a seeker after religious humbug, ascertained that the word 'repent', as used by Christ in the Aramaic (the language spoken by Christ) when translated into Greek meant 'metanoite', the Greek word that literally meant 'Change your mind'. It was an exhortation or an invitation to think again and change the base of your thinking. It had nothing to do with contrition or forgiveness. It did not mean that one had to rue, despoil one's value in supplication and guilt-ridden penitence. It encouraged the discovery of righteous value in whatever quandary you faced and a simple change of one's future thinking in line with this. A dignified and free choice to change one's mind in the light of a better, more rational alternative.

The original counsellors and administrators of the Christian Faith perhaps saw in this translation an interpretation that gave them an opportunity for awesome power of administration and control of the flock. One does not know whether this was done deliberately or not. (The subsequent treatment of Martin Luther by the Roman Church implies that it might well have been deliberate.) A difference of catastrophic consequence to the human psyche befell common moralistic thinking with this simple distortion. It provided for the depression of the human spirit, such that the vital change of perspective encouraged was immediately couched and surrounded by an air of perverse indulgence and, worst of all, fear.

A simple solicitation to 'see clearly and change one's mind' does not carry the sting that the stance of supplication and regret does. It doesn't include the perverse satisfaction of wallowing in self-pity and masochistic indulgence. Moreover, and this is the important point, it does not allow for a hold or control over the individual by a third party, such as the body politic of a Church. A guilt-ridden penitent is easier to control with the threat of damnation, especially if the expurgation of that guilt is joined into the fabric of ordained forgiveness under the total prerogative of the priests. Many of whom, at least in the early Christian church, were ecclesiastical refugees from life's hard ways at that time and nothing more special than that.

It is easy to see that the axiom, 'You have done something wrong, now make amends or you are damned' could get a lot of 'roubles' for a newly forming organization and more importantly its organizers. The obligation to depend for the future tenure of one's soul on the movement of a particularly blessed hand making the sign of the cross, while the palm of the other one is held flat upright and open is more to do with politics and accountancy than with the ethics of grace and righteousness. It passes immediate control of one's life and values to others who may then dictate henceforth a prescription for future behaviour. Stupefying effective control is the name of the game. All through the distortion of the meaning of one little word. And so the meaning of the word 'repent' as taught as a theosophical ethic grew to be the sword to smite the world with humbug. Humbug that has perhaps condemned millions to live in fear and guilt-ridden feelings and, worse than that, to die in this state.

You cannot go to heaven in my head and I cannot do it in yours. We as individuals are the ultimate guardians of our own destinies and that most precious and awesome phenomenon of connection to Godhead called a Soul. If someone else gets it wrong on our behalf, he she they or it may not be around to blame for the error when the chutes to hell are open for each of us. Preferment by proxy invites damnation by principle. It is true madness.

Words like 'hell' and 'damnation' have too often been the clue words for practitioners of religious deceit and debauchery through the ages. They define the anthem of the bogus holy men and religious charlatans that have led so many astray through the millennia. Many have mortgaged their very souls into the custody of such as these without a second thought about their investiture. Anyone who has switched on a television set in the USA or Canada cannot have failed to see parade after parade of phoney and beguiling platitudes pouring out of the mouths of armchair evangelists shouting, 'Praise the Lord and pass me the money'. The Bible is used as an instrument of fear soliciting belief in Jesus Christ under a twin axiom of carrot and stick. A heaven for favourites and courtiers and hellfire and damnation for the unbeliever. One wonders just how many of these well-groomed tailor's dummies with their plastic smiles and make-up adorned, media-cultured voices and faces would cope in the jungles of ignorance where mosquitoes bite with death and deadly abandon and sunlight burns the sweated brow. Where churches are built with bricks and mortar that actually tear and bruise hands connected to your own head. Where the stench of poverty, disease and death call for a few moments to be spent away from air-conditioned Waldorf Salads and iced tea.

We are and have to be our own masters. 'Mea culpa, mea culpa, mea maxima culpa' rings out loud and clear as the tenet that underlies Will and any resource to do anything. If reason has any meaning then each result of each decision is intrinsically and totally our own responsibility and no one else's. We all must, it seems, take the utmost care to know what adorns our Soul line to Godhead with strength and not weakness. It is crucial that we glean the knowledge of how this is done with objectivity and dispassionate zeal of the highest order through our individual state and not the proxy formulas of others. It simply invites outsiders to make our own individual disasters. We cannot for a single moment afford to be 'second-hand'. Our individuality is the most precious thing to no one but ourselves. We may observe, learn and borrow the best, but we can never afford to relinquish a particle of ourselves to another's keeping for a moment.

So how do we know who or what to follow? How do we know how to judge what is eternally right and wrong? 'By their fruits shall ye know them' a certain man of Nazareth once said. But against what final list of priorities may Truth be known? Where do we find the perfect scale that is safe and true?

The basic yardstick that says if you add, bring together, unite in total fit elemental parts, you simplify and make clear, and if you subtract, divide and set apart you complicate and obfuscate, is all one needs to know to set the compass points for any journey to enlightenment.

Ignorance is the paymaster of Hell. We welcome its demons as restriction. We settle on the shelves of damnation with Apathy. The cry of the billions in ignorance marks the nibs that have written the history of our species. A history forged in the blood of short-term sensory result despite so many warnings. So many sacrificial lambs on the altars of superior insight.

Yet we are still fair in eternal scope. Impossible though it may seem. The vastness of this giant conspiracy that has blinded us all through the millennia to our true predicament and destiny also gave us blessed pilots who have and will love our simple lost fold for as long as justice is eternal. They too were claimed because our ignorance caused them to be claimed.

A nail pierced the sweetest flesh and no finger did 'The Father' move. For such is love. Such is forgiveness. The sublimation of ignorance with wisdom. Such is the most powerful antidote to alien or any other malevolent influence. It is no empty platitude. It is reason itself.

The truth of the predicament of the alien beings and ours has to be demonstrated in love and forgiveness towards the representatives of these alien intelligences too. That truth rings loud and clear and says unequivocally and paradoxically that the strengthening of *our* soul retaining cordage with the Universe of the Whole comes as *their* most urgent priority too. With ultimate irony we are *their* Masters in still having the glorious dispensation of a Soul, as they don't. If finding a Soul is their quest they will have to help us to preserve ours. All extraterrestrial or indeed intra-terrestrial aliens have to be made to realize what a Soul really is. In doing so they will see that no single soul is open to being hijacked. That each one of us is connected to each other through karmic obligation somewhere along the line. The wasteful loss of a single one of us shakes the entire Tree of Life all through the Universe and beyond. That the Opening of the Universe of the Whole is in the hands of Compassion and Mercy personified. Therein, and only therein, is the final margin of all margins and in mutual understanding we may reach it more certainly, again in ultimate irony, together and not apart.

What does all of the foregoing finally imply for our collective family – Humanity? What does it say about our predicament and status as functioning beings now in our most contemporary stance as a species? In trying to answer my son's two questions my own spirit was led on a trail that for me at least threw up an insight into the whole existential paradigm that has left me concussed

with wonder and stunned with joy. It has also left me poised and
tantalized with a thundering concern and fear for our children's
tomorrow. I believe the ET factor, for so long so apparent yet
impossibly hidden from the sight and thus the affairs of men,
defined the very root of all our yesterdays and no one knew or
seemed to know. The reasons for how it could have happened
are now irrelevant. For me the thing that matters is that there
can be *no* doubt that it did happen and, more chillingly, it is still
happening and so few seem to care.

There can be no satisfactory resolutions to the premise 'Stop
the world, I want to get off.' There is nowhere else to go. The
Druids of expediency who advocate taking a hike into space as
our future for a clean new start and a better tomorrow carry
go–nowhere smart cards. They will have to know that all the real
estate is infected with the same seeds that poisoned the home they
have just left. Like the pioneers who leave for all promised lands
and soon discover that, alas, they have brought old heads into new
perspectives of hope. America has proved in a mere three hundred
years that the dreams of her pioneers have been dashed into the
fragments of the decadence, debauchery and superficiality you see
in any city there any second, minute, hour, day, or month of the
year. She claims to be the standpoint dream of civilization. The
American dream is touted as the highest masthead of social result
in the world today. It has turned instead into the hallmark recipe
from which all nightmares are made. Most thinking Americans
in their heart of hearts know this, as they know that it will be
the tub-thumping zealots of 'God Bless White America and pass
me the money' who will hold the societal smoking guns when the
song of the Greys is finally sung on the Earth.

Yet America is beautiful too. Awesomely beautiful as written
in the signatures of her sons: Washington, Jefferson, Lincoln,
Chomsky, Crosby, Disney. Yes, Crosby and Disney. The names
enshrine the glory of pleasant dreams. Decency, vision, romance,
sweetness, the fellowship of all life and living. It speaks of hallowed
margins. Margins defined in the scale of Godhead itself. A scale
that verified an American dream so different from what is seen now
laid out before us in any street of any city in the US of A. Disney
internalized the beautiful human dream. America externalized it
as a nightmare. Generations there once formed, and still do in

some remote regions, whole mental visionary quantums of decent lives led with decent rules of living. Wholesome forms and ethics spoke and of course still speak of better ways for us all to be. Stage and screen still assured millions of us that the Wizard of Oz and what was over the rainbow *was* America, while southern trees hid the deadly truth of the Cro-Magnon legacy with burning crosses and stretched black necks.

Do we ever learn our lessons? History unequivocally proves we don't. We always exchange righteous hopes and dreams for failure. Failures that each time result in parades of disappointment. Yet somewhat paradoxically we never cease to strive for the Rubicon, each time plastering the walls of previous failures with contrived reassurances that we'll get it right next time. The honest objective eye sees the truth of this as humbug. The subjective eye tells us our own truths as mostly lies. And surely it is here in this cushion of distortion and personal make-believe that the greatest threat to all our tomorrows has lain hidden right in the very bosom of humanity. Our genes.

The ET of Close Encounters turns out to be *the* most singular signal fire of doom for all reasoning life forms when judged against the scale of freedom that marks eternal standpoints. It seals us all with the punctuation of the finite. It writes on our future with a language of limit and seeks to steal our eternity with a subterfuge counted in millions of years.

Yet could it all have been different if we had spotted the subterfuge earlier, for what it was? We have always been confronted with this seemingly impossible paradox of a human nature that is instinctively tutored to save and at the same time to mindlessly destroy. Does the stance of natural Godhead in all of us urge us to save and the artificially implanted elements of the false and self-appointed ET God or gods of the atomic and thus physical Universe urge us to destroy? Would it have helped us to know that the destructive side to our nature is a constructed artefact alien to us in every sense of the word? Could we then have been more capable of being more watchful of its effect if we had known the true nature of its origin? I believe it would have made an awesome difference.

Imagine for a moment that you are standing at a vantage point in space and can see the entire universe arrayed before you. Billions of galaxies with trillions of suns and mega-trillions of planets. What price size? Our home the Earth is a tiny point among all these magnitudes and we as individuals are reduced further in size in such enormity to the smallest imaginable fractions of it all. Yet we instinctively magnify our size and place an importance on ourselves as beings to a scale that transcends these numbers and imperatives. It gives us Godlike importance. Tiny shapes on a tiny planet all going about their business, thinking their individual wants and needs are the most important things in all this panorama. We kill, we maim, we injure and practice the most heinous affronts to each other in the name of this tacit self-proclaimed idea that we are bigger and better than it all. We expect a Divine Being in all these numbers to take a personal interest in us. In all our specific individual affairs. Respond to our whims and fancies, however trite. In other words, be on our individual telephone line twenty-four hours a day, at our beck and call. How many of us ever asks the question: How?

If God existed and functioned for us personally in our personal private contexts and was referenced in terms of this Universe's spatially judged and sequentially tallied time, as I believe ninety-nine per cent of us expect and believe, then a most spectacular nonsense is revealed. God just won't have time for us all – personally. Just take a look at the numbers involved.

We have about 7,000,000,000 (seven billion) people on this Earth. If each one prayed to God and told the great deity his troubles, wants and wishes and gave him our usual personally marked shopping list – Gimme this, Gimme that, do this, do that etc. – just how much time is He/She going to have to listen and respond to us individually, say in a given year?

Let's do the sum. There are 60 seconds x 60 minutes x 24 hours x 365 days in a year. Multiply that all and we have 31,536,000 seconds in a year. That's thirty-one million, five hundred and thirty-six thousand seconds in one year. But there are *seven thousand million* people on this earth and only thirty-one million, five hundred and thirty-six thousand seconds available in any given year. That means that if the deity is fair, each one of us has just 31,536,000 divided by 7,000,000,000 = 0.450 of a second per person of God's time in any one year, or (0.450 x 70), a mere 31.5 seconds' worth of God's exclusive attention in an average lifetime.

Ah! I hear you say. This is ridiculous. Not all of us on Earth believe in God and not all of us who do will be all praying at the same time. True. You got me! . . . But a squirmy little thought is forming in my head. What if we are not alone in this Universe? Last time it looked, the Hubble space telescope told us that there may be more planets in the Universe than stars. Just a hundred more planets in the entire Universe like ours with *Homo Sapiens* equivalents among the billion that scientists now think might support our type of life, and God won't have one second in an entire lifetime to hear our personal pleas.

Ah, but I hear a few lone voices out there saying: Phew! That's a relief. We must be the only intelligent life in the Universe! (Let me say at this point that there are people who still believe seriously that the Earth is square.) Can anyone still believe that we are alone? I am tempted here to say, in the light of what I have discovered in researching and writing this book, I wish to God we were.

Is the lesson of all of this merely that we have to keep our prayers very short? (Ha! Ha!) Just think of all that wasted prayer-time that in any given moment is going adrift in our Universe. All that heartfelt, concentrated, deeply centred thought and will-power travelling at the speed of light and going to waste somewhere out there in the Universe.

But where is that somewhere? Where indeed is God? There has surely got to be a point from which a response can come. If we judge God by the laws of physics as we know them and he, she or it is too far away when our prayers leave us, we may have to wait thousands of millions of light years for an answer. That is, of course, presupposing, as scientists tell us, that nothing can travel faster than the speed of light. So is it any wonder that many prayers are not answered? At least, they may be answered but the answer may still be winging its way on a relatively slow postal service travelling at the speed of light and you, me and Uncle Tom next door may be grossly unable to care while little worms are finishing their fine dining exercises on our carcasses six feet under, when it finally arrives.

It all seems preposterous put this way, doesn't it? Yet that is just what it is. We continue to believe this nonsense. In fact many of us will fight and even kill to maintain belief in this humbug.

However, what it all does is to force us to see God as a concept that bears no relation to the atomically derived basic laws of physics.

It all implies that God is a phenomenon outside time, space and matter, perhaps akin to a giant telephone exchange. A huge quantum sponge, tuned into every point everywhere. Capable of isolating mega trillions of calls every instant and sorting it all out on an individual basis across the length and breadth of the Universe and able to respond instantly i.e. faster than the speed of light. If we thus put God outside the Universe in a totally different frame of existence and still claim that we are not isolated from God, then there has to be a way the two connect. The clear implication from this is that the mechanism that allows us to conceive all of this in the first place, and indeed reach and communicate with God, may indeed be Thought. It may be a capacity that can reach and exist outside the frames of Space and Time and indeed 'travel' faster than the speed of light.

So much for seeing the phenomenon of God in inappropriate anthropocentric terms. We fight and kill millions for little pieces of real estate we call countries, or ethnic enclaves that are so small when seen against the awesome context and grandeur of the size of the Universe as to shame the word 'minute' for giving a false impression of magnitude. This is the size of our madness. Our condition as a species. Yet we *can* love, can't we? How is it possible that we can do this when we are as humanity in such an apoplectic state of lunacy? They say that the other side of hate is love. Can it really be that the one can be the other at one and the same time? The most stunning contradiction of all terms. I do not believe it for an instant. I insist that while there's love there can be no hate. Love is Godhead and thus the bequest of Godhead and hate the legacy of that which is not in any way directly of it. I believe that hate came through the hypodermics or whatever may have been used by artificial machine-type extraterrestrial robots. A poisoned alien engine oil. A lethal alien genetic mulch that held no recipe for tenderness, compassion or grand references that told of an emotional sense, of feeling and caring. The Snake in the Adam and Eve story that tempted and brought down the whole edifice set up by God is an association with reptiles. Surprise surprise, many so-called 'abductees' describe these alien Greys and their cohort Clones who abduct them to be like 'Humanoid reptiles'. Food for thought, isn't it?

I believe hate is *in* us but not *of* us. It rises to a command we never see. A flash of invisible light. A pulse of cold microwave force. An unreasoned mental prompt. All centred on what is referred to as the R Complex of the brain. Hate is a prompt, the property of a deliberate genetic and unnatural alteration of our brain. A transceiving grey-mattered mechanism that receives, transmits, sorts and synthesizes signals through three distinct schemes of tissue and a series of fissures called sulchi. That is all of it. The plum that became a prune. Our curse. Original Sin.

We can envision and understand the Universe in a single swoop of our mind. The microbe on the Leviathan's pulse. Yet who really is the Giant? Haven't we got something the wrong way round here? Not a single one of those multi-trillion gargantuan points out there in space has the slightest idea themselves, out of themselves, that they are even there. That they in fact exist. But the spindly brown Sri Lankan beggar scuttling along the streets of Colombo can quote Tagore in awesome affirmation that it is the 'living' atom and not the 'dead' one that makes up all this size.

Yes, we are *of* Godstuff, but not *made out* of it. It is a fine and absolutely vital distinction. The stardust that scientists proclaim made us all is merely a decaying robe that encircles Godstuff. The robot-minded biologist who hysterically claims there is no Godstuff and that it all comes from a purely atomic derivation might well be saying it out of his particular 'alienized' programme of star-stuff. He has just, alas, switched off his Godstuff. That is all. And sadly for him or her that is everything.

A billion hungry stomachs. A million crying eyes. Ten thousand silos storing food, a trillion pounds of relief and no one moves a finger to wipe the pain away. When the legacy of supremacists, be they Cro-Magnon, Mongoloid, ET, Grey or whatever, is examined for its true nature amid the lies touted on a billion television screens daily, it is plain that it is a legacy that has given the world great suffering. It has also given rise to generations that hold the keys to the kingdom of hope for the whole world. Yet these keys are still turning to close the door of hope to many and open it for the few. It is their sin that remains. It is their gauntlet that all our souls have to run. It is my last behest in this work, that I attempt to show your son and mine a sight of it, perhaps before it is too late to matter. And if that is conceit, I humbly bow my head without an apology.

It may be said of this all that it is the singular purpose of the Universe to see to it that all that is there goes the way of death and decay. That it is truly inevitable, and that the En-forced Cosmos can do nothing else. The great mathematician and philosopher Bertrand Russell affirmed that the Universe was under a death sentence from the Second Law of Thermodynamics, and argued that all human life was ultimately futile and existed to no real higher purpose. As he put it: 'All the noonday brightness of the human genius' would count for nothing in the wake of the entropic process, if the Universe and all that was in it came to a final demise in an unimaginable void of heated nothing. It implies that it is the legacy of Godstuff in all planets to finally cede itself to this awesome and final behest. To sublimate all things in this Universe into a divided form that will be the last dispatch of Soul and life and thus the capacity for independence from it. It may well be true, but I for one *don't* believe it for a moment, if what we commonly call sense and meaning have any resource or recourse in the nature of our species. I believe Russell was right insofar as the atom was concerned. It is the atom that is damned. We, fortunately, are not just atoms. The existential blanket that makes for living being sparkles in every fraction with the quiet glorious En-light of eternal tenure. Godstuff. Our own personal 'godstuff' encoded with our individual restrictions making our own unique fingerprint emblazoned within Godhead called our Soul. Like a glass paperweight with the air bubbles (Godness) in it. The 'air-conditioned aeration' provided by Godhead in this Universe provides living paradigms with intelligence and thus the ability to make rational choices. Yes, we are both here in this Universe and there in God at the same time. Yet the likelihood of keeping some fraction of ourselves beyond the 'Margin of Forever' gets less and less likely the longer we linger in this Universe. We have to get out of this Hell. Fast. It is the imperative to end all imperatives if Gautama Buddha, Jesus Christ, the Prophet Mohammed, Confucius and all the great Prophets, Masters and Seers of logically derived existential Truth are to be believed. There can be no compromises with this engine of doom we call the Universe of enforced Parts. We have to go home to our true point of eternal belonging – Godhead itself – as soon as we can. We have, in other words, got to get the hell out of this Universe while we can make effective enough choices to do so, or slowly, inexorably, be damned by drifting into a state or living paradigm that does not allow for such effective choices to be made.

In my search for an added insight into the phenomenon of UFOs and so-called 'Flying Saucers', I have tried to demonstrate and verify that existentiality consists of *two* bases. Two final drifts. The first and most important base consists of all that *is* Godhead and out of it *naturally*. The second base is a derivation out of the first and is made up of all that is *created* and manufactured from it and out of it *unnaturally*. It is on this 'soul-less' second base that UFOs and flying saucers and Clones and roboids and all the rest of the 'artificial' negative and deadly paraphernalia in the Universe of Parts find an existential margin. In this 'Universe of enforced Parts' what is natural and what is created continually impinge on one another. Whatever the whole final truth might be of it *all*, one thing for me stands clear and veritable above all else. That is simply this: The vast majority of naturally existing beings (i.e entities with Soul) capable of making intelligent choices don't really know the difference between the two states. This vital, crucial, awesome difference is lost on so many that their respective eternities are seriously mortgaged. We systematically kill, maim and make impotent all those who still have enough insight into the difference to shout a warning to us all of the consequences of not knowing this contradiction. We thus drift into the oblivion of a future *in* atoms to finally exist *as* atoms, divided and damned.

If my children were to ask me what I might say as a last word of advice to them in a father's valedictory words of love, when I close my eyes for the last time, I would suggest a lesson. A lesson that might serve them well, if they would burn it into their minds. I would ask that they pay heed to logical sense alone. Nothing else. I would ask that they never listen with sanction or fear. There are no pipers to pay for pink elephants and tooth fairies. Above all I would ask that they never commit themselves to the behests of others, but only to behests on behalf of others. In that way the only piper one pays will be guaranteed to be present when the final payment is due. It will be you and only you alone that have earned the result, and if a blank go-nowhere eternity will be yours to reap, you and you alone would have chosen it to be so.

And so, when all the summaries are taken and all the totals are totted up, could it all have been a series of innocent incidental natural atmospheric events and secret military procedures of strictly terrestrial origin going on around the world? Could it be that these have been hitched and stitched together to form a preposterous paranoid conspiracy theory about an invasion of little green, or in this case little grey men from outer space? I'm sure many will think so. But what if it is not? What if it is *NOT*?

How would one begin to tell the world that an alien presence is already here if there is a conspiracy of silence of the size and power we have clearly had demonstrated as succeeding at Roswell and elsewhere in covering it all up, a conspiracy maintained by top secret government organizations? If you read this then you know there is at least one avenue still untainted and uncontrolled by the Alien Protective Conspiracy. I am convinced it won't be long before all adverse serious critical analysis and comment on the endeavours of the Clones and Greys will be covertly stopped before it can get to full and worldwide public exposure.

If all this is paranoia blended with a fertile imagination then, as I have said before, little harm will have been done to the general consensus of truth. It will have at worst been a horror story that cannot compare with the verifiable pictures of hell that have come out of Bosnia and Rwanda that are broadcast by the electronic and print media all over the world. But I would rather be paranoid and right than incredulous, cautious and wrong. I am thoroughly convinced that we as a species are at the rim of a cataclysm if we don't expose the presence of an alien influence in the affairs of humanity. It is for the simple citizen to find the truth of it for him or herself. Governments should never be trusted to do it. I believe most governments don't know how deeply they are penetrated and controlled by the agents of these insidious alien interlopers. After all, thousands of years of covert genetic culturing have given their hybrids human faces. I believe it will be almost impossible to spot the subterfuge now unless we are all as a species aware that it is going on. The vast majority of the people of this planet haven't a clue that such a thing as an alien interception of our species has been and still is going on. What I fear most of all is that most won't care.

In the final analysis it is the future of all our human children that counts. I believe, for what it's worth, that what I have discovered needs urgent exposure. Its veracity is for the reader to judge within the halls of his or her inalienable individuality and sense of what is true. It is vitally important, if true, for all our sakes, and particularly for the sake of the generations to come, that somehow the cat of an alien extraterrestrial possession of our future be let out of the bag. I have tried to lay before you informed opinion and, I hope, a prima facie case for it. It is the final courtesy I can pay to all my fellow human beings simply because we are all human and might want to stay in every way truly human.

Well, here goes folks . . . One more try . . . Wish me luck . . . Wish us all luck.

If you sing the song of the Little Grey Men, perhaps you will sing it now with a tinge of sadness and a little irony. It's a simple song. Anyone can sing it:

> 'Grey, Green, Yellow and Blue,
> We are here to take 'care' of you'

CONCEPTUAL DEFINITIONS

CENTRE GOD-NESS

If God-ness is the view of parts from the Universe of the Whole, then Centre God-ness is the view of the whole within the ultimate coalescence of all sentient being in perfect PEACE (i.e. unenforcedness) and the absolute and perfect union of all parts. As the perfect reconciliation of all difference in total fit, it can be seen as that ultimate point in which all absolutes are contained.

COMPLEXITY

Complexity is neither order nor chaos. It is the confluence of both.

ENLIGHT

This is my word for potentiality and therefore freedom and sentience within a physical universe of dead actuality, or static dependency. I present a case that our brains do not manufacture awareness, but that our bodies are living AERIALS that receive it through an antecedental line of un-enforcedness (SOUL) traced all the way to the big bang. So God-ness is how Enlight is resolved in the Universe of the Whole; Enlight is how God-ness touches the Universe of Parts. They are one and the same.

FIELD

In scientific parlance the term 'field' is used to denote any effect that has a set of contours joining points with equal amounts of what scientists call POTENTIAL. This is potential in the sense that an electrical voltage is a POTENTIAL DIFFERENCE and doesn't of itself imply lines of open potential in the sense of free choice, i.e. the freedom to 'Be' or not to 'Be'; not to be or what to be without compulsion by force. I have argued that force and therefore force potentials are, in fact, simply the derivative of true potentiality formed out of the choice for separation. So why do I use the term SOUL FIELD? Isn't that a contradiction in terms, if SOUL refers to the encapsulation of Enlight or potentiality of un-enforcedness and the term FIELD refers to the contours of enforcedness? It need not be a contradiction. As I have pointed out earlier, the power of a vacuum is its LACK of enforcedness? It is this when set against the huge (normally unnoticed) pressures surrounding a vacuum that define the 'VACUUM EFFECT'.

When you turn on a vacuum cleaner it is not, strictly speaking the vacuum that draws the air and rubbish into the machine, it is actually the surrounding atmospheric pressure that 'pushes' it in. 'Ah, got you!' you might say. If force dominates non-force then according to your definitions matter would dominate THOUGHTness and how could this be consistent with your postulation that the whole physical universe is just one little 'pimple on the face of God', so to speak?

The resolution of this *apparent* paradox into no paradox at all is actually very simple: If the vacuum effect in question has NO inherent enforced-ness, then it must be infinitely malleable in terms of the where, when and how of its intercession in force. 'Soul field' therefore refers to the individualized patterns of reception of Enlight and therefore the shapes of vacuum field effect, and therefore to the fulcrum points where the Thought-Awareness-Will continuum 'becomes' the Matter-Space-Time continuum and vice versa. What about what I have called, LIFE's fields and DEATH's fields? As I have said, the term 'field' is used to denote 'iso-contours' of like effect in the sense that iron filings, for example, trace the contours of a magnetic field around a bar magnet. What has that to do with 'life' and 'death'? What are their contours?

Consider, if you will, the structure of a sponge. The holes have their contours and the material of the sponge has its contours. Each is, in fact, in summary a picture or impression of the other. The holes have a kind of discreteness as separate holes although the sponge is one sponge. The sponge also has a kind of definition in fixture as the holes define location within the sponge such that it is not all-over 'sponge-ness'.

So what I call Life's fields are simply the writings of the 'vacuum pen' of Enlight or potentiality through and within atoms i.e. bodies of 'living' beings, or organisms. DEATH's fields, then, are simply the signature of discarnate SOUL field manifested and contoured through and within the various shells of tension in the space between atoms. In other words, I am suggesting that in the state of discarnacy that is often misleadingly referred to as death, our 'bodies' are our capsules of Thought-ness that keep us discrete from the universe of the whole. So that once the restrictions of outlook that maintain limit in separation are undone we could merge with the ALL of perfect fit and therefore balance, but that any tendencies we have towards separation may pull us back into a downward spiral of reincarnations into further and further exponencies of LOSS, to become any previous form of 'BEING'.

FORCE

Force is the 'Paradigm of Potential' for things or events to 'happen'. It defines the interface between what is of GODHEAD and what is not. It is an effect that occurs when what we term the abstraction 'WILL' as it exists in the state of GODHEAD is sublimated into the state of separation in the Universe of Parts or Portions.

Force may also be seen as the *summary quantum* of the potential difference that exists between the Universe of Parts (our Universe) and the Universe of the Whole (Godhead). In other words, FORCE defines the *lines of slippage* that favour events to happen such that the reconciliation of the two Universes, one with the other, occurs and a state of ultimate and absolute balance is achieved.

GOD-NESS

The view point of ALL TOGETHERNESS within the state of PERFECT UNION OF ALL PARTS and therefore the ultimate reach of the Universe of the Whole into the Universe of Parts, implying and defining what may be called God in you and me as sentient beings.

GODHEAD

Godhead is to Centre Godness as Enlight is to God-ness. While Enlight DOES, Godhead IS, if you like.

GRAVITATION

As I have said, Einstein's General Theory of Relativity defines gravity as the curved, bent and twisted contours of the Matter-Space-Time continuum (M.S.T.c.) that shapes the lines of 'happening' between the two poles of the M.S.T.c., i.e. the Big Bang at one end and the Heat-Death, or 'Big Crunch' at the other. According to many theoretical physicists the other 'fundamental' forces (electromagnetism and the two nuclear forces) are also contours of the M.S.T.c. If this is so, then it implies an implicate nine-dimensional space but if, as I have argued in Chapter Three, two dimensions imply four without four happening, then three can also imply nine (as three is the root of nine). If this is the case, then all the 'forces of nature' are implied derivatives of gravitation which is itself the line of connectedness from God-ness to nothingness and back.

HOLOGRAM

This is a word derived from the Greek, meaning a device for providing a whole picture. This picture or holograph is made by combining information from two light beams to provide a three-dimensional image viewable from all directions. This image has the property that if it is broken into small parts, each part retains the whole shape.

Electromagnetic radiation e.g. visible LIGHT

This is what Einstein inferred to be the matrix that sets and juxtaposes the axes (axial dimensions) of the matter-space-time continuum, its speed (or the square of its speed) a measure of the inextricable binding of these three elements one to the other. The equations of 'special relativity' define the inter-relatedness of matter, space and time, while those of 'general relativity' define what had previously been called GRAVITATIONAL FORCE. These are simply the contours of the matter-space-time Universal map defining the path of least action, or 'geodesic', between two points. Thus 'happening' or 'events' are mapped through geodesic 'WORLD LINES' of matter 'in' space and time. Matter makes and shapes space and time as actual effects when a further ingredient exists to give these elements a non-inertial, but non-ethereal reference frame of all references to exist against.

I suggest that the MATTER-SPACE-TIME CONTINUUM is no more than a sublimation of what I call the THOUGHT-AWARENESS-WILL CONTINUUM. A sublimation of where the elements of one take on the appearance of the other. A sublimation that is always a 'half-way house' because sublimation means no matter, space or time and total sublimation in an ultimate 'universal heat death' would also lead to a state of NOTHINGNESS and perhaps another 'big bang'. Let me explain:-

The simplest demonstration of this is through the example of TIME. As I have intimated, time, space and matter are one continuum, so in illustrating my thesis through the concept of time it will, I hope, become self-evident that matter and space are tied in with the same thread.

The law of MINIMUM ACTION TO MAXIMUM RESULT

This 'law' describes the process of becoming anything. It is the description of how the progression of events, or happening, will always at the most basic level follow the shortest possible path between any two points between the Pole of Absolute Order and the Pole of Absolute Chaos.

MOROID

This is a word I have used to denote Möbius toroid (see Chapter Three). A toroid is a shape like a doughnut with a hole in the middle and can be made by taking a cylinder and bending its central axis to form a circle thereby joining its two ends (see diagrams 5 & 6 in the illustrated section), or by taking a Möbius strip and spinning it about either or both axes, the shape of a toroid is traced out on space. So the 'moroid' is a suggestion as to how a Möbius-twisted design of space can be seen to take up all directions in separation.

ORDER and CHAOS

Chaos is the summary of a multitude of separate but interacting points of enforced-ness. Each point evolves in space and time according to 'The Law of Maximum Result in Minimum Action', but each point has its unique quantum of direction and parcelled tension. As all directions are possible, 'all over' directed-ess is inevitable, so in fulfilling this scope, chaos ultimately provides in summary a balance point or EQUILIBRIUM state of NO IMPLICIT POTENTIAL FOR CHANGE. This is what science predicts as the Heat-Death of the Universe. Along the way to it, sub-states of chaos make for homogenized 'soups' of diverse ingredients with apparently random but in fact finely-tuned fluctuations, hence the statement of mathematicians who study chaos that the flapping of a butterfly's wings can create a storm on the other side of the planet. Order, then, is the singular resolve of parts in union that implies 'all over'-ness, i.e. isotropic homogeneity through symmetry and all over-ness implicit also in the potential for dissolution or break up. Order, as seen within the Universe of Parts, implies concepts like together-ness, i.e. proximity, but the pole of absolute order is something different to this and implies a singularity of no-'thing'-ness in all potentials. It bears saying that though SEPARATION and CHAOS proceed out of this point of ORDER and state of perfect balance, (i.e. NOTHINGNESS gives birth to order), it is not subject and cannot be subject to what we call TIME. It therefore cannot be created or destroyed.

The Universe of PARTS (Physical Universe)

A phenomenon that occurs when a previous state of the Union of all Parts is disrupted into platforms of break-up and disorder. The Universe is this state of separation and therefore presents as what we call SPACE, TIME and MATTER. It is the summary of the CHOICE to *be* separate (i.e. the 'Big Bang'). It defines a state of ACTUALITY (potentiality actualized through implicit and explicit choice. This further implies that the prior state is an abstraction. A state of ALL KNOWING in a paradigm we might describe as THOUGHTNESS). The concept of NOW (TIME) is therefore the interface between the actual ('past') and what is potential ('future') within any observer (sentient being with the capacity to free choice) and therefore implies and points to the existence of: the universe of the whole together – Godhead.

SOMETHING from NOTHING and nothing from something

Physicists tell us that the whole physical universe came out of a prior state of nothingness and also that if you tot up the sum of all mass in the universe and set that against all the energy that there is precisely enough gravitational energy to balance out all the mass. In other words it still adds up to ZERO. This supports my assertion that matter, space and time are products of nothingness which proceed into nothingness and at any point on the way there their summary is nothingness and therefore that 'something-ness' is merely a blip or an anomaly that happens between 'forever' and 'never'. I have suggested that the MATTER-SPACE-TIME continuum (M.S.T.c.) is simply the exposition or outward manifestation of what I have called the THOUGHT-AWARENESS-WILL continuum into separation and therefore limit. I have also made a case that this sublimation into fixture is 'never' complete and I have coined the term ENLIGHT to describe the reach of potentiality into the state of exposed actuality. So, what then is the 'equation' for transfiguration? The equation that describes how the twist that 'freezes' matter, space and time in limit is undone to release them as Enlight. Mathematically I think it is best expressed as 0=0, ZERO EQUALS ZERO. We have alrea' seen that the final summary of physicality is zero and that the state of Enlight in potentiality prevails through a BALANCED state of no force and therefore No–Thing-ness. It is an interesting fact that until relatively recently in history, European mathematicians had no concept of a number zero. This concept was, in fact, introduced to them by Arab scholars: even the word 'algebra' is actually a word brought into the English language from the Arabic.

SOUL

Encapsulated Enlight with discreteness defined as memory through choices. The quality of reception of Enlight defines and is defined by the propensity of an individual towards UNION against SEPARATION. An important sign of the propensity towards union is CONSCIENCE, i.e. the implicit tacit recognition of ultimate value in all sentient being that can choose. Hence the suggestion of the great teachers 'Love thy neighbour as thyself'. Love is a word implying cherishment of focus in logically derived value of that which has subjective value, and therefore meaning to an individual. What you value or treasure is where your heart (or Will) is and therefore where what is YOU will be.

STEM CELLS

These are pluri-potent early progenitor cells. In other words, cells with the potential to make of themselves many cell types in a biological entity.

THOUGHT-ness

This is a term I have used to specify or personify, if you like, Awareness and Will through MEMORY, i.e. individualized action and experiences encoded as patterns of reception or filtering out of Enlight, so if the concept of NOW is the summary of what is commonly termed PAST, PRESENT and FUTURE then THOUGHT-ness is the past, AWARENESS the present and WILL the various Lines of Open Potential that comprises the FUTURE. The three together summarize Enlight which is the unchanging reference of total un-enforcedness.

TIME

Time is so central to all our experience that to find a way to define it has never been easy. Our attempts at a definition of time seem to be like the attempts of a fish to define the sea. A fish has no concept of anything outside its watery world, so it would be very difficult for a fish to speculate on what water might be, if you get my metaphorical drift. So, in deference to the philosophers who have pondered the subject of time, I shall now attempt to define a common-sense outlook on it which is, at least as far as I can see, consistent with logic and reason.

I suggest that what we call 'NOW' is simply the confluence between that which is actual and fixed, i.e. what we commonly call 'THE PAST', and that which exists as Lines of Open Potential, i.e. 'THE FUTURE'. Fixture, of course, implies sublimation outside of the eternal continuum of all potentials which I call the Thought-Awareness-Will continuum and 'Lines of Open Potentiality' are, of course, only open as long as there is an implicit potential for change from out of a prevailing situation. In other words, as long as there are still islands of Awareness and Will that can experience a 'now' in thought. So once total sublimation would be reached it would already have ended. Time is therefore the bridge between FOREVER and NEVER.

TRANSFIGURATION

This is the release mechanism from out of the twisted loophole that defines the transient existence of physicality for a soul manifesting Enlight. The capsule that maintains limit is dissolved and in so doing the loophole is partially untwisted THROUGHOUT the Matter-Space-Time continuum. Could this be what makes the vast voids in space detected by astronomers? What about all the 'missing mass'? Scientists say that the large-scale gravitational evolution of the universe implies that ninety per cent of the mass which 'should' exist in order to 'produce' this gravity is not visible and is therefore pronounced 'missing presumed as W.I.M.P.s' – Weakly Interacting Massive Particles (or WIMPs to their friends) are one attempt of theoretical physicists to explain the missing mass. If gravity is, as I have suggested, the lines that trace the pathways of relativity between the two poles of absoluteness, then the undoing of the knot that freezes potential in matter as mass doesn't break the line of connectedness which continues until the consummation of the state of separation.

This is no 'god of the gaps' philosophy. It really is not. I am suggesting that it is the physical universe itself which is the GAP if you like. If the equation that defines the dissolution of all limits is 0=0, then what happens if we rearrange this equation? If we divide both sides by zero we get $\frac{0}{0} = ?$ WHAT IS ZERO DIVIDED BY ZERO?

According to the 'big bang' theory, the whole universe came from nothing. A point with no size that existed for an instant of no duration divided itself to make space, time and matter including the raw materials that now make human bodies so that we are here now also as a result of it. But how do you split up or divide a point that has no size (or dimensions) to start with? There was no yardstick or measure in space and time to gauge division of this first point as space and time are themselves the products of its division. So all that was there to divide it was itself. In other words, 'Big Bangs' are what happens when zero is divided by zero.

Every mathematician I have asked, however, says that the question is meaningless and can't be answered. If they had been asked the same question some time ago in the past, many mathematicians would probably have replied: 'Zero? But what's that?' I think we can afford to take the mathematical law into our own hands, so to speak, and try to derive logically what the question and its answer might be about. So here goes. There are three simple algebraic rules which I use:

1. $\frac{0}{x} = 0$
2. $\frac{x}{x} = 1$
3. $\frac{x}{0} = \infty$ (∞ is the mathematical symbol for infinity!)

Substituting x with zero we have the result that: zero, one and infinity and therefore zero, unity and infinity are all different expressions of the same effect. In fact, you can further derive that if you can divide zero by zero all numbers are equivalent to each other. So is this why many mathematicians are reluctant to consider $\frac{0}{0}$? If all numbers are the same as all others then they're out of a job.

I'm joking, of course, but I wonder what mathematics really means to its experts? I mean REALLY? After the lights have gone out in the lecture theatre and all the students have gone home leaving the differential equations on the blackboard, what is it all about? Although I don't agree with everything in his book, Professor Penrose of Oxford, England, seems to be one mathematician who does at least try to see the relevance of pure mathematics to deeper, more philosophical questions and tries to make his subject accessible by the ordinary person. In his recent book *Shadows of the Mind* he uses simple mathematical reasoning to highlight certain critical differences between the human *mind* and a computer's capacity for information processing. He infers that what people call 'artificial intelligence' refers to the processing of information and not to the sentient experience of that information by a being with AWARENESS and WILL. The value of this to me is that it contrasts the sanctity of human life with the functional utility of a computer and therefore exposes as nonsense the notion of many scientists that people could be in a sense immortalized by having all their memories encoded in a self-maintaining computer program which could be sent into space carrying with it the 'mind' of the subject whose memory it copied in the hardware of self-replicating robots, perhaps. I call this nonsense because the encoded memories could never manufacture awareness and will. Their concept of our future sounds chillingly reminiscent of 'Planet of the Greys', don't you think?

To return to $\frac{0}{0} = ?$: I have implied that it is the formula defining all potentials being contained within the state of nothingness. It is interesting that it implies all extents through three roots: zero, one and infinity. If you think about it, I think you might agree that these three numbers, as well as the fact that there *are* three of them, summarize best of all numbers the perceived defining attributes of God in all the world's major religions. One central tenet of all the religions is that God is not a 'thing' and exists beyond the labels that apply to THINGS; beyond extent, size and limit and therefore able to prevail in a state described as 'void' or nothingness. Secondly, they are all agreed that 'God is ONE'. (The Hindu concept of 'gods' is said by Hindu scholars to be an attempt to describe the various attributes of a singular Godhead as it relates to human life. The Christian concept of the 'Trinity' is, likewise, seen as three discrete parallax views of a singular effect and not as three gods.)

Thirdly, all are united in their view that God is eternal and without limit. Hang on a minute, though, if $0 = 0$ implies $\frac{0}{0} = ?$ then why when I add one apple to another do I get two apples rather than, say, fifty-six? Yes, of course $1 + 1 = 2$ as long as there *is* a 1 and a 2, in other words within the state of the phenomenon we call separation. In what I have called Centre-Godness (see definition above), however, all potentials are summarized into nothingness, the one and the ALL, and I have suggested that it is this phenomenon of perfect union that proffers the potential for 'separation-ness'. I have also suggested that we all, as sentient beings, are the receivers of this $0 = 0$ effect in the Universe of Parts and that it is this that allows us to 'KNOW' that $1 + 1 = 2$. As Professor Penrose points out in his book, what we know as true is not computable through self-consistent formal systems of logic so that the fact that we can know it is proof that our minds are not the product of a point-to-point computational process. In the above, I have addressed the issue of TRANSFIGURATION through an equation, without yet putting this in a historical perspective. It is reported that Jesus Christ demonstrated a certain phenomenon to three of his closest friends. They went with him up a mountain and saw him glow 'brighter than the SUN', but remarked that it didn't hurt their eyes to behold him. A second time the same thing is said to have happened except this time his body is said to have disappeared. This is usually called 'the Ascension'. As I have tried to show, I believe that if a big bang is possible, i.e. the condensation of matter, space and time out of nothing but pure potentiality through the action of choice, then its opposite, i.e. transfiguration, must also be possible. One clue to the nature of this phenomenon is, I believe, that witnesses saw him glowing brighter than the sun without hurting their eyes. Sunlight is electromagnetic radiation released out of the encapsulated mass-energy of a star through nuclear fusion as summarized in Einstein's famous equation $E=mc^2$. (The same basic processes underlie the flash, blast and electromagnetic pulse of an atom bomb.) If $E=mc^2$ is the equation for stars and atom bombs to shine then what is the equation for transfiguration? Why, if all the mass-energy of his body was released (he is said to have disappeared), is there no record of a devastating explosion?

$E=mc^2$ implies that a tiny piece of matter has enough locked-in energy to move a mountain if all the mass-energy were released. So what would have happened to the Mount of Olives and to Judea and, indeed, the surrounding continents of Asia, Africa and Europe if about 70 kg of mass-energy were suddenly released? Perhaps the light that they saw is what I have called Enlight, so that by uniting at each point of choice (see definition of 'soul' above) he was simply undoing the bonds of separation and therefore undoing the twist that makes the image of matter-space-time out of Enlight. By undoing the twist, he released the Enlight which is, of course, totally un-enforced, which is why there was no explosion.

$$0 = 0$$

$$\tfrac{0}{0} = 0, 1 \text{ AND } \infty$$

$$\tfrac{0}{0} = \tfrac{0}{0}$$

therefore: $0 = \infty = 1$

$$1$$
$$\diagup \quad \diagdown$$
$$0 \quad = \quad \infty$$

The Universe of the WHOLE

The state of perfect union of all parts in perfect peace (unenforcedness) or stillness. It is therefore the summary of all POTENTIALITY, TO BE OR NOT TO BE. Potentiality is the implicit product of the total absence of Force (compulsion). It is potentiality expressed through 'THOUGHTNESS', which is itself expressed as Awareness and Will, and provides an insight into how at the big bang 'somethingness' or every*thing* can be spontaneously generated out of NOTHINGNESS. Nothingness implies the total absence of force to make anything happen, in any given direction.

BIBLIOGRAPHY

CHAPTER 1

1 Mack, John E.: *Abduction* (pp 115–117) (Simon & Schuster, 1994)
2 Randles, Jenny: *UFOs and How to See Them* (pp 70–71) (Anaya Publishers Ltd, 1992)
3 Jacobs, David M.: Interview, *UFO Magazine* (pp 5–8) Nov/Dec 1995

CHAPTER 2

1 Stannard, Russell: *Doing Away with God* (pp 78–79) (Marshall Pickering, 1993)

CHAPTER 3

1 Stannard, Russell: *Doing Away with God* (pp 72–73) (Marshall Pickering, 1993)
2 'Death Wish': *Horizon* B.B.C. Television 17–1–94
    Wyllie, A.H.: 'Death from Inside Out: an Overview' *Philosophical Transactions of the Royal Society of London*, Aug 1994 345 (1313): 237–41
    Wyllie, A.H., Bellamay, C.O., Malcomson R.D., Harrison, D.J.: 'Cell Death in Health and Disease: the Biology & Regulation of Apoptosis' Seminars in Cancer Biology, Feb 1995 6(1):3–16

CHAPTER 9

1 Coptic Gnostic Library: *Pistis Sophia* (Book II, ch 100, p.249). Edited by Carl Schmidt (Leiden: E.J. Brill, 1978)

CHAPTER 10

1 'Chips Full of Protein': Newell, John *The Guardian* 9–8–91
2 'Living Factories': *New Scientist* 3–2–96
3 'Silicon Cells with a Life of Their Own': *New Scientist* 18–11–95
4 *Daily Telegraph* 18–7–96
5 *The Nag Hammadi Library in English* (Leiden: E. J. Brill, 1984)
     'The Hypostasis of the Archons' (II 4: 86, 94)
6 'Aeronautics, a Manuscript from the Prehistoric Past' *International Academy of Sanskrit Research, Mysore, India* (1976). As quoted in *Secrets of the Last Races*, Rene Noorbergen, New English Library, 1977
7 Crawford, Ian: 'Some Thoughts on the Implications of Faster than Light Interstellar Space Travel' (*Royal Astronomical Society Quarterly*, 1995)
8 Warwick, Kevin (Professor of Cybernetics at Reading University): 'Beware the Robot Slave Masters' *The Times* 12–9–95
     'Machines Could Take Over Planet' *The Independent* 12–9–95
9 Pearson, Ian: 'Terror Robots Need to be Curbed' *The Engineer* 21–9–95

CHAPTER 12

1 'Reptiles Don't Leave Evolution to Chance' *New Scientist* 16–9–95
2 'Making Evolution Run Backwards' *New Scientist* 28–10–95
3 'In the Beginning': *Scientific American*, Feb 1991
4 Hoyle, Fred: *The Intelligent Universe* (pp 12, 19) (Michael Joseph Ltd, 1983)

CHAPTER 13

1 Easteal, Simon: Australian National University DNA Profile Conference, Canberra (16–11–94)
2 'Monkey Murders may be Falsely Accused' *New Scientist* 15–7–95
3 'Neanderthals': *National Geographic*, Vol. 189 Jan 1996 (pp 2–36)

CHAPTER 14

1 Randles, Jenny: *UFOs and How to See Them* (pp 72–73) (Anaya Publishers Ltd, 1992)
2 Jacobs, David M.: *Secret Life* (p 191) (Simon & Schuster, 1992)

CHAPTER 15

1 'Creators of the Forty-Seventh Chromosome' *New Scientist* 11–11–95
2 'Living Factories' *New Scientist* 03–02–96

3 Arthur, Charles: 'Eating New Food May Change Your Genes' *Independent* 3-1-97
4 'Did Genetic Garbage Spur Primate Evolution?' *New Scientist* 16–9–95
5 'Message in a Genome' *New Scientist* 12–8–95
6 'When DNA Turns Traitor' *New Scientist* 25–3–95
7 'India Looks Farther East for its Ancestors' *New Scientist* 8–3–97

CHAPTER 16

1 Jacobs, David M.: *Secret Life* (p 243) (Simon & Schuster, 1992)
2 Spurdle, A.B., Jenkins, T.: 'The Y Chromosome as a Tool for Studying Human Evolution' *Current Opinion in Genetics & Development* (1992 2: 487–491)
3 Ritte, Neufeld, Broit, Shavit, Motro: 'The Differences among Jewish Communities – Maternal & Paternal Contribution' (*Journal of Molecular Evolution* – 1993 37: 435–440)
4 The Dead Sea Scrolls: 'The Ages of the Creation' (40 180)
5 *The Old Testament Pseudepigrapha* (Darton, Longman & Todd, 1983) (Edited by James Charlesworth) Appendix to 3 Enoch Ch 15 B.
6 The Old Testament of The Bible: Exodus Ch. 39, v.2–3
7 The Old Testament of The Bible: Leviticus Ch. 21
8 The Old Testament of The Bible: Ezekiel Ch. 27
9 *Mysteries of the Unknown: Mystic Places* (pp 151–152) (Time/Life Books, 1987)

CHAPTER 17

1 Bauval R., Gilbert A.: *The Orion Mystery* (pp 7–9) (Heinemann)

CHAPTER 18

1 *The Nag Hammadi Library in English* (Leiden: E.J. Brill, 1984) The Gospel of Philip II 3:81

CHAPTER 19

1 Cheetham, Erika: *The Further Prophecies of Nostradamus* (Corgi, 1985)
2 Jacobs, David M.: *Secret Life* (p 170) (Simon & Schuster, 1992)

CHAPTER 20

1 *The Nag Hammadi Library in English* (Leiden: E.J. Brill, 1984) 'The Dialogue of the Saviour' III. 122.
2 The New Testament: St. Luke, Ch. 4, V.8.

CHAPTER 21

1 *The Nag Hammadi* (see reference above) 'The Dialogue of the Saviour' III, 5:142
2 *The Old Testament Pseudepigrapha* (Darton, Longman & Todd, 1983) (Edited by James Charlesworth) 1 Enoch Ch. 6–8
3 *The Nag Hammadi* (see reference above) (Leiden: E.J. Brill, 1984) 'Apochryphon of John' III, 1:9–13
4 *The Nag Hammadi* (see reference above) 'Sophia of Jesus Christ' III, 4:117–122
5 *The Nag Hammadi* (see reference above) 'First Apocalypse of James' V, 3:32–33
6 *The Nag Hammadi* (see reference above) 'Apochryphon of John' II, 1:28
7 Fange, Erich Von: 'Strange Fire on the Earth' *Creation Research Society Quarterly*, Dec 1975
8 The Old Testament of the Bible: Genesis Ch. 18–19
9 'Robot Are Us': *Asiaweek* 10–8–94

CHAPTER 22

1 Maclean, Paul: 'Ritual and Deceit' *Science Digest* Nov/Dec, 1980

CHAPTER 23

1 'The Way of Logic': *New Scientist* 2–12–95
2 'Onward Cyber Soldiers': *Time Magazine* 21–8–95

CHAPTER 25

1 'Go On, Read My Mind': *New Scientist* 16–12–95
2 Mack, John E.: *Abduction* (pp 360–361) (Simon & Schuster, 1994)
3 Verschuur, Gerrit: *Impact* (Oxford University Press, 1996)

CHAPTER 26

1 Jacobs, David M.: *Secret Life* (p 172) (Simon & Schuster 1992)
2 'The Boy Whose Blood has no Father' *New Scientist* 7–10–95
3 Randles, Jenny: *UFOs and How to See Them* (p 72) (Anaya Publishers Ltd)
4 Jacobs, David M.: Secret Life (p 316) (Simon & Schuster, 1992)

CHAPTER 27

1 The Old Testament of The Bible: Ezekiel Ch. 1,V. 4–19

CHAPTER 28

1 'Doctors Urged to Fight Genetics Weapons Threat' *Daily Telegraph* 30–9–96

CHAPTER 29

1 Forum: 'I Hiss Therefore I Am': *New Scientist* 11–11–95